Singapore's Real Estate
50 Years of Transformation

World Scientific Series on Singapore's 50 Years of Nation-Building

Published

50 Years of Social Issues in Singapore
   edited by David Chan

Our Lives to Live: Putting a Woman's Face to Change in Singapore
   edited by Kanwaljit Soin and Margaret Thomas

50 Years of Singapore–Europe Relations: Celebrating Singapore's Connections with Europe
   edited by Yeo Lay Hwee and Barnard Turner

Perspectives on the Security of Singapore: The First 50 Years
   edited by Barry Desker and Cheng Guan Ang

50 Years of Singapore and the United Nations
   edited by Tommy Koh, Li Lin Chang and Joanna Koh

50 Years of Environment: Singapore's Journey Towards Environmental Sustainability
   edited by Tan Yong Soon

50 Years of the Chinese Community in Singapore
   edited by Pang Cheng Lian

Singapore–China Relations: 50 Years
   edited by Zheng Yongnian and Lye Liang Fook

Singapore's Economic Development: Retrospection and Reflections
   edited by Linda Y. C. Lim

Food, Foodways and Foodscapes: Culture, Community and Consumption in Post-Colonial Singapore
   edited by Lily Kong and Vineeta Sinha

Singapore's Health Care System: What 50 Years Have Achieved
   edited by Chien Earn Lee and K. Satku

Singapore's Real Estate: 50 Years of Transformation
   edited by Ngee Huat Seek, Tien Foo Sing and Shi Ming Yu

The complete list of titles in the series can be found at
http://www.worldscientific.com/series/wss50ynb

**World Scientific Series on
Singapore's 50 Years of Nation-Building**

Singapore's Real Estate

50 Years of Transformation

Editors

**Seek Ngee Huat
Sing Tien Foo
Yu Shi Ming**

National University of Singapore, Singapore

NEW JERSEY · LONDON · SINGAPORE · BEIJING · SHANGHAI · HONG KONG · TAIPEI · CHENNAI · TOKYO

Published by

World Scientific Publishing Co. Pte. Ltd.

5 Toh Tuck Link, Singapore 596224

USA office: 27 Warren Street, Suite 401-402, Hackensack, NJ 07601

UK office: 57 Shelton Street, Covent Garden, London WC2H 9HE

Library of Congress Cataloging-in-Publication Data
Names: Seek, Ngee Huat, author. | Sing, Tien Foo, author. | Yu, Shi Ming, author.
Title: Singapore's real estate : 50 years of transformation / Ngee Huat Seek (NUS, Singapore),
    Tien Foo Sing (NUS, Singapore), Shi Ming Yu (NUS, Singapore).
Other titles: World Scientific series on Singapore's 50 years of nation-building.
Description: New Jersey ; Singapore : World Scientific, 2016. |
    Series: World Scientific series on Singapore's 50 years of nation-building |
    Includes bibliographical references.
Identifiers: LCCN 2015044560| ISBN 9789814689250 | ISBN 9789814689267
Subjects: LCSH: Real estate business--Singapore.
Classification: LCC HD890.67.Z63 S44 2016 | DDC 333.3095957--dc23
LC record available at http://lccn.loc.gov/2015044560

British Library Cataloguing-in-Publication Data
A catalogue record for this book is available from the British Library.

Cover Image (Clifford Pier): Ministry of Information and the Arts Collection, courtesy of National Archives of Singapore

Copyright © 2016 by Seek Ngee Huat, Sing Tien Foo and Yu Shi Ming

All rights reserved.

In-house Editor: Shreya Gopi

Typeset by Stallion Press
Email: enquiries@stallionpress.com

Printed in Singapore

Contents

Foreword	Mr Lawrence Wong Minister for National Development	vii
Preface	Professor Tan Chorh Chuan President, National University of Singapore	ix
Introduction	Professor Deng Yongheng Director, Institute of Real Estate Studies, NUS Head, Department of Real Estate, NUS	xi
Acknowledgements		xiii
About the Editors		xv

Part A   The Making of a Global City   1

Chapter 1	Evolution of the Real Estate Industry in Singapore *Seek Ngee Huat*	3
Chapter 2	Transforming a Nation: Role of Government Agencies *Yu Shi Ming & Sing Tien Foo*	19
Chapter 3	Changing Skyline: Real Estate Development Industry in Singapore *Sing Tien Foo*	55
Chapter 4	Role of Real Estate Service Providers in Growing the Real Estate Industry *Yu Shi Ming*	101

Part B   A Global Real Estate Market Place   113

Chapter 5	Singapore Commercial Real Estate Industry in a Global Context *Seek Ngee Huat*	115
Chapter 6	Exporting Singapore's Experiences in Real Estate Development and Urban Planning *Sing Tien Foo & Yu Shi Ming*	137

Part C Real Estate Capital Markets — 159

Chapter 7 The Rise of Singapore's Real Estate Investment Trust (SREIT) Market — 161
Sing Tien Foo

Chapter 8 Bridging the Gap between Capital and Real Estate Markets — 207
Sing Tien Foo

Part D 50 Years of Grooming Real Estate Talents — 239

Chapter 9 Real Estate Education — 241
Yu Shi Ming

Chapter 10 Transforming Singapore's Real Estate: Building on Firm Foundation — 253
Sing Tien Foo & Yu Shi Ming

Foreword

Mr Lawrence Wong
Minister for National Development

Since 1969, the National University of Singapore's Department of Real Estate has been deepening our understanding of the real estate sector and nurturing generations of industry leaders.

The Institute of Real Estate Studies has played a similarly important role in promoting research and analysis, often through collaboration with the industry, to offer new perspectives on the increasingly intricate dynamics of the domestic, regional and global property marketplace.

Singapore's Real Estate: 50 Years of Transformation is a valuable addition to their extensive body of publications.

For those interested in tracing the development of Singapore's real estate industry and its impact on Singapore's physical landscape, this book provides several concise and astute observations, most notably on the respective roles played by Singapore's pioneering decision makers and property development firms.

In the opening chapter, Dr Seek Ngee Huat discusses the robust land use planning guidelines and building approval processes which have facilitated Singapore's rise as a distinctive global city; urban renewal policies which fostered the expansion of the commercial real estate sector, and the far sightedness of a public housing programme which has enabled a vast majority of the population to own homes.

Much information is also provided on the contributions of those in the private sector. The readiness and eagerness of firms to embrace technological innovations and respond to the changing needs of Singaporeans have reaped the sophisticated and vibrant property development industry of which we are now rightly proud.

It is my hope that the synergistic public-private partnership we have enjoyed over the last 50 years will continue to serve Singapore well in the years ahead.

Preface

Professor Tan Chorh Chuan
President, National University of Singapore

"Singapore's Real Estate: 50 Years of Transformation", prepared by NUS' Institute of Real Estate (IRES) and the Department of Real Estate, is a timely and excellent contribution to the commemorative series of SG50 books.

The physical landscape and infrastructure of Singapore has indeed been transformed over the past half-century. From a backwater colonial trading post, we have emerged as a First-World nation and leading global city. Our real estate industry has not merely kept pace with this remarkable change, but played a vital role in enabling and supporting Singapore's development into a thriving metropolis and globally-connected economy.

One key factor that has underpinned the industry's continued ability to adapt, despite the rate of change, has been the strong partnership between the public and private sectors. The public sector's remarkable capabilities in long-term planning, transparent policies and excellent implementation, are complemented by the entrepreneurial energy and innovation of the market and industry.

The results have been clear and impressive. There have been several distinct phases of development: at the onset of independence, our primary and urgent concerns were shelter, housing and infrastructure; later, the use of land for industry and manufacturing helped jumpstart our economy, and set Singapore on the path of rapid development; and as Singapore become more global, the real estate industry transitioned from domestic concerns to a globalised approach, tapping into new sources of funding, developing a deep pool of human talent, and venturing into overseas markets.

However, the most important and enduring impact the real estate sector has helped achieve is the creation of a highly liveable and sustainable environment. Singapore has consistently ranked well in surveys of liveable cities, and we are known throughout the world for our sound infrastructure, a balance between living and working amenities, and our lush, green, landscaped spaces. Our hard-earned expertise in urban planning and sustainable development has been honed into a competitive niche, a global calling card of our competence and abilities.

"Singapore's Real Estate: 50 Years of Transformation" charts this extraordinary half-century of transformation, and serves as a rich and insightful guide and resource for real estate professionals, as well as interested members of the public. Besides the contributions of academics and policy makers, the book uniquely incorporates the views of leading industry practitioners, many of whom are our NUS alumni.

As Singapore moves into the next phase of growth, the real estate industry will need to remain highly adaptive and continue to build fresh capabilities. New challenges include climate change, high density living, demographic shifts, and the volatile global economy. To continue its enabling role in Singapore's development, and to stay globally competitive, the real estate industry will have to draw on the qualities of excellence, innovation, resourcefulness and resilience it has so successfully demonstrated over the past 50 years.

Introduction

Professor Deng Yongheng
Director, Institute of Real Estate Studies, NUS
Head, Department of Real Estate, NUS

Foremost, I would like to congratulate the editorial team of this SG50 book, comprising Dr Seek Ngee Huat, Chairman of the Institute of Real Estate Studies (IRES), and two of my colleagues (Sing Tien Foo and Yu Shi Ming) at IRES and the Department of Real Estate, for publishing a timely and relevant book in commemoration of the 50 years of Singapore's nation building.

World Scientific Publishing first approached Tien Foo with the idea of publishing a book regarding the real estate market in Singapore as part of its SG50 commemorative book series. This book proposal was aligned with Dr Seek's idea to have IRES produce a book which will document important lessons and experiences arising from the transformation of Singapore's real estate market since the country gained independence.

Clearly, Singapore's growth story is well-recognised and acknowledged by policy makers and urban planners; and the strategies behind the urbanisation process have likewise attracted keen interest among the academic community. To varying extents, many countries, both emerging and developed alike, have also emulated Singapore's urbanisation experience even as they relentlessly pursue their quests in creating sustainable and livable utopias within their respective sovereign contexts. However, there is a dearth of published books which document developments and transformations in Singapore's real estate market. Information on the real estate market during Singapore's transformative years are fragmented and scattered. Consequently, the recollection of such information is often only gathered through the narrative accounts provided by a handful of industry veterans and pioneers who have sailed through the sea of change over the years. To conserve the rich reservoir of experiences and perspectives for future generations to come and as a way to contribute to the local real estate industry, IRES endorsed and supported the initiative of penning this book.

The team commenced brainstorming and conceptualising a book outline as early as August 2014. The underlying principle centres on the need for a book that will prove as a useful reference for people to learn and appreciate the various thought processes, motivations and influencing factors that shaped the real estate market in Singapore. The editorial team leveraged on the valuable resources of some very experienced and influential thought-leaders in Singapore's real estate industry, and through structured interview processes, it was able to draw on their reservoir of knowledge. Another interesting feature in this book is that it sought the inputs of 30 distinguished Real Estate alumni of the National University of Singapore (NUS). The team incorporated their remarks, comments and views to provide a more coherent piece of Singapore's real estate story. Essentially, this has created a compilation of insights from industry captains that will add to the real estate heritage in Singapore.

Two broad themes have been identified that will aptly represent the development of the real estate market in Singapore. These are, namely, the local to globalisation drive in real estate, and the increased integration of real estate and capital markets.

Exporting the traditionally not-so-"portable" real estate expertise has been challenging. The small size of Singapore has not restricted its competitiveness in the area of international real estate business. The country has been able to establish a strong reputation through efficiency and professionalism when competing for projects overseas. Many Singaporean real estate firms including institutional investors, developers, consultants and associated professional service providers (architects, engineers, urban planners) have been expanding and exploring new business opportunities in real estate markets overseas.

As a regional and global financial hub centered in Asia, Singapore is also a forerunner in adopting changes and embracing new financial technologies that help to integrate real estate with capital markets. The emergence of the real estate investment trust (REIT) market in 2002, and its rapid growth that saw its capitalisation reaching S$70.35 billion as of May 2015, has been remarkable.

Globalisation and securitisation (a term that is commonly used in the real estate capital markets to describe the process of converting illiquid real estate cash flow into tradeable instruments) are twin engines that will continue to drive the future growth of Singapore's real estate market. This book: **"Singapore's Real Estate: 50 Years of Transformation"**, will not just be a comprehensive reference that reflects past developments; I certainly hope it will also contain useful learning points that will guide the growth of Singapore's real estate market in the next 50 years and beyond.

Acknowledgements

The writing of this book has been a challenging journey. It would have been even more daunting without the willing support and assistance given to us. We would like to thank the following people for helping us in completing this book.

Mr Lawrence Wong, Minister for National Development, for the Foreword.

Professor Tan Chorh Chuan, President of the National University of Singapore (NUS), for the Preface.

Professor Deng Yongheng, Director, Institute of Real Estate Studies (IREA) and Head of Department, National University of Singapore, for the Introduction.

We would like to thank DP Architects for proposing the idea for the book cover design. We would like to thank Urban Redevelopment Authority (URA) for sharing the Downtown@Marina Bay photo in Chapter 2; City Developments Limited CapitaLand Limited, Far East Organization, and Keppel Land for sharing the photos of their condominium projects in Chapter 3 and 7, as well as CapitaLand for the photos of IMM Building in Chapter 7.

For their generous contributions of materials for Chapters 3 and 4, developers and consultants from the real estate industry: City Developments Limited, CapitaLand Limited, Far East Organization, GuocoLand Limited, Keppel Land, Perennial Real Estate Holdings Limited; ERA Realty Network Pte Ltd, CBRE Pte. Ltd., DTZ, JLL, and Knight Frank Private Limited.

The following persons, who have kindly granted us precious interviews, despite their busy schedules, and shared with us their insights of interesting stories of Singapore's Real Estate in the book: Mr Ang Wee Gee, Mr Chia Boon Kuah, Mr Chia Ngiang Hong, Ms Chong Siak Ching, Mr Jack Chua, Mr Chris Fossick, Ms Pauline Goh, Mr Eugene Lim, Mr Philip Ng, Mrs Ong Choon Fah, Mr Ong Teck Hui, Mr Pua Seck Guan, Mr Willy Shee, Mr Tan Tiong Cheng, Mr Edmund Tie, and Mr Danny Yeo.

For their generous assistance on Chapter 5: Wendy Wong and Noel Neo. We also thank Peter Verwer for writing a case of the Australian REIT market in Chapter 7.

For the concluding Chapter 10, we are grateful for the contributions and valuable inputs by the members of the NUS real estate alumni: Chang Yoke Ping Frances, Chia Ngiang Hong, Chng Shih Hian, Chong Siak Ching, Choo Kian Koon Steven,

Chua Yang Liang, Goh Pauline, Kwok Wai Keong, Lee How Cheng Gerard, Leong Hong Yew, Lim Swe Guan, Lim Tong Weng Eugene, Liow Kim Hiang, Muhammad Faishal Ibrahim, Ng Seng Tat Michael, Ong Choon Fah, Ooi Thian Leong Joseph, Phua Jimmy, Poh Boon Kher Melvin, Pua Seck Guan, Sum Siok Chun Patricia, Tan Bee Kim, Tan Chew Ling, Tan Swee Yiow, Tan Tin Kwang William, Tan Wee Kiong Augustine, Tay Kah Poh, Yap Neng Tong Jonathan, Yeo Eng Ching Danny, and Yeo Huang Kiat Dennis.

We also thank our research assistant, Jeanette Yeo, for providing effective research support and assistance.

For supporting the production of this book, IRES, NUS, and the publication team at World Scientific.

We also gratefully acknowledge those whose names may not have been included in this list, but whose assistance in one way or another, has made the completion of the book possible.

Finally, we thank our families for their unfailing support and understanding. This book is dedicated to you all!

Seek Ngee Huat
Sing Tien Foo
Yu Shi Ming

About the Editors

Seek Ngee Huat is Chairman of the Institute of Real Estate at the National University of Singapore (NUS), where he is also an Adjunct Professor of Real Estate. He is also Chairman of Global Logistic Properties Ltd., a Board Director of Brookfield Asset Management Inc., Canada and a Senior Advisor to Frasers Centrepoint Ltd.

Dr Seek retired in 2011 as President of GIC Real Estate Pte. Ltd. after fifteen years, following which he served a further two years as Advisor to the GIC Group Executive Committee and a Board Director of GIC Real Estate. Before joining GIC, he was a Senior Partner at Jones Lang Wootton in Sydney. He served on the advisory boards of Guanghua School of Management, Peking University and Fundacao Dom Cabral, Brazil and the real estate advisory boards of Cambridge University and Harvard University. He was also a Board Director of the Pension Real Estate Association, USA.

Dr Seek was conferred the Singapore Public Administration Gold Medal in 2007, the NUS Outstanding Service Award in 2015 and the NUS Distinguished Alumni Service Award in 2011. He holds a BSc (Estate Management), University of Singapore; MSc (Business Administration), University of British Columbia; and a PhD (Urban Research), Australian National University.

Sing Tien Foo is the Dean's Chair Associate Professor and the Deputy Head (Administration and Finance) at the Department of Real Estate. He also serves as the Deputy Director at the Institute of Real Estate Studies (IRES) at the National University of Singapore. He sits on the Asian Real Estate Society (AsRES) Board (since 2000) and the Global Chinese Real Estate Congress (GCREC) Board (since 2008). He serves as a member of the panel of assessors for the Appeal Board (Land Acquisition), Ministry of Law (2010–present). He is the Co-Principal Investigator for the NUS-REDAS Real Estate Sentiment Index.

In NUS, he teaches real estate finance and investment modules at both undergraduate and post-graduate courses. His research interests include housing policies, real estate finance, and securitisation. Tien Foo obtained a PhD degree from University of Cambridge, UK in 1999 under the Cambridge Commonwealth Trust scholarship and the Overseas Research Students award. He holds a Master of

Philosophy degree in Land Economy from University of Cambridge, UK and a Bachelor of Science degree with First Class Honors in Estate Management from the National University of Singapore. He graduated from Ngee Ann Polytechnic with a Diploma in Building Management (Silver Medal) in 1989.

Yu Shi Ming obtained his undergraduate education in Urban Valuation from the University of Auckland, New Zealand, under the Colombo Plan Scholarship. He obtained his Master's degree and PhD from the University of Reading, UK. He joined NUS as a Senior Tutor in 1981 and since then has extensive teaching, research, and consultancy experience over the last 30 years. He has taught and published in the areas of real estate appraisal, housing, and urban and facilities management. He has also presented papers at many international conferences and conducted executive courses in Asia, Middle East, and Africa.

Yu Shi Ming has served as a member of several government organisations including the Housing and Development Board (HDB), the Council of Estate Agencies (CEA), the Resource Acquisition and Compensation Panel, the Valuation Review Board, and the West Coast Town Council. At NUS, he was Vice-Dean of the School of Design and Environment from 2000–2007 and Head of the Department of Real Estate from 2007–2013.

Part A
The Making of a Global City

Chapter 1

Evolution of the Real Estate Industry in Singapore

Seek Ngee Huat

Singapore's transformation since Independence in 1965, from a poor port city of the Third World to a modern world-class metropolis with one of the most developed and sophisticated real estate markets in the world, is truly remarkable. Very few markets in the world can claim the distinction of achieving so much as rapidly as Singapore has. This 50-year journey, made not without trials and tribulations, reflects in many ways a successful public-private partnership, combining pragmatic government policies with the entrepreneurship of the private sector. This book traces the evolution of the Singapore real estate industry and identifies the contributory factors to the successful partnership. The introductory chapter is an overarching summary of the book and subsequent chapters discuss in more detail the roles played by the government and the private sector — developers, investors, financiers, fund managers and consultants and other intermediaries — in this transformational journey from the simple beginning of a locally focused bricks-and-mortar market, building largely for owner-occupation through to globalisation and securitisation of real estate. The last two chapters look into the role of real estate education and collate the views and comments from the alumni of the NUS Real Estate school, on the future of Singapore real estate.

Supported by strong and sustained economic expansion, the public-private partnership has worked well for Singapore. Economic growth was the fuel that drove the public-private engine, and in combination created value as manifested in the multifold increase in property values. Sustained strong economic growth, with per capita GDP rising from S$1,580 in 1965 to S$71,318 in 2014,[1] accompanied by increasing demand for more and better quality space to live, work or play in, and growth in wealth and purchasing power, continued to push up the values of both residential and commercial real estate. Singapore has joined the league of "global superstar cities", including New York, London, Paris and Hong Kong, which share the common trait of rising home prices over a long period of time, reflecting the strong demand from

---

[1] At current market prices. Singapore Department of Statistics.

local and international investors.[2] Savvy international investors' selection of investment destinations is indicative of their confidence in the continuous strength of these markets. Singapore is one such favoured market. While each of these markets goes through its own boom and bust cycles, they have all shown secular upward trends both in real and nominal terms. For example, residential property values in Singapore increased by close to 23 times between 1965 and 2014.[3] However, property value only measures the performance of the market; it does not explain the workings of the underlying drivers that transformed the Singapore market.

Economic growth is a necessary but not sufficient condition to achieve the sophistication of a developed and mature real estate market. Over the last 50 years, increasing demand from economic expansion for all types of real estate for occupation and investment was met through a synergistic interplay between a private sector, which brought to bear its market knowledge, business skills, capital and willingness to take risks, and a public sector with the competence to effectively execute sound economic and social policies. This public-private synergy has served Singapore real estate well and provided a robust framework for the private real estate industry to grow, innovate and adapt to changing local and international conditions.

The Role of Government

Being a young nation, the Singapore government has played an active role since the country's formative years. It has been involved indirectly through its various agencies in providing and managing the hard and soft infrastructure as well as being the policy maker and regulator, and directly as a provider of physical real estate, being the largest land owner and supplier of housing.[4]

A key responsibility of government is the provision of hard infrastructure, including transportation, communications network, public utilities — including water, electricity, sewerage and waste collection — and public amenities such as parks and other recreation spaces. Singapore's urban planning and hard infrastructure are amongst the best in the world and it has been voted regularly as one of the most liveable cities in the world. Much has been written about the quality of Singapore's built environment but its soft infrastructure is of an equally high standard. Effective and efficient urban management carried out through the various ministries and government agencies and a strict enforcement of its laws and regulations are examples of the importance of soft infrastructure. In addition, unambiguous land use planning

---

[2] Phang Sock Yong, "Home prices and inequality: Singapore versus other global superstar cities", The Straits Times, 3 April 2015.
[3] See Chapter 3 for data sources.
[4] Chapter 2 details the roles of various government agencies.

guidelines and development, and building approval procedures and processes, reduce the uncertainties and associated risks for the private sector in making investment decisions. Another example of reducing uncertainty is the master planning approach adopted by Singapore. Drawing on the long range directions of 40–50 years set out in the Concept Plan (reviewed every ten years), the Master Plan, which is reviewed every five years, details land use plans in Singapore; this is supplemented by Development Guide Plans which stipulate planning objectives for 55 planning areas and specify the zoning, height limit and development intensity. This approach provides developers with clarity regarding what they are allowed to build in the medium term, and yet retains the flexibility to meet longer term changing needs.

In addition to being the provider of infrastructure, the government is also the regulator ensuring that all market players work within Singapore's legal framework, which is largely inherited from the British. Over time, new laws were enacted and existing ones amended to effect specific government policies. In the early years of independence, the Land Acquisition Act (1966) was enacted with sweeping powers to readily clear slums and resettle displaced residents, while the Controlled Premises (Special Provisions) Act (1969) allowed owners to repossess their rent-controlled premises for re-development purposes. Both pieces of legislation helped to accelerate the urban renewal programme in the 1970s following the recommendations of a team of United Nations (UN) experts in 1963. The complete abolition of rent control in 2001 paved the way for the redevelopment of privately owned buildings. Since those early years, the Central Business District (CBD) skyline and the many public housing estates today are an outcome of swift and considered legislative changes. When policy makers decided to encourage higher density living, the Land Titles (Strata) Act (LTSA) and the Buildings and Common Property (Maintenance and Management) Act were introduced in 1967 and 1973 respectively to enable the subdivision and ownership of strata space, and the management of common property. In 2004, this regime was given a major overhaul with the enactment of the Building Management and Strata Management Act which further provided for a two-tier management corporation framework for the management of common property in mixed developments. The LTSA also provided a regulatory framework for the collective sale of condominium units which allows strata unit owners to sell their old or physically obsolete property "en-bloc" for redevelopment.

The government has also demonstrated that it would not hesitate to intervene if the property market failed to meet its policy objectives. To alleviate the social ills and waste associated with the boom and bust cycles of the residential property market, the government has on a number of occasions introduced macro-prudential measures to moderate extreme market volatility. The most recent measures involved further increases in Additional Buyers' Stamp Duty (ABSD) and tightening of loan requirements implemented in 2013. While the government strived to meet its economic and social objectives, it also has shown to be cognizant of not stifling the entrepreneurial spirit and the market mechanism as an efficient allocator of scarce resources. For instance, in the run up to the last market peak in 2013, the government's preference was to release more land supply in the hope of moderating price increases through the market mechanism. Admittedly, the timing of any intervention is not always ideal, which may result in a sub-optimal outcome.

Another example is the government's proactive involvement in providing a business-friendly framework for the successful development of a Singapore Real Estate Investment Trust (REIT) — S-REIT market. As part of its comprehensive programme to enhance the role of Singapore as a key financial centre in Asia, if not the world, and sensing the growing demand for securitisation of real estate, it worked with local developers and fund managers to put in place regulations and appropriate tax concessions to encourage the setting up of public REITs.

The role of the government as provider and manager of infrastructure, regulator or even policy maker is essentially passive in nature. It provides an enabling framework for the private sector to carry out its activities. What is unique to Singapore is the government taking the role of an active participant in real estate development. In at least two areas, namely the supply of land for development purposes and public housing, government participation has significantly impacted the way the Singapore real estate market has developed.

The State is the largest land owner in Singapore. In addition to owning large tracts of land since Singapore's independence and through land reclamation exercises, the government is empowered, on behalf of the State, to compulsorily acquire land. Land parcels are released periodically by the government to the market for development under the "Sale of Sites" programme administered by the Urban Redevelopment Authority (URA) since the 1960s. Each land parcel is designated for a specific use or as a "white site", allowing a developer to decide the best mix of uses. The timing, location, frequency, pricing (by setting a reserved price) and number of land releases have an impact on developers' decisions on when, what, how much and where to develop as well as the pricing of completed buildings.

The control of public land supply is a powerful policy instrument. For example, between 1967 and 1969, 46 parcels of land were released under the Urban Renewal Department's Sale of Sites programme for commercial redevelopment[5] to accelerate the urban renewal programme recommended by a team of UN experts. The success of the programme depended on the ability of the URA to provide cleared sites in prime locations and on the private sector to apply its entrepreneurial skills, commit capital and take risks. Many of the commercial skyscrapers in the Singapore CBD skyline

---

[5] Singapore: A Pictorial History, 1819–2000, Gretchen Liu, Psychology Press, 2001, at pg 324.

today are the products of this partnership in the 1970s and 1980s. The subsequent clusters of developments at the Marina Centre[6] and Marina Bay[7] areas are mostly of mixed-use, intended for meeting the planning objective of bringing life to the city after office hours. The Marina Bay area has also met the planning objective of extending the CBD to the south of Raffles Place. Similarly, the planned releases of land for the development of regional centres across the island have seen the growth of Tampines, Jurong, Woodlands and Seletar, and met the policy objectives of decentralising commercial activities from the CBD.

Through Jurong Town Corporation (JTC), which was initially set up for implementing its industrialisation programme as part of the government's overall economic development plan, the government controls most of the industrial land in Singapore. It has developed over 7,000 hectares of land and built four million square metres of industry-related space. JTC has grown beyond its humble beginning of building simple factories and warehouses for manufacturing, to developing sophisticated facilities for high value-added end-users, including various biomedical and high-tech establishments, and more recently, Biopolis and Fusionopolis, to further Singapore's ambition of becoming a centre for knowledge-based industries.

Another uniquely Singaporean phenomenon is the demonstrated leadership of the government in proactively promoting the expansion of economic growth to the neighboring countries by developing the so-called "external wing" of the Singapore economy, key exports being its know-how in urban and township development, management and planning, riding on Singapore's reputation as a well-planned and efficiently managed modern world-class metropolis. To manage the risks associated with large scale greenfield development projects and to align interests, the government adopted the model of pooling resources and capital by forming consortia comprising government linked companies (GLCs) and the host countries' state-owned or private companies. Two of the most prominent successes from such collaborative projects are the Suzhou Industrial Park (SIP) and the Bangalore IT Park (BITP). They are also examples of how their successes were built on overcoming immense difficulties in the initial years. The SIP, launched in 1994, was the first government-to-government (G2G) developmental project between Singapore and China. This was followed by the Tianjin Eco-city in 2008 and more recently the Guangzhou Knowledge City and Sino-Singapore Food Zone. In the case of BITP, whilst it was initiated by the two governments, the project was led by Tata Corporation, the giant Indian conglomerate and Singapore's Ascendas, a subsidiary of JTC. Such G2G initiatives opened doors and provided the leadership and confidence for Singapore

---

[6] "The Changing Face of Singapore: Marina Centre", URA, Skyline Jan–Feb 2000.
[7] "Realising the Marina Bay Vision", URA, Skyline Jul–Aug 2008.

developers and investors to make substantial investment in real estate in China, Southeast Asia and India in subsequent years.[8]

The government is also the largest housing developer. Ownership of large tracts of land enabled the implementation of an ambitious public housing programme since the beginning of nationhood. Singapore's public housing, managed by the Housing Development Board (HDB), is the envy of the world. Built and managed to a high standard, albeit progressively improved over the years, HDB estates now house close to 80% of the population, of which 91.6% own their flats.[9] The government has more than met its social policy objective of satisfying the basic housing needs of the population, although meeting aspirational needs for even higher quality housing in recent times has been more challenging. Upgrading of existing HDB estates and building new higher quality flats can only meet such aspirations to an extent. To cater to the sandwiched class that is ineligible for public housing and unable to afford private housing, it introduced in 1995 a hybrid form of housing, called the Executive Condominium (EC). Nevertheless, many so-called "upgraders" continue to look to the private housing market to meet their higher aspirations. The public segment itself has a secondary market which allows owners, who have lived in their flats more than five years, to trade them in the open market. Many sell their HDB flats and use the proceeds to buy into the private market. This overlap is an important link between the public and private segments. It is another uniquely Singapore feature — a housing market with a public segment that overwhelms the private segment. Notwithstanding the fact that private housing accounts for approximately only 20% of the total housing stock, it plays the important function of providing housing for those who are ineligible for public housing, for HDB upgraders and for a large expatriate community.

Growth of the Real Estate Development Industry

Fifty years ago, real estate was a relatively simple and under-capitalised industry driven by entrepreneurs with little specialist knowledge in real estate. Most of the current home-grown developers started in the residential sector before Independence and evolved into developing commercial real estate much later. While the nature of the business may have changed somewhat over time for some of the largest and oldest companies, such as the Far East Organisation and the Hong Leong/CDL Group, the bulk of their business remains in residential development. In fact, the top 10 developers currently share more than 75% of the private housing market and the top five more than 50%.[10]

---

[8] See Chapter 6 for a more detailed account of the experience of Singapore in exporting real estate development and urban planning expertise.
[9] Yearbook of Statistics Singapore, 2015.
[10] See Chapter 3 for an analysis of market share.

In the early years, with limited capital, developers bought small land parcels to build mostly terrace and semi-detached houses. These were quickly sold in order to roll the capital into larger housing projects. It was in the 1970s that they were better capitalised and started building high-rise apartments mostly in the prime areas of Bukit Timah, Cairnhill, River Valley and Grange Road. Although the condominium concept was introduced in mid-1970s, it did not take off until the 1980s when developers began to respond with a slew of condo projects. The first condo development was Beverly Mai, a 28-storey tower at Tomlinson completed in 1974, followed by the Pearl Bank Apartments in Pearl Hills in 1976 and Pandan Valley, a 625-unit project completed by DBS Realty Pte Ltd (an entity which subsequently merged with Pidemco to form CapitaLand) in 1978. The Approved Residential Properties Scheme, introduced in 1981, which allowed members of the Central Provident Fund (CPF) to draw on their CPF savings to buy private properties, contributed to the rise in condo demand. In 1980, 32% of households[11] lived in private housing, and only 4% resided in condominiums and apartments; by 2014, 20% of households lived in private housing, and 14% lived in condominiums and apartments.[12]

The residential property market went through three distinct cycles, peaking in 1983/84, 1996 and 2013. The last cycle was precipitated by the Asian Financial Crisis (AFC) in 1997 and prices did not return to the last peak until 2008/2009 when it was hit by the Global Financial Crisis (GFC), which only caused a temporarily decline. The market resumed its upward movement until macro-prudential measures were introduced in 2013. Residential development is a cyclical business requiring developers to have the resilience and resources to weather a severe downturn. Many smaller developers did not survive it. In line with its policy of moderating extreme cyclical swings, while the government has imposed measures to cool down the market, it has conversely introduced measures to boost demand during severe downturns, such as suspending sale of land, deferring stamp duty and property tax rebates, for example.

Throughout the up and down cycles, developers continue to adapt to changing demands and demographics. While it was fashionable to build large units of over 2,000 sq ft in the 1970s and 1980s, partly constrained by rising cost and partly to accommodate changing needs and affordability, smaller units became the norm in the 1990s, to the extent that by the 2000s, "shoe-box" units of 500 to 600 sq ft began to flood the market. The quality of design and construction also continued to improve, especially since the 1990s, when the Building and Construction Authority, formed in 1989, introduced a standard quality assessment system, and assessment of projects built on all URA and HDB sites became mandatory.

---

[11] "Household" refers to a household headed by a resident (i.e. Singapore citizen or permanent resident). See Chapter 3 for a more detailed examination of Singapore's residential market.
[12] Singapore Department of Statistics.

Almost all the leading real estate companies in Singapore started their business in residential development and only moved to developing commercial projects in the 1970s when Singapore's urban renewal programme took off. Not unlike other real estate markets in the world, the Singapore market was quite unsophisticated in the 1960s. Most commercial buildings were built by individuals, families or corporates, mainly for their own use. In 1965, there were only a handful of prominent office buildings in the CBD and the Asia Insurance Building (now converted to a block of serviced apartments operated by Ascott), built in 1954, was the tallest with 20 storeys. The urban renewal programme rapidly transformed Singapore's skyline and by the 1970s, skyscrapers started to appear in Shenton Way and around Raffles Place: Robina House (1973), UIC Building (1973), Shenton House (1973), Ocean Building (1974), Hong Leong Building (1975), DBS Building (1975) and OCBC Building (1976).[13] Interestingly, some of these have already gone through a complete cycle of obsolescence and have been redeveloped or extensively upgraded. The URA initiative started the renewal momentum and the next cluster of high-rise office towers and hotels were built in the 1980s, notably Chartered Bank Building (1984), Raffles City (1984), OUB Centre (1988). During this and subsequent phases of renewal, many of these redevelopment projects were however not on URA sites. Recent clusters of modern buildings were built to higher specifications on reclaimed land in the Marina Bay areas.

Commercial real estate development activities in the first 25 years of Singapore's founding were constrained by limited capital resources. Singapore did not have the benefit of a home-grown institutional investment market the likes of which was being established during the 1970s and 1980s in the developed markets of the US, UK and Australia.[14] Hampered by inadequate capital and the absence of institutional support, developers had to find innovative ways to fund their projects. In the 1970s, developers were able to recycle scarce capital by sub-dividing their shopping centres and office buildings into strata-titled units and selling the individual units in the retail market to individual buyers either for investment or their own business use. Examples of such strata-titled commercial buildings at prime locations which still exist today include Lucky Plaza and Far East Shopping Centre around Orchard Road, International Plaza at Anson Road, and Golden Mile Complex, Golden Mile Tower and The Plaza along Beach Road.[15] This method of recycling capital has continued to the present time. However, since the 1970s, as developers have progressively become better capitalised, with many becoming listed as public companies, they have increasingly been able to

---

[13] Singapore Then & Now, Ray Tyers, revised by Siow Kin Hua, Landmark Books (1993).
[14] See Chapter 4 for details.
[15] Colliers International White Paper "Bright Spot in Singapore Property Market: Strata-titled Office", March 2012.

hold their developments for longer investment periods. Some of the early publicly listed property development companies in Singapore include United Engineers Limited and City Developments Limited, Singapore Land Limited, Boustead Singapore Limited, and GuocoLand Limited. Not surprisingly, as their capital positions have improved over time, so has the quality of the commercial developments built. The advent of REITs in the 2000s provided another avenue for recycling capital.

Moving from the developer/entrepreneur phase into the 1990s and 2000s, the Singapore real estate industry further developed by leveraging on the twin trends of globalisation and the securitisation of real estate equity and debt.

From Local to Global

Fifty years ago, real estate was basically a bricks-and-mortar industry driven by developers/entrepreneurs focusing on their domestic markets anywhere in the world. Very few ventured offshore. It was in the 1990s that the real estate business showed signs of becoming truly global, in terms of the scale and flows of capital across borders. Singapore has been a beneficiary of this trend, both as an importer of capital from foreign investors and as an exporter through the offshore investment activities of its home grown investment institutions and developers.

Cross-border investing in real estate was not a new phenomenon. Up until the 1990s, the scale of fund flows was relatively small and it happened in waves, each of which was largely driven by a dominant developed economy and the movement of funds was between developed markets. It was the British in the 1960s, followed by the Dutch in 1970s and then the Japanese in the 1980s. By the 1990s, multi-directional flows of investible funds into real estate became visible, and the Chinese emerged as the new significant foreign investors in the 2010s.

There are three main reasons for the surge in cross-border investment activities in the last 20 years. First, the development of an institutional real estate investment market in the developed economies from the 1970s through the 1980s is a phase not experienced in Singapore. Real estate was included formally as an alternative asset class, offering the benefits of risk diversification, inflationary hedge and stable long term returns, in a multi-asset investment portfolio. It led to a massive injection of capital into real estate in their domestic markets and the consequential increase in the quality of real estate investment management and the talent pool of investment professionals. Second, a huge growth in organised savings in the world has forced institutional investment managers to search for better risk-adjusted returns offshore in an increasingly competitive global market. According to a PwC Report, the combined global asset under management (AUM) of pension funds, insurance companies and sovereign wealth funds is estimated to reach US$101.7 trillion by 2020 from

US$63.9 trillion in 2014, a 63% increase over a period of just six years.[16] The third reason was an expanding real estate investment universe. Over the last 20 years, more markets have opened to foreign investment and institutional grade real estate, including those in emerging markets, has continued to grow alongside new investment choices in REITs and debt instruments.

Interestingly, the Government of Singapore Investment Corporation (GIC) began to diversify its investments to more countries from the late 1990s. The journey it took since its formation reflects in many ways the changes in the global arena. Save for the Dutch and Middle Eastern institutions, it was also one of the first institutional investors in the world to be given a mandate to invest in foreign real estate. Although it was established in 1982, almost all its investments in the initial years were in the US as it was then the only market with the depth and breadth to meet the conservative risk appetite of a prudent investment institution. It gradually diversified to other geographies. Modest attempts were made to invest in Europe in the late 1980s. Investment in Asia came much later in the mid-to-late 1990s. It was from this point onwards that its portfolio became truly "globalised" and it continued to expand its global portfolio. Today, it has investments in more than 30 countries.

GIC was not the only Singapore entity that ventured overseas. By the 1990s, other Singapore-based entities were also being carried by the globalisation trend. Home-grown companies including Singapore Land, Far East, Temasek, Capitaland and its predecessors (DBS Land and Pidemco), Keppel Land, Ascendas, GuocoLand and CDL made forays into foreign markets, targeting mostly emerging Asia, including China, Hong Kong, India, Korea and Southeast Asia and to a lesser extent, the developed markets of the UK, Australia, Japan and the US. However, the main business focus of these property companies was still the Singapore market. As at 2013, overseas real estate investment by Singapore companies stood at S$44.2 billion or 8.3% of Singapore's total direct investment abroad, of which China was a favoured destination, attracting S$23.3 billion.[17] In line with this global trend, whilst Singapore investors were venturing abroad, Singapore too was becoming a destination for capital flows from other countries. International investors initially sought to acquire physical real estate but later expanded into property securities as the market for REITs in Singapore developed.

Foreign developers and investors also began investing in Singapore in the 1990s. One of the most prominent development projects at the time was Suntec City, completed in 1997 by a Hong Kong consortium led by Cheung Kong Holdings. A slew of other foreign developers from Hong Kong, Australia, Indonesia, Malaysia, Japan and China, followed with investments in both residential and commercial projects, either

---

[16] "Real Estate 2020: Building the Future", PwC, 2014.
[17] Singapore Department of Statistics.

on their own or in joint ventures with local developers. Two major recent large mixed use developments in the new CBD were Asia Square and the Marina Business and Financial Center (MBFC). Asia Square was completed in 2013 by Macquarie Global Property Advisors and the development of MBFC by Hongkong Land, Keppel Land and the Cheung Kong Group was completed in 2012.

The globalisation trend also manifested itself in another way, with an influx of international fund managers and other intermediaries setting up regional offices in Singapore. Many are attracted to Singapore's position as a key financial centre with a stable political environment and strong and reliable hard and soft infrastructures. It also has a pool of skilled and experienced human resources trained in a sophisticated real estate industry. Tax concessions given to qualified regional offices are an added incentive. Its strategic location in Asia serves as a natural launching platform for their real estate investment programmes in Asia.

A number of investment managers have established their regional headquarters in Singapore including Pramerica, the Asian subsidiary of Prudential US, Eastspring Investment (wholly owned by UK-based Prudential plc), Chartered Investment Management, LaSalle Investment Management, SEB, and AVIVA (acquired by JP Morgan recently). Institutional investors like La Caisse de dépôt et placement du Québec, the Investment Company of People's Republic of China, and Norges Bank Investment Management have also set up offices in Singapore.[18] As the number of investment professionals such as portfolio managers, investment analysts, traders and economists operating out of Singapore increased by almost four-fold, from 814 in 1997 to 3,312 as at 2012, Singapore appears poised to become a regional hub for this sector.[19]

Intermediaries provide much needed information to assist investment decision-making. Away from the comfort and familiarity of their home markets, foreign investors are faced with unfamiliar market fundamentals and structures, business practices and regulatory and taxation frameworks. Not surprisingly, there has been a proliferation of specialist real estate intermediaries, including banks, fund managers, asset managers, lawyers, accountants and consultants and brokers servicing the information needs of investors. With increasing competition from other service providers, international real estate consultants and brokerage houses in particular, including Jones Lang LaSalle, CBRE, Knight Frank, DTZ and Colliers, established over the last 40 years, appear to be holding their own and continue to grow with the Singapore market and strengthen their operations to service both local and international clients.

---

[18] "2014 Singapore Asset Management Survey, Singapore — Global City, World of Opportunities", Monetary Authority of Singapore.
[19] Singapore Asset Management Industry Surveys 1998–2012, Monetary Authority of Singapore.

From Bricks-and-Mortar to Capital Markets

Singapore is a beneficiary of the global trend of the integration of real estate with the capital markets. The commercial property investment model of building or buying an asset to hold and collect rent has remained unchanged for a long time and the capital structure of this model commonly comprises a combination of private equity and a bank loan, not unlike how most individuals finance their homes. While this funding structure is still prevalent, innovations in the real estate industry and the capital markets over the last 20 years have enabled all parts of the underlying capital structure of real estate to become tradeable both in the private and public markets. This transformational change has resulted in a vastly expanded range of real estate investment instruments and vehicles in the markets. Instead of buying and selling physical assets as has been the practice since time immemorial, new thinking and innovations in the capital markets have allowed the equity and debt components in the capital structure to be bought and sold. This so-called four-quadrant approach has become an integral part of modern real estate investment practice in developed markets; the four quadrants being private and public debt and equity.

Use of innovative debt instruments, initially confined to the US, later spread to the more developed markets in Europe. Save for Japan and Australia to a limited extent, the real estate debt market remains under-developed in Asia. In Singapore, the first commercial mortgage backed bonds (CMBB) was a small issuance of S$18.5 million backed by a mortgage of the Hong Leong Building, but in the property boom years of 1994–1997 that followed, 16 CMBB with a total value of S$2.32 billion were issued. When the AFC hit in 1997, developers facing financial stress transferred their assets into Special Purpose Vehicles (SPVs) which in turn issued commercial real estate backed securities (CREBS) with fixed coupon yields. Singapore's nascent development of a real estate debt investment market was virtually vanquished by the GFC, although by 2006, 31 tranches of CMBS totalling S$5.91 billion were arranged. No further issuances have been made since then. However, more recently, a structured debt deal made between Blackstone and CDL for a property in Sentosa is perhaps an indication of innovative debt instruments becoming more readily available as traditional lending sources tighten.[20]

On the equity side, the breakthrough was the introduction of REITs, which led to a surge in the securitisation of public real estate equity and private (or sometimes called unlisted) equity funds throughout the world. In terms of scale and impact, the modern REIT era started in the early 1990s in the US during the Savings and Loans Crisis as a way for distressed owners to raise capital when the market for real estate financing was very tight. It quickly gained acceptance and grew rapidly to the extent

---

[20] See Chapter 8 which traces the development of Singapore's debt market.

that by the end of the decade more than 60 REITs were publicly listed in the US with a market cap of US$118 billion.

The proliferation of the REIT model globally to 37 countries[21] marks an important transformational change in the real estate industry. It not only presents investors with another investment avenue but also greater liquidity to those who perceive real estate as lumpy and illiquid. It allows smaller investors to access commercial real estate and provides developers and asset owners with another means to recycle capital.

Singapore entered the REIT market much later in 2002 with the launching of CapitaLand Mall Trust (CMT) as the first S-REIT, but it has grown rapidly since then. In 2005, there were five S-REITs with a total market capitalisation of S$5.2 billion.[22] It has grown by more than 12 times to around S$66.7 billion with 28 listed REITs and six stapled listed property trusts today.[23]

The development of the REIT market in Singapore provides an important additional source of funding for equity real estate, and contributes to the deepening of the commercial real estate market. Developers now have another reliable vehicle to recycle capital, while small investors can invest through REITs to own a share of large commercial properties, which were previously beyond their reach. S-REITs have become attractive investments for investors looking for indirect exposure to Singapore commercial real estate as well other Asian markets.

Singapore REITs, not unlike similar vehicles in other markets, were introduced as an investment vehicle principally for local real estate. However, the S-REITs have since evolved uniquely to have a substantial exposure to foreign real estate, which is not surprising given Singapore's limited market size. Of the 28 REITs, at least ten[24] have some exposure to foreign real estate and at least six[25] are entirely foreign. The fact that Singapore has established a fully functional REIT market in advance of many other Asian countries helps to draw foreign players to list in Singapore. This unique characteristic is partly the efforts of REIT managers, who being constrained by size of the Singapore market, scour for assets in other countries.

Another international phenomenon is the growth of real estate private equity funds in the last 20 years. The volume of funds raised by private equity vehicles

---

[21] European Public Real Estate Association (EPREA), http://www.epra.com/regulation-and-reporting/taxation/reit-survey/, accessed on 11 November 2015.
[22] The Growth of REIT Markets in Asia, Joseph T. L. Ooi, Graeme Newell and Sing Tien Foo (2006), Journal of Real Estate Literature, Volume 14 No. 2, pp. 203-222
[23] Singapore Exchange.
[24] CDL Hospitality Trust, Ascendas Real Estate Investment Trust, Ascendas Hospitality Trust, Ascott Residence Trust, First Real Estate Investment Trust, Keppel REIT, Frasers Commercial Trust, OUE Commercial REIT, ParkwayLife REIT and Suntec REIT.
[25] Fortune REIT, CapitaRetail China Trust, Mapletree Greater China Comm, Saizen REIT, Lippo Malls Indonesia Retail Trust and IREIT Global.

peaked in 2007 at US$760 billion,[26] but they were severely tested during the GFC and many were found wanting and did not survive the crisis. Fund raising had been difficult in the years after the GFC, during which only the larger, more established global funds were able to raise money more readily. In the last few years, however, fund raising activities have risen significantly, indicating the return of confidence by investors in private funds. Preqin reported funds raised in 2014 stood at US$103.5 billion, a significant rebound from the post-GFC quantum of US$52.7 billion in 2009.[27]

The first Singapore-based fund was a 1994 three-party joint venture between US Prudential, Jones Lang Wootton and GIC, called the South East Asian Property Co (SEAPAC). Subsequent to that, Singapore real estate companies also saw the potential of the private fund management business as an extension of being managers of public REITs. In 2003, Keppel Land's real estate investment arm, Alpha Investment Partners, set up a close-end fund, the Asia No. 1 Property Fund[28] and CapitaLand launched its first integrated development private equity fund, the Raffles City China Fund, in China in 2008.[29] Many more fund management entities were formed in subsequent years in Singapore, including ARA Asset Management, Pacific Star Financial, Perennial Real Estate, Prudential Real Estate Investors Asia Pacific and Global Logistic Properties.[30] Given the size constraint of the Singapore market, most of these funds adopted a mandate of investing beyond Singapore covering markets largely in Asia.

Conclusion

From its humble bricks-and-mortar beginnings, the Singapore real estate industry has grown to a high level of sophistication, offering a range of investment choices in both the public and private markets, and securing its position as a regional hub for real estate fund management activities in Asia. The public-private formula has worked well for Singapore real estate, allowing the private developers and investors to achieve their profit motive, while satisfying the government policy agenda. Through both design and good fortune, this partnership has proven to be effective in capitalising on opportunities and overcoming challenges.

The real estate industry has shown resilience, innovation, and adaptability in transforming itself in the last 50 years. It hopefully will be just as adept at meeting

---

[26] Preqin.
[27] Preqin.
[28] "Alpha raises $1.6b for its latest fund", Business Times Singapore, 16 July 2008.
[29] "CapitaLand sets up first integrated development private equity fund in China", CapitaLand, News Release, 16 July 2008.
[30] Preqin.

future challenges. It has to learn to accommodate the needs of an ageing population, changing demographics, increasing affluence with demands for better work-life balance, work place and style changes and more stringent sustainability requirements, with new design and construction. Information technology and e-commerce, which are already changing traditional shopping habits and rendering some shopping centres obsolete, will continue to have a profound influence on what and where we work, live and play. In many capital market initiatives, such as REITs and fund and wealth management, Singapore has had a head start, but its pre-eminence as a hub for investment management activities will be challenged by other cities in the region. There are indeed many challenges ahead. What has worked in the last 50 years may not for the next 50 years. A new formula will need to be found.

Chapter 2

Transforming a Nation: Role of Government Agencies

Yu Shi Ming and Sing Tien Foo

1. Introduction

Since independence, the Singapore government has spearheaded the country's economic development including the real estate industry through its agencies. Any documentation of the transformation of the Singapore real estate market and industry over the last 50 years must therefore acknowledge the significant contributions of the various government agencies. In fact, a number of these agencies were already established before independence — some of them were set up when the country obtained self-rule in 1959. One of these is the Housing and Development Board (HDB), which was established in 1960. By the time Singapore gained independence in 1965, substantial breakthrough in the provision of public housing had already been attained. Today, the HDB is the largest public housing developer, providing housing for more than 80% of Singapore's population. This achievement is but one of the many that clearly illustrate the key roles that government agencies have played in the transformation of the real estate industry.

Indeed, the role of government agencies cannot be over-emphasised; quite often, they needed to take the lead before the private sector could enter the fray. The close public and private partnership is a significant factor in the rapid development of the real estate industry. Each government agency's involvement and contributions have been well documented. This chapter therefore only intends to provide an overview of the critical roles played by these agencies in the transformation of Singapore's urban landscape. It will start with outlining the roles of the various public agencies in the real estate development life cycle. It then highlights the significant roles of the government in the three key areas of planning and development, housing and industrial and economic developments. The chapter concludes by reiterating the importance of the partnership between the government and the private sector in the development of the real estate industry over the last 50 years.

Real estate is a multi-faceted and complex subject. It provides shelter, which is a basic human need, and its attendant amenities and facilities. It supports and drives economic growth and development through its industrial and office sectors. It underpins the tourism and leisure industry through hotels, serviced apartments and tourist attractions. Indeed, it covers all types of buildings and institutions including schools, hospitals, utility buildings and also extends to parks, green spaces, and sports and recreation facilities. Given the diversity and wide spectrum, it is therefore not surprising that at least six of the 16 ministries in Singapore have a direct impact on the real estate industry. These are the Ministries of National Development, Trade and Industry, Environment and Water Resources, Finance, Law and Transport. The specific roles of the various statutory boards and agencies will be discussed under different phases of a real estate development cycle. It must be noted that there are other government agencies, which will have an indirect impact on real estate activities. For example, the Ministry of Manpower (MOM) oversees the employment of foreign workers who form a substantial portion of the construction industry's human resource. So while the MOM's overall policies and regulations would generally have no direct impact on the real estate industry, the specific policy regulating the employment of foreign workers would.

2. Role of Government Agencies in the Real Estate Development Life Cycle

A real estate development life cycle comprises six main phases. Starting with a vacant site (land assembly and preparation) through planning, construction, occupation and eventual redevelopment, the government plays multiple roles in each phase of the lifecycle.

2.1 *Land Assembly and Preparation*

In this initial phase of a real estate development cycle, Singapore is unique compared to other countries that gained independence at around the same time. As a small island-state and nation, Singapore's land regulatory framework has the advantage of having the oversight of a single level of authority in all matters dealing with real estate developments. The size constraint, however, necessitates the need to expand physical land mass through reclamation. Today, key infrastructure and real estate projects, such as the Changi Airport and the Marina Bay, sit on reclaimed land. Land acquisition was carried out during the 1960s and the 1970s in furtherance of public projects involving housing, transportation and schools. Indeed, the Land Acquisition Act was one of the most important pieces of

Figure 1. Real estate development life cycle.

legislation passed in the 1960s when the framework for Singapore's urban transformation was being laid. While some countries may share similar constraints, using the power of eminent domain has created the Singapore of today, where land is largely state-owned and yet private sector developments are simultaneously and actively encouraged.

One of the most critical problems at the time of independence was the living conditions of the Central Area. The Urban Renewal Unit (URU) was set up in 1964 to undertake comprehensive urban renewal and redevelopment of the Central Area. Its task was to remake the Central Area into a vibrant, modern commercial centre. This required finding new homes for residents and new locations for industries. Redeveloping the Central Area was an uphill and daunting task. The lack of control and planning since the early days of Singapore had resulted in clusters of shophouse settlements in the Central Area, which had deteriorated into veritable slums. Sites were fragmented making it difficult for the URU to assemble into meaningful modern developments. Shophouses were overcrowded and obsolete; streets were narrow; and, the most challenging obstacle was the extensive resettlement of residents from the Central Area to the outer regions of Singapore. The URU was renamed the Urban Renewal Department (URD) in 1966. Its officers took the challenge head-on. They went on site visits to get a feel of ground sentiments and conditions; and worked in tandem with the planners for public housing. Central Area slum dwellers were gradually resettled into first-generation HDB flats with modern conveniences such as running water, electricity and sanitation. More importantly, residents had more space of their own — home was no longer a temporary shophouse cubicle shared with another household. After addressing these housing needs, the URD could begin the redevelopment of downtown Singapore.

In 1966, the passing of the Land Acquisition Act eased the way forward for the URD enabling it to acquire, clear and assemble fragmented land lots for development, to build up the State's land reserves, and to resettle displaced residents. By 1967, the URD had successfully sold 13 sites under the "Sale of Sites" programme. The "Sale of Sites" programme helped the URD to realise its vision for downtown Singapore. One of the first completed developments was People's Park Complex — Southeast Asia's first modern, international class multi-use building with shops, offices and residential apartments. Through the '70s and the '80s, the URD's (and later the Urban Redevelopment Authority's (URA)) land sales function helped to transform the Central Area from a motley collection of shophouses to the downtown of a new nation making its mark in the world.

The "Sale of Sites" successor, the Government Land Sales (GLS) programme, forged partnerships between the Government and the private sector. The Government planned and implemented key infrastructure before releasing land for development lands for sale by tender; the private sector provided the capital investment and market expertise to develop those land parcels. As the main land sales agent of the Government, the URA has facilitated the rejuvenation of the historic Singapore River area into a vibrant commercial, recreational and entertainment precinct, and transformed Tanjong Rhu into a quality waterfront living area. The successful development of Marina Bay, Singapore's new financial district, with key developments such as the Marina Bay Financial Centre and Asia Square, and the development of new growth centres at Jurong Lake District and Paya Lebar Central, were made possible through the GLS programme.

Land assembled for development needs to be prepared with basic infrastructure such as the provision of water, electricity, sewerage and other amenities. This is a necessary condition for real estate development and in the case of Singapore, largely undertaken by the government agencies. As a result, real estate developments in Singapore can be successfully completed on time, which helped to speed up the pace of urban development. Another important infrastructure development is land transport. Real estate is about location and thus accessibility, which is determined by the transportation network. The Land Transport Authority (LTA) is responsible for

Co-location of Mass Rapid Transit (MRT) Station, bus interchange and residential/commercial developments
E.g. Clementi and Toa Payoh new towns

Horizontal Integration

Combining similar land uses by utilising underground space to optimize land use
E.g. Dhoby Ghaut MRT interchange

Vertical Integration

Physical Integration

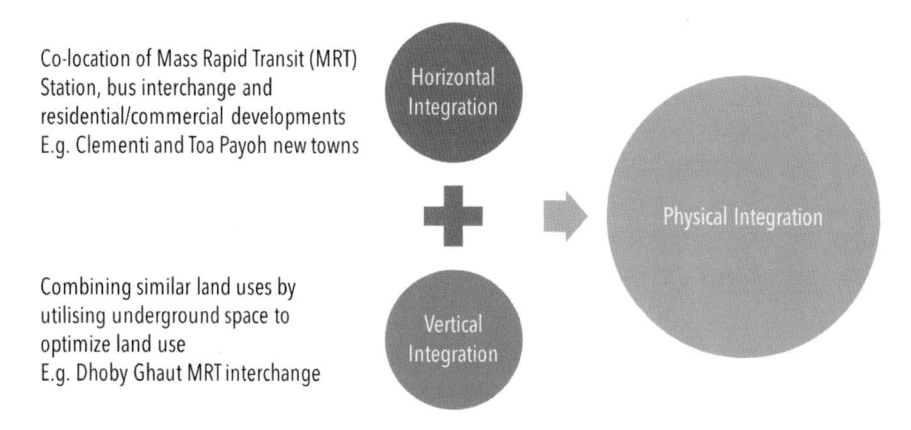

Figure 2. Integration of Transport Hub and real estate developments.

planning, operating, and maintaining Singapore's land transport infrastructure and systems. More specifically, road and rail are the two components of land transport and their developments form part of infrastructure to support real estate developments.

Achieving integration of land use and transport has been paramount in planning for real estate development in Singapore. Over the years, there has been an increase in physical integration (see Figure 2), both horizontal and vertical, depending on land use, site constraints and construction costs.

Roads are the primary means of access for real estate developments in Singapore. If poorly managed, negative externalities such as congestion and noise may result. Singapore has made significant investments in road infrastructure over the years. Given the land constraints, fiscal measures such as the Certificate of Entitlements and Electronic Road Pricing have been introduced to limit the growth in the number of vehicles as well as their usage. To overcome land scarcity, Singapore developed her underground space for transportation. Examples include the Kallang-Paya Lebar Expressway (KPE) with nine kilometres of highway constructed entirely underground, and the Marina Coastal Expressway (MCE). Rapid transit has also come a long way since 1982. A rapid transit system — the Mass Rapid Transit (MRT) — commenced operations with sections of the North-South Line in 1988, followed by the completion of East-West Line and North-South Line in 1990. The MRT has proven to be an effective means of public transport, especially with seamless integration with buses, and hence the addition of new lines and stations. It has been an important part of the Concept Plan and all property developments benefit from having an MRT station in their vicinity. Over the last two decades, properties sited near MRT stations have experienced an increase in value as a result of commuting convenience.

2.2 Planning and Approval

Being small is a double-edged sword in urban planning terms. Whilst easier to plan and control, it is also subject to constraints given that the use of land is limited. Planning and development control is one of the most fundamental critical success factors in the transformation of Singapore's real estate industry.

The Urban Redevelopment Authority (URA) is the lead agency that is entrusted with ensuring that the use of limited lands is optimised. Singapore adopts a two-tier system in land use planning. This consists of the Concept Plan, which is a long-term strategic plan addressing broader national concerns on social, economic and environmental issues, and the Master Plan, which prescribes detailed parameters for every land parcel, such as land use type, density, road networks, open spaces, building form and height, taking into consideration local development needs. Together, the plans address housing needs as well as community, commercial, industrial, transport and recreational facilities for the population of each area. Both long term and detailed planning have become a hallmark of Singapore's development. A Master Plan Committee, which represents all the key users of land in Singapore, deliberates on the Concept and Master Plans. Besides allocation of land uses, the URA also oversees all aspects of development control including the conservation of land and buildings. Physical planning in Singapore is therefore supported by a comprehensive system of planning and development control parameters and legislation.

The first Concept Plan was formulated in 1971 with the technical assistance of the United Nations Development Programme. It follows a "ring-shaped" plan with high density developments separated by green buffers surrounding the central water catchment areas. Major developments, such as Changi Airport, Mass Rapid Transit (MRT), the Central Business District (CBD) and others, are some of the outcomes outlined in the first Concept Plan. The Concept Plans were reviewed every 10 years in 1991, 2001 and 2011 to keep pace with rapid changing environments and also to meet population and economic growth in the future. In 2003, the URA also unveiled an ambitious plan to propel Singapore into a world class Business Centre by seamlessly integrating the Downtown Marina South with the existing CBD in the Raffles Place, Shenton Way and Marina Centre areas (Case Study 1).

The Master Plan first introduced in 1958 is the statutory land use plan, which guides Singapore's development in the medium term over the next 10 to 15 years. It is reviewed every five years so that local development activities can be guided dynamically to realise the long-term objectives of the Concept Plan. The planning parameters are clearly specified to provide certainty and transparency in property development activities for developers and prospective investors. In 1987, the URA

Case Study 1: The Making of a New CBD in the Marina Downtown[1]

In Jun 2003, the Urban Redevelopment Authority (URA) unveiled the latest master plan for the Downtown @ Marina Bay, which aimed to transform Singapore into an international business and financial hub (Figure CS1-1). The Downtown @ Marina Bay serves as a seamless extension of the current Singapore's Central Business District at Raffles Place, Shenton Way and Marina Centre create a distinctive and global location for business, living, working and leisure surrounding the Bay area.

The new Marina Downtown consists of 360 hectares of lands reclaimed in the 1970s and 1980s in anticipation of the potential growth of the CBD. It is planned as a vibrant, mixed-use residential district with round-the-clock activities based on sustainable development strategies. The area is connected to 4 Rapid Transit System (RTS) lines and 9 Mass Rapid Transit (MRT) stations, and also planned with a network of dedicated cycling lanes. A comprehensive pedestrian system of landscaped boulevards, covered walkways, underground link malls and high-level links are built to allow pedestrians to move comfortably around the bay area. Attached to the sale of the Marina Business and Financial Centre site, 1.8 ha underground malls were built linking Raffles Place MRT Station to the basements of Marina Business and Financial Centre, One Raffles Quay, and other surrounding developments. It is equipped with the state-of-the-art infrastructure, which include hub car parks, common services tunnels and centralized refuse disposal systems.

The majority of land parcels within the Downtown @ Marina Bay are zoned "white" to give flexibility for mixed-use developments with a variety of office, hotel, residential, retail and entertainment facilities. High-density, high-rise residential developments are also planned to offer quality options for city living. The reclaimed sites fronting Marina Bay will be released progressively for developments of around 1.27 million sqm of gross floor area and 1,150 residential units to support the next 15–20 years' growth.

Figure CS1-1. A world-class city in the making — Downtown @ Marina Bay.
(Photo Courtesy of the Urban Redevelopment Authority)

---

[1] Source: the Urban Redevelopment Authority (URA), Singapore. (https://www.ura.gov.sg/uol/master-plan/View-Master-Plan/master-plan-2014/Growth-Area/City-Centre/Marina-Bay-Marina-South.aspx)

introduced the development guide plans (DGPs), which were detailed land plans for 55 subdivided areas in the island, as part of its initiative to systematically and comprehensively review of the 1985 Master Plan. All the 55 DGPs were completed in December 1998, and they were gazetted into the new Master Plan. The new Master Plan has since evolved from being a static prescriptive planning document into a forward-looking plan. One of the unique features of the DGPs was the introduction of the "white site" concept in October 1995. From the planning authority's viewpoint, the concept is a positive move to ensure that land use planning is responsive to market conditions. For land parcels zoned as "white sites", developers are given the discretion to choose the mix of uses and the quantum of floor space of each use as long as the total permissible gross floor area (GFA) for the site is not exceeded. Developers are permitted to switch uses at any time during the life of the project without having to pay the differential premium, which is imposed when a change to a higher value land use is involved. Such an innovative approach also reflects how the Singapore government has responded to the constraints of size (Case Study 2).

Today, Singapore is economically vibrant and one of the most liveable cities in the world. This is a result of the comprehensive and long-term approach in land use planning. This integrated approach is needed to optimise the use of Singapore's limited land, and to meet current and future needs of the people. Being small, the integrated approach is necessary to ensure that all current and future needs are

---

Case Study 2: "White Sites"

With the flexibility afforded by developers are able to respond swiftly to changing market conditions thus minimizing the risks of mismatching usage with market demand.[1] This built-in flexibility confers a premium on white sites, which is valuable in highly volatile and dynamic property markets.[2] Table CS2-1 shows a list of white sites sold through the government's sales of sites programme.[3]

---

[1] Ong, S.E., Sing, T.F. and Malone-Lee, L.C., (2004) "Strategy Considerations in Land Use Planning: The Case of Singaporean White Site" *Journal of Property Research*, 21:3, 235–253.
[2] Sing, T.F., Yu, S.M. and Ong, S.E. (2002) ""White" Site Valuation: A Real Option Approach," *Pacific Rim Property Research Journal*, 8:2, pp. 140–157.
[3] A site with a conservation building at Cheang Jim Chwan Place at Prinsep Street has also been sold with a white site zoning.

(*Continued*)

CHAPTER 2 | Transforming a Nation: Role of Government Agencies   27

Table CS2-1. White sites sold by URA.

S/N	Date of award	Location (DGP)	Type of development allowed	Site area (m²)	GPR	GFA (m²)	Lease (yrs)	Successful tenderer	Successful tender price ($psm /GFA)
1	13-Mar-96	Middle Road/ Prinsep Sreet (Rochor)	Commercial or Hotel or Commercial/ Residential	2,600.6	4.2	10,923	99	IOI Properties Berhad	$52,222,222 ($4,780.94)
2	13-Mar-96	China Square (Downtown Core)	Commercial or Hotel or Commercial/ Residential	3,077.5	13.9	42,655	99	The Development Bank of Singapore Ltd	$367,310,736 ($8,611.20)
3	16-Sep-96	Esplanade Mall (Raffles Link/Raffles Boulevard/Nicoll Highway) (Downtown Core)	Commercial or Commercial & Residential or Hotel with underground shopping mall	17,992.6	3.5#	36,740	99	HKL (Marina) Ltd	$292,005,000 ($7,947.92)
4	21-Oct-96	Tekka Corner (A) (Serangoon Road/ Sungei Road) (Rochor)	Commercial or Hotel or Commercial & Residential and Carpark Station	6,332.0	3.5	22,162	99	Hicom Properties Sdn Bhd	$84,000,000 ($3,790.27)
5	6-Nov-96	China Square (F) (South Bridge Road/ Cross Street/China Street/Nankin Street) (Downtown Core)	Commercial or Commercial & Residential or Hotel	13,981.7	3.5	48,550	99	Merevale Holdings Pte Ltd	$308,000,100 ($6,343.98)

(Continued)

Table CS2-1. (Continued)

S/N	Date of award	Location (DGP)	Type of development allowed	Site area (m^2)	GPR	GFA (m^2)	Lease (yrs)	Successful tenderer	Successful tender price ($psm/GFA)
6	4-Jun-97	China Square G (South Bridge Road/ Pickering Street/ China Street/ Nankin Street) (Downtown Core)	White Site (permitted uses are Commercial and/or Residential and/or Hotel and/or Medical Centre (Excluding Hospital & Sanatorium)	13,554.1	3.0	40,300	99	Merevale Holdings Pte Ltd & The Great Eastern Life Assurance Co Ltd	$340,050,000 ($8,437.97)
7	21-Feb-00	Clarke Quay MRT Station (Singapore River)	White Site (Commercial and/or hotel and/or Residential (Serviced Apartments are allowed)	15,302.3	5.6&	77,577.36	99	Arts Associate Company Pte Ltd	$340,800,000 ($4,393.03)
8	16-Mar-01	Raffles Quay/Marina Boulevard (Downtown Core)	White Site (Commercial/ Hotel/Residential) Underground Pedestrian Mall with activity-generating uses.	11,366.9	13.0	147,770	99	Boulevard Development Pte Ltd, Comina Investment Limited & Freyland Pte Ltd	$461,816,800 ($3,125.24)
9	14-May-02	Marina Boulevard (B) (Downtown Core)	White Site (Commercial/Hotel/ Residential)	9,090.9	13.0	118,182	99	Glengary Pte Ltd	$288,900,000 ($2,444.53)
10	31-May-02	Sinaran Drive (Novena)	White Site (Commercial/Hotel/ Residential/Civic and Community Institution)	7,822.6	4.2	32,855	99	Glory Realty Co Pte Ltd	$100,800,000 ($3,068.03)

11	14-Jul-05	Marina Boulevard/ Central Boulevard (BFC) (Downtown Core)	Development of a business and financial centre, with at least 60% of the maximum permissible GFA to be used for office. The remaining GFA may be used for complementary uses such as hotel, residential, recreation/ entertainment.	35,515.2	12.3	438,000	99	Bayfront Development Pte Ltd, Choicewide Group Limited and Sageland Pte Ltd	$1,908,315,094.77 ($4,356.88)
12	25-May-07	Belilios Road/Klang Lane (Rochor)	Commercial/Hotel/ Residential and Car Park Station	3,086.7	3.5	10,803	99	Hotel Grand Central Ltd	$48,888,888 ($4,525.49)
13	25-Sep-07	Marina View (Land Parcel A) (Downtown Core)	Commercial/Hotel/ Residential	10,238.4	13.0	133,120	99	MGP Berth Pte. Limited	$2,018,888,988 ($15,165.93)
14	1-Oct-07	Race Course Road/ Rangoon Road (Rochor)	Hotel/Commercial/ Residential/Hospital use (with at least 40% of the max perm GFA for hotel use)	13,625.0	4.2	57,225	99	Singapore Healthpartners Pte Ltd	$265,265,000 ($4,635.47)
15	5-Dec-07	Marina View (Land Parcel B) (Downtown Core)	Commercial/Hotel/ Residential	8,735.7	13.0	113,580	99	MGP Kimi Pte. Limited	$952,888,888 ($8,389.58)

(continued)

Table CS2-1. (Continued)

S/N	Date of award	Location (DGP)	Type of development allowed	Site area (m²)	GPR	GFA (m²)	Lease (yrs)	Successful tenderer	Successful tender price ($psm/GFA)
16	28-Jun-10	Jurong Gateway Road (Jurong East)	Commercial/Hotel/Residential	19,124.5	5.6	107,098	99	Lend Lease Retail Investments 3 Pte. Ltd. and Lend Lease Commercial Investments Pte. Ltd.	$748,888,000 ($6,992.55)
17	22-Nov-10	Peck Seah Street/Choon Guan Street (Downtown Core)	Commercial/Hotel/Residential	15,022.6	10.5	157,738	99	Perfect Eagle Pte. Ltd., Guston Pte. Ltd. And Belmeth Pte. Ltd.	$1,708,080,000 ($10,828.59)
18	30-May-11	Boon Lay Way (Jurong East)	Commercial/Hotel/Residential	18,159.1	4.9	88,980	99	JG Trustee Pte. Ltd. (in its capacity as trustee of Infinity Mall Trust) and JG2 Trustee Pte. Ltd. (in its capacity as trustee of Infinity Office Trust)	$968,999,999 ($10,890.09)
19	7-Dec-12	Thomson Road/Irrawaddy Road (Novena)	Hotel/residential, office, retail	6,676.8	4.2	28,043	99	Hoi Hup Realty Pte Ltd, Sunway Developments Pte. Ltd. and Hoi Hup J.V. Development Pte Ltd	$492,500,000 ($17,562.32)

Source: Urban Redevelopment Authority (URA), Singapore.
Based on LPA1: 8,782.8 sqm & Based on Land Parcel A1:11,321.5 sqm and A2:2,531.6 sqm.

looked into, and from every stakeholder. Both the Concept and Master Plans are only finalised after public consultation and feedback. This is important to achieve the vision of an inclusive, highly liveable, economically vibrant and green home for all Singaporeans.

Another responsibility of the URA is to provide and implement control guidelines to facilitate development works in an orderly manner that is consistent with the Master Plan. In this regard, the URA conducts regular reviews with industry professionals and the general public to ensure that policies are business and user-friendly and relevant to prevailing needs. Over the years, many development control guidelines have been simplified and revised to give greater flexibility, and to be responsive to new trends. For example, to improve customer service, the Electronic Development and Application system was introduced for increased convenience and efficiency, enabling online submission of development applications and amendments.

2.3 *Construction and Project Management*

The construction phase of the real estate development is a production phase — what we see around us. The control and management of construction is obviously very significant, not least for the fact that what is produced will be around for some time. While the architects, engineers and other professionals are responsible for the design, aesthetics and quality of the buildings, the government. through the Building and Construction Authority (BCA) plays the critical behind-the-scenes roles of controlling and managing the construction process. Safety is a top priority in construction, especially in the aftermath of the collapse of the Hotel New World in 1986. Checks and accountability by professional engineers were stepped up to ensure that buildings in Singapore are designed, constructed and maintained to high standards of safety through its building regulatory system. The BCA oversees the approval of building and structural plans, periodic structural inspection for existing buildings, as well as the regulation of excavation works, unauthorised building works, civil defence shelters, exterior features of buildings, and outdoor advertisement signs. It also issues builders' licences to ensure that building works adhere to professional standards.

Besides controls and regulations, the BCA needs to embrace technology and promote innovations to overcome the market constraints of being small and limited in natural resources. Measures such as stock piling, reliance on technology and raising productivity have been implemented to develop and promote a construction industry that delivers a safe, high quality, sustainable and user-friendly built environment for Singapore.

However, despite the government's efforts over the years, the construction industry in Singapore is still faced with the challenges of professionalism, productivity and quality of construction, relative to most of the developed countries. Over-reliance on cheap foreign workers has resulted in low productivity and poorer quality of construction. Main and sub-contractors very often compete on price, resulting in some cases the inability to complete projects. Less professional standards and behaviour are often the cause of poor workmanship and, even worse outcomes, such as spalling concrete, choked pipes and leakages. While the government agencies, including the MOM, have pushed for greater professionalism, higher productivity and better quality, the industry as a whole would need to work with developers and owners as well as potential buyers and users to change and adopt better policies and practices.

2.4 *Marketing and Leasing*

This phase of the development life cycle is important primarily for matching demand with supply, both for sale and lease transactions. While properties can be transacted at any time throughout their life cycle, typically, new developments would require greater efforts in marketing and leasing. This is because successful marketing is a critical part of the overall success of the project. For residential projects, developers would conduct their own marketing or engage real estate service providers or brokers to market on their behalf. Under the Housing Developers (Control and Licensing) Act, developers of new projects would typically launch the projects once the sale licence is obtained. The marketing process would require show flats and teams of salespersons to attend to potential buyers as the projects are sold "off-the-plan", i.e., before construction even commences on the site. For commercial projects such as office and retail malls, the marketing process is even more crucial as developers and owners would want to ensure that the project attracts targeted tenants or buyers so as to attain the intended image and reputation of the projects.

Besides the owners/developers and the potential buyers, the key player in the marketing and leasing phase is the real estate consultant or service provider (see Chapter 4). They play an intermediary role that brings the sellers and buyers together. It requires professional knowledge of the property being transacted as well as the legal framework that covers the transaction. To provide such professional advice and services, these service providers or house agents need to be licensed. Prior to 2010, the licence was issued by the Inland Revenue Authority of Singapore (IRAS). The issuance of licence was also the extent of the government's involvement in the marketing and leasing of properties. However, as real estate deals increased in volume and value, the government decided that it would need to play a greater role to ensure that consumers' interests are well protected. This is especially so for more complex properties such as commercial, industrial and foreign properties. This led to the amendments of the Estate Agents Act in 2010, and the setting up of the Council for Estate Agencies (CEA) as a statutory board under the Ministry of National Development. The CEA is empowered to administer the new regulatory framework for the real estate agency industry. It is committed to raising the professionalism of the real estate agency industry through collaborative efforts with the industry on industry development programmes and protecting the interests of the consumers through targeted public education schemes. As real estate transactions increase in both price and volume, it is timely that a more comprehensive regulatory system is set in place. It also helps to enhance professionalism in the real estate industry.

While real estate agents serve all secondary market transactions, the Singapore Land Authority (SLA), a statutory board under the Ministry of Law, is responsible for managing state land through land sales, leases, acquisitions and allocations. As the government authority, it also develops and markets state properties to optimise their use for the benefit of all stakeholders. In optimising land use, the SLA maintains the national land information database. It plays a leading role in developing geospatial data infrastructure and policies, enabling knowledge and value creation for the Government, enterprise and community. From the regulatory perspective, the SLA is the national land registration authority and looks after the registration of property transactions in Singapore. It is also responsible for the management and maintenance of the national land survey system.

As discussed further in Chapter 4, information is crucial for the efficient functioning of the real estate market. In this regard, Singapore stands out as a trusted and reliable market for information provision even in its early years of development. The SLA and its predecessors have been committed to sharing timely and accurate information on market transactions, which has helped all stakeholders to better understand the market.

2.5 Occupation and Use

Proper maintenance and management is probably the most crucial and often overlooked aspect of real estate practice. Unlike other investments, real estate needs to be professionally managed. Obviously, this is easier said than done. Managing properties involves getting the right tenants, ensuring that the property is well maintained and requires not only the owners, but all users and other stakeholders to play their part. In fact, several government agencies are involved in this phase.

The government's role in this phase of the development life cycle has been clear and unambiguous. Starting with the ownership of property, the burdens and responsibilities need to be clearly stated and understood. Given that real estate is wealth, property tax is levied by IRAS on property owners for two reasons. Property tax is an important source of revenue to the government and although this is pooled as a consolidated fund, it helps to pay for infrastructure and amenities which benefit property owners. It is also a wealth tax and a progressive tax structure is applied to residential properties to ensure that higher value properties are taxed at higher rates. A key pillar of the property tax system is its simplicity and clarity. Except for owner-occupied residential properties, the tax is levied based on 10% of the annual value, which is the gross annual rent the property is capable of achieving. In relation to the occupation and use of real estate, there are other various types of taxes including goods and service tax, income tax, development charge and differential premium.

Besides the tax burden, owners are also responsible for the physical state of the properties they own. The BCA sets out rules and regulations to ensure owners abide by fire safety regulations as well as keep building facades and roofs clean and well maintained. In the case of multiple-ownership such as strata-titled properties, a management corporation must be set up to undertake these responsibilities. For public housing, town councils have been set up since 1990 to look after the common areas of public housing estates including the proper maintenance and management of areas such as common corridors, void decks, lift lobbies, roof tops as well as gardens, playgrounds and other facilities.

For the HDB housing estates where more than 80% of the population live, the maintenance and management of the common property within the estates is the responsibility of the town councils set up since 1988 under the Town Councils Act. Prior to this, the HDB was responsible for not only developing the flats but also managing the common areas. The town councils are set up along electoral boundaries where one to three constituencies (single member as well as group representation) can come together to form a town after each general election. The idea behind this is to let the elected Members of Parliament (MPs) take over the responsibility of the common areas of the public housing estates within their constituencies. The elected MPs can also appoint from six to 10 members each comprising at least two-thirds who are residents in the housing estates as town councillors. Together, the council can either engage a professional team of managers (usually from township or property management companies) or hire their own staff to manage the estates. In this way, the management of the housing estates is decentralised and the council can effect its authority on how the town is to be managed. This also allows some resident participation at the council or sub-committee levels. To manage the estates, which include the amenities at the block and precinct level such as lifts, water tanks, playgrounds, etc., the council is empowered to collect service and conservancy charges from all the HDB units within the town. Some of the monies collected must be put into sinking funds to be used for long term cyclical maintenance such as repair and redecoration, lift replacements and other electrical and mechanical installations.

A town council management report has been instituted by the Ministry of National Development since 2011 to assess the performance of each town council under the areas of cleanliness, maintenance, lifts and service charge arrears management. So far, almost all the town councils have been able to achieve satisfactory scores in the biannual report. At the national level, the significance is that housing estates are well looked after to ensure that they are liveable and the HDB flats are able to maintain their capital values.

For the environment, the National Environment Agency (NEA) is responsible for improving and sustaining a clean and green environment in Singapore. The NEA develops and spearheads environmental initiatives and programmes and is committed to motivating every individual to take up environmental ownership and to care for the environment as a way of life. By protecting Singapore's resources from pollution, maintaining a high level of public health and providing timely meteorological information, the NEA endeavours to ensure sustainable development and a quality living environment for present and future generations.

The built environment in Singapore today is certainly well maintained and managed. The government agencies, working with owners and all stakeholders, have helped to achieve this, and this should not be taken for granted but needs to be sustained into the future. In many developing countries that have seen rapid real estate developments, buildings have deteriorated quickly due to poor maintenance and management. Going forward, it would be imperative that even greater emphasis is paid to this aspect as building stock ages across the island. Recognition must be given to ensure that property and facility management becomes more professional.

2.6 *Upgrading, Renewal and Redevelopment*

The last phase of the real estate development cycle extends existing buildings through upgrading and enhancement to demolition and redevelopment. Both decisions have implications not only for the owners but the entire urban landscape and, hence, the roles of government agencies.

In the early years, the emphasis was on redevelopment. This led to many new developments and projects, and resulted in the loss of some history and heritage. From around the 1980s, Singapore was economically in a position to give greater attention to conservation; the URA embarked on a conservation programme to restore many of the older parts of Singapore especially in the central area. Many of these projects involve the protection of historic facades while redeveloping the interior or having new buildings blend into the conservation project. Old shophouses and buildings of historical significance have now been conserved with new life and uses created. For major conservation projects, the URA introduced a two-envelope tender system: the first stage requiring developers to satisfy a design requirement; the second stage involving shortlisted proposals having their bid price considered. This approach has helped the government to rejuvenate key precincts in the central area while retaining some of the history and heritage of the place.

For strata-titled privately owned properties, the government has also introduced legislation that encourages redevelopment. For properties more than 20 years old, only 80% consent from the owners is required to carry out an *en bloc* sale or redevelopment. For properties between 10 and 20 years old, 90% consent would be required. For public housing, the HDB has embarked on various upgrading and redevelopment projects since the 1990s (see upcoming section on HDB). For commercial properties, especially retail, a recent trend has been the regular upgrading and enhancement carried out in these properties. Typically, these are owned by real estate investment trusts which carry out periodic asset enhancement exercises to boost rental income. It is therefore not surprising that visitors to Singapore see an ever-changing city as new and redevelopment projects constantly crop up with changing skylines and landscape.

In the process of refurbishment and redevelopment, the government has embedded strategies to keep buildings sustainable and user friendly. The Code on Barrier Free Accessibility introduced in 1990 by the BCA, for example, aimed to reshape the accessibility landscape of the built environment by improving interconnectivity between buildings and upgrading existing buildings to make them more accessible. With an ageing population, barrier-free accessibility has become an imperative for Singapore's built environment. As we push ahead with new developments, there is growing emphasis on environmental sustainability. Given that buildings account for as much as 40% of the total energy consumption, it is important that new buildings are more environmentally friendly. In this regard, the BCA established the Green Mark scheme in 2005 and set an objective to achieve green mark certification of 80% of all buildings in Singapore by 2030. To achieve this, BCA actively promotes the use of green building technologies and designs through the Green Building Masterplan and other various initiatives. These include the BCA Green Mark Scheme, which assesses the environmental friendliness and energy efficiencies of buildings, as well as the Green Mark Incentive Schemes and Building Retrofit Energy Efficiency Financing (BREEF) Scheme to encourage building owners to build with green features and retrofit existing buildings to achieve greater energy efficiency.

3. Supporting Real Estate Developments

Besides the specific roles played by the various government agencies throughout the real estate development life cycle, two overarching strategies which the Singapore government has adopted over the last 50 years have been significant for real estate developments. The first is that of long term planning by the Government, especially in enhancing strategic areas such as the Changi Airport and the maritime port. This provides a future scenario, which the real estate industry can look forward to. The second is the enhancement of the environment through parks and water bodies, both of which are positively important to real estate developments.

Over the last 50 years, the real estate landscape in Singapore has indeed been transformed. In the downtown area, a new financial hub is emerging in the Marina Bay area. The older Shenton Way is witnessing an increase in residential uses while Tanjong Pagar is being revitalised with the upcoming Tanjong Pagar Centre which will be the tallest building in Singapore when completed. Orchard Road, the main shopping district, has several new malls, and plans for more underground links and pedestrianisation of part of the strip are still being worked out while the Bras Basah-Bugis area is on its way to becoming Singapore's arts, cultural, learning and entertainment hub.

The decentralisation and creation of regional centres as envisaged in the 1991 Concept Plan is slowly but surely becoming a reality. The Tampines Regional Centre in the east has been successfully developed into a vibrant business and commercial hub while the Woodlands regional centre in the north is also seeing new commercial developments. In the west, more plans have been revealed recently to develop a regional centre around the Jurong Lake District, which will become a unique lakeside destination for business and leisure in the next 10 to 15 years. Plans are also afoot to develop more commercial and mixed-use hubs at Kallang Riverside and Paya Lebar Central.

While many of the above plans are still being implemented, more exciting plans have been revealed for the next 20–30 years. These include the relocation of the Paya Lebar airbase and the Tanjong Pagar port. For the former, the redevelopment potential is not limited to the large piece of land after the airbase has decanted but would also allow surrounding developments to be freed from height restrictions enforced by the airbase. Similarly, the existing port at Tanjong Pagar not only has a sizeable land area, but the waterfront location would definitely magnify its development potential.

It is therefore interesting that despite limited land, real estate developments in Singapore have continued unabated over the last 50 years and will continue well into the future. The life cycle of real estate development discussed above is indeed a continuous cycle and as the country goes through economic and social changes, the physical landscape will also need to evolve to meet these on-going changes.

Amidst all the real estate developments mushrooming all over the island, there are more parks, green spaces and waterbodies today than at the time of independence. Interestingly, as development increases, the proportion of land kept for green actually increases (see Table 1).

Table 1. Green space and waterbodies in Singapore.

	2009	2013
Amount of skyrise greenery (ha)	10	61
Amount of green space (ha)	3,602	4,040
Length of park connectors (km)	113	216
Amount of waterbodies open for recreational activity (ha)	650	959
Length of waterways open for recreational activity (km)	72	93

Source: Sustainable Singapore Blueprint 2015, Ministry of the Environment and Water Resources and Ministry of National Development.

Right from the onset in the 1960s, Singapore's first Prime Minister Lee Kuan Yew envisioned Singapore as a Garden City in the heart of Asia. He pioneered efforts to green the island, recognising that greenery would help soften the harshness of urbanisation, improve people's quality of life and attract international investment. Singapore's first tree-planting campaign was launched back in 1963. Within a year, some 15,000 trees of 50 varieties were planted. Within five years, that number grew to almost one million. The initial focus was to green up the island as quickly as possible, with plantings on retaining walls, pedestrian overhead bridges, viaducts and car parks. Open spaces were turned into parks and gardens, most of which were close to the city and residential neighbourhoods. Flowering plants and fruit trees were subsequently planted to add more colour to Singapore's burgeoning landscape.

Instrumental to this endeavour has been the National Parks Board (NParks) — from merely creating a green environment, to the development of about 200 kilometres of greenways, or park connectors, linking housing estates to parks, nature sites and waterbodies. A good example is the transformation and development of the Southern Ridges, a nine kilometre-long chain of green, open spaces spanning the rolling hills of Mount Faber Park, Telok Blangah Hill Park and Kent Ridge Park, before ending at West Coast Park. Today, the vision of NParks has extended from developing a garden city to transforming Singapore into a city in a garden.

Besides parks and green spaces, proximity to waterbodies is highly sought for residential developments. The national water agency, the Public Utilities Board (PUB), has under its Active, Beautiful and Clean Waters (ABC Waters) programme converted canals and drains into attractive waterways which are accessible and in some cases, used for recreational activities. Together with NParks, the Green and Blue Plan aimed to bring parks and waterbodies closer to developments and enhance the living environment. Projects such as the Woodlands Waterfront, the Punggol Waterway and the Labrador Nature and Coastal Walk, certainly bring people closer to nature and the coastal areas in Singapore.

It can be seen that real estate developments in Singapore benefit hugely from the entirety of the government's efforts in creating a green and liveable environment. While such an objective is set in many other cities and countries, three key features are worth highlighting. First is the ability to turn ideas into reality. The Marina Barrage, for example, was a suggestion made by Mr Lee to tackle Singapore's water needs. By damming the rivers to create reservoirs, a larger body of water storage could be created. The outcome is that there are now more than 10 reservoirs (including the three well-known ones in the central catchment area — MacRitchie, Pierce and Seletar). These water bodies are not only a main source of water supply but also provide a place for leisure and recreation. Second is the deliberate plan to ensure that access to parks and waterbodies is open to the public, which means that the positive benefits brought about by such spaces can be enjoyed by everyone. Third is the continuous efforts undertaken in maintaining and improving these amenities so that future generations can continue to enjoy them.

4. Government's Role in Housing

Housing as a basic human need is often viewed as a social good, the provision of which a responsible government should play a part in. As highlighted earlier, in the case of Singapore, public housing development has grown in tandem with the urban transformation over the 50 years and one of the most distinctive and ubiquitous features of Singapore's urban landscape is blocks of HDB flats. Indeed, public housing built by HDB is synonymous with the physical development of Singapore.

Singapore's public housing programme has its roots in the 1960s, when the acute housing shortage called for a low-cost housing model that could meet the people's accommodation needs in the shortest possible time. Housing designs were kept simple and utilitarian — slab blocks of one-, two- and three-room flats came with basic amenities such as piped water and electricity. Although spartan by today's standards, these flats were far better than the slums and rural huts of the past. Following the first Concept Plan for Singapore in 1971, the HDB designed its public housing estates on two basic principles:

- Optimisation of scarce land resources to meet long-term housing demands which led to the building of high-rise, high-density public housing.
- Provision of a total living environment with educational, social and community facilities in sustainable and self-contained new towns.

Rising affluence in the 1980s brought greater social aspirations and higher expectations for public housing. Town planning began to consider factors such as urban form, town structure, and the provision of regional facilities such as parks and open spaces. There was greater emphasis on streetscape and the building of point-block apartments. The "precinct" concept was introduced, to provide each precinct with communal spaces and recreational facilities — like playgrounds and fitness corners, to facilitate community interaction. In the 1990s, greater emphasis was placed on creating a quality living environment and on building up the identities of precincts, neighbourhoods and towns. Landmark buildings, landscaping, open spaces and special architectural features were incorporated to achieve a strong visual identity. New residential concepts such as the "Punggol 21" waterfront town were also developed in response to changing lifestyles and aspirations. To meet the changing needs and lifestyles of Singaporeans, public housing has evolved over the years from the basic low-cost housing units of the 1960s to the high quality, reasonably priced apartments that are the hallmark of Singapore's urban landscape today.

Housing is not just a consumption good, but is also deemed by many as an investment good. Households do not trade houses as frequently as other financial assets because of high transaction costs. Increases in housing prices generate positive wealth effects and induce households' upward mobility on a housing ladder.[1] Households will move to new and larger houses if increases in prices of their existing HDB flats are large enough to cover their outstanding balances for existing mortgages and down payments for new houses. These households are more reluctant to move in a declining market.

In Singapore, there exists a dual structure in the public housing market, which includes a regulated primary market and a *laissez-faire* secondary market. Owners who purchase subsidised flats directly from HDB can only sell their flats after meeting the minimum five-year occupation requirement. Differences in prices between new HDB flats and resale HDB flats allow HDB flat owners to accumulate significant wealth when selling public flats in the secondary market. This process enables them to realise their "dream" of upgrading from public to private housing.

Figure 3 overlays selected public housing and CPF policies on the private residential property price trends, and details on each of the policies are summarised in Table 2. It is not surprising to find that these policies significantly influence the HDB resale price changes.[2] However, some empirical studies show that private

---

[1] Ortalo-Magne, F. and Rady, S., 2006. "Housing Market Dynamics: On the contribution of Income shocks and credit constraints," *Review of Economic Studies*, 73, 459–485.
[2] Tu, Yong and Wong, Grace K.M., 2002, Public Policies and Public Resale Housing Prices in Singapore, *International Real Estate Review*, 5:1, 115–132.

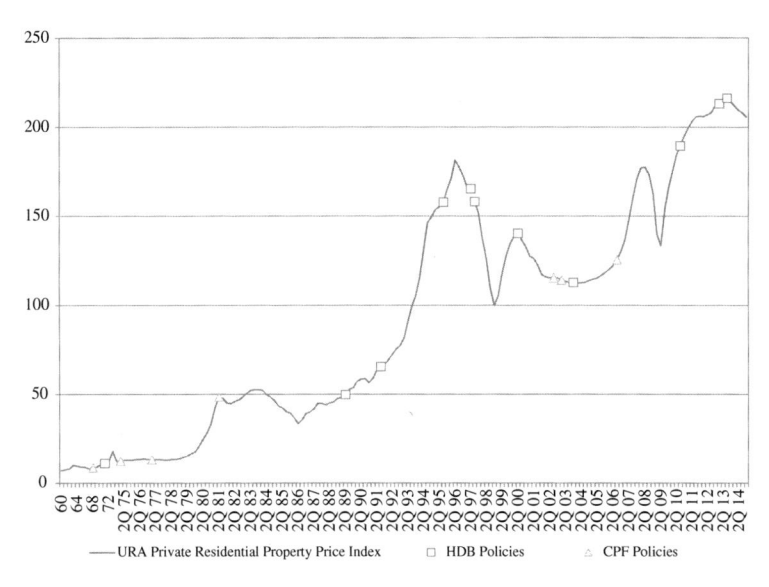

Figure 3. Effects of public housing and CPF policies on private housing prices.
Source: Realis, Urban Redevelopment Authority (URA), Singapore, REDAS, CDL, and the Author

housing price dynamics are highly sensitive to changes to public housing policies.[3] There are significant price discovery effects between the private and the resale public housing markets in Singapore.[4]

In 1995, the government introduced a new form of hybrid public housing known as executive condominiums (ECs) aimed to ease the demand side pressure caused by the sharp rising price in the private residential property markets. ECs are 99-year leasehold strata-titled condominium units built and sold by developers to eligible Singaporean buyers, who meet the income criteria imposed by HDB.[5] ECs are subject to the same five-year minimum occupation period (MOP) as HDB flats; and they can be freely transferrable in the open market after 10 years. At the beginning, government linked companies, such as the former Pidemco Land and NTUC Choice Homes, were entrusted to build and sell ECs on allocated state lands. The exclusiveness of the government linked companies was subsequently removed in 1997. EC lands have since been sold through competitive bidding exercises. Lum Chang Building Construction was awarded the EC land at Boon Lay Way in June 1997,

---

[3] Sing, Tien Foo, Tsai, I-Chun and Chen, Ming-Chi, (2007), "Price Dynamics in Public and Private Housing Markets in Singapore" *Journal of Housing Economics*, Vol. 15, No. 4, pp. 305–320.

[4] Ong, Seow Eng and Sing, Tien Foo, 2002, "Price Discovery between Private and Public Housing Markets," *Urban Studies*, 39(1), 57–67.

[5] The income ceiling was set at S$10,000 per month when ECs were first introduced. The income ceiling has been revised to S$12,000 per month with effect from 15 Aug 2011.

Table 2. Selected public housing and CPF policies that may have impact on the private housing market.

Year	HDB rules	CPF rules
Apr-1968		CPF Home Ownership Scheme
Mar-1971	HDB resale market was established	
Mar-1975		Use of CPF on HUDC flats
Mar-1977		Use of CPF on Ministry of Defense Housing
Jun-1981		CPF Approved Residential Property Scheme
Aug-1989	HDB resale rules were relaxed	
Oct-1991	Single Singapore Citizen Scheme	
Aug-1995	EC scheme was introduced	
Apr-1997	Regulations on HDB mortgage finance	
Sep-1997	5 years MOP to buy private properties	
Jun-2000	Rules of private property purchases by HDB owners	
Jul-2002		Revision of CPF withdrawal rules on housing purchases
Mar-2003		CPF minimum sum limit raised on 1 July 2003
Oct-2003	Relaxing of HDB subletting rules	
Jul-2006		Restrictions on multiple property purchases; Phasing Out of Non-Residential Properties Scheme (NRPS)
Aug-2010	Concurrent ownership of HDB and private within MOP is not allowed	
Jan-2013	PRs not allowed to sublet whole flats; PRs must sell HDB flat within 6 months of purchasing private properties; SSR on industrial properties and land: 15%, 10% and 5% if sold in 1st, 2nd and 3rd year respectively	
Aug-2013	Mortgage servicing ratio; PRs to wait 3 years before buying resale HDB flats	

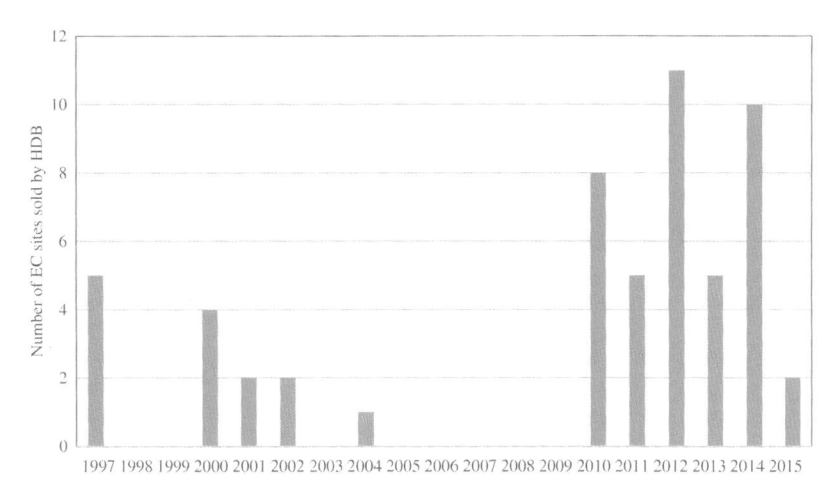

Figure 4. Sales of EC sites by HDB.
Source: HDB.

which was developed into Summerdale EC. Figure 4 shows the distribution of EC lands sold through competitive tender for the period from 1997 to 2015.

Today, more than 80% of the population lives in HDB flats and more than 90% own their of them own flat. This makes public housing in Singapore unique in three ways, relative to the social housing found in many other countries.

First, public housing has played a central role in nation-building. As early as 1964, the government envisaged that home ownership was needed to attract a migrant population to settle and build families in Singapore. Today, only citizen families have the privilege of buying new flats at subsidised prices from HDB under its Build-to-Order (BTO) scheme. Second, public housing is seen not only as a social good in that it provides shelter, it is also a real estate asset that can be monetised for future needs such as retirement. Since HDB owners were allowed to sell their flats after a minimum occupation period after 1981, a secondary resale HDB market has emerged. Relative to their original purchase price, owners typically can achieve capital gains in the resale market. Third, that the resale value is maintained largely due to proper maintenance and management of the public housing estates. Since 1990, town councils have been established to manage common areas in public housing estates based on electoral areas. This allows elected Members of Parliament and residents to make decisions in the running of the town councils. With enforceable legislation and clear regulations, the public housing estates today are generally well maintained.

Besides physical planning, HDB regularly reviews the type of flats and housing forms to be built based on the changing demography and life-cycle housing needs of the population. Housing policies have evolved to respond to the changing needs, aspirations and circumstances of Singaporeans over time. With evidence of an ageing population and a widening income disparity in Singapore, more attention is now being paid to meet the housing needs of the elderly and low-income flat buyers. Studio Apartments (SAs), for example, were launched in 1998 to provide the elderly with an alternative housing option. The SAs feature a compact design and elder-friendly safety fittings such as grab bars, bigger switches and an alert alarm system. In recent years, HDB re-introduced new two- and three-room flats to cater to the housing needs of lower-income groups. Additional subsidies are also given to aid the purchase, ensuring that up to 90% of the population can continue to afford a HDB flat. With more Singaporeans remaining single, the nucleus family rule has also been amended to allow singles over 35 years to buy new two-room HDB flats.

Another key emphasis of Singapore's public housing policy is estate renewal and rejuvenation. In the 1990s, the Estate Renewal Strategy (ERS) — comprising the Main Upgrading, Interim Upgrading and Lift Upgrading Programmes — was introduced to bring older towns up to the standard of newer ones. The Selective En bloc Redevelopment Scheme (SERS) was also introduced to enable HDB to acquire older flats for redevelopment, thereby releasing land in prime location that could be more optimally utilised. Residents affected by SERS are offered new replacement flats nearby so that they can enjoy modern amenities and a fresh lease of 99 years, while retaining communal ties in a familiar neighbourhood. In the next decade, as the number of HDB flats aged 40 to 50 years grows, the need to upgrade and redevelop the older estates will take on greater urgency. One priority area was lift upgrading so that residents of these blocks can enjoy lift access on every floor; the improved accessibility was much needed as the resident population ages. The lift upgrading programme has largely been completed and the focus has shifted to neighbourhood renewal as well as internal improvements to existing flats.

While public housing in the 21st century will evolve to encompass a wider spectrum of housing types, the mission of providing Singaporeans with affordable homes in cohesive communities will remain a top priority. And there will always be challenges such as matching supply to demand, adapting to socio-economic changes as well as continued economic growth in order to keep public housing affordable.

5. Housing Market Intervention

As the information flows in the property market are less perfect and inefficient relative to other asset markets, market distortions could be created by irrational investors. Speculators or informed investors could make use of their information advantages to

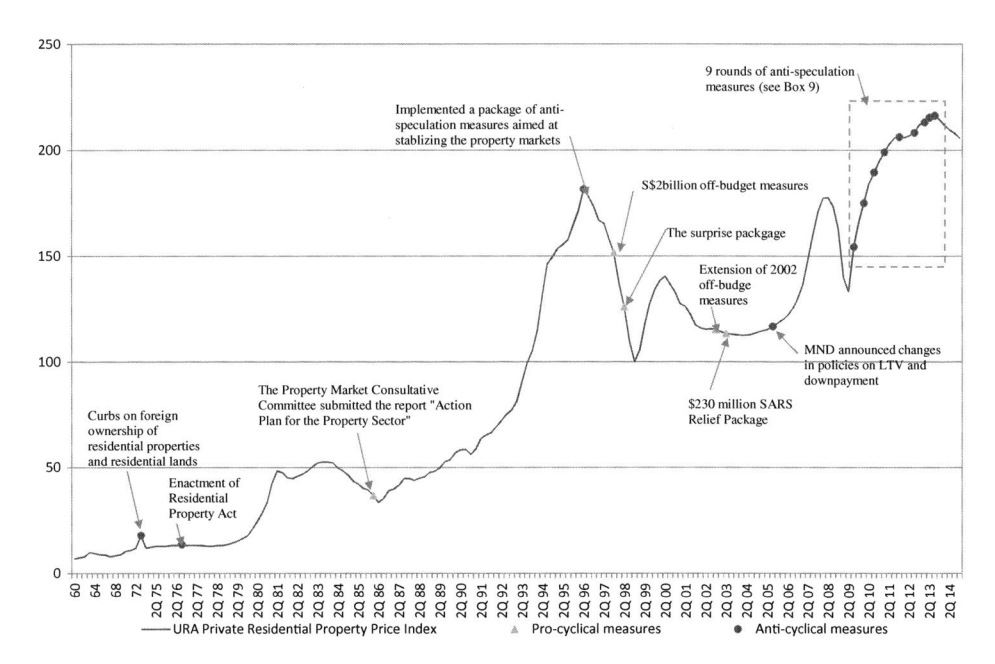

Figure 5. Government interventions in the private residential property market.
Source: Realis, Urban Redevelopment Authority (URA), Singapore, REDAS, CDL, the Author.

earn abnormal profits. If left alone without restraints, prices in the private property markets could deviate far from the fundamentals causing large losses economically and socially for some home buyers. Therefore, the government takes a pro-active approach from time to time to intervene in the market to smooth out unnecessary and extreme volatility in the market. Figure 5 shows the past government interventions in the private residential property markets, and Table 3 provides details of the policy measures.

In 1985, Singapore experienced its first most serious economic recession in the post-independence period. The Minister for Finance formed a Property Market Consultative Committee (PMCC) composed of representatives from government agencies, private sectors, and academia, to evaluate the problems facing the property markets and provide recommendations. In February 1986, the committee chaired by Dr Toh Peng Kiat, the then Director at the Revenue Division, Ministry of Finance, submitted its report — *"The Action Plan for the Property Sector"*, that proposed three-pronged strategies to address the depressed property market (Case Study 3). Real estate investment trusts (REITs) were mooted as one of the strategies to boost demand in the market, but the REIT market did not take off till July 2002. The turnaround of the private property market started in 2Q1986 shortly after the PMCC's report was submitted.

Table 3. The government's property market stimulus measures.

Year	Pro-cyclical measures	Policy details
Nov-1997	The surprise package	Government sale sites deferred; review set for 2H1998. Extended PCP for residential projects from 4–5 years to 8 years; private residential land sale sites to be sold in 1998 and 1999 would be tendered out with PCP of 8 years. Also, extension of PCP for foreign companies by up to 2 years. Premium of 5% of land price per year of extension applies unless there are technical grounds for the delay. Suspension of stamp duty surcharge on sale of properties within 3 years of purchase on or after 19 Nov 1997.
Jun-1998	S$2 billion off-budget measures	To suspend government's land sale till 1999, and to defer stamp duty payments till TOP or completion for the purchase of uncompleted properties
Dec-2002	Extension of 2002 off-budget measures	GLS Confirmed List suspension extended to 1H2003. Defer the release of BFC site for sale in 1H2003; fixed rebate of up to $8,000 per year for all commercial and industrial properties; 30% rebate for the remaining property tax payable.
Apr-2003	$230 million SARS Relief Package	Additional property tax rebates for commercial properties. The existing property tax rebates for commercial properties will be enhanced by an additional rebate of $2,000 plus 10% of the balance property tax payable in 2003.

Compared to 1986, the market downturns after the 1997 Asian Financial Crisis were prolonged and sticky. Beset by multiple negative events, the private property market witnessed two consecutive price declines: 3Q1996 — 4Q1998 and 3Q2000 — 1Q2004, lasting two years and four years, respectively. The private residential market dropped into the doldrums with 18,205 unsold condominiums units in the pipeline as at 2Q2001 (*Source: The Urban Redevelopment Authority, URA*). The government introduced four rounds of pro-cyclical stimuli to revive the markets, which include the 2002 off-budget, the surprise package, the extension of the off-budget package and the SARS relief packages. Then Minister of National Development of Singapore, who oversees the property market activities, commented after the announcement of the off-budget measures:

> "..*off-budget measures to stabilize the property market will not have an immediate effect, but will help boost confidence and help the real estate industry ride out the downturn.*

Case Study 3: Property Market Consultative Committee's Report

In the report "Action Plan for the Property Sector" published on 6 February 1986, the Property Market Consultative Committee proposed a multi-pronged approach to address problems besetting the property markets. The strategies covering three aspects, namely controlling supply, stimulating demand and improving market confidence are summarized below:

A) Strategies to control supply

- Withdrawal of competition by the public sector by refraining from letting out space to privte tenants, unless absolutely necessary; and from leading the market in prices and rentals
- Deferment, suspension, reduction in scale or abandonment of property development plans, both in private and public sectors
- Deferment of URA land sales for residential, commercial and industrial sectors
- Conversion of surplus properties into institutional, recreational and other users in both public and private sectors

B) Strategies to stimulate demand

- Deregulation, which includes giving more time for HDB home owners to sell their HDB homes before upgrading to private housing; relaxing guidelines for foreign ownership or properties and others
- Provision of tax incentives, such as allowing deduction of operating losses on their homes and interest on mortgage loans for owner-occupied homes against personal income tax, reducing stamp duties, providing depreciation allowances for commercial properties
- Reductions in government changes and fees for conveyancing and mortgages
- Enhancement of affordability via the relaxation on CPF rules on withdrawal and downpayment for property purchases
- Marketing and publicity of international competitiveness of property prices and rentals
- Inducement of foreign demand
- Introduction real estate investment trusts (REITs) to facilitate investments

C) Strategies to improve confidence

- Improvement in standards of workmanship
- Preservation of market orderliness through the licensing of all estate agents as well as the regulation of their operations
- Maximum objectivity in media reporting on the property market
- A high sense of discrimination by developers, owners, buyers, financers, intermediaries and members of the public when interpreting daily events or prevalent sentiments
- An enlightened approach to lending by financial institutions
- Introduction of facilitating instruments like REITs
- The improvement in the availability, analysis, presentation and publication of property data
- Greater clarity and certainty in government policy, especially in respect of land usage, such as land acquisition and compensation rates
- The establishment of a coherent government machinery
- Greater recognition of the property sector by the government in relation to other sectors.

> *The measures will not on their own help the real estate industry to recover. Ultimately, the recovery of the real estate sector will depend on the recovery of the economy as a whole."*
>
> Mr Mah Bow Tan, Minister for National Development
The Business Times, Singapore (Rashiwala, 2001)

In the last 50-year private property cycles, the government only intervened twice in the market via anti-cyclical measures in 1995 and then between 2009 and 2013. The periods starting from 1Q1991 to the peak in 2Q1996 witnessed the longest consecutive quarter-to-quarter growth in the URA private residential property price index. The price index doubled between 2Q1993 and 2Q1996; and on a compounding basis, the growth rate was computed at 23.8%. The unprecedented rate of growth in the private property prices significantly dwarfed the compounded quarterly growth of 5.92% in earnings over the same period (*Source: The Central Provident Fund (CPF) Board Statistics*).

The government acted swiftly and decisively by introducing a slew of measures to cool the overheated market on 15 May 1996.[6] The measures included restricting loan-to-value ratio of property loans to 80%,[7] and imposing capital gain tax and seller's stamp duty on residential properties sold within three years of purchase. The government also stepped up its sales of state lands programme to increase the private housing supply from 6,000 units to 7,000–8,000 units. These anti-speculation measures coupled with the 1997 Asian Financial Crisis contributed significantly to the decline in private residential property prices. The prices dropped by 44.9% from the peak of 181.0 points in 3Q1996 to 100 points in 4Q1998.

The second bubble in the private residential property market started to form from 2Q2004, but was interrupted by the Subprime Crisis and the bankruptcy of Lehman Brothers in 2008 (resulting in the Global Financial Crisis). However, the private residential property prices took a V-shaped rebound in 3Q2009 culminating in the peak in 3Q2013. During the strong build up in the private residential property prices from 2009 to 2013, the government introduced nine rounds of cooling measures (Table 4), which included various macro-prudential tools (such as the LTV limits, total debt servicing ratio (TDSR), mortgage servicing ratio) and transaction taxes (such as seller's stamp duty (SSD) and additional buyer's stamp duty (ABSD)). These were aimed at curbing irrational market activities that cause overheating in prices.

---

[6] The measures implement by the government to check the sharp rise in private residential property prices include imposition of a 80% loan-to-value limit on bank loan, levies of capital gain tax and seller's stamp duty for residential properties sold within three years of purchase.

[7] Prior to the May 1996, loans of up-to 90% of valuation were provided by banks to purchasers of private properties.

5. The Government's Role in Other Real Estate Sectors

Besides the multiple roles played by the government throughout the real estate development life cycle and its direct role in the housing market, the Singapore government has also left indelible marks on the industrial sector through the Jurong Town Corporation (JTC) and the hospitality sector through the Singapore Tourism Board (STB). Indeed, the establishment of JTC in 1968 was part of the government's industrialisation programme to drive the economy. Similarly, the Singapore Tourist Promotion Board (STPB, now STB) was set up in 1964 to develop Singapore's tourism industry.

Table 4. The government's anti-cyclical measures.

Year	Anti-speculation measures	Policy details
Oct-1976	Enactment of Residential Property Act	Foreigners are only allowed to buy private apartments in buildings of six levels or more, or flats in condominiums where ownership is by strata title. Permanent Residents (PRs) can apply to the Law Minister to buy landed properties.
May-1996	Implemented a package of anti-speculation measures aimed at stabilising the property markets.	80% financing restriction for property purchase; 7,000–8,000 residential units to be released in 1997; 30-month project completion period (PCP) for private developments under QC scheme; 5% p.a. penalty imposition for PCP extension; stamp duty extended to buyers of all sales and sub-sales of uncompleted properties; new stamp duty on those who sell properties within 3 years; tax on gains from properties sold within 3 years of purchase.
Jul-2005	MND announced rules on downpayment and loan-to-value (LTV).	MND announced changes in policies affecting property market: To raise loan-to-value ratio from 80% to 90%; to reduce cash downpayment from 10% to 5%; to allow unrelated singles to jointly use their CPF savings to buy private residential properties; to phase out the non-residential properties scheme in July 2016; and restrict the use of CPF on multiple property purchases.
Sep-2009	Round 1 Anti-speculation: Removal of Interest Absorption Scheme (IOS) and Interest Only Mortgage (IOM)	

(*Continued*)

Table 4. *(Continued)*

Year	Anti-speculation measures	Policy details
Feb-2010	Round 2: LTV and Seller's Stamp Duty	
Aug-2010	Round 3: Extension of SSD periods	
Jan-2011	Round 4: Enhance SSD rate and periods/LTV	
Dec-2011	Round 5: Additional Buyer's Stamp (ABSD)	
Oct-2012	Round 6: Loan tenure and LTV	
Jan-2013	Round 7: ABSD rate increase and LTV further tightened	
Jun-2013	Round 8: Total Debt servicing ratio (TDSR)	
Aug-2013	Round 9: Maximum loan term and Mortgage Servicing Ratio	

5.1 JTC — Agency for Industrial Real Estate

The JTC Corporation (JTC) is the main agency spearheading the planning, promotion and development of industrial space in Singapore. Since its inception in 1968, JTC has played a major role in Singapore's economic development journey by developing land and space to support the transformation of industries and create employment. Together with the Economic Development Board (EDB), JTC has been instrumental in the industrialisation of Singapore right from the onset. While the former strategises and attracts foreign investments, the latter provides and manages the space required by various industries and investments. Given the limited resources, especially land, JTC has indeed managed to continuously cater to the changing needs of industrial space over the last five decades.

In the early years of independence, manufacturing was an important part of the economy. JTC built factories for various industries and leased industrial lands for industries with specific needs. Over the decades, JTC has pioneered cutting-edge industrial infrastructure solutions to meet the evolving needs of companies with each phase of industrialisation. In terms of industrial space, JTC has developed over 7,000 hectares of industrial land and 4 million square metres of ready-built facilities. Apart from developing Singapore's first industrial township, Jurong Industrial Estate, from swampland, other key projects that JTC has developed include a chemical hub on Jurong Island; business and industrial parks such as the Airport Logistics Park of

Singapore, International and Changi Business Parks, Seletar Aerospace Park, CleanTech Park, Tuas Biomedical Park, and one-north, a cluster for knowledge-based industries with key developments like Biopolis, Fusionopolis and Mediapolis. Ascendas, a leading regional business park developer today, was started by JTC as New Technology Park in the 1990s.

Today, JTC continues to break new ground with pioneering projects that not only support the changing needs of today's industries but also anticipate the future needs of new industries. The Jurong Rock Caverns look to subterranean depths to optimise land use; the Tukang Innovation Park supports the growth of new industry clusters in innovation activities; and the Jurong Island initiative plans to enhance competitiveness of the chemicals hub.

Amongst the various real estate uses, the industrial sector is probably the most dynamic, given the constantly changing economic and industrial landscape. The life cycle of industrial properties is typically short (hence, the shorter leases) as industries continuously change and innovate. JTC's contribution exemplifies the dynamic nature of industries in their role as provider of industrial infrastructure. As Singapore transforms itself for the future, JTC will continue to develop specialised land and new innovative space to support and catalyse new industry clusters, in order to support the growth and transformation of industries and enterprises.

5.2 STB — *Hospitality and Tourism*

The Singapore Tourist Promotion Board (STPB) was established in 1964 to market Singapore as a tourist destination, and seek to contribute to the growth of the young economy. STPB started by working with various government agencies and industry stakeholders to build more hotels, the first being four luxury hotels along Tanglin Road and Orchard Road. The Raffles Landing Tourist Project and the Merlion Project were undertaken in 1970, in collaboration with the URU, to develop and conserve Singapore's historic sights. A slew of other tourism infrastructure projects quickly followed: the Jurong Bird Park in 1971, the Singapore Zoological Gardens in 1973, and the development of Pulau Blakang Mati (now known as Sentosa) as a resort island for tourists and locals in 1972. These early projects are still very much part of the tourist landscape today and fit into the hospitality sector.

In 1986, STPB unveiled Singapore's very first tourism master plan, the S$1 billion Tourism Development Plan, with the objectives of increasing visitor arrivals, length of stay and tourist expenditure. The plan comprised five major themes: positioning Singapore as a tropical island resort, a clean and green garden city, one rich with colonial heritage, a showcase of the exotic east and a host to international sporting and other events. It set the direction for developments in the Singapore tourism landscape for the next decade. A number of significant achievements arose from this plan, including the revitalisation of cultural precincts, conservation of historic landmarks such as Alkaff Mansion and Raffles Hotel, rejuvenation of Bugis Street, and redevelopment of Boat Quay and Clarke Quay.

To capitalise on the rising tourism potential within the Asia-Pacific region in the 1990s, STPB rolled out the 'Tourism 21' master plan to transform Singapore into a global tourism capital. It championed the ideas of tourism as a key economic driver for Singapore and developing tourism as a business, and called for the repackaging of existing tourism offerings such as Chinatown and Orchard Road into various "thematic districts" to enhance visitor experience. One of the strategic thrusts under Tourism 21 was to grow regional tourism to add to Singapore's attractiveness as a regional tourism hub and business centre. Also key to this master plan was the forging of partnerships amongst the public sector, private entities and local residents to transform Singapore into a vibrant and livable city to be proud of, underpinned by the belief that tourism is not just for tourists, but also for all Singaporeans. To better reflect the expansion of its roles and its status as the economic agency fully responsible for the tourism sector, STPB was also renamed Singapore Tourism Board in 1997.

The Tourism 2015 roadmap was drawn up in 2004 to strengthen Singapore as a leading convention and exhibition city in Asia with a strong and dynamic business environment. At the same time, Singapore would be developed as a leisure and services centre of the region. This master plan launched mega tourism projects such as the Formula One Singapore Grand Prix, Integrated Resorts with casinos and the Singapore Flyer. These, along with others, helped to establish Singapore as a compelling destination replete with world-class amenities and lifestyle events.

Today, the hospitality and tourism sector is an important part of the economy as travel becomes easier and more commonplace amid increasing affluence across the world. Whilst many of the projects are privately owned, the government plays a crucial role in the planning as well as initiating many of the projects such as the Integrated Resort, the implementation of which was debated thoroughly. The public-private partnership has certainly served to transform this important real estate sector over the last 50 years.

6. Conclusion

In the course of 50 years of development, five themes stand out:

1. The extensive involvement of, and intervention from, the State, especially in the residential sector where housing is regarded as a social good, and often used as a policy tool to achieve socio-economic and political goals. Besides providing housing for more than 80% of the population through the HDB, it regulates the

market through the supply mechanism as well as macro-prudential policies. For the other real estate sectors, the government typically takes the lead, sets the tone and brings in the private sector to operationalise the strategies and objectives in the transformation of the real estate industry.

2. Since independence, economic development and growth have always been imperative to the country's well-being, which lead to the rapid growth of the commercial and industrial sectors, as real estate demand is a derived demand. The office sector has been driven by the strategy to develop Singapore into a global financial centre. The retail and hospitality sectors have grown as a result of the government's effort to make Changi an aviation hub while increasing the number of visitors. The industrial sector, led by JTC, has seen transformation from manufacturing to high value-add industries.

3. Given that real estate investment is more risky, relative to other investments, it is important that the macro-environment should mitigate political and legal risks. In this, the Singapore government has provided stability, which is often seen as one of the key success factors, especially by foreign investors. That the rule of law is totally observed and followed has reduced much of the uncertainties that investors need to be wary of especially in cross-border investments.

4. The Singapore government's strategy of maintaining an open economy has encouraged the inflow of foreign funds. Foreign investments have certainly boosted the real estate markets. This is, however, a double-edged sword in that while it helped to drive an active market, it also contributed to the escalation of property prices especially in the residential property market. The last residential market boom was due to foreign buyers amongst other reasons.

5. The strategy of long term planning, whether with respect to transportation, land supply, greening or developing a smart nation, the Singapore government plans ahead to ensure that all stakeholders are fully aware of the future opportunities. A case in point being the development of the Marina Bay area. Land reclamation started in the 1970s, and in the 80s, interim uses for periods of 12 to 15 years were implemented, and only through the 90s and in the new millennium was it that the present Marina Bay began to take shape. Thus, over a period of more than 30 years, plans were developed and implemented gradually. Government agencies adopted a long-term approach whilst constantly adjusting for near-term changes brought about by changing economic and social trends. The HDB, for example, moved to allow singles to buy new flats, a policy which would not have been contemplated as recently as 10 years ago.

The role of the government in the transformation of the real estate industry in Singapore over the last 50 years is clearly evident. From housing to industrial properties, the government has not only supported all types of real estate development projects but also has taken the leading role as a developer where it is necessary and advantageous. In public housing and industrial developments, for example, the government has been the primary developer that guides the development of these sectors. In other real estate sectors, it plays a key role throughout the phases of the project life cycle. Above all, the government sets the tone and tenor under which an active and growing real estate industry can thrive. Political stability and economic growth achieved over the period have been fundamental in the development and growth of the real estate industry in Singapore.

In terms of the future, technology will have a significant impact on real estate developments. All buildings, whether they are schools, residential, commercial or industrial, will not only be green, but be connected technologically as Singapore aims to become the world's first smart nation.

References

CEA http://www.cea.gov.sg/cea/content/aboutus/overview.html
Government Land Sales http://www.mnd.gov.sg/MND_Handbook/MND_English/files/assets/common/downloads/publication.pdf
HDB https://www.cscollege.gov.sg/Knowledge/ethos/Issue%202%20Apr%202007/Pages/Homes-for-a-Nation-Public-Housing-in-Singapore.aspx
http://www.iras.gov.sg/irasHome/page04.aspx?id=5676
http://www.mnd.gov.sg/MND_Handbook/MND_English/files/assets/common/downloads/publication.pdf
http://www.mnd.gov.sg/MND_Handbook/MND_English/files/assets/common/downloads/publicatio
JTC Corporation http://www.jtc.gov.sg/About-JTC/Pages/default.aspx
Land Acquisition http://www.ura.gov.sg/skyline/skyline09/skyline09-02/text/01_2.htm
Master Plan 2014 http://www.ura.gov.sg/uol/master-plan/view-master-plan/master-plan-2014/master-plan/Introduction.aspx
NEA http://www.nea.gov.sg/corporate-functions/about-nea/overview
SLA http://www.sla.gov.sg/AboutSLA.aspx#.VR_28PmUd1Y
STB https://www.stbtrc.com.sg/PASSPORT/STB_ANNUAL_REPORT%202013%202014.PDF
URA http://www.mnd.gov.sg/MND_Handbook/MND_English/files/assets/common/downloads/publication.pdf

CHAPTER 3

Changing Skyline: Real Estate Development Industry in Singapore

Sing Tien Foo

1. Introduction

The beautiful skyline of Singapore today has not come by chance. The high rise skyscrapers dominating the central business district (CBD) symbolise the economic growth and wealth creation of the city state. They have been the results of the collaborative efforts of the private sector and the public sector in the last 50 years.

The government master-plans major land uses and undertakes major infrastructure developments, which include airport, seaports, highways and public amenities, such as schools, parks, markets and others. Private real estate developers play the entrepreneurial roles of pooling capital and taking market risks in transforming the urban blueprints of Singapore into reality. They buy lands via the government's sales of sites programmes, and then develop them into productive space for commercial and industrial users; and living space for local residents and foreigners who want a roof over their heads.

Whilst the business aspect of real estate development is subject to market competition among private developers; the social aspect of providing affordable housing remains the key responsibility of the government. The Singapore government started the ambitious Home Ownership for the People Scheme in 1964. Since then, the government's public housing authority, Housing and Development Board (HDB), has embarked on large-scale public housing building programmes to meet housing needs for the nation. It has systematically rolled out more than a million units of public housing flats, which provide affordable housing to more than 90% of the citizens today. The achievement of the public housing programme in Singapore is enviable to many countries.

This chapter aims to discuss the private property markets in Singapore. It starts with a macro-analysis of the dynamics of residential property market in Singapore. It then covers some micro-level discussions of the property developers that are active in Singapore. Land supply activities and the commercial markets are also discussed before the concluding chapter.

2. Residential Property Market in Singapore

Singapore has a unique dual market structure for the residential property markets, consisting of a subsidised public housing market,[1] and a fully *laissez-faire* private housing market. Figure 1 shows the compositions of housing stocks in the two markets from 1980 to 2014. The fraction of the public housing units in the total housing stocks hit the peak of 88.07% in 1995. The total housing stocks, based on the number of dwelling units for resident households, have expanded significantly from 472,700 units in 1980 to about 1,200,000 in 2014. The intensive public housing programmes in the 1980s have contributed to the rapid expansion of the housing stocks. The home ownership rate in public housing reached a high of 89.8% in 1990, and has stayed above the 90% level since then (Figure 2).

After fulfilling the housing needs for the majority of the residents, the focus has shifted to providing a variety of housing choices to meet housing aspirations of a population with rising affluence. The government has allocated and sold more residential lands via its sales of sites programme for private developers to build private housing units. From 1995 to 2009, the shares of the private housing stocks (both

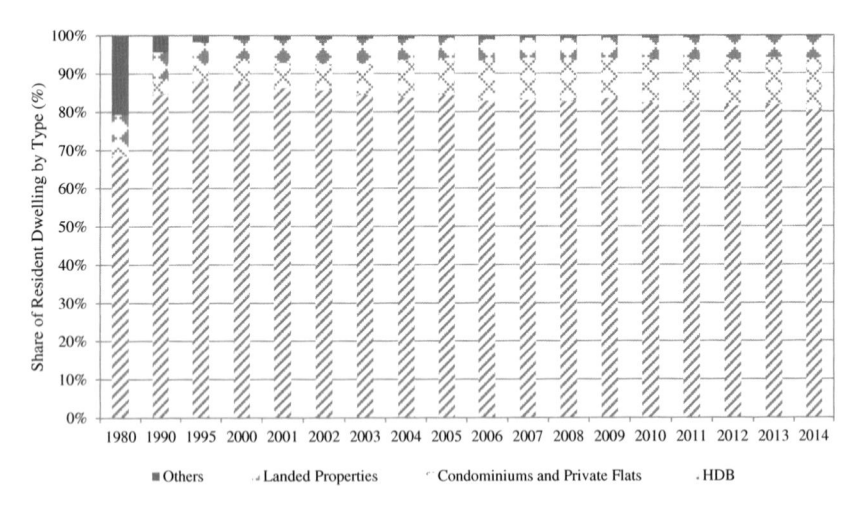

Figure 1. Composition of residential dwelling by type: 1980 to 2014.
Source: *Department of Statistics, Singapore.*

---

[1] The government via its public housing agency, Housing and Development Board (HDB), plans, builds, and sells public housing flats at concessionary prices to eligible Singapore citizens, whose gross monthly household income does not exceed S$12,000 with effect from 24 August 2015.

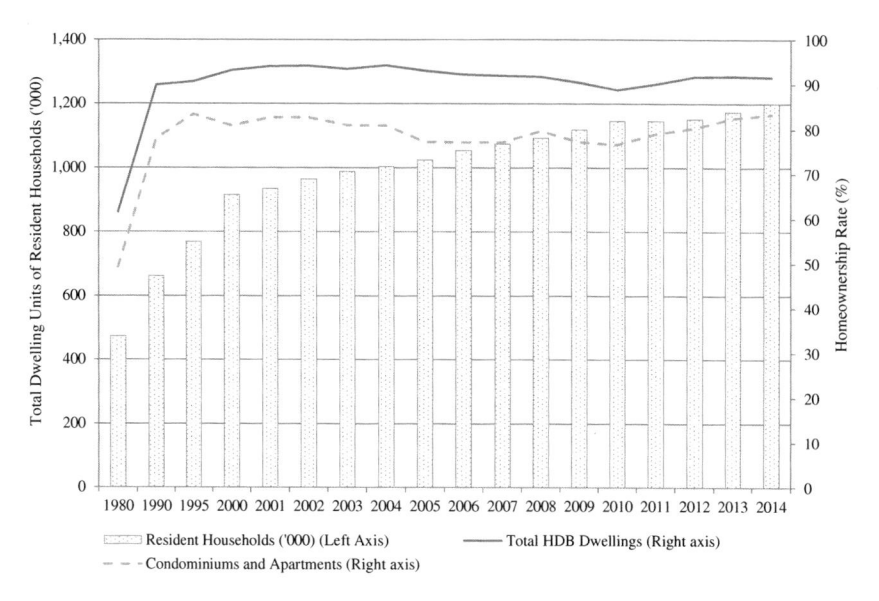

Figure 2. Total housing stocks and homeownership rates.
Source: Department of Statistics, Singapore.

landed and non-landed housing units) have increased steadily from 11.08% in 1990 to 19.27% in 2014 (Figure 1). The increases in the private housing stocks come mainly from the non-housing units, which include condominiums and apartments. Due to land scarcity constraints, many landed housing lands have been redeveloped into high density non-landed developments. The share of landed housing dwelling units declined from 7.0% in 1990 to 3.6% in 2014. However, non-landed housing stocks have increased from 4.08% to 13.48% over the same periods. As of 2014, 70% of the private housing stocks are made up of non-landed housing dwelling units. Many private developers have become active in non-landed developments, which consist mainly of strata-titled units with shared facilities, to meet the rising housing aspiration of more affluent residents.

Housing is an asset with a good hedge against inflation. Housing values increase with inflation, and protect owners/investors against erosion of purchasing power of money. Empirical results in Singapore and many countries have shown that real estate provides strong and positive inflation hedges compared to other asset classes, such as bonds and stocks.[2] In Singapore, private landed residential properties are found to have stronger hedge against inflation than non-landed residential properties.

---

[2] Sing, Tien Foo and Low, Swee Hiang Yvonne, 2001, "A Comparative Analysis of Inflation-Hedging Characteristics of Property and Non-Property Assets in Singapore," *Journal of Real Estate Portfolio Management*, Vol. 6, No. 4, pp. 373-386.

2.1 Private Housing Stocks

In land-scarce Singapore, the non-landed private residential properties, which include condominium and apartment units,[3] are the most popular housing form. Figure 3 plots the distributions of available stocks of private residential properties, based on the Urban Redevelopment Authority (URA)[4] statistics. The non-landed private residential properties constitute two-third of the accumulated private residential stocks in Singapore. As of 2Q2015, the total available private housing stocks in the market stand at 318,524 units composed of 71,699 (77.5%) landed housing units and 246,835 (22.5%) non-landed housing units. The structural shift in the composition of the private residential property market started after the peak of the property cycle in 2Q1996. The shares of housing stocks in all categories have declined since then, except for condominiums. Condominium units that accounted for only

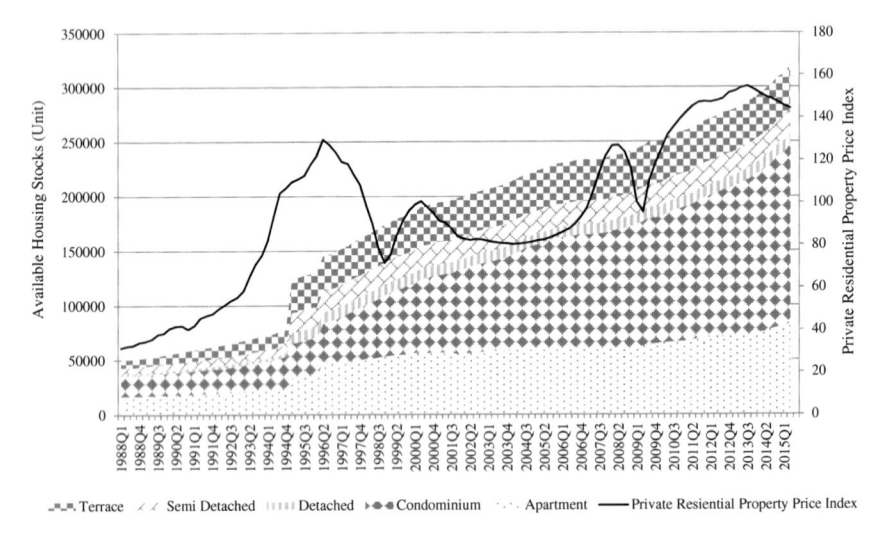

Figure 3. Available stocks by housing type.
Source: Realis, Urban Redevelopment Authority (URA), Singapore.

---

[3] Apartments and condominiums are two property types that make-up the non-landed private residential property sector in Singapore. Condominium is a strata-titled development with a full-range of facilities provided within a minimum land area of 0.4 hectare. Apartments are also a multi-unit project built on smaller parcel of land. There is a restriction on re-sale to foreigners for apartments less than six storeys high. Apartment units also include apartments above shops and privatised apartments previously under the Government Housing schemes for employees.

[4] The Urban Redevelopment Authority (URA) is the national planning authority of Singapore, which is entrusted with the responsibility of planning the physical development and optimisation of the scarce land resource in Singapore. The URA provides comprehensive and up-to-date data and information on the real estate market to improve efficiency and transparency of the real estate market.

25.0% of the total available private residential stocks in 2Q1996 expanded rapidly and doubled the share to 51.4% as of 2Q2015.

Figure 3 groups the housing type into the landed and non-landed categories and shows the shares of the two categories of private residential properties, for the period from 1988 to 2015. The line represents the private residential property price index. The total non-landed housing stocks increased by more than 6.89 times from 35,802 units in 1Q1998, to 246,835 units in 2Q2015; the landed housing stocks also increased by 5.07 times from 14,132 units to 71,699 units over the same period. One interesting observation is that during the run-up in private housing prices from 1Q1988, the shares of landed housing stocks increased gradually from 28.3% to 39.2% in 3Q1992. Large increases in all categories of landed housing stocks (including terrace, semi-detached and detached houses) from 24,583 units in 4Q1994 to 58,955 units in 1Q1995 pushed the landed housing share up to the peak of 47.4%. After the peak in the prices for the private residential properties in 2Q1996, more non-landed housing units were built, bringing down the share of landed housing stocks to 22.5% in 2Q2015. This coincides with the government's concerted efforts in the intensification of the scarce land resource in Singapore. Looking at the ownership status (See Figure 1), the ownership rates of the non-landed housing units by Singaporean households range between 77% and 88.3% for the period from 1995 to 2014. This reflects Singaporeans' aspiration to own a condominium.

2.2 *Major Crises and Trends in Private Residential Property Market*

Figure 4 shows three distinct cycles in the private residential property market for the periods from 1960 to 2014. Three peaks in the property cycles were clearly found in 1983/1984, 1996 and 2013. The trend line shows that the private residential property prices have grown steadily at an average quarterly rate of 0.19% since 1975. Despite the short-term volatility, the prices increased by approximately 23 times from the 9 points in the URA private property price index in 1965 to 205.7 points in 2014.

Many of the down cycles in the last 50 years were precipitated by major economic crises in the markets, including the oil crisis in the 1970s, the great economic recession in 1985, the Asian Currency Crisis in 1997 and the US subprime crisis in 2007. Major events, such as the Gulf War, the Iraq War and the terrorist attack of the New York's World Trade Centre, and the outbreaks of SARS and the tragedy of the 2004 tsunami, were also found to have had dampening effects on the private property price trends. These unanticipated shocks could have broader adverse economic impacts, spilling over into the housing market and causing short-term price declines in the private residential property markets.

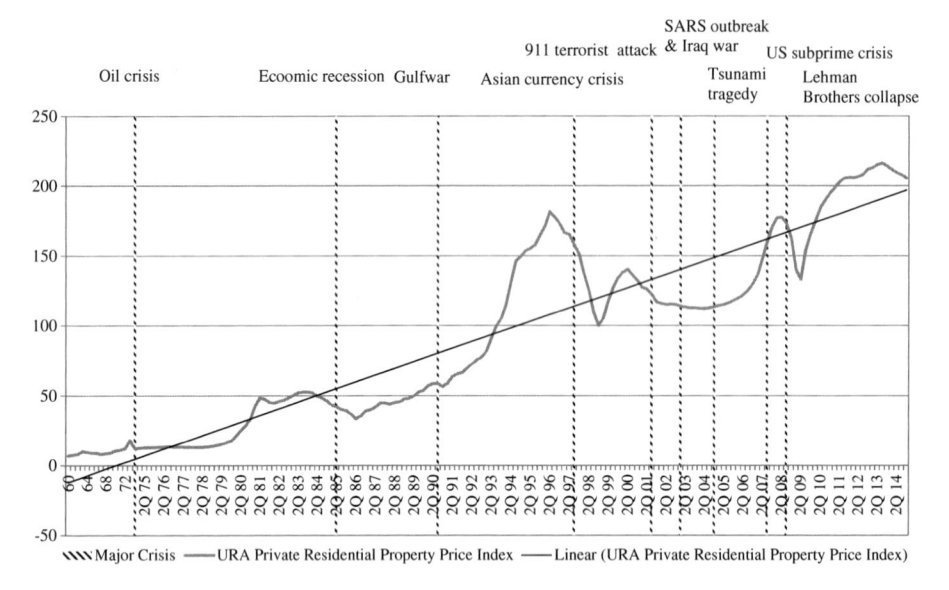

Figure 4. Major crises and private residential property price trends.
Source: Realis, Urban Redevelopment Authority (URA), Singapore, REDAS, CDL, the Author.

2.3 Condominium Concept — A New High-Rise Strata-Titled Living in Singapore

The condominium is a new housing concept with shared facilities, that was first brought into Singapore in 1974. The communal living concept appeals to middle-income young professional couples, who consider owning a condominium a desirable path in the social mobility cycle.[5] The high-rise and high-density nature of condominium development bodes well for the planning strategy aimed at optimising the scarce land resource in Singapore.

In 1972, DBS Realty Pte Ltd bought a large freehold site off Ulu Pandan / Holland Road for S$7 psf to build the largest private condominium development in Singapore — Pandan Valley Condominium. The 625-units project was considered to be the first condominium in Singapore, though the project was completed later in 1978.[6] The first super high-rise condominium project — Pearl Bank Apartment, developed by Hock Seng Enterprises Pte Ltd, was completed earlier in 1976.[7] Mr Tan Cheng Siong was the architect for the two earliest condominium projects in

---

[5] Sing, Tien Foo, 2001, "Dynamics of Condominium Market in Singapore," *International Real Estate Review*, Vol. 4, No. 1, pp. 135-158.
[6] Knight Frank, The Evolution of Singapore Real Estate — Journey to the Past and Future: 1940-2015, 2015, Page 57.
[7] Whang, Rennie, "Plotting the 'high life' at low cost," *The Straits Times*, Saturday, Oct 04, 2014.

Singapore.[8] However, by the completion date, Beverly Mai, a 28-storey tower at Tomlinson Road completed in 1974, would claim the accolade of being the first condominium development in Singapore.[9] The condominium project was built on a site of 7,230 square metres (sqm) by Pontiac Trading Co. Limited. In 2006, the project was sold en bloc to Hotel Properties Limited for S$238 million.[10] The Futura at Leonie Hill Road built by Prestige Homes Pte Ltd in 1976 was the second condominium project in Singapore, going by the completion date. The project was also sold en bloc to City Development Limited (CDL) for S$287.3 in October 2006[11].

Condominium housing started off slowly in the 1970s due to unfamiliarity with the communal living concept. Private developers were unsure of buyers' reception, and at the time, learnt to understand preferences of potential buyers. Economic forces were a major factor driving the first phase of growth in condominium housing market in Singapore.[12] The rapid growth of Singapore's economy coupled with the influx of multinational corporations and foreign talents increased the demand for condominium housing in the earlier 1980s. The Approved Residential Properties Scheme (ARPS) implemented in 1981, which allows members of the Central Provident Fund (CPF) account to draw on ordinary account savings to buy private properties, was also an important factor driving up the condominium demand.

The 1985 economic recession, however, put a halt to the rising condominium demand and caused the condominium price index to plunge into the trough in 2Q1986. The condominium market was highly resilient, with condominium prices rebounding in 3Q1986 and then growing on an average quarter-to-quarter rate of 4.27%, culminating to the peak in 2Q1996. The two largest quarterly growths of 18.7% and 11.7% were recorded in 2Q1994 and 2Q1996, respectively. The government promptly intervened into the overheating private residential markets by introducing a slew of anti-speculation measures for the first time in May 1996. The first reversal in the upward price trend occurred in 3Q1996. The outbreak of the Asian Finance Crisis in July 1997 following a series of attacks on the currencies of several Asian countries, including South Korea, Thailand and Indonesia and Malaysia, brought the condominium market to the doldrums with four consecutive quarters of declines in condominium prices by between 7.15% and 10.10% in 1998.

---

[8] Liew, Christine, "Holding the Skye, Tan Cheng Siong, Archurban Architects Planners," *Architecture and Environment*, a magazine of Singapore Architect, SA280 Issue,
[9] Au Yong, J., "Is S'pore's first condo worth preserving?" *The Straits Times,* September 24 2006.
[10] Kalpana, R., "HPL bags Beverly Mai for $238m," *The Business Times,* April 27 2006.
[11] The Futura's site will be replaced by a brand new freehold condominium, known as New Futura, which is due for completion by 2021.
[12] Ho, C.W. and Sim, L.L. (1992), *Studies on the Property Market*, Singapore University Press.

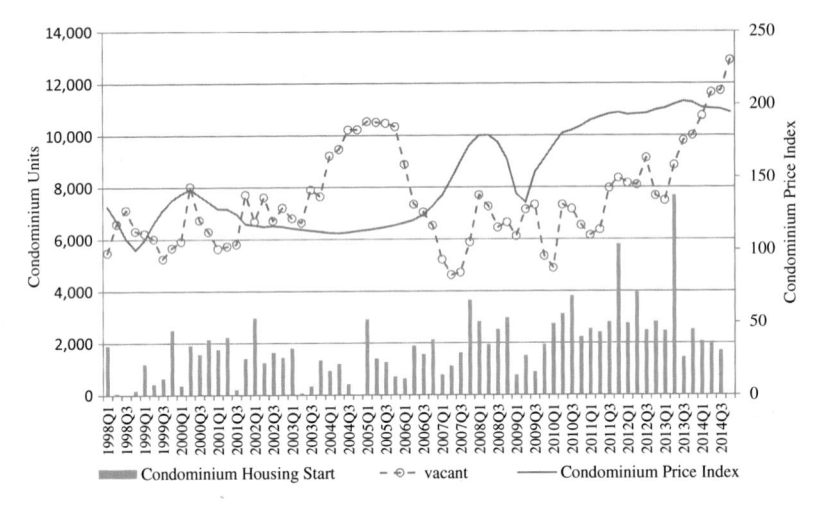

Figure 5. Vacant stock and new supply of condominiums.
Source: Realis, Urban Redevelopment Authority (URA), Singapore.

Figure 5 shows the new condominium construction start (supply), and the unoccupied (vacant) stocks in the condominium market in the post-crisis periods in 1998. Despite the weak condominium prices in the post-crisis periods, an average of 1,651 units of new condominium construction commenced each quarter. The vacant stocks of below 6,600 units were recorded between 1999 and 2003. The outbreak of the severe acute respiratory syndrome (SARS) epidemic in Singapore on 1 March 2003 has significantly dampened the activities in the condominium market. New commencement of condominium construction dipped to 609 units per quarter, and the vacant stocks went up to 8,760 units in the two years between 2003 and 2004. The normalisation resumed in the market after 2005, and stayed till the occurrence of the US subprime crisis in 2007. The effects of the US crisis were short-lived, and signs of the market overheating emerged again after 2009. The periods between 2009 and 2014 saw more than 3,021 units of new condominium commencing construction, and the excess supply rose to 1,385 units on average per quarter. The vacant condominium stocks increased to 12,885 units as at 4Q2014.

3. Characteristics of Singapore's Developers

3.1 *Local Developers — The "dreamers" and "empire builders"*

Real estate development is a venture that requires an entrepreneurial and risk-taking spirit. Developers assemble a team of in-house or third-party professionals to undertake development and derive the highest and best use value of a land parcel. By virtue of the inherent characteristics of real estate, which are heterogeneity, fixity in location, and being capital intensive, real estate development business is usually local in nature. Local developers are in a better position to harness home-turf advantages in terms of scale economics, local knowledge and reputation, in expanding their share in the local market. The late Mr Ng Teng Fong, the founder of Far East Organization, commented during an interview with Apple Daily in 1996[13] that

> "If you want to be in the property business, it is not possible to invest in every region. You open the map. If you can't see the place (because it's too small) but only the name, that's the place to invest in ... Singapore and Hong Kong are the best examples."[14]

Based on the statistics of 102,318 units of new private housing sales from 393 non-landed residential development projects in Singapore for the period from 1995 to 2009, a developer's market share is computed by dividing the cumulative new unit launches by the developer over the aggregate new housing units for all developments in the market. Table 1[15] summarises the top 10 developers by the market shares of the total non-landed housing units launched. City Developments Limited and its parent firm, Hong Leong Holdings, are the largest developers with a market share of 18.22% and a total of 18,638 new units launched. Far East Organization (with its listed vehicle Orchard Parade Holdings) is the second-largest developer, selling a total of 16,691 new units (16.31%) in the market. The two government linked real estate companies, CapitaLand (Appendix-A) and Keppel Land (Appendix-E), rank in the third and fourth positions with a market share of 8.82% and 5.10%, respectively. GuocoLand Limited (Appendix-D), which is the real estate vehicle of Mr Quek Leng Chan's Hong Leong Group (Malaysia), built and sold about 4.87% of the total private non-landed residential property units in Singapore between 1995 and 2009.

In Singapore, developers are broadly organised either as a public listed entity or a private company. Many private real estate development companies in Singapore are owned and controlled by families, such as the late Mr Ng Teng Fong's Far East Organization (currently helmed by Mr Philip Ng) (Appendix-C), the Kwee brothers' Pontiac Land, Mr Raj Kumar and Kishin RK's Royal Holdings and RB Capital, Mr Tao Shing Pee's Shing Kwan Group and Mr Wee Cho Yaw's Kheng Leong

---

[13] The comments were abstracted from an article published in *The Business Times*. (Source: Lee Meixian, "For Singapore's wealthiest, land is riches," *The Business Times*, 8-9 August, 2015.)

[14] Mr Ng's remarks also imply that the small size of the local market may drive developers to look for development opportunities beyond the home shore.

[15] Coulson, N. Edward, Dong, Zhi and Sing, Tien Foo, (2015), "Estimating Hedonic Cost Functions: Case of Singapore's private residential property markets," NUS Institute of Real Estate Studies (IRES), Working paper.

Table 1. The top 10 developers in Singapore by market share (1995–2009).

	Name	Total units	Market share	Cumulative market share
1	City Development Ltd + Hong Leong Group	18,638	18.22%	18.22%
2	Far East Organization	16,691	16.31%	34.53%
3	CapitaLand	9,021	8.82%	43.34%
4	Frasers Centrepoint Ltd	8,930	8.73%	52.07%
5	Keppel Land Ltd	5,219	5.10%	57.17%
6	GuocoLand Ltd	4,983	4.87%	62.04%
7	Wing Tai Holdings Ltd Singapore	4,491	4.39%	66.43%
8	MCL Land Ltd	3,931	3.84%	70.27%
9	Allgreen Properties Ltd	3,534	3.45%	73.73%
10	Ho Bee Group	2,371	2.32%	76.04%

Note: The cumulative market share is the sum of the developers' market share in order of their ranking.
Source: Edward N. Coulson, Zhi Dong and Tien Foo Sing (2015) "Estimating Hedonic Cost Functions: Case of Singapore's Private Residential Property Markets," NUS IRES Working Paper.

Group. Some developers use public listed vehicles to run their property development businesses, such as Mr Kwek Leng Beng's City Developments Limited (CDL) (Appendix-B), Mr Quek Leng Chan's GuocoLand, the late Mr Tan Chin Tuan's Straits Trading Company (currently helmed by Ms Chew Gek Khim) and Mr Wee Cho Yaw's UOL Group. The third group of property developers consists of government-linked companies, which include publicly listed CapitaLand, Keppel Land; and unlisted vehicles such as Mapletree, Ascendas Group, and NTUC Choice Home.

Many of the first generation property tycoons in Singapore share a similar story in the early years of formation. Most of them migrated to Singapore in the pre-independence period, and their forays into real estate businesses were not by chance. The late Mr Ng Teng Fong's entry into property business was not without challenges, and his experience was described in the Far East Organization's 50th anniversary commemorative book, "Landmarks" published in 2010, which states that "*Against his father's wishes, he pursued his dream of developing property when he was still in his twenties, starting with terraces and semi-detached houses in Lowland Road, Figaro Street and Highland Road, among others.*" (page 2, paragraph 4).

The success stories behind the property empires would not have had been possible without the persistence and foresights of the founders. "*It has always been my ambition to acquire land and develop property. Even as an apprentice, I often looked at the shop houses lining the banks of the Singapore River and imagined my own towering building in their midst,*" envisioned the late founder of CDL, Mr Kwek Hong

Png.[16] The trait of being diligent, inherent in these first generation entrepreneurs, was another important factor underpinning the drive to succeed in real estate businesses.

3.2 Private Residential Property Market

The growth in property businesses of the successful local developers mirrors the economic growth story of Singapore. In the 1960s and the early post-independence period of Singapore, with limited capital, these developers bought small land parcels and built terrace and semi-detached houses. They sold those projects, and rolled the capital into buying new and more lands to build larger and more landed units. Keeping abreast with the rapid phase of the public housing programme in 1970s, private developers started to build high-rise apartments with large floor space, which were then described as "bungalows in the sky". These projects including Beverly Hill, Lucky Tower, Honolulu Tower and others are mainly located in the prime areas near Bukit Timah Road, Carnhill, Grange Road and River Valley. In the 1980s, the condominium living concept, where large-scale residential development with landscaped open spaces, and communal and recreational facilities, became a popular housing form in Singapore.

In 1990s, private developers started to put more emphasis on reputation building, elevating construction quality and delivering enhanced value to customers. The quality drive was facilitated by the introduction of the Construction Quality Assessment System (CONQUAS ®), a standard assessment system on the quality of building projects, by the Building and Construction Authority (BCA) in 1989. The construction quality assessment is mandatory for projects built on land parcels sold by URA and HDB via SOSPs.

This period also witnessed three major merger and acquisition (M&A) events involving property companies in Singapore. In April 1990, United Industrial Corporation (UIC), the detergent manufacturer turned investment vehicle of Mr Oei Hong Leong, mounted a hostile bid to take over Singapore Land (SingLand),[17] which was at the time a listed property company with 20% stake owned by the chairman Mr S P Tao and family. SingLand held a large portfolio of premium commercial properties in town, which include Marina Square, the Gateway at Beach Road, Shell Towers, Clifford Centre and Shing Kwan House at the Raffles Place-Shenton Way area.[18]

---

[16] The one man's vision behind the creation of "Property Empire" of the Hong Leong Group and CDL was encapsulated in the 50th year commemorative book of CDL, "A Lasting Impression," published in 2013.
[17] "SingLand urges shareholders to reject UIC offer," *Business Times Singapore*, 1 May 1990.
[18] Magdalene Ng, "SingLand advises acceptance of UIC bid," *Business Times Singapore*, 15 May 1990.

In 1995, another tussle took place between the Mr Quek Leng Chan-led consortium and Mr Ng Teng Fong's Orchard Parade Holdings Limited (OPHL), to win control of a food and beverage group, Yeo Hiap Seng (YHS). The consortium led by Mr Quek's investment vehicle, Camerlin, was composed of Mr Quek's First Capital Corporation (FCC) with 40% majority stake, and Sembawang Corporation, Haw Par Brothers, and Indonesian Salim Group, each held 20% stake.[19] Mr Ng's OPHL had started to amass YHS shares in the open market since 9 July 1995,[20] and successfully took a controlling stake of 82.98% of YHS in September 1995. In an interview,[21] Mr Philip Ng explains the motivation of Far East Organization in acquiring YHS: *"we were interested in the Yeo's brand and its beverage and food businesses ... (After acquisition) we leveraged on our property development infrastructure at Far East to assist Yeo's in developing the two parcels of land — at Dunearn Road (where the YHS factories were sited). The monetisation of these projects allowed capital to be deployed back to YHS' manufacturing business, to expand its business in China, Indonesia, Malaysia and Cambodia."*

Case Study 1: Merger of Pidemco and DBS Land

In 1996, Temasek Holdings Private Limited, an investment company owned by the Government of Singapore, transferred Pidemco Land Limited ("Pidemco") with a collection of URA resettlement projects in its portfolio to Singapore Technologies ("ST") at the peak of market valuation. Pidemco, with total assets of S$8.2 billion as at 31 December 1999, had a significant presence overseas with investments in 24 cities in 12 countries including key gateway cities in the Asia Pacific region and in the United Kingdom.

Pidemco recognised that scale economics would give an additional competitive advantage when venturing abroad. In early 2000, an opportunity to create scale economics opened up when DBS Bank was evaluating the divestment option for its listed property arm — DBS Land (DBSL), which was a spin-off from its in-house property department. DBSL was the second-largest property company listed on the main board of the Singapore Exchange ("SGX") with a market capitalisation of S$3.5 billion as at 11 July 2000. Based in Singapore, it had total assets of S$7.5 billion as at 31 December 1999 with operations spanning 11 countries in Asia Pacific and Europe.

(Continued)

---

[19] Joyce Quek, "Alan Yeo tells employees why he backed Wing Tai," *Business Times Singapore*, 17 May 1994.
[20] Genevieve Cua, "YHS tells shareholders not to act pending advice," *Business Times Singapore*, 28 June 1995.
[21] The editorial team (Sing Tien Foo and Jeanette Yeo) conducted an interview with Mr Philip Ng, the CEO of Far East Organization, at his office at Far East Plaza on 22 January 2015.

(Continued)

ST made an unsolicited offer to DBS Bank, which was about to close some serious offers from international suitors on the DBS Land stake. ST's offer outbid other international suitors, leading to the successful acquisition of DBS Bank's stake in DBS Land. The DBS Land acquisition paved the way for the subsequent merger of Pidemco and DBS Land to form CapitaLand. On July 12, 2000, Pidemco and listed DBS Land Limited entered into a merger agreement to create the largest listed property company in Southeast Asia, with total assets of approximately S$18 billion. The merger allowed the new entity — CapitaLand, to skill up and scale up to compete as an effective international player. In the merger arrangement, DBS Land was turned into a wholly-owned subsidiary of Pidemco through a share swap arrangement, where each DBS Land ordinary share was exchanged for 0.928 new Pidemco ordinary shares, based on the relative NAV per share of each company. DBS Land would then be delisted from, and Pidemco would be listed as CapitaLand by way of introduction on, SGX.

Rationale for the Merger:

The merger should result in significant benefits to both companies including:

a. Enlarged company size; significant scale in core sectors

The merged company, which was the largest listed property company in Southeast Asia with a combined asset base of S$18 billion, was well positioned to expand internationally. The merged company with enlarged revenue base and significant scale in core businesses could significantly improve operational efficiency and flexibility when pursuing growth opportunities abroad.

b. Larger market capitalisation

The merged company's enlarged capital base of approximately S$7 billion as of 31 December, 1999 would enable it to compete more effectively for acquisitions with other large property companies. Its increased international visibility would enhance its ability to attract deals and partners. The larger market capitalisation would attract stronger investor interest from funds from a wider potential investor base.

c. Broader geographic presence

The merged company with market presence in 31 cities in 15 countries, including Singapore, Malaysia, China, Australia, New Zealand and the United Kingdom, could enjoy geographic diversification and reduce the over-reliance on any single market, tenant, asset or asset class.

d. Operational synergies and economies of scale

The merged company could access a larger international pool of talent and expertise. It could also reap operational synergies in the development of human resources, the identification and adoption of best practices, and the increased negotiation and purchasing power.

The private residential property market activities were sluggish in the first half of the 2000s, clouded by multiple external shocks such as the terrorist attack that crashed the twin towers of the World Trade Centre in New York in 2001 (Figure 6). The private residential property market recovered in 2004 and 2005 followed by sharp increases in private housing prices before its growth momentum was halted by the 2007 subprime crisis in the US. The dip in private housing prices did not prolong, and a v-shaped rebound was observed in 2009, which prompted the government to intervene into the private residential market at the end of 2009. There were three interesting trends observed in the booming private residential market after 2005.

First, the Far East Organization project — "The Bayshore", which was completed in 1996, was the largest condominium development with a total of 1,038 units, prior to 2005. After that, many large-scale projects with more than 1,000 units were developed, which include the two CapitaLand projects — d'Leedon (1,715 units) and The Interlace (1,040 units), built on sites bought from the en bloc sales of HUDC projects, the Keppel's Reflection by Keppel Bay built on the old shipyard and dock sites at Telok Blangah area, and the Sail @ Marina Bay (1,111 units) by CDL built on the URA's site downtown. Second, more local developers engaged renowned foreign architects to create iconic designs in the private residential market, especially after 2000s (Case Study 2).[22]

The third trend is seen in the mushrooming of shoebox units, which generally refer to units having gross floor areas of less than 50 square metres (or approximately 538 square feet), after the run-up in housing prices in 2009. The government projected an exponential increase in the number of shoebox units from 2,400 units in 2012 to 11,000 units by 2015.[23] On 4 November 2012, the URA acted swiftly to curb the spreading of the shoebox units to outside the Central Area by imposing a rule that limits the average unit size to 70 sqm.[24]

3.3 *Foreign developers*

Foreign developers' entry into Singapore's private residential property market goes as far back as the 1970s. Japanese developers were among the earliest foreign firms to

---

[22] One of the earliest foreign architects engaged to design residential projects in Singapore was the late Paul Rudolph, who designed The Colonade (1986), a 90-unit condominium project at Grange Road.
[23] Agarwal, Sumit, Deng, Yongheng and Sing, Tien Foo, "The Rise and Rise of Shoebox Units," *The Straits Times*, NUS Expert Series, 12 September 2012.
[24] Kalpana Rashiwala, "Govt to act to contain rash of shoebox units," *Business Times Singapore*, 5 September 2012.

Case Study 2: Increased Presence of World-Renowned Architects

World-renowned architects, such as the late Paul Rudolph, the late Kenzo Tange and I.M Pei, among others, put their marks on the skyline of Singapore in 1980s and 1990s. The earlier projects designed by the foreign architects were mainly high-rise commercial projects located in prime CBD areas (I.M Pei's projects: Raffles City Singapore, OCBC Centre, the Gateway, Suntec City; Kenzo Tange's projects: UOB Plaza, OUB Centre (now renamed One Raffles Place); Paul Rudolph's project: The Concourse). In the residential projects, the late Paul Rudolph designed the iconic Colonnade Condominium at 82 Grange Road (completed in 1986), and the late Kenzo Tange designed the Linear apartment at Upper Bukit Timah Road (completed in 2006).

During the run-up of the property market in 2000s, more developers turned to renowned foreign architects to add brand cachet to their residential projects. With intense competition in the market, reputable architects could bring new and fresh design ideas to residential projects; some analysts believe that the reputation of the foreign architects could bring brand effects that could add premium to projects. In the mid-2000s, big developers, such as CapitaLand, City Development, Keppel Land and Far East Organization, roped in illustrious foreign architects including Ole Scheeren, Daniel Libeskind, Moshe Safdie, and others, to lend their names to their local residential projects (see Table A1). Safdie's design for CapitaLand's Sky Habitat, which features two tower blocks connected by three bridges, has created an iconic landmark to the heartlands of Bishan. However, the premium associated with his landmark design is hard to verify though one analyst attached a 30 to 35% premium to Safdie's name.[1]

There is also no lack of Singapore architects, who have designed award-winning iconic projects including the Pinnacle at Duxton. Some developers, such as SC Global, have put more faith in local architects in designing their projects. The ultra-luxury project of SC Global — The Marq on Peterson Hill, which set a record sale price of S$5,842 psf in August 2011, was designed by a local architect, Chan Soo Khian.[2] SC Global's CEO, Mr Simon Cheong, commented that "local architects have a better understanding of our environment and living conditions and are better able to express this in their designs".

The entry of foreign architects may have brought diversity and variety in the architecture of high-rise condominiums in Singapore; and also introduced healthy competition that spurs local architecture to constantly innovate and embrace new technology in residential projects. Foreign architects may not come cheap, however, and it would be important to find out if buyers are willing to pay premiums for owning a home designed by foreign architects. Developers, too, will probably be eager to find out if branding through having iconic designs by renowned architects does translate into better sales for their projects. While these still remain puzzles, however, increased housing price is expected to increase the number of projects designed by renowned foreign architects in Singapore.

(Continued)

---

[1] "Renowned foreign architects spice up Singapore's building design landscape," Channel News Asia, 21 June, 2012.
[2] Tay, Suan Chiang, "Local architects make their Marq - Singapore architects can give foreign ones a run for their money in designing condos," The Straits Times - August 6, 2011

(*Continued*)

Table A1. Residential projects designed by foreign architects in the 2000s.

No	Residential project name	Location	No of residential units	Site area (sqm)	(Expected) completion date	Foreign architect/ architecture firm	Developer
1	DUO Residences	Ophir Road/Rochor Road/Beach Road	660	26,688	2017	Buro Ole Scheeren	M+ S Ptd Ltd (Malaysia's Khazanah Nasional and Singapore's Temasek Holdings)
2	Marina One Residence	Marina Way	1042	26,200	2017	Christoph Ingenhoven	M+ S Ptd Ltd (Malaysia's Khazanah Nasional and Singapore's Temasek Holdings)
3	V on Shenton	5A Shenton Way	510	6,778	2017	Ben van Berkel/ UNStudio	United Industrial Corporation, UIC)
4	South Beach	Beach Road	190	35,000	2016	Lord Norman Foster/ Foster and Partners	City Developments Limited and IOI Group
5	Wallich Residence at Tanjong Pagar Centre	Peck Seah Street/ Choon Guan Street	181	15,023	2016	Skidmore, Owings & Merrill (SOM)	Guocoland Ltd
6	The Scotts Tower	38 Scott Road	231	6,100	2016	Ben van Berkel/ UNStudio	Far East Organization
7	Eden Residences Capitol	North Bridge Road/ Stamford Road	39	n.a.	2015	Richard Meier	Capitol Investment Holdings (JV of Perennial Real Estate Holdings: 24%, fotiac Land; 50%, and Osim International: 26%)
8	HANA	8 Tomlinson Road	29	n.a.	2015	Kerry Hill	Pontiac Land Group

CHAPTER 3 | Changing Skyline: Real Estate Development Industry in Singapore

9	Sky Habitat	Bishan Street 15	509	11,997	2015	Moshe Safdie, Safdie Architects/DCA Architects Pte Ltd	CapitaLand Limited, Mitsubishi Estate Asia Pte. Ltd. and Shimizu Investment (Asia) Pte. Ltd.
10	d'Leedon	Farrer Road	1715	78,043	2014	Zaha Hadid, Zaha Hadid Architects/RSP Architects Planners & Engineers (Pte) Ltd	CapitaLand Limited, Hotel Properties Limited and two other shareholders
11	Admore Residence	7 Ardmore Park	58	5,625	2013	Ben van Berkel/UNStudio	Pontiac Land Group
12	The Interlace	Depot Road	1040	81,000	2013	OMA/Ole Scheeren/RSP Architects Planners & Engineers (Pte) Ltd	CapitaLand Limited, Hotel Properties Limited
13	Reflections at Keppel Bay	Keppel Bay	1129	84,000	2011	Daniel Libeskind	Keppel Bay Pte Ltd (a subsidiary of Keppel Land)
14	The Rochester	Rochester Drive	366	14,331	2011	Paul Noritaka Tange	UE One-North Developments Pte Ltd
15	The Clift	21 McCallum Street	312	1,820	2011	Japanese Super Potato	Far East Organization
16	The Sail @ Marina Bay	Marina Boulevard	1111	90,909	2008	Peter Pran and Timothy Johnson/NBBJ	City Developments Limited (CDL) and AIG Global Real Estate
17	Orchard Scotts Residences	Anthony Road/Peck Hay Road/	205	25,000	2007	Arquitectonica	Golden Development Pte Ltd (Far East Organization)/Far East Orchard Limited
18	The Linear	880 Upper Bukit Timah Road	221	n.a.	2006	Kenzo Tange Associates	Creative Investments Pte Ltd (a subsidiary of Amara Holdings Ltd)

Source: Compiled by the author (the list is not exhaustive).

come to Singapore. TID Pte Ltd (previously named Trade and Industrial Development Private Limited), is a joint venture (JV) formed in 1966 between Mitsui Fudosan and Hong Leong Group, which develops residential projects, such as Parc Emily, the Trevose and Goodwood Gardens. Sekisui Houses, the largest homebuilders in Japan, also formed JVs with local developers such as Far East Organization and Frasers Centrepoint Limited in several projects in Singapore, such as QBay Residences in Tampines, Watertown in Punggol and eCO at Bedok South.

Hong Kong's developers entered Singapore's real estate market in the 1990s. In 1988, 11 renowned and successful Hong Kong tycoons led by Tan Sri Frank Tsao, together with Dato' Dr Cheng Yu-Teng, Dr Lee Shau Kee, Dr Li Ka-Shing, Sir Run Run Shaw, Dr Chou Wen Hsien, Mr Chow Chung Kai, Dr Li Dak Sum, Mr George Y.V. King, Mr Robert W.H. Wang and Mr Anthony Y.C. Yeh led by Mr Li Ka-Shing, formed a consortium, Suntec Development Pte Ltd, bought a parcel of land from URA, and built and completed Suntec City in 1997. Hong Kong's Cheung Kong Holdings and Hong Kong Land partnered local developer, Keppel Land, to develop two other commercial projects — One Raffles Quay (completed in 2006), and the Marina Business and Financial Centre (completed in 2012). Mr Li Ka-Shing's private vehicle, Pacific Enterprise Development (PED), developed private condominium projects, such as Thomson 800 and Costa del Sol. It experimented the innovative price appreciation and rental guarantee schemes in the marketing of the Costa del Sol project, which was completed in the midst of weak property market in 2004 (Case Study 3).

Large conglomerates from Indonesia and Malaysia entered into Singapore's real estate markets through the 2000s. In 2010, Indonesia's Lippo Group acquired the majority stake in Overseas Union Enterprises Ltd (OUE),[25] which owned prime commercial properties such as One Raffles Place, OUE Bayfront, OUE Tower and OUE Link. It also acquired the former DBS Headquarter at Shenton Way, and carried out major transformation work to turn the twin towers into a mixed-use development, known OUE Downtown. Malaysia's YTL Group purchased Westwood Apartments through an en bloc arrangement, and took over Starhill Global REIT, which holds part of the prime Orchard Road shop space in Ngee Ann City and Wisma Atria. Other Malaysian developers that are active in Singapore's property markets include SP Setia Group (projects include such as 18 Woodsville and Eco Sanctuary), Hoi Hup Sunway Group (many residential projects in Singapore), and IOI Group (projects include the JV project with CDL - South Beach, the Trilinq, Citiscape).

---

[25] INDONESIA'S Lippo Group bought the key stake in Singapore's listed Overseas Union Enterprise (OUE) from Malaysian tycoon Ananda Krishnan in a deal worth S$957 million in March 2010. (Source: Lee, Su Shyan, "Lippo Group buys tycoon's stake in OUE," *The Straits Times*, 10 March 2010.

Case Study 3:   Innovation in Real Estate Project Financing

Case fact: In 1994, URA planned to rejuvenate the Bukit Timah and Hillview areas by rezoning some freehold industry sites in the areas into residential use. In August 1994, Orchard Parade Holdings (OPH) and Wing Tai Holdings (WTH) set up a 60%:40% joint venture (JV) entity to purchase a 373,277 square feet (sf) freehold industry site located off Bukit Timah Road, a prime residential district in Singapore, for S$218 million, or S$584 per sq foot (psf).[1] The freehold site was occupied by Tien Wah Press with a tenancy agreement ending in March 1997. The OPH-WTH JV proposed to develop the site that had been given an enhanced plot ratio of 2.07 into a 467-unit condominium project, known as Blissville Condominium, after Tien Wah Press had vacated the site.

In November 1997, OPH issued S$93 million via its subsidiary OPH Orion Ltd five-year secured medium-term notes (MTNs) bearing a coupon of six percent a year.[2] OPH planned to use a part of the fund raised to redeem OPH's S$51.5 million outstanding bonds in 1998, and the balance to partially finance the Blissville project.[3] The MTNs were issued with three layers of credit enhancement, which include a guarantee by OPH, a collateral in the form of 60% of OPH's share of the site, and an explicit put option underwritten by Pidemco Land. The MTNs were structured by Credit Agricole Indosuez Merchant Bank, which gave an estimated yield to maturity of about seven percent.

The put option underwritten by Pidemco Land was a kind of financial innovation used by property companies as a credit enhancement to the MTN issuance in a sluggish market. The put option underwritten by Pidemco on the collateral value of S$90 million by setting the strike price at 50% of the equivalent of OPH's 60% share in Blissville project.[4] The put option will only be *in-the-money* (exercised), if the project value drops by more than 50%. In return, Pidemco earned an undisclosed fee for taking the downside risk in the project.[5] In the event of default, bondholders' rights to redeem the bonds at par are protected; and by exercising the put option, Pidemco Land, the underwriter, is obliged to purchase the notes or the OPH shares in the project at not less than the par value of S$90 million.[6]

Case fact: Mr Li Ka-Shing's Cheung Kong Holdings made the debut into Singapore's residential property market by developing its first condominium project — Thomson 800.

(*Continued*)

---

[1] Williams, Ann, "Orchard Parade, Wing Tai buy Tien Wah site" *The Straits Times*, 4 August 1994.
[2] Abdul Hadhi, "Orchard Parade, Wing Tai to Refinance Tien Wah Site Purchase," *Business Times* Singapore, 5 November 1994.
[3] WTH separately issued S$62 million of "plain vanilla" five-year secured floating rate notes bearing quarterly coupons at an interest rate of one per cent above the three-month Singapore Interbank Offered Rate to refinance its share in the land deal.
[4] Based on an estimated project value of S$302 million, the 60% OPH stake in the joint venture was estimated at about S$181.2 million.
[5] "Time will tell if Pidemco's OPH deal is profitable," *Business Times Singapore*, 3 October 1998.
[6] Rashiwala, Kalpana, "Pidemco guarantees OPH bonds," *The Straits Times*, 2 October 1998.

(*Continued*)

Mr Li via its solely-owned local property vehicle, Pacific Enterprise Development (PED), developed Costa del Sol, the second condominium project located at Bayshore Road, which is opposite East Coast Park.

The leasehold project has seven 30-storey high-rise blocks comprising 906 two- to four-bedroom units with gross floor areas (GFAs) ranging from 950 square feet (sqf) to 1,800 sqf, and 23 penthouses with GFA ranging from 2,800 sqf to 3,500 sqf. The project was soft-launched in May 2000 at an average price of S$8,234 per square meter (psm) (S$765 per sqf (psf)).[7]

In the Phase 2 launch on 22 March 2002, PED released 50 new units at an average price of S$8,428 psm (S$783 psf). It offered potential buyers/investors a price appreciation guarantee option on the upside potential of the development.[8,9] This option is a forward contract, in which PED promises a minimum price appreciation of 10% for buyers of Costa del Sol at the end of a specified period.[10] If the value of the Costa del Sol units did not increase by at least 10% of the original purchase price in 2002, PED was obliged to pay the buyers the shortfalls of the 10% guaranteed price appreciation, which is defined as the difference between the valuation at the expiry on 30 December 2003 and the original purchase price.[11] PED introduced an alternative rental guarantee forward contract to potential buyers of Costa del Sol.[12] Under the contracts, PED guarantees at least a five percent rental yield for two years. Buyers can only choose either the price appreciation option or the rental guarantee option.

Based on the transaction data collected from the Realis database, the average sale price for Costa del Sol units was estimated at S$9,242 psm (S$859 psf) (as indicated by the first dotted line in Figure A1), which was 32.3% and 34.3% higher than the average unit sale price of Sanctuary Green (S$6,256 psm or S$581 psf) and Water Place (S$7,096 psm or S$659 psf), respectively. Figure A1 also shows that the average prices of Costa del Sol units increased significantly with the price gaps widening to 47.2% and 52.6% vis-à-vis Sanctuary Green and Water Place, respectively, at the end of the option period in 4Q2003 (as indicated by the second dotted line to the right). The simple average growth in the unit prices for Costa del Sol for the two-year period was estimated at 12.53% exceeding the 10% range set for the price appreciation options. The options may have been lapsed unexercised, based on the transaction evidence.

---

[7] Ms Annie Loke, the PED general manager, said at the soft-launch that the below the market price offered ".. *is our way of rewarding our loyal supporters who have been waiting for this launch.*" (Source: "First Costa del Sol units are a bargain, developer admits," *The Straits Times*, 31 May 2000.)

[8] "Costa del Sol developer guarantees up to 10% cash gain, *The Straits Times*, 22 March 2002.

[9] "Buy a Costa del Sol unit and get price appreciation guarantee," *Business Times*, 22 March 2002,

[10] Andrea Tan, "Buy a Costa del Sol unit and get price appreciation guarantee," *Business Times Singapore*, 22 March 2002.

[11] "Few takers for Costa del Sol," *The Straits Times*, 25 March 2002.

[12] "Costa del Sol offers 5% rental yield guarantee," *Business Times*, 2 May 2002.

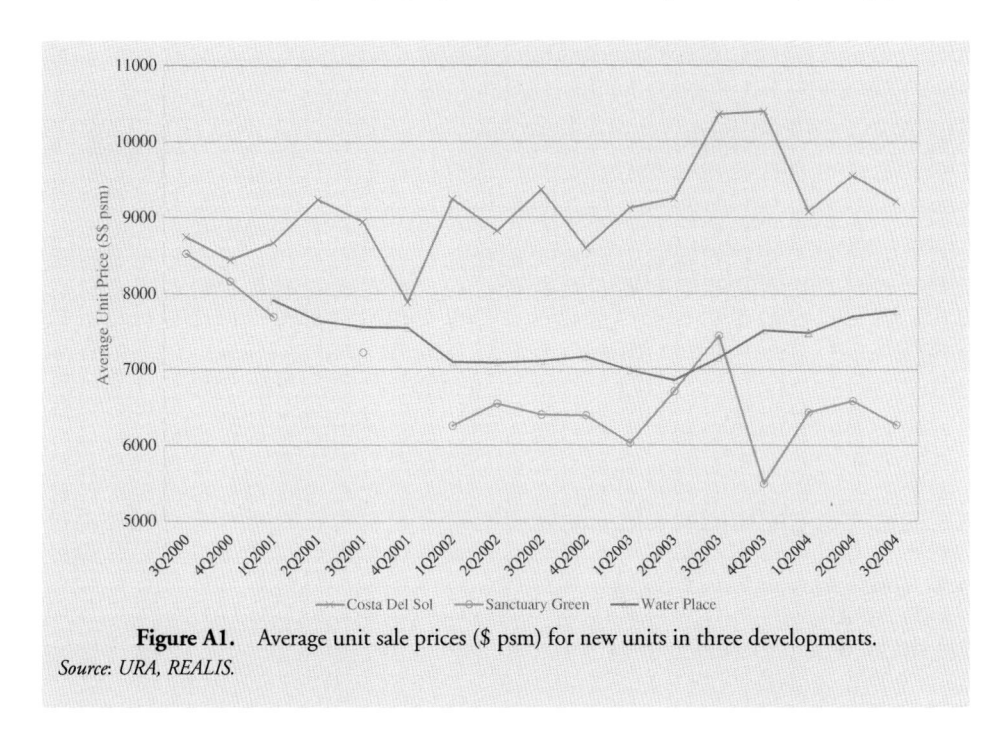

Figure A1. Average unit sale prices ($ psm) for new units in three developments.
Source: URA, REALIS.

China's developers only entered Singapore's property market in 2009 after a strong run-up of prices in Singapore's housing market.[26] China's developers, such as Qianjian Group, Kingsford Development and MCC Land have been aggressive in bidding for residential lands via URA's sales of sites programme.[27] Some new strategic alliances have been formed, such as China Vanke and Keppel Land, which jointly developed the Glades, a condominium project at Tanah Merah.

In May 2010,[28] the governments of Singapore and Malaysia entered a landmark land-swap agreement that led to the cessation of the Keratapi Tanah Melayu (KTM) railway services in Singapore. The agreement signed on 28 June 2011 paved the way for the relocation of Tanjong Pagar railway station to a site next to the Woodlands CIQ and Checkpoint. The KTM lands at Tanjong Pagar, Kranji, Bukit Timah, and Woodlands stations and along the railway tracks were returned to Singapore. The Singaporean government in exchange allocated four parcels of land in Marina South

---

[26] Nicholas Mak and Jenene Wong, "Competition from foreign developers" *Business Times Singapore*, Property 2014, 13 March 2014.

[27] Cheryl Ong, "China developers' interest heating up," *The Straits Times*, 13 September 2014.

[28] We use this date (May 2010) in which the agreement to enter into the land-swap deal between the two Prime Ministers was announced as the "announcement" date in our empirical design discussed in subsequent section.

(2.62 ha) and two parcels of land in Ophir-Rochor (2.67 ha) to a joint-venture firm, M+S Private Limited,[29] set up by the two countries to develop the lands. M+S Private Limited is a 40:60 joint venture between Singapore investment firm Temasek Holdings and Malaysian sovereign wealth fund Khazanah Nasional. M+S Private Limited started two mixed-use development projects — Duo at the Bugis Road/Ophir Road area and Marina One at downtown Marina in 2013. When completed in 2017, Duo will consist of DUO Residences, a 49-storey residential block of 660 units, DUO Tower, a 39-storey commercial and hotel complex and DUO Galleria, a unique retail gallery with basement carparks. Marina One comprises two 30-storey office towers: Marina One East Tower and Marina One West Tower, and two 34-storey residential blocks of 1,042 units, known as Marina One Residences.

4. Land Supply for Development

4.1 *Government Land Sales*

On the land-scarce island state of Singapore, more than three-quarters of developable lands are state-owned and held by custodian — the Singapore Land Authority (SLA). The sales of sites programmes (SOSPs) have been used to spur economic growth in stable markets by supplying new business space to meet demand derived from economic activities in Singapore. The government sells state lands via competitive bidding processes to private developers for the construction of private housing units and commercial spaces. URA and HDB are the two government land sale agencies that administer the SOSPs.

In Singapore, the first-price sealed-bid auction is widely used for the SOSPs. However, innovative land tender systems have also been used in some cases, which include the land option method for the Marina Business and Financial Centre site (Case Study 4), and the two-envelope system. The innovative two-envelope system may take the form of a Concept and Price Revenue and/or Fixed-Price Request-for-Proposal tenders, and is used for selected strategic sites to encourage high quality architectural designs and unique business concepts to be incorporated into future developments on the sites. Since 2005, four government sites have been sold through the two-envelope (Concept and Price Revenue) system. They include the Urban Entertainment Centre site (the former Iluma, which has been renamed Bugis+ after being acquired by CapitaLand Mall Trust), the Collyer Quay site (Fullerton Heritage),

---

[29] M+S Private Limited is a joint venture company set up by the governments of Malaysia and Singapore to undertake developments of the lands in Marina South and Ophir-Rochor. The company has a 60% and 40% shareholding structure held by Malaysia's Khazanah Nasional and Singapore's Temasek Holdings, which are the investment arms of the two governments.

Case Study 4: An Innovative Land Tender Scheme — the Marina Downtown International Business and Finance Centre

Case fact: In July 2005, the Urban Redevelopment Authority (URA) sold a "white site" at the Downtown Marina South for the proposed Marina Bay Financial Center (MBFC) development via the government's sales of sites programme (SOSP). The 3.55-hectare (ha) site is connected to the Raffles Place mass rapid transit (MRT) interchange through 1.8 hectares of subterranean space. The subterranean space can be developed into an underground pedestrian mall with shops, restaurants, and other commercial facilities. Upon completion, the development yields a total of 438,000 square meters (sqm) of gross commercial space.

In the MBFC land tender launched on 27 May 2004, the URA introduced an innovative "option-based" tender scheme for the first time. The new scheme gives the successful bidder the flexibility to develop the project in phases. During the tender submission, each bidder indicates his/her bid on a unit gross floor area (GFA) basis, instead of the usual lump sum bid, in a sealed envelope. He/she has to indicate the GFA for the initial phase of the development, which is not less than 100,000 sqm. For the second phase of the development, he/she is also required to choose upfront one of the three option schemes as in Table A2 below:

Table A2. Option scheme in tender of Marina Business and Financial Centre (MBFC) land.

Option scheme	Option period (Years)*	Option fee (%)
A	6	6
B	8	8
C	10	10

Period from the date of award of BFC tender to the expiry of the option.

Upon the award of the land, the winning bidder pays an option fee ranging from 6% to 10% based on the bid price for the land set aside for the Phase 2 development. The option gives the winning bidder the right to purchase the land at an agreed price in a future date ranging from 6 years to 10 years. The option fee is not refundable, if the winning bidder chooses not to exercise the option to purchase the subsequent phase, or when the option term lapses, whichever is the later. The option fee is not a security deposit. Part of the option fee, that is, 3% of the land price can be used to pay for the land price in the later phase. The maximum project completion period for each phase is capped at eight years. Therefore, the project completion period for the subject development could technically be stretched up to a maximum of 18 years, if the 10-year option scheme is chosen.

(Continued)

> *(Continued)*
>
> The MBFC site was awarded on 14 July 2005 to a consortium comprising Hong Kong Land, Cheung Kong (Holdings) Ltd/Hutchison Whampoa and Keppel Land, which submitted the highest unit price of S$4,101 psm. The proposed first phase of development covers a total GFA of 244,000 sqm (or an equivalent of 56% of the total permitted GFA of 438,000 sqm), which comprises 180,000 sqm of office space, 55,000 sqm of residential space, and 9,000 sqm for retail space. The consortium also took up an eight-year option (Option Scheme B) for the remaining 194,000 sqm of GFA on the site. On 16 February 2007, the consortium exercised the option to purchase the Phase 2 land with a GFA of 194,000 sqm for a sum of S$883.8 million[1]. Upon the full completion, the MBFC development yields a total GFA of 438,000 sqm, which include three office towers with nearly 300,000 sqm of Grade "A" office space, two residential towers of 649 luxury apartments and penthouses, and 176,000 sqf of retail space.
>
> ---
>
> [1] The unit bid price for the Phase 2 land is estimated based on the development charge rates for commercial sector in the core CBD segments published by the Inland Revenue Authority of Singapore.

the Beach Road site (South Beach) and the Capitol site at Stamford Road/North Bridge Road.[30] The Fixed-Price Request-for-Proposal system was used in the sale of the two integrated resort projects at Marina Bay Sands and Resort World at Sentosa in 2005 and 2006, respectively.

Figure 6 shows the cumulative number of land parcels by year sold by URA and HDB based on the tender award date. The land sale data from the SOSPs by the URA and the HDB are aggregated in plotting the charts. The residential land sales include only the sales non-landed sites, which are sold for apartments and condominiums developments. The commercial sites used in the graph include white sites and commercial sites that can be used for office, commercial, and mixed uses.

The government has also used the SOSPs as an effective supply-side tool to regulate overheating housing prices in boom markets. The government stepped up sales of state lands during the residential property price booms in the 1994–1997 and 2009–2014 periods with the intent to alleviate imbalances in demand and supply in the private residential property market. The URA and HDB jointly sold 66 and 97 land parcels for residential developments during the two boom periods, respectively. In terms of per square metre built-up area, the two projects could be translated into a total 2.63 million square metres in the 1994-1997 period, and 4.61 million square metres in the 2009–2014 period. Based on a typical unit gross floor area of 110 square metres, the lands sold could be developed into a total of 23,884 units (1994–1997)

---

[30] Serene Tng, "Capito Sale Site: Concept & Price Revenue Tender," Skyline, May/June 2011.

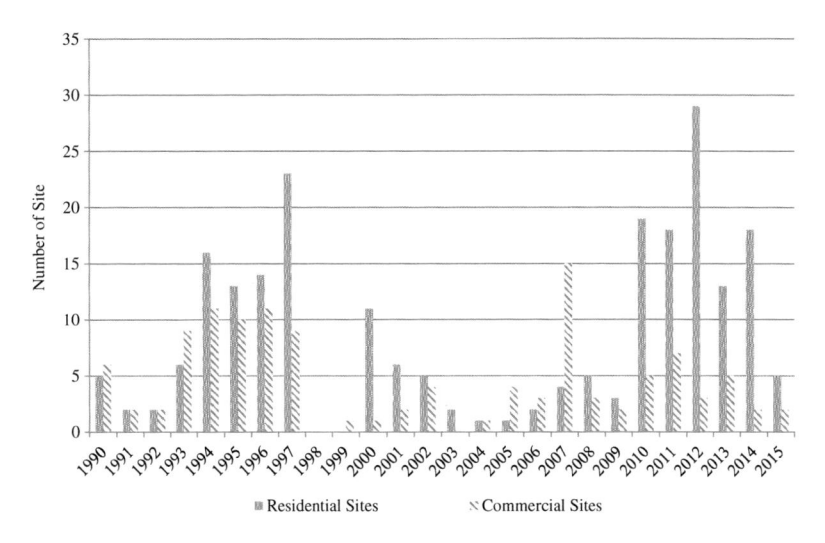

Figure 6. Government's sales of sites.
Source: Urban Redevelopment Authority (URA) and Housing and Development Board (HDB).

and 41,941 units (2009–2014), respectively, which could ease the supply crunch in the non-landed residential properties during the two boom periods.

The government could by suspending state land sales, temporarily *"turn off"* supply to control excessive stocks in the periods of weakening private housing markets. In 2001, a "Reserve List" system was introduced as a more flexible way to balance the demand and the supply in the markets. A site in the reserve list can be called out by an interested developer, if he/she submits an offer price that is close to the Government's Reserve Price for the site.

4.2 *Collective Sales*

Development Guide Plans (DGPs) have been a key planning tool used by URA to turn the long-term vision defined in the 1991 Concept Plan into reality. After the 55 DGPs were completed between 1993 and 1998, and gazetted as the new Master Plan for Singapore on 22 January 1999, land use intensity in many DGP regions has been reviewed upward, which significantly increases development potentials of many older residential developments. These planning initiatives coupled with depreciating values of ageing structures on lands motivate en bloc sales of the developments. Cosy Mansion was the first collective sale in 1994 followed by the transactions of Changi Heights in the same year. For the period from 1995–2013, there were 491 en bloc transactions which were estimated in value term to be S$31.5 billion (Figure 7). The

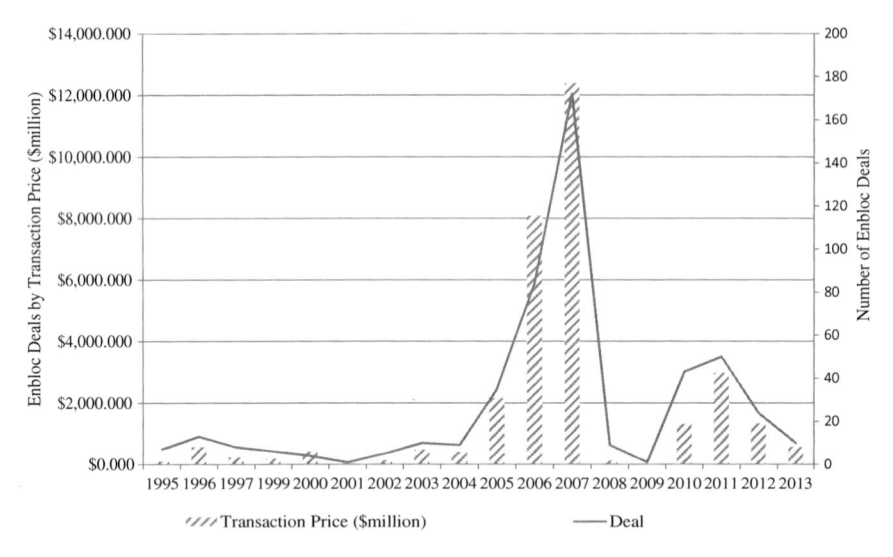

Figure 7. En bloc sales of strata-titled and landed properties.
Source: Urban Redevelopment Authority (URA).

en bloc transaction activities were the most active in the two years of 2006 and 2007. En bloc sales are an important process in urban renewal, and they are an alternative source of supply of private residential development lands for developers.

Collective sales, or en bloc sales, are a unique phenomenon in the local residential property market. In a collective sale, more than one private owner from either a strata-titled residential development or contiguous landed developments come together to jointly sell their properties. (Case Study 5) They reap significant windfalls if redevelopment potential on a land exceeds the combined value of the land and any physical improvement thereon.

The amendment to Land Title (Strata) (Amendment) Act taking effect from 11 October 1999 removes unanimous consents from the owners that may lead to potential "hold up" problems in a collective sale process. In the amended rule, majority consent is applied. For a development that is less than 10 years old, 90% of the share values, whereas for a development that is more than 10 years old, 80% of the share values are required to form a majority decision. Two more amendments were subsequently made in 2007 and 2010 to ensure a fair and transparent en bloc process for both the pro-en bloc and anti-en bloc groups of owners. The 2007 amendments provide that, in addition to the specified majority (based on share value, share in land or notional share), there must also be a specified majority of the total area of all the lots in a strata development to constitute the majority consents. For a development of less than 10 years old, owners of 90% of the total area of all lots, and for a development of 10 years old or

Case Study 5:   Processes in a Typical Collective Sale in Singapore

Property owners, developers and property agents are "*deal-makers*" in a typical collective sale. The collective sale process is usually triggered off by a group of enthusiastic owners who are motivated by the windfall potential of their development. However, in some cases, developers may initiative the negotiation process with owner representatives.

Under the Land Titles (Strata) Act (Chapter 158) 1985 and the Land Titles (Strata) (Amendment) Act 1987,[1] it was necessary to obtain unanimous consensus from owners of strata-titled properties in a collective sale process. A deal could be aborted as long as one owner disagrees to sell his/her unit. It created serious hold-up problems, where minority owners ask for higher payoffs in order to cooperate in a transaction. In a 1999 amendment to the Land Strata Titles acts and two subsequent amendments in 2007 and 2010, the unanimous consensus condition was replaced by the majority rules.[2]

The collective sale process starts with the formation of a collective sale committee comprising between three and 14 members who must be elected at a general meeting of the management corporation. The committee will then appoint a team of professionals, which includes a marketing agent/property consultant and a legal adviser, to advise on procedural matters. It will obtain a valuation report for the whole development from an independent valuer, which is used as a reference on a reasonable reserve price. It will work concurrently with the inputs of the marketing agent and the legal advisor on issues relating to apportionment of sale proceeds, options to repurchase properties in the redeveloped property, relocation of existing owners, outlined planning permission, estimation of development charges[3] and other terms and conditions for the collective sale. The next important step is to obtain the requisite majority consent within 12 months for the collective sale. Failure to do so will result in the dissolution of the committee. Based on the advice of the marketing agent, it will decide on the method of sale either by tender, or auction or private treaty, then evaluate and negotiate with prospective buyers on offer prices and terms of sale, and finally, enter into a conditional sale and purchase agreement with potential buyers.

The committee then submits an application on behalf of the consenting majority property owners to the strata titles board to confirm the proposed collective sale. It needs

(*Continued*)

---

[1] These two acts are enacted to facilitate the strata-titles subdivision and registration of the joint and common interests of development involving multiple ownerships, so that each owner has an exclusive ownership to the strata space of individual units and at the same time, they also jointly own the common areas within the boundary of the strata-titled plan.

[2] Prior to October 1999, a unanimous resolution is required to pass through the motion of collective sale. The requirement has been relaxed in the amendments made to the Land Titles Strata Act in 1999, whereby a majority of 80% to 90% of the owners' consents is sufficed for passing the resolution to collectively sell the strata-titled property.

[3] Development charge is a form of betterment levy imposed by the government and administered by the Urban Redevelopment Authority (URA), which allows the government to cream off 50% of the enhancement value of the land created by the planning initiatives that leads to an upgrading of the permitted zoning and density of development.

(*Continued*)

to serve a notice of the application to all owners and mortgagees, chargees or other persons (other than a lessee) with an estate or interest in the unit by registered post. A dissenting minority owner may lodge an application with the strata titles board stating the grounds for objection within 21 days from the date the application for approval. The strata titles board will make the decision within four to six months from the date of application. If the application is successful, all units and land in the development will be sold collectively.

The apportionment method for net sale proceeds is an important factor that can break a collective sale deal. The net sale proceeds could be apportioned based on built-up area, share value, or independent valuation of each unit. Owners sometimes bring in factors like the renovations carried out, the premium view and frontage enjoyed by the units, etc., in the negotiation. The time taken in a collective sale process from negotiation till the delivery of vacant possession may take from few months to years. In the case of the Changi Height sale, the 58 owners waited nine months to receive the last payment because of the delay in obtaining the outline planning permission to redevelop the site.

more, owners of 80% of the total area of all lots must agree to sell in order for an en bloc sale to be approved by the Strata Titles Board (STB).

5. Commercial Real Estate Markets

Singapore is an economy that relies heavily on manufacturing and services outputs to generate its economic growth. As of 1Q2015, 67.37% of the country's gross domestic product (GDP) (current market price) is made up of goods and services produced by manufacturing (16.34%), wholesale and retail trade (15.26%), business services (15.23%), and finance and insurance (12.53%). The four key sectors of economic activities create significant demand for commercial real estate. Private developers are the main suppliers of commercial real estate space, which include office, retail, hotels and hospitality, and industrial space. The public agencies like JTC and HDB supply industrial land and customised factory space for industrial users.[31] By the available stocks in the market as at 1Q2015, the market shares of the private sector by the available space in factory, office and shop are estimated at 85.1%, 83.0% and 69.8%, respectively.

The commercial real estate markets are highly competitive, where private developers engage in a full range of development activities from land purchase, design and construction, financing and leasing activities. Commercial real estate developers

---

[31] The government's agency, Jurong Town Corporation (JTC), is the main supplier for industry lands and the developer for custom-built factories.

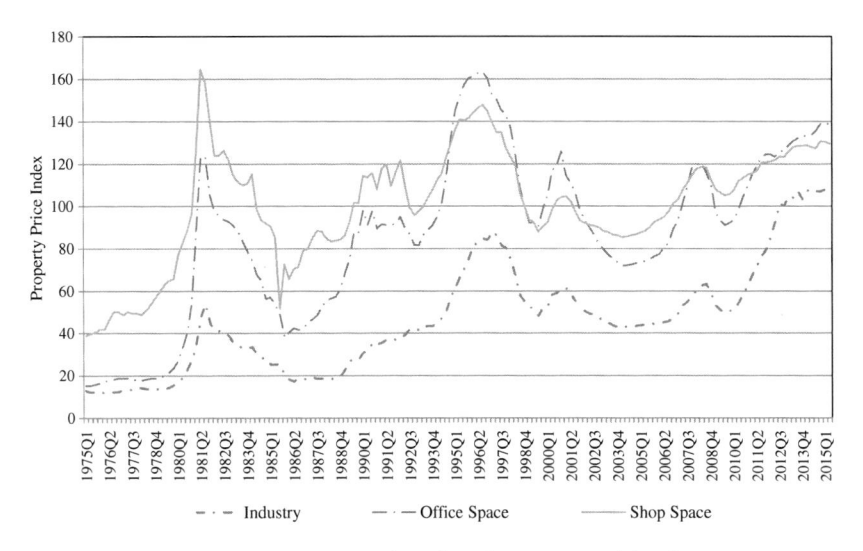

Figure 8. Property price indices for private commercial real estate.
Source: Realis, Urban Redevelopment Authority (URA).

adopt either a *"build to hold"* or a *"build to sell"* development strategy. Prime commercial properties, such as office buildings and shopping malls, are usually held by developers for long-term rental income purposes. Developers could choose an "exit" by selling commercial properties either en bloc or by strata-titled sales. In strata-titled sales, individual investors own sub-divided commercial space coupled with joint interests of the land thereon.[32] With the emergence of REITs after July 2002, many developers set up REIT vehicles and sell their investment-grade commercial properties to affiliated REITs.

Currently, the URA transaction-based private commercial real estate indices are constructed based on transactions of strata-title commercial space.[33] The URA has published four price indices for office, shop and industry properties since 1975.[34] Figure 8 shows the historical trends of the URA property price (nominal) indices for office, shop and multiple-user factory for the period from 1Q1975 to 1Q2015.

---

[32] Unlike prime-grade commercial properties held by a single institutional investor, strata-titled space includes subdivided units and floors in commercial buildings that are sold separately to individual users/occupiers. The land on which the buildings are constructed is jointly owned by multiple strata-titled owners.

[33] The URA indices are quality-constant median price indices published on a quarterly basis. The indices are weighted using a 12-quarter moving average from a basket of transactions. Smoothing in the median price indices may occur, if trading activities of the strata-titled commercial real estate are thin in some areas. (See Deng, Y.H., McMilen, D.P. and Sing, T.F. (2014) "Matching Indices for Thinly-Traded Commercial Real Estate in Singapore" *Regional Science and Urban Economics*, 47, 86-98.)

[34] The industrial property price sub-indices for the multiple-user factories and multiple-user warehouse are published after 1990.

The three markets move together, though short-term variations are observed over the sample period. Singapore's commercial real estate markets witnessed three peaks in 1981, 1996, and 2007. Positive economic factors, which include strong economic growth, large investment inflows and low interest rates, create buoyant commercial property markets in the mid-1990s. Over a three-year period from 2Q1993 to 3Q1996, the URA property price indices for the industry, shop and office sectors increased by 96.3%, 47.8% and 88.6%, respectively. The Asian Financial Crisis in 1997 caused commercial real estate markets to plunge into recessions in 1999. Two short booms were experienced in 2000 and 2008. The rise in commercial real estate prices in 2008 was derailed by the Subprime Crisis in the US. A strong rebound in all sectors was observed in 2009, with the industrial sector showing the strongest growth as the industry property price index surpassed the office and shop indices in 2011.

5.1 *Converting CBD Office Space into Luxury Condominiums*

The government of Singapore started land reclamation around the Marina Bay area in 1970s and 1980s in anticipation of the future expansion of the CBD. It reclaimed 360-hectare prime sites at the Marina Bay area, which integrate seamlessly with the existing Raffles Place CBD. Unlike the Raffles Place CBD, the Mariana Bay area is not just a hub for global businesses and financial institutions; it will showcase a sustainable model for a total live-work-play, which is integrated with quality housing, recreational and leisure facilities. The expansion of the existing CBD into the Marina Bay area is expected to propel Singapore into becoming a thriving and vibrant world-class city.

The development process started through the sales of state lands via the URA SOSP. The first parcel of land in the area was sold to a consortium consisting of Cheung Kong Holdings, Hong Kong Land and Keppel Land in March 2001. One Raffles Quay, a project consisting of a 50-storey North Tower and a 29-storey South Tower, was built on the site. The adjacent site was sold in a separate URA SOSP tender exercise in 2002 to a consortium of City Development Limited (CDL) and American International Group Global Real Estate (AIG) (Table 2). The CDL-AIG site was developed into the tallest luxury condominium tower, and the first residential project — the Sail @ Marina Bay, to offer the downtown living experience.[35] The decision to use the "white site" at the Marina Bay for residential development has been considered a bold move.[36]

---

[35] Arthur Sim, "The imbalance seen in CBD space supply, demand," *Business Times*, 27 March 2007.
[36] Kalpana Rashiwala, "Why rivals hope CDL won't do office project," *Business Times*, 16 May 2002.

Table 2. Details of the earlier Marina white sites sold.

	Site 1	Site 2
Successful Tenderer	Boulevard Development Pte Ltd, Comina Investment Limited & Freylnd Pte Ltd	Glengary Pte Ltd
Consortium / Joint venture	Cheung Kong Holdings, Hong Kong Land, Keppel Land	City Development Limited, AIG Global Real Estate
Site Area (m2)	11,367	9,091
Gross Plot Ratio	13	13
Permissible Gross Floor Area (m2)	147,770	118,182
Date of Award	16 March 2001	14 May 2002
Tender Price	S$461,816,800	S$288,900,000
Price per square meter per plot ratio	S$3,125	S$2,445
Completed project	One Raffles Quay	The Sail @ Marina Bay
Development	Office	Residential/Retail
Construction Start	—	2005
Completion Date	2007	Marina Bay: 2008/ Central Park: 2009

Source: Compiled from press reports.

The success of CDL-AIG's project has triggered a slew of conversion of old office buildings into luxury condominiums along the Shenton Way and Tanjong Pagar areas. Some of the conversion projects include V on Shenton, (formerly the UIC Shenton), Eon Shenton (formerly the Marina House), and the conversion of 76 Shenton Way and One Shenton. As more CBD office buildings were converted into residential use, office space crunch, especially in the Central Area, was experienced when the demand picked up in 2007. Businesses forced out of the converted office buildings had difficulty finding alternative office space in the CBD area. On 21 May 2007, URA issued a circular to temporarily curb conversion of office use until 31 December 2009 to prevent depletion of the existing office stocks in the Central Area.[37]

In July 2005, URA launched the sale of a large plot of 3.5 hectares at Marina Boulevard/Central Boulevard earmarked for the Marina Business and Financial

---

[37] A media statement by the URA "*URA to Temporarily Disallow Conversion of Office Use in the Central Area to Other Uses,*" published on 21 May 2007.

Centre (MBFC). The MBFC site includes a 1.8-hectare subterranean space with underground retail space connecting the area with the waterfront promenade, the Raffles Place MRT station and the Downtown MRT station. An innovative land option system was adopted in the sale of the MBFC site by URA (see Case Study 4).

The newest development in the Marina Bay area — Marina One by the M+S group, when completed in 2017, together with the MBFC and other major projects (One Raffles Quay, The Sails@ Marina Bay, One Marina Boulevard, Asia Square) will form a critical mass to draw business activities to the Marina Bay area.

6. Retail Mall Developments

Singapore's retail scene has undergone significant changes in the last 50 years.[38] As modern Singapore's history started with the commercial activities that took place at the mouth of the Singapore River, the early retail concentration was found mainly in the central area surrounding Raffles Place and its vicinity. Several sub-centres like High Street, Chinatown, Middle Road, Serangoon Road, Arab Street and Geylang were the main retail nodes in the early 1950s. The Orchard thoroughfare had developed into an important commercial ribbon in the late 1950s, and together with Raffles Place and High Street, provided retail facilities catering mainly to international clientele. There were sub-centres serving various ethnic groups, such as Chinatown for Chinese, Serangoon Road for Indians, Geylang Serai for Malays, and Arab Street for a mixture of Indians and Malays, and also outlying community centres along major traffic arterials. These included clusters of shops along Bukit Timah Road and Bukit Panjang Road (popular among shoppers from Peninsular Malaysia), Changi Village, Seletar, Nee Soon and Holland Village (with a presence mainly associated with the proximity to the British military bases).

After the 1960s, the rapid public housing programmes spearheaded by HDB saw the mushrooming of many new towns with self-sustainable neighbourhoods and community centres, which provided basic shopping facilities and amenities such as supermarkets, restaurants, banks, and convenience goods to residents in the public housing estates. These HDB neighbourhoods and community centres supplemented the regional and national centres located in the central areas. In the 1970s and 1980s, the urban renewal activities were systematically implemented in a rapid pace by URA, which was created out of HDB's Urban Renewal Department in 1974. Under the urban renewal programme, many small plots of land were acquired and combined into larger plots and sold by tender to private developers. Many shop houses and old

---

[38] More details on shopping centres development in Singapore could be referred to the book by Sim, Loo Lee, *A Study of Planned Shopping Centers in Singapore*, 1984, Singapore University Press.

buildings in the Central Area were demolished to make way for planned shopping centers and modern high-rise buildings.

The URA uses the government's SOSPs to attract private developers to take active part in the effort of modernising retail facilities in the Central Area. Planned shopping centres, which provide one-stop shopping convenience on a comprehensive scale in a standalone building, became popular in the 1970s. There were four distinct phases of growth for the shopping centres in Singapore. The first planned shopping centre built on the SOSP site was the People's Park Complex in 1969. Completed in the same year, Supreme House, located along Penang Road (now the refurbished Park Mall), was the first shopping centre in the Orchard Road area. In the first phase of development from 1969 to 1977, 22 shopping centres were completed. Several one-stop air-conditioned shopping centres were built in the Orchard Road area (Tanglin Shopping Centre, The Orchard, Specialist Centre, Shaw Centre, Plaza Singapura, Far East Shopping Centre, Orchard Towers, Lucky Plaza, and others). New shopping centres were also built in the Chinatown area (such as the People's Park Centre, Pearl Centre and the People's Park Complex); in the High Street area (such as Peninsula Shopping Centre, Colombo Court, High Street Shopping Centre, Peninsula Plaza); in the Selegie-Serangoon area (such as Selegie Complex, Peace Centre, Parklane Shopping Mall and the President Shopping Centre); and the Beach Road area (such as the Golden Mile Shopping Centre, Golden Mile Tower, and Textile Centre). Other suburban shopping centres were also built, such as Holland Road Shopping Centre (1971), Katong Shopping Centre (1971) and Queensway Shopping Centre (1975).

In the second phase of development between 1975 and 1983, 29 shopping centres were built, and more than half of them were located in the Orchard Road area. During this period, the two most comprehensive developments that integrated shopping, hotel, office and entertainment facilities were developed — Raffles City Singapore and Marina Square. Suburban shopping centres such as Parkway Parade and Goldhill Square (now United Square) were also built during this period. In the third phase during the 1990s, with the opening of the MRT lines coupled with the decentralisation strategies in the 1991 Concept Plan, many new suburban and regional shopping centres were built near MRT stations (Table 3).[39] Mega shopping malls with a space of more than a million square feet were built, such as Suntec City (1997) and Ngee Ann City (1993).

In the 2000s, the emergence of retail REITs significantly transformed the retail scene in Singapore. REITs actively carried out asset enhancement initiatives to facelift the shopping malls to enhance rental yields and shopper traffic. Turnover leases are increasingly being adopted in most of the REIT-owned shopping malls.

---

[39] Joanna Chen, "The changing retail landscape, *Business Times*, 23 Sep 2010

Table 3. Planned shopping centres built in the 1990s.

Development	Net floor area (sqf)	Year of completion	Developer
North:			
Northpoint Shopping Centre	145,313	1993	Centrepoint Properties Limited/ Cold Storage Holdings
Hougang Point	79,922	1997	Hiap Hoe Holdings
Hougang Lifestyle Centre	160,005	1996	NTUC
Junction 8	200,209	1993	Singapore Technologies Industrial Corporation Pte Ltd & Liang Court Holdings
Causeway Point	441,320	1998	Centrepoint
East:			
Century Square	200,000	1995	First Capital Corporation
Tampines Mall	312,153	1995	DBS Land/Pernas International/ NTUC
East Point	190,000	1996	Far East Organization
White Sands	143,483	1996	OCBC (Whitesands Development)
West:			
Ginza Plaza	141,362	1992	Far East Organization
Jurong Point	349,999	1996	Guthrie GTS & Lee Kim Tah Holdings Limited
Lot 1	220,003	1996	Isrich Property Pte Ltd (CDL)
West Mall	207,593	1997	Alprop Pte Ltd (UIC & RMA Land)
Bukit Panjang Plaza	161,459	1998	Superbowl Holdings
Jurong Lifestyle Centre	79,997	1996	NTUC/SLF
Central:			
Anchorpoint	70,999	1996	Centrepoint Properties Limited

Source: Knight Frank Consultancy & Research.

Suburban shopping malls continue to be in the interests of REITs and private institutional funds with several new shopping malls, such as JEM and Westgate being built around Jurong MRT and interchange. Together with the redeveloped JCube (formerly the Jurong Entertainment Centre) and the refurbished IMM Building, the shopping space known as Jurong Gateway forms the largest shopping cluster outside the Central Area. New developments along the Orchard Road, which include ION Orchard, 313@Somerset, Orchard Central and *Scape, also add vibrancy to Singapore's most popular shopping belt.

7. Conclusion

The private residential property market has fulfilled the dreams of many Singaporeans, who aspire to upgrade from public housing flats to private non-landed, and then to landed housing units. The housing ladder will continue to serve its function facilitating the upward mobility of a society with one of the highest ownership rate in the world — where one in nine HDB dwellers own the flats they live in. The collaborative arrangement between private developers and the government's planners has been tested and proven to deliver the city growth of Singapore in the last 50 years. Under this framework, the government undertakes long-term planning and carries out various infrastructure developments. It also covers the subsidised housing segment to ensure that housing affordability is not compromised, while giving private developers the free-hand in the private housing market activities. Private developers use their equity and capital raised from stock and debt markets to translate the long-term "blue-print" of the city into reality.

Moving forward, the proven formula is expected to continue to guide future developments, transforming the island state into a sustainable and liveable city that will be a model for other cities to emulate.

The private property market will become competitive and crowded with the entrance of more foreign developers. Local developers have been actively exploring new opportunities outside the country. Scalability, diversification and local knowledge, though the last two are opposing forces, are three ingredients that local real estate firms will have to properly manage and balance in order to compete globally with foreign developers who are bigger and stronger. Collaborating with foreign developers and cross-sharing local know-how through strategic alliance is likely to deliver win-win outcomes.

The importance of real estate capital cannot be under-stated in the next phase of development of the local property market. Capital flows into real estate markets could improve efficiency and transparency in the market on the one hand; local markets could, on the other hand, be more susceptible to external shocks when inter-country flows of funds into real estate become less restrictive. Adapting to new changes, facing new risks and innovating in the product lifecycle are skills that need to be embedded in the perspective of local developers.

Appendix: Major Developers in Singapore

(A) CapitaLand Limited (www.capitaland.com)

CapitaLand is one of Asia's largest real estate companies headquartered and listed in Singapore. The company leverages its significant asset base, design and development capabilities, active capital management strategies, extensive market network and operational capabilities to develop high-quality real estate products and services. Its diversified global real estate portfolio includes integrated developments, shopping malls, serviced residences, offices and homes. Its two core markets are Singapore and China, while Indonesia, Malaysia and Vietnam have been identified as new growth markets. The company also has one of the largest real estate fund management businesses with assets located in Asia.

CapitaLand's listed real estate investment trusts are CapitaLand Mall Trust, CapitaLand Commercial Trust, Ascott Residence Trust, CapitaLand Retail China Trust and CapitaLand Malaysia Mall Trust.

(B) City Developments Limited (CDL) (http://www.cdl.com.sg/app/cdl/company/corporate_profile.xml)

Since its inception in 1963, City Developments Limited (CDL) has been Singapore's property pioneer. Today, CDL is a Singapore-listed international property and hospitality conglomerate with businesses in real estate development and investment, hotel ownership and management, facilities management and the provision of hospitality solutions. It is one of Singapore's largest companies by market capitalisation and has a global presence of 91 locations in 25 countries.

With an extensive network of more than 400 subsidiaries and associated companies under its wings, CDL has five companies listed on notable stock exchanges in New Zealand, Hong Kong, London and Philippines. The Group currently owns and manages a solid portfolio of residential and investment properties, in addition to hotels, across Asia, Europe, the Middle East, North America and New Zealand/Australia.

CDL holds an impressive track record of having developed over 36,000 luxurious and quality homes across diverse market segments. As one of Singapore's biggest landlords, it owns close to 7.2 million square feet of floor/lettable area of office, industrial, retail, residential and hotel space locally and globally. Amongst private developers in Singapore, the Group possesses one of the largest land banks, with more than 2.7 million square feet, which can be potentially developed into over 7.6 million square feet of gross floor area.

The Group's global presence is led by its diversification into hospitality management and the acquisition of hotel assets through CDL's London-listed subsidiary, Millennium & Copthorne Hotels plc (M&C). As one of the world's largest global hospitality management and real estate group, M&C owns, asset manages and/or operates 120 hotels globally. The Group was also the first to establish a hospitality trust in 2006. CDL Hospitality Trusts currently owns hotels in Singapore, Australia, New Zealand, Japan, the UK and the Maldives. CDL's China division and wholly-owned subsidiary, CDL China Limited, has been strategically making inroads in China's key cities. CDL has also established a real estate platform in the United Kingdom which focuses on acquisitions of real estate in Greater and Central London for development and investment.

As a socially responsible corporation, CDL is fully committed towards environmental stewardship and has been taking the lead in shaping Singapore's built environment for over two decades. To date, CDL has developed more than 80 Green Mark buildings.

Testament to its commitment towards social responsibility and sustainable development, CDL was honoured with the President's Social Service Award and President's Award for the Environment in 2007. It was also the only developer to be accorded the Built Environment Leadership Platinum Award in 2009 and Green Mark Platinum Champion Award in 2011 by the Building and Construction Authority, the governing authority for Singapore's built environment.

CDL is the first Singapore company to be listed on three of the world's sustainability benchmarks — FTSE4Good Index Series (since 2002), Global 100 Most Sustainable Corporations in the World (since 2010) and the Dow Jones Sustainability Indices (since 2011). In 2016, CDL was ranked Top Real Estate Company in the Global 100 Most Sustainable Corporations in the World listing. Since 2014, it has been ranked Top Asian Developer in the Channel NewsAsia Sustainability Ranking.

(C) Far East Organization (http://www.fareast.com.sg/)

Far East Organization is the largest private property developer in Singapore. Since its establishment in 1960 by the late Mr Ng Teng Fong, Far East Organization has been contributing to the transformation of Singapore's urban landscape with over 760 developments in the residential, hospitality, retail, commercial, healthcare and industrial space segments, including 49,000 or one in six private homes in Singapore. It is also the city-state's largest private residential landlord and largest hotels and serviced residences operator.

Far East Organization includes three listed entities: Far East Orchard Limited, a hospitality and property group, Far East Hospitality Trust which consists of Far East Hospitality Real Estate Investment Trust and Far East Hospitality Business Trust, and Yeo Hiap Seng Limited, a 115-year-old industry pioneer of processed food and beverage products in Southeast Asia.

Far East Hospitality, the hospitality arm of listed Far East Orchard Limited, specialises in the mid-tier to upscale hospitality segments and has a combined portfolio of more than 13,000 rooms under management across 90 hotels and serviced residences in seven countries.

Far East Organization's Corporate Real Estate Business Group manages a large and diverse portfolio of quality real estate for lease to suit different business and individual needs. The Retail Business Group manages over 1.4 million square feet of leasable retail space in established as well as new growth areas in Singapore across 21 malls and retail properties. Far East Organization's restaurant and franchise food arm, Kitchen Language and The Big Idea, a homegrown food and beverage company acquired by the group, operate a portfolio of 16 food and beverage concepts across 30 outlets.

Continuing its entrepreneurial heritage to seek new avenues for growth, Far East Organization has built a growing portfolio of quality investment properties and development sites in prime locations across Australia. Today, the Organization has a significant presence in the hospitality, residential and commercial sectors in Australia, having invested A$1.9 billion in acquisitions and joint ventures since 2013.

As a Christian enterprise, Far East Organization is guided by its values to seek the welfare of the city, support the causes of the needy and show love to its neighbours. Through space philanthropy facilitated by the Government's Community/Sports Facilities Scheme, Far East Organization has gifted purpose-built spaces at its developments for community use. These gifted spaces are located at Clarke Quay Central above Clarke Quay MRT station, Novena Specialist Center, SBF Center, Orchard Central and Junction 10.

Far East Organization is the only developer in the world to be bestowed eight FIABCI Prix d'Excellence Awards, underscoring its unique achievements in the international real estate arena.

(D) GuocoLand (https://www.guocoland.com.sg/index.shtml)

GuocoLand is an award-winning property developer with operations and investments in key markets around the region including Singapore, China, Malaysia and Vietnam. Headquartered in Singapore and listed in the Singapore Exchange, GuocoLand is part of the Hong Leong Group, a leading conglomerate with a portfolio of diversified businesses.

An established developer with more than two decades of experience, GuocoLand's projects are distinguished by quality and thoughtful design. From residential to commercial properties and integrated developments, GuocoLand has delivered premium properties sited in prime locations across different markets that have been well-received by the industry and the general populace.

In Singapore, GuocoLand has successfully developed 33 residential projects yielding more than 9,000 apartments and homes over the last 25 years. Widely-recognised for its eco-friendly award-winning developments, GuocoLand has received the prestigious Building and Construction Authority (BCA) Green Mark Platinum Award, the highest honour for a green building in Singapore, for its most recent developments being Goodwood Residence and Sophia Residence within the residential portfolio. Wallich Residence at Tanjong Pagar Centre, Leedon Residence, Elliot at the East Coast, The Quartz and The Waterline have also won Green Mark Awards. In addition, Goodwood Residence was conferred the prestigious Outstanding award for Excellence by the Singapore Landscape Architecture Awards (SILA) in 2014. GuocoLand's commercial developments have also set the benchmark for environmental sustainability with Guoco Tower at Tanjong Pagar Centre achieving the LEED (CS) (Leadership in Energy and Environmental Design) Platinum Precertification. LEED (CS), an internationally renowned award recognising eco-friendly buildings in the world. Guoco Tower, as well as the hotel and retail components, has also been conferred the Singapore BCA (Building and Construction Authority) Green Mark (Platinum) award.

To further its vision of becoming a premier property developer in the region, GuocoLand will continue to build on its success by championing sustainable development and by developing choice properties that create a lasting legacy.

(E) Keppel Land Limited (http://www.keppelland.com.sg/)

Keppel Land is the property arm of the Keppel Group, one of Singapore's largest multinational groups with key businesses in offshore and marine, infrastructure as well as property.

One of Asia's premier property companies, Keppel Land is recognised for its sterling portfolio of award-winning residential developments and investment-grade commercial properties as well as high standards of corporate governance and transparency.

The Company is geographically diversified in Asia, with Singapore and China as its core markets as well as Vietnam and Indonesia as its growth markets. It focuses on a two-pronged strategy of property development for sale and property fund management.

A leading prime office developer in Singapore, Keppel Land contributes to enhancing the city's skyline with landmark developments such as Marina Bay Financial Centre, Ocean Financial Centre and One Raffles Quay.

Keppel Land is Asia's premier home developer with world-class iconic waterfront residences at Keppel Bay and Marina Bay in Singapore. With a pipeline of over

70,000 homes in Singapore and overseas as well as an increasing commercial presence in the region, Keppel Land is well-positioned to meet the growing demands for quality residential, office and mixed-use developments.

Keppel Land is committed to creating value for all stakeholders through innovative real estate solutions, shaping the best for future generations. Adopting a proactive approach towards environmental management and protection, the Company strives to create sustainable and optimal live-work-play environments in all its properties, celebrated for their quality and innovation.

Keppel Land has also been conferred many sustainability accolades. In 2015, it was listed in Corporate Knights' prestigious Global 100 Most Sustainable Corporations in the World for the second consecutive year. The Company was ranked 4th, placing it first in Asia and real estate companies worldwide.

Keppel Land was previously a component of the Dow Jones Sustainability World and Asia Pacific Indices prior to its delisting. It was featured in the RobecoSAM Sustainability Yearbook for five consecutive years as one of the top 15% of companies worldwide in sustainability leadership. Keppel Land is also a constituent of the Morgan Stanley International (MSCI) Global Sustainability and Socially Responsible Indices.

Other notable recent awards include being named winner in the Large Organisations category at the Singapore Apex CSR Awards in 2015, one of the winners under the category of Business Leadership in Sustainability at the inaugural Asia Pacific Regional Network Leadership Awards in Green Building by the World Green Building Council as well as winner in the Energy Management category at the Sustainable Business Awards in 2014.

Iconic Residential Buildings Designed by World-Renowned Architects/Architecture Firms

Reflections at Keppel Bay, designed by Daniel Libeskind
(Photo courtesy of Keppel Land)

The Sail @ Marina Bay, designed by Peter Pran and Timothy Johnson / NBBJ
(Photo courtesy of City Developments Limited)

CHAPTER 3 | Changing Skyline: Real Estate Development Industry in Singapore 97

The Scotts Tower, designed by Ben van Berkel / UNStudio
(Photo courtesy of Far East Organization)

98   *Iconic Residential Buildings*

Sky Habitat designed by Moshe Safdie
(Photograph by Edward Hendricks, courtesy of CapitaLand)

CHAPTER 3 | Changing Skyline: Real Estate Development Industry in Singapore   99

Wallich Residence at Tanjong Pagar Centre, designed by Skidmore, Owings & Merrill (SOM)
(Photo courtesy of GuocoLand)

Chapter 4

Role of Real Estate Service Providers in Growing the Real Estate Industry

Yu Shi Ming

Introduction

Consultants or real estate service providers are often called the purveyors of information. For real estate, given its unique and complex characteristics, information is fundamental to a better understanding of the market. It plays a critical role, which in turn drives the need for professional experts whose principal role is one of information intermediation. Typically, real estate services centre around information through collection of information, structuring information flows, synthesising information and helping their clients reduce information costs and match information requirements.

Real estate service providers therefore play an important role in ensuring the real estate market functions efficiently and effectively. This was especially significant in the early days of Singapore's independence when market information was scarce and fragmented. Typically, the consultants provided valuation, auction, brokerage and property management services, which were introduced by the British who governed Singapore since its founding in 1819 until 1959. While many of these services are still being provided today, the scope and range of consultancy services have, like other industries, changed significantly over the last 50 years.

As with most developed economies, real estate services typically cover valuation, auction, brokerage for both sale and lease transactions, feasibility and financial consultancies, tax advisory, research consultancies and property management. Each of these services is important due primarily to the characteristics of real estate. The heterogeneity of real estate interests means that professional advice would be required to understand the different types of values that exist within a specific real estate interest. While most valuations are undertaken to determine the open market value of an interest in real estate at a specific date, there are also other purposes of valuations and valuation of unique and special properties which are more complex. Similarly, an auctioneer's or an estate agent's services would be required because of the increasing complexity of real estate transactions, even in today's market where information is much more accessible than it was in the past. With market knowledge about local areas and property market activities (which the lay person cannot easily access), the real estate agent helps to reduce client costs of searching for matching parties to close a transaction whether for purchase or lease. The physical aspects of real estate also imply that maintenance and management by professionals would be required in order that the property continues to be functional and that its value can be sustained, or even enhanced over the long term. Most of all, real estate service providers seek to add value to their clients, be it through research and consultancy, financial advice or asset management.

This chapter traces the role of the real estate service providers in Singapore and the main changes over the last 50 years in five phases. Starting from the early years of the 60s and 70s, through the growth years of the 80s, the periods of change and competition from the management consultants and the investment banks in the 90s up to the global financial crisis in 2008, it is clear that much has changed and most of this can be attributed to global changes especially in the financial sector. Singapore, as a small market, was perhaps more affected and the real estate service providers needed to evolve to remain relevant. Most of the information was sieved through interviews with a few of the leading real estate consultants in Singapore, namely, CB Richard Ellis (CBRE), DTZ Debenham Tie Leung, Jones Lang Lasalle (JLL), Knight Frank Singapore and ERA Real Estate.

The chapter then discusses the key trends and changes in the real estate services sector, ranging from client profiles and types of real estate space to service solutions. With more pervasive information through technology and communication, clients have become more demanding and would expect that users' needs are matched in leasing and other property services. Tenants are looking not only for premium floor space but also tailored services that add value to their core operations. Buildings have also become more sophisticated; retail space is not only about shopping but also about providing a "lifestyle experience" for the shoppers with an increased focus on events and entertainment. In addition, green office buildings have become a requirement for some global companies. Valuation methods have also evolved to meet growing expectations of financial standards. Real estate is no longer just bricks and mortar, but a financial asset that is traded in capital and financial markets. This, coupled with competition from financial advisors, has also shaped the organisation and human resource of real estate service providers especially over the last 15 years. The chapter concludes with a discussion of what to expect in the future. As with the past 50 years, changes will remain a constant and the real estate services industry will likely see other forces affecting its businesses.

Phases of Development and Growth

The five main phases of development and growth in the real estate services industry can be broadly defined as the early years of the 60s and 70s; the growing years of the late 70s to the 80s; the consolidation years of the 90s up to the Asian Financial Crisis in 1997; the globalisation years from 1998 through the 2000s; and lastly, the current phase from post-Global Financial Crisis to present. Although these phases can be redefined in many different periods, these five phases are chosen as they coincide with major events or milestones which have a significant impact on the property services industry.

Early Years of the 60s and 70s

Prior to Singapore's independence in 1965, there were already property consultancy firms introduced by the British chartered surveying practices. The period of the 60s to 70s was largely characterised by small-scale operations, typically sole proprietorships and partnerships. Many of these were run by the British, including Messrs CH Williams and John Carter. These sole proprietors and partnerships focused mainly on the provision of valuation, auction, brokerage and property management services. Amongst the big consultancy firms today, Knight Frank was one of the first to set up its real estate business in Singapore under Cheong Hock Chye & Company which operated from a small office at the corner of Chulia Street and Raffles Place in 1940. It had a staff count of six men providing valuation and auctioneering services. Another the big consultancy firm today, CB Richard Ellis (renamed after CB Commercial's acquisition of Richard Ellis), started in 1958 at the old Hongkong Bank Chambers office under CH Williams. Similarly, the focus was mainly on valuation and later expanded to include property management.

The business in this early period was largely successful due to the small pool of professionals available. As discussed in the chapter on education (Chapter 9), the early training was provided by the local polytechnic while the university only started its estate management course in 1969. This limited pool of graduates was supplemented by those who obtained their professional qualifications from overseas such as the Royal Institution of Chartered Surveyors (RICS), while the public sector had relied on local scholars trained in New Zealand. The success of the property consultancy business led to the entry of foreign companies such as Richard Ellis (1977) and Knight Frank (1983). These British firms established their business in Singapore as the property market became more established. Similarly, Jones Lang Wootton (JLW) started in 1973, but unlike the other two, did not acquire a local business. Today, CBRE, JLL, DTZ and Knight Frank have all grown from small teams of a few professionals to multi-national companies with a few thousand staff just in Singapore alone. Other international British real estate consultancy firms including Debenham, Colliers and Chesterton also started operations in Singapore through various collaborations and franchises.

These early services were crucial as Singapore started its urban renewal programme and developed its infrastructure. Land acquisition was carried out to assemble the land needed for public housing, schools, and other public goods. With the introduction of legislation to remove the protection accorded to tenants of controlled premises, which were mainly located in the city centre, the redevelopment of the central area was able to be undertaken. The Golden Shoe area, which saw the sprouting of new offices, came to design the Central Business District (CBD). Valuation was necessary as land owners needed advice when their land was compulsorily acquired. Brokerage services for property transactions were also important and auction was quite commonly used to sell properties. Property services expanded to include project management and property management in the late 70s. Richard Ellis, for example, project managed the Hong Kong Shanghai Bank Building when it was rebuilt in 1978. This then led to property management including leasing.

Property consultancy services were also crucial during this period as the market was largely characterised by heavy regulations and was not so transparent, particularly in cases of compulsory acquisition. Services such as valuation were therefore important to help the private sector participate in real estate activities. Furthermore, with the first URA sale of sites conducted in 1967, property development which required property advisory, feasibility studies and marketing began in fervour. These were confined largely to the commercial sector as real estate developments in the public sector were focused on public housing and industry with the establishment of HDB and JTC.

Second Phase — Late 70s-80s

From the late 70s through to the 80s, the Singapore economy grew rapidly under the political leadership's visionary drive to open Singapore up as an open market and a fertile ground for foreign investments. The late 70s also witnessed the introduction of condominium living in Singapore as well as new retail centres and hotels being built in the Orchard Road area. New developments were also coming up in the Beach Road and Marina area with the establishment of major office and retail projects such as The Gateway and Marina Square. These new large development projects were important to the property consultants who enjoyed significant growth during this period as their services were required for project management, leasing and marketing. In fact, these became the main source of revenue for the consultants.

The rapid growth of the private residential market also led to the founding of ERA Real Estate in 1982, the largest real estate agency in Singapore today. Brought in as a franchise of the US company, ERA's primary focus has been residential brokerage. Yet, it was able to grow from a few agents into an international company with branches in Asia Pacific and about 6,000 salespersons in Singapore. This rapid growth came to a halt as the country faced its first recession in 1985. Both external factors such as the slowdown of the US economy, and the high operating costs arising from the high wage policy in 1979, were the main causes of the recession. This led to new strategies to revitalise the economy, and a property market consultative committee was set up to recommend measures to stimulate the property sector.

The changes in legislation had also helped to generate business for property consultants. The changes to the development charge system in 1979, for example, provided opportunities for consultants to advise owners and developers. With the successful renewal of the central area, the lifting of the rent control was expanded to more areas in conjunction with the trend towards conservation. These led to the rise in the potential for redevelopment of land as well as the refurbishment of conservation buildings. Property consultants as well as other kindred professionals such as architects, engineers and quantity surveyors flourished with the increase in workload. The collapse of Hotel New World in 1986 resulted in a slew of measures to ensure safety in construction, which also meant more checks and certifications required by engineers and surveyors.

On the other hand, the booming real estate services sector also attracted the entry of other consultants and advisories such as management consultants and investment banks. These intermediaries, while not able to perform real estate core services such as valuation and property management, could offer financial analyses particularly for global capital markets.

Third Phase — 90s up to the 1997 Asian Financial Crisis

The 90s saw a change in leadership for the country and some major shifts in economic strategies. A key thrust was the need to grow an external wing for the economy through regionalisation of the government-linked companies and other Singapore-based businesses. Another was the need to restructure the industrial sector with the development of the science and business parks leading the way for a shift towards a knowledge-intensive phase of industrialisation. The 1991 Concept Plan also spelt out the decentralisation of commercial activities to the regional centres in Tampines, Seletar, Woodlands and Jurong East as well as the extension of the downtown from Raffles Place to the newly developed Marina Bay. The scale of developments in the 90s was also substantially bigger and faster. As a benchmark, while it took about

25 years for Marina Square to be established, the Marina Bay development has taken a much shorter period but on a far larger scale.

In conjunction with the 1991 Concept Plan was the introduction of micro-zone plans called development guide plans. Focusing on smaller areas, they spelt out more detailed plans for developments especially allowing for higher plot ratios. Lands with existing buildings had densities increased to the extent that owners found it profitable to come together to sell their properties to a developer willing to redevelop the property. This en bloc or collective sale fever was particularly prevalent in the residential market. Again, it provided a golden opportunity for property consultants to deliver their services in such multi-faceted transactions. In terms of market performance, the 90s provided a further boost for the real estate service providers or consultants, especially with the booming residential sector. The changes to the HDB resale flats transaction regulations in 1993, for example, fuelled a huge increase in HDB resale transaction volume as well as prices, which then fed the private residential market. This led to the establishment of many real estate brokerage firms and agencies. While this further consolidated the growth of the real estate services business, it also sowed the seeds of rising cost of space.

The escalating spiral of property prices eventually led to the introduction of anti-speculative measures including a levy on capital gains for properties re-sold within a period of three years. Whether these anti-speculative measures were effective became a moot point when a few Asian countries' financial systems ran afoul. This sparked the Asian Financial Crisis in 1997. In any case, the measures imposed in 1996 and the onset of the AFC proved to be a double whammy for Singapore's property market as prices and rentals fell across all sectors. As with most economic recessions, the reaction from the Singapore government was to introduce measures to stimulate the market, including the reduction in CPF contribution rates and corporate and property tax rebates.

This period was certainly a boon for real estate businesses. Real estate service providers and agents benefitted from the active transaction market in both HDB resale flats as well as private residential developments. Big commercial projects and en bloc sales meant high commissions from investment sales. In fact, all aspects of the real estate consultancy business witnessed strong growth during the period.

Fourth Phase — 98–2000s

This period is significant for three key events and trends. The first is the globalisation of the real estate consultancy business; the second is the emergence of Singapore as a financial hub and the launch of the Real Estate Investment Trusts (REITs); and, the third is the Global Financial Crisis.

While the top real estate service providers such as JLW and Richard Ellis were already global with offices all over the world by the 80s, mergers and collaborations with the big real estate firms in the US such as Lasalle, Coldwell Banker and Cushman and Wakefield in the late 90s saw the establishment of global real estate service providers in the form of Jones Lang Lasalle and CBRE, which had a presence in Singapore. These mergers opened the doors for the real estate service providers in Singapore to the markets in the rest of the world including the key markets in Europe and the Americas. The globalisation trend in the real estate consultancy business emerged mainly from the need to service the multi-national companies which had already gone global, and given the local characteristics of real estate markets, the acquisition of local real estate consultancies was the logical solution. The prospects for growth became very bright, albeit the climate at that time was gloomy in the wake of the Asian Financial Crisis and in the run-up to the dot-com crash at the dawn of the new millennium.

Post the Asian Financial Crisis, the real estate market in Singapore recovered with government policies aiding the process. As part of the recovery strategies from the Asian Financial Crisis, the government drafted plans to establish the REITs market with the intention to launch it in 2001. However, external events such as the dot-com bust and 9/11 pushed the launch of the first Singapore REIT to 2002. Since then, Singapore has become one of the leading REIT markets in Asia and this has helped to create and expand real estate consultancy businesses, especially for valuation and asset management.

The period of the millennium witnessed rapidly increasing liquidity, and financial engineering became fashionable. This culminated with the sub-prime crisis in the US which subsequently was blown into a full-scale global financial crisis (GFC). While the effects of the crisis were very much mitigated by government economic strategies, it nevertheless had a direct impact on real estate businesses. It also had ramifications on real estate mortgage and finance, which real estate consultants needed to be cognizant with.

For the real estate industry, this period also witnessed significant developments, which continue to shape and impact market activities and consultancy business. The launch of the two integrated resorts in Sentosa and Marina Bay has set the tourism industry on a new path of growth. The whole of Marina Bay has evolved into an international attraction with the hosting of the Formula 1 Grand Prix and the opening of the Gardens by the Bay. New residential projects such as waterfront housing at Sentosa Cove and The Sail @ Marina Bay have also added diversity to the housing market. The commercial and industrial markets similarly witnessed major changes and growth during this period.

Current Phase — Post-GFC

This current phase started with the rapid emergence from the GFC, especially in the case of the Asian economies including Singapore. Governments had to intervene and keep interest rates at artificially low rates, which spurred real estate activities. In fact, the short downturn was followed by a strong rebound in the Singapore economy in 2010. Rapidly escalating prices of real estate across all sectors, especially residential, resulted in the Singapore government introducing a series of macro-prudential measures to curb speculative activities and prevent further exuberance. The booming market also meant more activities for real estate consultants, especially the real estate salespersons and agents. To ensure that they would abide by professional practices and regulations, the Council of Estate Agencies was established in 2010.

The GFC has changed real estate markets in more ways than one. From the financial perspective, there is increasing flexibility to the financial structure in deals while investors are spreading their interests across multiple assets and asset classes. The investment services have also witnessed an increasingly competitive environment with the "big four" management consultants such as PWC and investment banks such as JP Morgan seeking involvement in real estate deals.

More than a decade since the internationalisation of the major consultants in the late 90s, the Singapore real estate market has diversified and globalised multiple-fold. Today, the major consultants are an integral part of the world's premier, full-service real estate services companies, operating across the world with offices in hundreds of cities and staff numbering tens of thousands. While 50 years is a relatively short time frame in the history of most countries, Singapore's transformation from a third-world port to a first-world city is reflected in the progress of the economy, including real estate services.

Key Trends

There are five key trends in the growth and evolution of the real estate consultancy services in Singapore that can be observed over the last 50 years.

Growth and Globalisation

Evidently, the first is the tremendous growth in terms of the size and capacity of the consultancy firms. Since independence, most of the major consultancy firms have grown from a team of a handful of staff to more than a thousand. Estate agents grew even more in terms of the number of salespersons. Since its founding in 1982 with a few staff, ERA, for example, has about 6,000 salespersons at present. Besides size, the major firms have also gone global. CBRE and JLL are now global companies with worldwide networks. Ownerships of the major firms have also changed as global funds seek investment opportunities.

Scope of Services

The scope of services provided has also expanded significantly. From the core business of valuation, brokerage and management, most of the major firms now provide services ranging from fund management (e.g. Lasalle Investment Management and CBRE Global Investors) to capital markets, and capital advisory to global corporate services which include occupier consulting, project management and facilities management. Many of these new services came about to meet changes in the industry as well as competition from those outside the traditional boundaries of real estate. With securitisation and new financial products, capital markets and capital advisory have emerged to fill the gap. The growth of the REITs market has similarly provided more opportunities for valuation as it extends to the international arena. Even while the core services have remained, the methods by which these services are carried out have changed. In valuation, for example, one cannot simply rely on a single method such as comparison but must incorporate more sophisticated financial methods to analyse cashflows and justify returns. This change is in part due to more demanding clients; as the base of investors grows from equity funds to financial institutions and institutional funds, the demand for greater substantiation and analysis has increased.

Changing Client Profile

In the early days, consultancy firms' clients were mainly the landlords and potential investors. The work was focused around owners and investors and providing valuation, brokerage and property management. Most of the consultancy firms were really representing owners in search of tenants and they would act as leasing agents. From the 90s, a major shift in clients took place as a greater percentage of clients became occupiers instead of owners. In fact, one of the most significant trends in consultancy services has been the development of tenant representative services. Prior to the 1990s, as much as 95% of work was for owners and investors and only 5% for occupiers; now, the breakdown is closer to 50-50. This change can be attributed to the changing profile of property ownership. In the early days, most of the foreign companies which operated in Singapore were owners and not occupiers. These included foreign banks such as HSBC and Standard Chartered. Even the emerging local companies were owners as they expanded their business, such as Straits Trading, Fraser & Neave and Inchcape. During the 1990s, the consultancy firms started to see a new profile of tenants who were not owners but occupiers, and some of the older companies who were owners shedding their ownership of properties. Both MNCs and local companies began to focus on their core business and elected to lease rather than own, which led to a large increase of work under corporate solutions where companies engaged the consultants to look after their work space. This includes space planning, lease management, and facilities management. This outsourcing of real estate needs is not unique to Singapore but is a global trend, with signs of strengthening into the foreseeable future. This tenant representation is also growing amongst retailers as they seek to open new markets.

Data and Technology

As mentioned in the introduction, consultants are really purveyors of information. As information and data become more pervasive and widely available with enhancements in technology, this has become a significant challenge to the real estate consultants. In the early days, data such as transaction prices were not easily available and consultants had to collect and establish their own databank, especially for valuation. The market was largely information inefficient. It was not until the 80s that the professional body, the Singapore Institute of Surveyors and Valuers (SISV), started to collate data from official sources and disseminate to members. Fast forward to today — transaction prices are posted on real estate portals by real estate agents, data providers as well as official sources including the URA, HDB and SLA. Besides the proliferation of data, there is a myriad supply of statistics, analyses and indices which claim to track market movement and performance. The biggest challenge from this is how consultants can continue to justify a fee for their service. As a case in point, with large amounts of data, some data providers are able to claim that they can disburse indicative valuations free of charge.

Communications technology has also enhanced to the point where consultants are expected to use the latest technology to help them advise their clients and keep them updated. The use of video for virtual tours has become *de rigueur* for salespersons. Other technical applications such as GIS (geographic information system) maps are commonly used to enhance service provisions.

Complexity and Scale of Real Estate

The complexity and scale of real estate developments have increased exponentially over the last five decades. Buildings have become more sophisticated and typically have multiple uses. With the emphasis on conservation, many projects have to deliver creative designs that incorporate the heritage identity while providing new and large spaces that justify the investment. Developments at transit hubs have to take advantage of the large footfall to connect the retail spaces to the stations. The pace of construction and development has also quickened. As a comparison, while the whole of Marina Square took 25 years to be completed, the Marina Bay development will probably be completed in half the time.

Besides, developers and owners are now more concerned with what occupiers want, such as greater emphasis on practical, efficient, and regular floor design. There is also a lot more pressure from occupiers in wanting green buildings, such as multinational occupiers who want to attract talent. These changes in demand for space mean that consultants need to get more involved in the design of the building and understand best practices in construction.

Shaping the Future

Given the nature of the key trends that have emerged over the last 50 years, some of these will likely continue to shape the future. The following are some of the issues which warrant the real estate services providers' attention.

First, the shift in client profile from owners to occupiers is likely to continue. This means that real estate service providers need to focus even more on corporate solutions. Occupiers would want more advice on how to best use their space as cost increases. In fact, an increase in the percentage of revenue coming from "contract businesses", such as a five-year contract with a large-sized corporation — which could range from major banks to international MNCs — to provide medium-to-long term corporate real estate solutions for the organisation's global operations, as opposed to the traditional focus on brokerage-related businesses, could bode well for the real estate service providers, especially during a market downturn.

Second, real estate will likely remain as a unique asset class in that while its physical aspects cannot be overlooked, its attraction as an investment asset will continue to increase. As developing countries open up their markets, more real estate investment opportunities will emerge. Service providers need to better understand real estate as an asset from the financing and returns perspectives and how it fits into the greater investment market. Regarding the physical aspects, real estate service providers would need to be more involved in design and construction so that they can offer better advice to their clients as occupiers and users.

Third, the increasingly competitive environment will necessitate that real estate service providers also offer the full range of financial services including equity placement, debt and structured finance, loan servicing and financial consulting, which have been the domain of the management consultants and investment banks. However, such capital market advisory personnel need to emphasise their strength as specialists in real estate across sectors and geography, supported by agency and asset management expertise.

Following from the above would mean that real estate service providers need to hire real estate graduates with new skill sets such as in the areas of investment and finance. They will need to know not only the real estate asset as their main differentiation but also about indirect real estate such as buying into funds and securities. Their skill sets must therefore include real estate capital raising, transaction structuring, tax advisory and so on. The real estate service providers will also need employees with engineering and design capabilities to address occupiers' needs.

Last but not least, changes in technology will likely have the greatest impact in the future. They will shape the buildings and developments in areas such as the application of smart technology, the increasing demand for green and sustainable construction and the scale and speed of new projects. Online platforms will continue to have an impact on the use of office and retail space as workers can work from anywhere and shoppers make purchases electronically. Technology will also affect client demand in that clients will expect better and faster delivery of services.

Notwithstanding these challenges, real estate service providers can continue to play an important role in the future. The core services of valuation, brokerage and management are unlikely to be phased out as long as consultants continue to adapt their methods and make use of technology to ensure relevance. With additional focus on real estate capital markets services, capital raising and indirect real estate advisory, amongst others, real estate service providers will be capable of providing a total solution to the clients, potentially edging out the investment banks. And of course, they will also need to be vigilant about new challenges that can emerge in the future.

PART B
A Global Real Estate Market Place

Chapter 5

Singapore Commercial Real Estate Industry in a Global Context

Seek Ngee Huat

The global real estate industry has evolved and innovated over the last 50 years and is much more complex and sophisticated today. Lagging behind in the early years, Singapore has largely caught up with the developed markets, where not only has real estate become a global business, it is now fully integrated with the capital markets. Fifty years ago, commercial real estate investment was a relatively unsophisticated business: entirely local in nature, focused on bricks-and-mortar and quite detached from the world of finance. It has since evolved from this simple beginning of building largely for owner-occupation through to the development of investment markets with institutional participation, and then to globalisation with increased cross-border investments and eventually to securitised real estate equity and debt in both private and public markets.

This chapter traces the evolution of the commercial real estate industry in Singapore in the context of the transformational changes which took place in the broader global arena. It shows how Singapore adapted and transformed itself into a sophisticated market, not only by attracting global investors to its property assets and publicly listed real estate securities, but also in establishing itself as a regional hub for fund managers investing in Asia. In addition, it discusses the pioneering role played by Singapore's home grown institutions and property developers in globalising real estate investments.

From Owner-Occupation to Investment Market

Two intertwined global trends in the last 25 years led to impactful and accelerated changes to real estates markets around the world. First, the movement away from a purely domestic-focused business to internationalisation with increasing cross border investments amongst institutional investors. Second, the integration of real estate with the capital markets, resulting in a broadening of investment choices. These trends vastly expanded the range and variety of investment opportunities globally and set the scene for how real estate business is practised today.

However, a critical enabling market development phase, which was largely by-passed in Singapore, was the establishment of an institutional investment market in the 1970s through the 1980s in the developed markets. It set the stage for further innovations which evolved into the two global trends mentioned above. During this period, institutional investors, such as insurance companies and pension funds, formally added commercial real estate to their investment portfolios. Such investment activities gave depth and breadth to the market, and paved the way for the emergence of a nascent commercial real estate investment market. Real estate was included as a strategic asset class amongst the more traditional classes of public equities and fixed-income securities in a mixed asset investment portfolio as it was seen to offer the benefits of risk diversification, inflationary hedge and long term returns from stable income and moderate growth.

Prior to the 1970s in the US, there was little, if any, institutional participation in real estate investment. Commercial real estate was owned largely by individuals, families and corporates for their own occupation. Hampered by a lack of quality information and investment professionals and vehicles, the market was deal oriented and driven by entrepreneurs. Institutional investors considered real estate as too illiquid, lumpy, risky and entrepreneurial. From the late 1960s and early 1970s, high inflation and interest rates began to depress returns from bonds and stocks, and provided the impetus for institutional investors to look for higher risk-adjusted returns from alternative asset classes. A case for including real estate in an institutional portfolio emerged amongst portfolio managers, who were keen to advocate the application of Modern Portfolio Theory, arguing for the inclusion of real estate for the benefits of diversification, inflation hedging, stable income yield and exploitation of market inefficiencies.

Concerns for the dearth of professional portfolio managers and the perceived risks of real estate were eschewed with the passing of a key piece of legislation in the US — the Employees Retirement Income Security Act (ERISA) in 1974, which set off institutional investment in real estate on an unprecedented scale. It gave institutions managing retirement plans the mandate to diversify investment portfolios. Pension money started to flow into commercial real estate in the mid-1970s, with the establishment of Prudential's PRISA (Prudential Property Investment Separate Account) in 1970 (as the first open-end real estate fund for tax-exempt investors) and Lazard Freres's Corporate Property Investors in 1971. These were two of the earliest real estate specialist funds. With the passing of ERISA, many more investment managers and investors emerged with increased participation from insurance companies, banks, pension funds and real estate specialist funds. For example, Rosenberg Real Estate Equity Fund (RREEF), the first closed-end real estate fund, was set up in 1975.

However, some pension funds chose not to embrace the new investment approach for many years. For example, CalPERS (California Public Employees' Retirement System), a major US pension fund, was not authorised to invest in real estate until the early 1980s. The flow of institutional funds accelerated throughout the 1980s, which also saw the entry of Japanese investors into the US. In the 1970s, pension fund investment in real estate was only approximately US$5 billion. By the end of the 1990s it had grown to approximately US$200 billion. The number of pension investors grew from around 70 to 500 and the number of investment managers from about 15 to 150 during the same 20-year period. The number and range of investment vehicles expanded in response to increasing demand.[1]

Before the First World War, insurance companies in the UK were way ahead of their US counterparts. They started holding real estate investment portfolios on a relatively small scale, largely consisting of ground rents, buildings occupied for their own use and properties from mortgage defaults. Direct investment in income producing real estate came much later. By the 1930s, real estate was seen as a stable asset class given the volatility in public equities, and direct property investment increased in significance. Following the devastation of London during the Second World War, British investment institutions became involved in funding the reconstruction of the city. However, like in the US, the surge in real estate investment in the modern era occurred in the second half of the 1970s through most of the 1980s, following the property market crash between 1973 and 1974, when British pension funds and insurance companies, like their US counterparts, looked to real estate as the asset class for stable long-term returns and diversification. However, the scale of institutional investment in real estate in the UK was relatively small compared to that in the US following the passing of ERISA in mid-1970s.[2] In Australia, further to the recommendations of the Australia Financial System Inquiry (known as the Campbell Inquiry), investment restrictions on insurance companies and pension funds were progressively lifted for most of the 1980s and 1990s.[3] This together with and the search for higher risk-adjusted returns from alternative asset classes for investment led to a surge in institutional real estate investment around that time.

The 1970s marked the establishment of an institutional investment sector in developed markets. With increased flows of institutional capital into real estate in the 1980s, the market responded with an increased supply of investment grade property

---

[1] NCREIF (2011), "Nuts and Bolts of Institutional Real Estate".
[2] Peter Scott (1996), The Property Masters: A History of the British Commercial Property Sector, London: E & FN Spon.
[3] Monica Keneley (2004), "Adaptation and Change in the Australia Life Insurance Industry: An Historical Perspective", Accounting, Business & Financial History, Volume 14, No. 1, March 2004, pp. 91–109, at pg. 102.

assets, which was the precursor to the disastrous over-supply of commercial real estate in developed markets in the late 80s and early 90s. On the other hand, an important far-reaching outcome of this heightened interest was a demand for higher standards in real estate investment management. The net result was the creation of a deeper and broader investment market accompanied by enhanced professionalism and rigour in investment analysis and management with a more pervasive use of modern finance methods and techniques. It also spurred a proliferation of specialist intermediaries, including consultants, bankers, advisors and fund managers providing a range of real estate related services and products.

The establishment of a well-oiled investment market with its constituent players set the stage for the transformational changes in the next 30 years. Although these changes spread to other parts of the world at different points in time, they were anything but smooth-sailing. While some of the changes were responses to new opportunities and market developments, others were adaptations to severe market upheavals and traumas which the real estate industry had to endure periodically since the late 1980s.

In the early years, not unlike the developed real estate markets in the world, the Singapore industry was quite simple and unsophisticated. Most commercial real estate was built and owned by individuals, families or corporates, mainly for their own use. For example, in 1965, there were only a handful of significant office buildings, including Bank of China, Asia Insurance, Shell House, Denmark House, Crosby House and Hong Kong and Shanghai Bank in the CBD. Most of these were owned and occupied by corporates, and by current standards, all of them were relatively small. For example, in 1954, the 20-storey[4] Asia Insurance Building (which is now a block of serviced apartments operated as Ascott Raffles Place), an Art Deco influenced building was the tallest commercial building. By the 1970s, many of these older buildings were replaced by modern skyscrapers when urban renewal of the CBD began in earnest.

One of the main reasons for the rapid renewal of Singapore's CBD is the role played by government. The Singapore government embarked on an urban renewal programme which had been recommended by a three-man United Nations team of experts in 1963 to assist Singapore in the redevelopment of the central parts of Singapore and revitalise the financial and banking district located in the "Golden Shoe" area which covered Shenton Way, Telok Ayer Street, South Canal Road, Fullerton Quay, Collyer Quay and Boat Quay.[5]

---

[4] URA Planning Decision Number P160614-55B2-Z000.
[5] URA, "Redevelopment of Golden Shoe", Skyline August 2002, HistorySG, http://eresources.nlb.gov.sg/, accessed on 14 May 2015.

Using the Land Acquisition Act (1966) to compulsorily acquire land and the Controlled Premises (Special Provisions) Act (1969) to allow owners to repossess their rent-controlled properties, the Government was able to successfully clear slums and re-parcel land for redevelopment purposes in the CBD. Between 1967 and 1969, the Urban Renewal Department tendered out 46 sites on 99-year leases to the private sector for commercial redevelopment.[6] This was carried out via what was known as the "sale of sites" programme. The urban renewal programme rapidly transformed the skyline of the central area of the city. By the mid-1970s, many of the older buildings along Shenton Way were replaced with skyscrapers. The first wave of construction saw the development of commercial buildings such as Robina House (1973), Shenton House (1973), UIC Building (1973), Ocean Building (1974), Hong Leong Building (1975), DBS Building (1975) and OCBC Building (1976).[7]

In the 1980s, another cluster of high-rise office towers was built: Chartered Bank Building (1984), Raffles City (1984), Marina Centre (1984), Monetary Authority of Singapore Building (1985), Treasury Building (1986) and Overseas Union Bank Centre (1988).[8] The supply of commercial land was further enhanced by the completion of extensive land reclamation works at Marina Centre and Marina South. At the end of 1983, 17 hectares of land at Marina Centre had been sold by the URA, which resulted in the completion of Suntec City and several 5-star hotels in Marina South[9].

During the first 20–25 years or so since 1965, Singapore had neither the capital nor the number of home-grown institutional investors to develop an institutional investment market. Its commercial real estate market was driven mainly by entrepreneurs/developers. Hampered by the lack of capital and without institution support, developers had to find innovative ways to fund their projects. In the 1970s, developers were able to recycle scarce capital by sub-dividing their shopping centres and office buildings into strata-titled units and selling the individual units in the retail market to buyers either for investment or their own business use. Examples of such strata-titled commercial buildings at prime locations which still exist today include Lucky Plaza and Far East Shopping Centre around Orchard Road, International Plaza at Anson Road, and Golden Mile Complex, Golden Mile Tower and The Plaza along Beach Road.[10] This method of recycling developers' capital has continued to the present time.

---

[6] Gretchen Liu (2001), Singapore: A Pictorial History, 1819–2000, Psychology Press, at pg. 324.
[7] Ray Tyers, revised by Siow Kin Hua (1993), Singapore Then & Now, Landmark Books.
[8] Ibid.
[9] Wong Tai-Chee and Yap Lian-Ho Adriel (2004), Four Decades of Transformation, Land Use in Singapore, 1960–2000, Marshall Cavendish, at pg. 21.
[10] Colliers International White Paper "Bright Spot in Singapore Property Market: Strata-titled Office", March 2012.

As developers became progressively better capitalised, with many like United Engineers Limited and City Developments Limited,[11] Singapore Land Limited (1963, acquired by United Industrial Corporation Limited in 1990), Bukit Sembawang Estates Ltd (1968), Boustead Singapore Limited (1975), and GuocoLand Limited (1978) becoming listed as public companies, they were able to hold their developments for longer terms. Not surprisingly, over time as their capital positions have improved, so has the quality of the commercial developments built. The advent of REITs in 2000s provided a further avenue for recycling capital.[12]

Moving away from the developer/entrepreneur phase into the 1990s and 2000s, the Singapore real estate industry developed further by harvesting the fruit of the global changes to become a sophisticated and attractive real estate investment hub to cross-border investors. This next phase of industry development happened without its own home grown foundation of an institutional investment market. Instead it drew on the experience and knowledge garnered from the evolution of strong investment markets in the US, UK and Australia. The next few sections discuss how Singapore has adapted and taken advantage of these global trends in the last 20 years or so.

From Local to Global

Fifty years ago, real estate was not only about bricks-and-mortar but also local in focus. Very few investors ventured outside their domestic markets. It was in the late 1990s that real estate started to show signs of becoming truly globalised in terms of the scale and flows of capital across borders. Singapore was a beneficiary of the globalisation trend, although it had a taste of this in the late 1980s when Japanese investors made their first major acquisitions in Singapore.

Cross-border investing in foreign real estate was not however a new phenomenon. Up until the 1990s, the scale of cross-border investment activity was relatively small and occurred in waves. Each wave was driven largely by a single dominant developed market moving capital to other developed markets. The multi-directional cross-border flows of capital into real estate happened much later. For example, in the 1960s, a number of British property companies such as British Land, Hammersons, MEPC and Grosvenor started to invest in Canada and Australia. Almost all of them, except Grosvenor, retreated back to the UK and Europe in the 1990s or earlier. Dutch institutional investors followed in the 1970s investing in the US and other European markets, but incurred substantial losses in the late 1980s and early 1990s, when the developed markets in the West suffered one of the worst property market slumps ever — largely due to overbuilding. Subsequent to this bad experience with physical property, they

---

[11] Both of which were listed on the then joint stock exchange of Singapore and Malaya.
[12] See Chapter 7 for a detailed discussion of the REIT market in Singapore.

switched their investments into US REITs, which were perceived to give better liquidity than lumpy physical assets. The support of the Dutch institutions was instrumental in the growth of the US REIT market in the 1990s.

In the 1980s, Japanese investors, propelled by huge foreign account surpluses and the strength of its economy during the bubble era, scoured the world for investment properties. Unfortunately, their foray into foreign markets was quite untimely and they paid inflated prices in rising markets. Most had to pull back from their overseas ventures when their domestic bubble burst in the early 1990s. The new major exporters of capital into real estate in the 2010s are the Chinese, who like the Japanese then, have accumulated massive surpluses and are beginning to make acquisitions all over the world. Chinese investors have been paying record prices based on recent transactions. For example, two record-setting hotel acquisition deals were carried out by Chinese insurance companies in the last two years. In June 2014, Anbang Insurance Group was reported to have paid US$1.95 billion for the Waldorf Astoria Hotel.[13] This works out to approximately US$1.4 million per room and was a record in absolute terms paid for a hotel in the US. In February 2015, China Sunshine Insurance Company bought the Baccarat Hotel, also in New York, for over US$230 million or US$2 million per room, the highest on record, beating the previous record for the sale of the Plaza Hotel to by India's Sahara Group in 2012. Like the Japanese investors in the 1980s, Chinese investors, large and small, have been scouring the world for real estate investments. Is this another passing phase as reflected in previous waves?

There was a quantum change in the scale and directions of cross-border investments in the late 1990s and early 2000s which marked the beginning of real estate being truly globalised. This trend continues to the present day, except for a pause after the Global Financial Crisis (GFC) following the collapse of Lehman Brothers in 2008. Unlike previous waves, there were no dominant exporters of capital. Investors originated from many countries and invested in both developed and emerging markets around the world. The volume of transactions was several folds higher than previous waves. For example, total global commercial property transaction volume reached a peak of US$760 billion in 2007 before it collapsed during the GFC. Today, activity has hit US$333 billion in the first half of 2015 alone.[14]

Asian real estate markets (excluding Japan) started to attract foreign investors' interest following the Asian Financial Crisis (AFC) in 1997. The initial interest was in distressed assets from vulture funds, mainly in Thailand, Korea and Indonesia, although similar funds had already been working the Japanese market in the post-bubble era in

---

[13] Forbes, "Chinese Insurer Buys Waldorf Astoria for a Record $1.95B", 6 October 2014. Source: http://www.forbes.com/sites/michaelcole/2014/10/06/chinese-insurer-buys-waldorf-astoria-for-a-record-1-95b/, accessed on 12 November 2015.

[14] Preqin Ltd.

the 1990s. As the Asian economies repaired themselves from the AFC and the Chinese economy was showing sustained high growth rates, more capital from the developed markets was attracted to Asia. However, the volume of cross-border transactions in Asia was still relatively small compared to developed markets, although its proportionate share of global commercial transaction volumes increased significantly post GFC. According to Preqin, in 2003, the volume of transactions in Asia accounted for only 1% of the global total of US$350 billion and reached 3% when the GFC reduced the global volume drastically to US$195 billion. By 2014, global volume had almost returned to the pre-GFC peak of over US$700 billion, of which Asia accounted for 5%.[15]

Interestingly, the Government of Singapore Investment Corporation (GIC) began to diversify its investments to more countries from the late 1990s. Its journey since its formation reflects in many ways the changes in the global arena. It was a pioneering SWF (this term was not coined until in the 2000s when more countries set up such national funds and increased their visibility with increased investment activities around the world) and real estate was amongst the first asset classes formally established in GIC. It was also one of the first institutional investors in the world to be given a mandate to invest in foreign real estate. Except for the Dutch and Middle Eastern institutions, there were few others in the 1980s. Although it was established in 1982, almost all its investments in the initial years were in the US as it was then the only market with the depth and breadth to meet the conservative risk appetite of a prudent investment institution. As it learnt more about other markets, it gradually diversified to other geographies. Modest attempts were made to invest in Europe in the late 1980s; investment in Asia came much later in the mid-to-late 1990s. It was from this point onwards that its portfolio became truly "globalised" and it continued to expand its global portfolio. Today, it has investments in more than 30 countries.

GIC was not the only Singapore entity that ventured overseas, although it was probably the earliest. By the 1990s other Singapore based entities were also being carried by the globalisation trend. Home grown companies including Singapore Land, Far East, Temasek, CapitaLand and its predecessors (DBS Land and Pidemco), Keppel Land, Ascendas, CDL, GuocoLand and Frasers Centrepoint made forays into foreign markets, targeting mostly emerging Asia, including China, Hong Kong, India, Korea and Southeast Asia and to a lesser extent, developed markets of the UK, Australia, Japan and the US. However, the main business focus of these property companies remained Singapore.

---

[15] Preqin Ltd.

As at 2013, overseas real estate investment by Singapore companies stood at S$44.2 billion, or 8.3% of Singapore's total direct investment abroad, of which China was a favoured destination, attracting S$23.3 billion.[16] In line with this global trend, whilst Singapore investors were venturing abroad, Singapore too was becoming a destination for capital flows from other countries. In 1989, a Japanese company, Kowa Real Estate Company, entered the Singapore real estate market with a 50% stake in Savu Investments, an investment company established by Ong Beng Seng which held two Collyer Quay properties — Rubber House and Winchester House.[17] One of the most prominent development projects at the time was Suntec City, completed in 1997 by a Hong Kong consortium led by Cheung Kong Holdings. Two major recent large mixed use developments in the new CBD also involved foreign players: Asia Square and the Marina Business and Financial Center (MBFC). Asia Square was completed in 2013 by Macquarie Global Property Advisors and MBFC, which was completed in 2012, was by developed by Hongkong Land, Keppel Land and the Cheung Kong Group. International investors initially sought to acquire physical real estate but later expanded into property securities as the market for REITs in Singapore developed.

The globalisation trend also manifested itself in another way with an influx of international fund managers setting up regional offices in Singapore. Many were attracted to Singapore's position as a key financial centre with a stable political environment and strong and reliable hard and soft infrastructures. It also had a pool of skilled and experienced human resources trained in a sophisticated real estate industry. Tax concessions given to qualified regional offices were an added incentive. Singapore had become a hub in Asia, competing against Hong Kong, for international fund managers. Its strategic location in Asia serves as a natural launching platform for their real estate programmes in Asia. A number of fund managers have since come and gone depending on their ability to weather the regional and global financial crises in the last 20 years. Between 1998 and 2013, assets under management in Singapore grew from S$150 billion to over $1.8 trillion,[18] of which direct and indirect real estate accounted for S$108 billion in 2013 (Figure 1).

---

[16] Singapore Department of Statistics.

[17] "Ong Beng Seng ropes in Japanese developer", *The Straits Times*, 12 May 1989, pg. 25; "Ong Beng Seng sells half share in Rubber House, Winchester House, *Business Times Singapore*, 12 May 1989, pg. 3.

[18] "Looking Back, Looking Forward", Opening Address by Mrs Josephine Teo, Minister of State for Finance and Transport at the Investment Management Association of Singapore 16th Annual Conference, 26 March 2015.

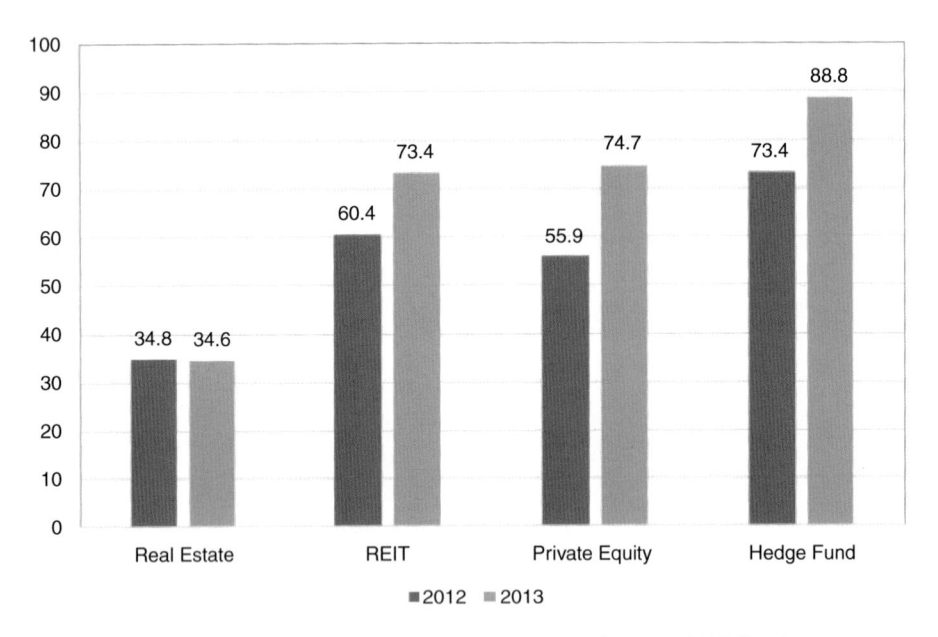

Figure 1. Asset under management in Singapore by sector (S$ billion).
Source: Singapore Asset Management Industry Surveys, Monetary Authority of Singapore.

Drivers of Globalisation

Most investors' comfort zone is their domestic markets as real estate is traditionally viewed as local in nature. They tend therefore to perceive foreign real estate markets as having higher risks. Investing beyond their national borders would only be considered if such foreign investments are expected to produce higher risk-adjusted returns than domestic investments. In addition to superior returns, cross-border investments also have the additional benefit of geographical diversification. For a long time institutional investors were deterred by the perceived executional difficulties of investing in unfamiliar markets. Much of the issues were centred on overcoming the local-global divide. A number of push and pull factors led to a quantum leap in foreign investment activities since the 1990s.

Several macro forces helped to accelerate the increased flows of capital across borders. There has been a huge growth in organised savings in the world. Started in the developed economies and copied in many emerging economies, compulsory savings schemes managed by the private sector or the state, such as the CPF in Singapore, gained popularity over the last 50 years. Total assets under management (AUM) held by pension funds globally is expected to grow by more than 2.5 times to US$56.5 trillion from 2014 to 2020 according to a recent study undertaken by PwC. In the same study, if the AUM of insurance companies and sovereign wealth funds (SWFs) are included, the figure in 2020 will swell to more than US$100 trillion (Figure 2). Even if

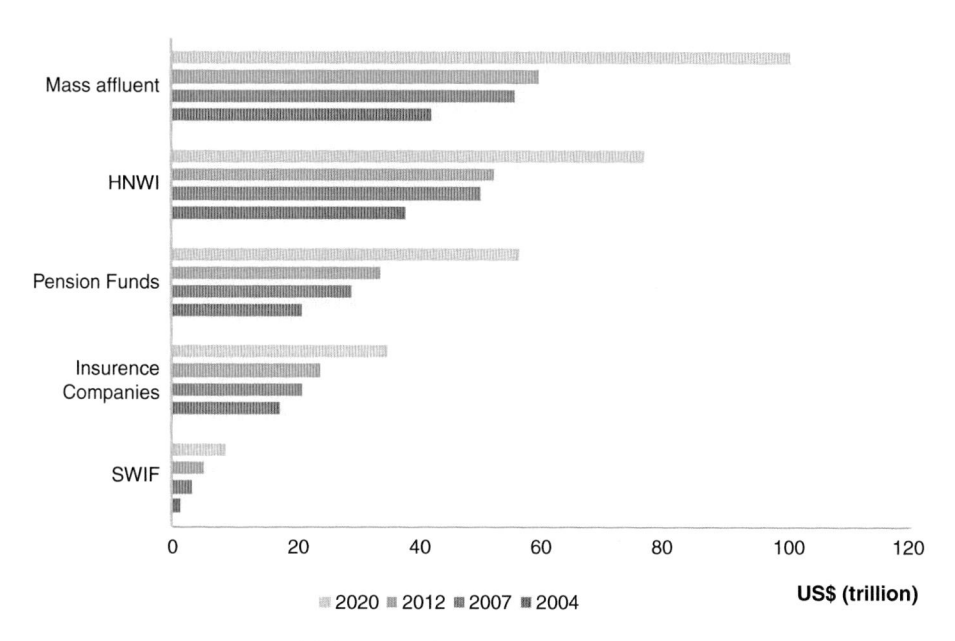

CHAPTER 5 | Singapore Commercial Real Estate Industry in a Global Context   125

Figure 2. Global Asset under Management (AUM) (US$ trillion).
Source: PwC (2014), "Real Estate 2020: Building the Future".

only 10% of the total investable funds is allocated to real estate, it is not difficult to see the impact of capital flows crossing borders in search of investment opportunities.

Managers are constantly being challenged to produce above-benchmark returns, and have little choice but to break from their comfort zone and expand their opportunity set to include foreign markets for higher risk-adjusted returns and greater diversification.[19] According to the 2014 Institutional Real Estate Allocations Monitor produced by Cornell University and Hodes Weill & Associates, global institutional investors have been allocating 9.38% of their AUM portfolio to real estate, and have indicated an intention to increase their average target allocation for real estate assets. PwC expects the global stock of institutional-grade real estate to increase by more than 55% from US$29 trillion in 2012 to US$45.3 trillion in 2020.[20]

Western institutions typically allocate 5–10% of their AUM to real estate. Although Asian fund investment in real estate is presently relatively small compared to its western counterpart, there is significant potential for growth.[21] The South Korean National Pension Service (NPS) acquired six major office properties valued at

---

[19] PwC (2014), "Asset Management 2020 — A Brave New World.
[20] PwC (2014), "Real Estate 2020: Building the Future".
[21] APREA (2014), "The Increasing Importance of Real Estate in Asian Pension Funds" and APREA (2013), "Asia Pacific Listed Real Estate: A Contextual Performance Analysis", July 2013.

US$3.6 billion between 2009 and 2014. APREA reported that 67% of Asian pension funds regarded real estate as an essential component in their portfolio, with 73% and 30% of them planning to increase their allocations to unlisted and listed real estate respectively between 2015 and 2016.[22]

In recent years, new, very large investors have been making forays into the global market. Relatively new players, who until a few years ago either did not exist or were purely domestically focused, are institutions such as China Investment Corporation (CIC), State Administration of Foreign Exchange (SAFE), Korea Investment Corporation (KIC), Qatar Investment Authority (QIA), Australia Future Fund (AFF), NPS and Norges Bank Investment Management (Norges), with the latest major SWF to join being Japan's Government Pension Investment Fund with US$1.3 trillion in AUM. The build-up of investable funds globally in search of investment opportunities throughout the world has become a main driving force behind the massive increase in cross-border investment. This also means competition for investment opportunities has intensified.

Diminished investment opportunities in domestic markets have compounded the problem of managing large pools of accumulated investable funds, particularly in mature economies where growth has been slow for decades. The supply side responded to lower aggregate demand for space in a slow growth environment by maintaining a smaller inventory of new assets. Investment managers have therefore been forced to look beyond their shores, including emerging markets, for better opportunities. China, for example, has the largest retail construction pipeline in the world. According to a survey undertaken by CBRE in 2014,[23] Chinese cities accounted for half of the retail centre space under construction globally in the 180 cities surveyed. Shanghai alone with 3.3 million square metres of retail space under construction exceeded the combined pipeline of the 86 European cities (excluding those in Russia and Turkey) surveyed.

Over the last 20 years, a number of markets, which were previously closed, allowed foreign investors in real estate for different reasons. Forced by necessity, Korea opened its market following the devastation caused by the Asia Financial Crisis in 1997. In the case of Japan, while there was no foreign investment regulatory restriction, prime real estate was tightly held by a small number of conglomerates. Their stranglehold was only broken during the post-Bubble period, starting from the early 1990s. Foreigner investors could then find meaningful acquisitions of good quality assets. The growth of the Chinese economy at an average of rate of about 10% for 20 years up to 2013 and the opportunities presented by its vast and developing real

---

[22] APREA (2014), "The Increasing Importance of Real Estate in Asian Pension Funds".
[23] CBRE (2014), "Shopping Centre Development — The Most Active Cities Globally, Global ViewPoint", April 2014.

estate market attracted much foreign investment. The joining of the EU by Central and Eastern European countries in 2004 opened up their borders for investment, particularly from Western Europe. These structural changes increased the number of markets considerably for cross-border investors in the last 20 years.

Apart from geography, the spectrum of investment grade assets has also expanded. China alone for example has created at a break-neck pace a massive increase in the number of property assets in all its cities. The real estate landscape has totally transformed in just 20 years. Whereas there were hardly any modern high-rise residential buildings in the early-to-mid 1990s, and whatever that were built were of rudimentary quality, today, it boasts some of the best designed and constructed residential accommodation in the world. Starting from virtually no modern retail facilities, it now has the entire hierarchy, ranging from neighbourhood shopping centres to super-regional malls, not to mentioned high quality offices in the major cities. However, China's retail bricks-and-mortar will continue to evolve as it adapts to the onslaught of e-commerce. This unprecedented growth phenomenon has also been happening in other emerging markets, although not in the same scale or pace. There are now so many more choices in different markets open to cross-border investors.

While real estate technical skills are portable, cross-border investing presented a whole new set of considerations. Away from the comfort and familiarity of their home markets, investors are faced with different market fundamentals and structures, business practices and regulatory and taxation frameworks. Investing in emerging markets presents additional complications, principally relating to the lack of transparency and reliable information. Not surprisingly, there has been a proliferation of specialist real estate intermediaries, including banks, fund managers, asset managers, lawyers, accountants and consultants in response to the demand for a range of professional services arising from increased off-shore interests. Based on surveys of the asset management industry for 1997 to 2012 conducted by the Monetary Authority of Singapore, the number of investment professionals such as portfolio managers, investment analysts, traders and economists operating out of Singapore increased by almost four fold, from 814 in 1997 to 3,312 as at 2012 (Figure 3).[24]

Through these services, the intermediaries, who are essentially appointed to overcome executional issues, further lubricate the flows of capital across borders. The role of fund managers who are conduits of investable funds will be further discussed in the next section. Intermediaries provide much needed information to assist investment decision making. One of the impediments to real estate investing, particularly in foreign markets, has been the lack of reliable information. The quality of information has improved overtime as markets mature and this has given investors more confidence in making acquisition or disposition decisions. In the early years, the

---

[24] Monetary Authority of Singapore, Singapore Asset Management Industry Surveys.

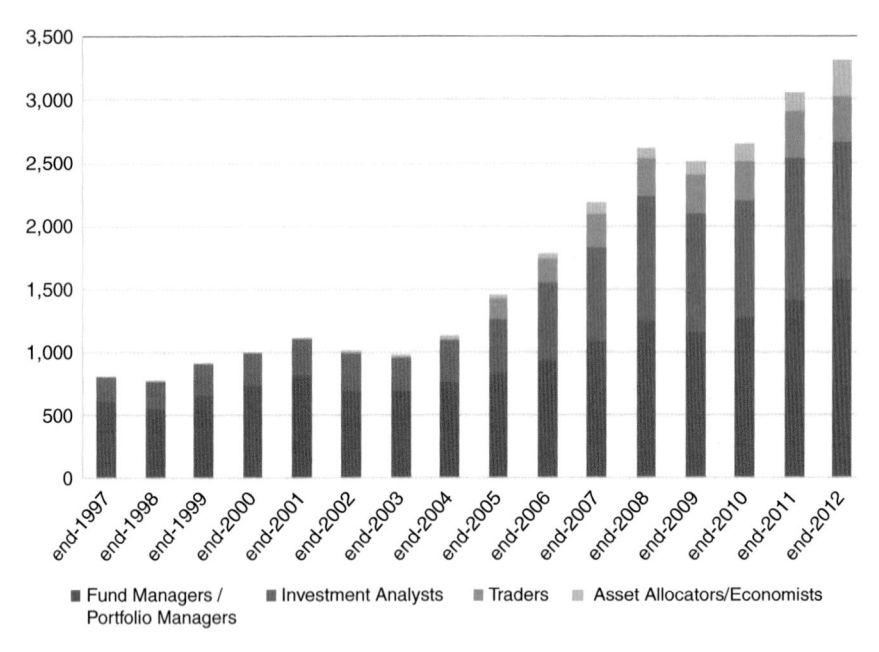

Figure 3. Investment professionals in Singapore.
Source: Singapore Asset Management Industry Surveys, Monetary Authority of Singapore.

problem was simply about collecting reliable information, before it advanced to more value-adding research, applying analytical and forecasting tools to better understand the markets. The most significant development, in terms of its impact on institutional investment, was the introduction of property indices in the developed markets. This was quite instrumental in attracting institutional money to real estate as investment managers needed to compare the performance of real estate to other asset classes in their portfolios. However, as real estate indices are mostly valuation based and tend to understate the volatility of the returns, questions were raised on their use in asset allocation models. Further refinement was made possible when Fisher, Geltner and Webb[25] introduced the techniques to unsmooth the volatility of returns to overcome one of the methodological weaknesses of index computation. The quality of information and research has continued to improve in all markets, both mature and emerging. However, emerging markets have yet to reach a level of maturity and transparency required to enable a reliable property index to be constructed. Hence, a truly representative global index equivalent to the MSIC equity index still does not exist.

---

[25] Fisher, J.D., D.M. Geltner, and R.B. Webb. (1994), Value Indices of Commercial Real Estate: A Comparison of Index Construction Methods, *Journal of Real Estate Finance and Economics*, Volume 9, pp. 137–164.

Nevertheless, improved information over the last 20 years is another enabling factor for increased institutional allocations to real estate in general.

Another reason for the growth in cross border investment is market innovations which have led to an expanded range of investment vehicles or instruments becoming available in a greater number of countries. Real Estate Investment Trusts (REITs), Commercial Mortgage-backed Securities (CMBS), private or unlisted funds presented international investors with investment choices previously absent and showed signs of growth from the early 2000s throughout Asia. These new investment products are the result of the real estate industry drawing on the resources of capital markets and also adapting to major market upheavals in the last 20 to 30 years. The next section shows how the industry moved away from bricks-and-mortar towards integration with the capital markets.

From Bricks-and-Mortar to Capital Markets

The commercial property investment model of building or buying an asset to hold and collect rent has remained unchanged for a long time and the capital structure of this model is commonly comprised of a combination of private equity and a bank loan, not unlike how most individuals finance their homes. While this funding structure is still prevalent, innovations in the real estate industry and the capital markets over the last 20 years have enabled all parts of the underlying capital structure of real estate to become tradable both in the private and public markets. This transformational change has resulted in a vastly expanded range of real estate investment instruments and vehicles in the markets. Instead of buying and selling physical assets as have been the practice since time immemorial, new thinking and innovations in the capital markets have allowed the equity and debt components in the capital structure to be bought and sold. Figure 4 shows the four-quadrant approach to real estate investment. The four quadrants are private and public debt, and private and public equity.

The four quadrant approach has become an integral part of modern real estate practice in developed markets, particularly the US. Both Commercial Mortgage-backed Securities (CMBS) in the public debt quadrant and REITs in the public equity quadrant arose as innovative solutions to alleviate problems associated with the massive build-up of non-performing assets during the Savings and Loans (S&L) crisis in the US following the collapse of the property market in the late 1980s. The CMBS market grew from US$5 billion in 1990 to a peak at US$230 billion in 2007 before collapsing to a low of US$3 billion during the GFC in 2009. It has since revived and in 2015 stood at US$101 billion. While the CMBS market was being established, the private debt market continued to innovate by sub-dividing real estate debt into tradeable tranches, ranging from investment grade to equity-like mezzanine, to appeal to investors with varying risk-return appetites. Singapore's nascent development of a real

	EQUITY	DEBT
PRIVATE	• Physical Assets • Private Real Estate Development Companies	• Commercial Mortgages • Construction Loans • Mezzanine Loans
PUBLIC	• Real Estate Investment Trusts (RFITS) • Listed Real Estate Development Companies	• Asset Backed Securities / Commercial Mortgage Backed Securities

Figure 4. The four quadrant model.

estate debt market was virtually vanquished by the GFC, although by 2006, 31 tranches of CMBS totalling SG$5.91 billion were arranged.[26]

On the equity side, the breakthrough was the introduction of REITs, which led to a surge in the securitisation of public real estate equity and private (or sometimes called unlisted) equity funds throughout the world.

The modern REIT era started in the US in the terms of its scale and impact. It came into being during the S&L Crisis as a way for distressed owners to raise capital when the market for real estate financing was very tight. KIMCO's IPO in 1991 marked the beginning of the modern equity REIT market in the US. It quickly gained acceptance and grew rapidly to the extent that by the end of the decade more than 60 REITs were publicly listed with a market cap of US$118 billion (Figure 5). The growth in the REIT market was helped by the UP-REIT structure which allows owners to defer taxes. Since then, the REIT model has spread internationally and still expanding.[27]

The successive application of the REIT model globally marked an important transformational change in the real estate industry. It not only gave investors another investment avenue but also greater liquidity to those who perceived real estate as lumpy and illiquid. It allowed smaller investors to access commercial real estate and provided developers and asset owners with another avenue to recycle capital.

---

[26] See Chapter 8 for the Singapore experience in real estate debt.
[27] NACRIEF, "Nuts and Bolts" conference paper.

Singapore entered the REIT market much later in 2002 with the launching of CapitaLand Mall Trust (CMT) as the first S-REIT, but it has grown rapidly since then. In 2005, with five S-REITs, it had a total market capitalisation of S$5.2 billion.[28] It has grown by more than 12 times to around S$66.7 billion with 28 listed REITs and six stapled listed property trusts today.

The development of the REIT market in Singapore provides an important additional source of funding for equity real estate, and contributes to the deepening of the commercial real estate market.[29] Developers now have another reliable vehicle to recycle capital, while small investors can invest through REITs to own a share of large commercial properties, which were previously beyond their reach. S-REITs have become attractive investments for investors looking for indirect exposure to Singapore commercial real estate as well in other Asian markets.

Singapore REITs, not unlike similar vehicles in other markets, were introduced as an investment vehicle principally for local real estate. However, the S-REITs have since evolved uniquely to have a substantial exposure to foreign real estate, which is not surprising given Singapore's limited market size. Of the 28 REITs, at least 10[30] have some exposure to foreign real estate and at least six[31] are entirely foreign. The fact that Singapore has established a fully functional REIT market in advance of many other Asian countries helps to draw foreign players to list in Singapore. This unique characteristic is partly the efforts of REIT managers who, being constrained by size of the Singapore market, scour for assets in other countries. Set up in 2003, ARA's Fortune REIT whose portfolio consists of entirely Hong Kong retail properties, is one such example.

Apart from being the catalyst to the growth of the modern REIT market in the US, the Savings and Loans Crisis (S&L Crisis) also precipitated the expansion of real estate private equity funds internationally. The first batch was opportunity funds created to take advantage of distressed assets accumulated by the Resolution Trust Corporation (RTC). Since then, the private fund industry continued to innovate and create new products in addition to opportunity funds. Over time, a vastly expanded array of funds offering a variety of risk-return characteristics to meet different investor demands, including core private, value-added, opportunity, global and emerging markets, emerged (Figure 6).[32]

---

[28] Joseph T. L. Ooi, Graeme Newell and Sing Tien Foo (2006), "The Growth of REIT Markets in Asia", *Journal of Real Estate Literature*, Volume 14, No. 2, pp. 203–222.
[29] Chapter 7 examines the growth of the S-REIT market in detail.
[30] CDL Hospitality Trust, Ascendas Real Estate Investment Trust, Ascendas Hospitality Trust, Ascott Residence Trust, First Real Estate Investment Trust, Keppel REIT, Frasers Commercial Trust, OUE Commercial REIT, ParkwayLife REIT and Suntec REIT.
[31] Fortune REIT, CapitaRetail China Trust, Mapletree Greater China Comm, Saizen REIT, Lippo Malls Indonesia Retail Trust and IREIT Global.
[32] INREV (2014), "The Investment Case for Core Non-Listed Real Estate Funds", September 2014.

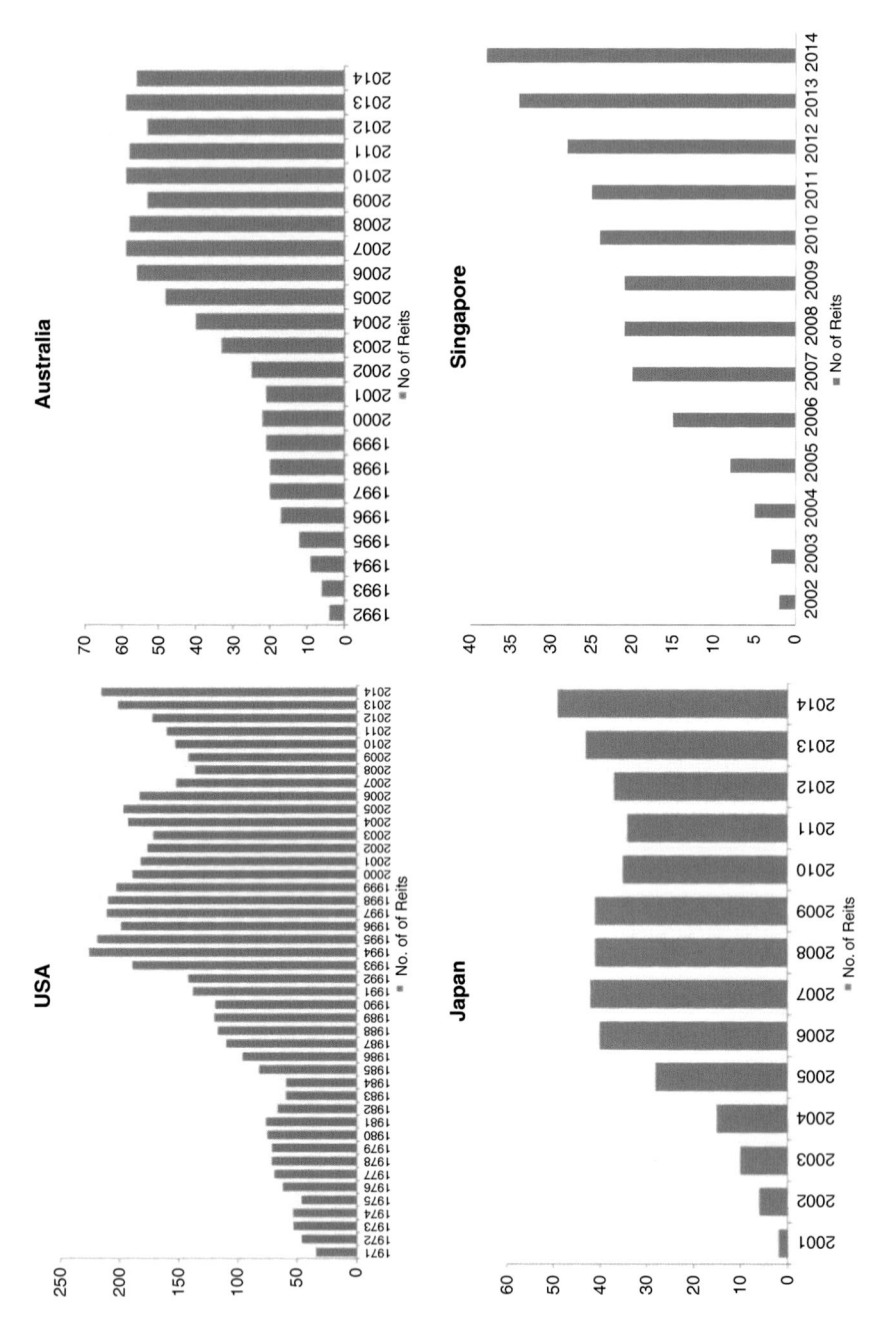

Figure 5. Growth of REITs in USA, Australia, Japan and Singapore.

Source: NAREIT, Morgan Stanley Research.
Source: Bloomberg, Morgan Stanley Research.
Source: Bloomberg, Morgan Stanley Research.
Source: Bloomberg and Sing Tien Foo.

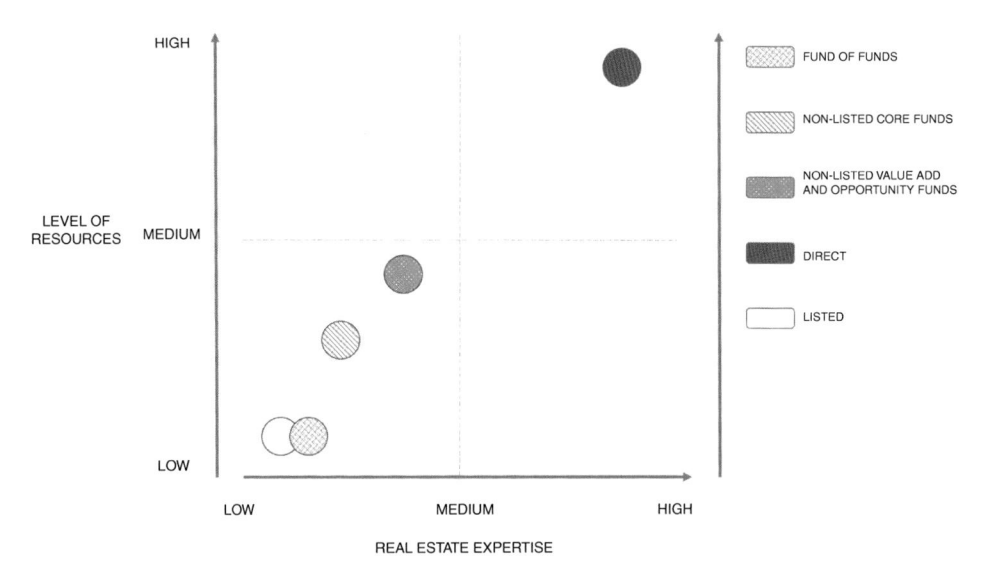

Figure 6. Range of real estate investment vehicles.
Source: INREV, "The Investment Case for Core Non-Listed Real Estate Funds".

The fund management industry grew rapidly as operators in other countries soon followed those in the US, although most of these funds were focused on their domestic markets in the first decade. It was not however until the 2000s that funds offering cross border opportunities emerged in response to growing interest amongst institutional investors looking to foreign markets for higher returns and diversification.

The volume of funds raised by private equity vehicles peaked in 2007 at US$760 billion (Figure 7). During the Global Financial Crisis (GFC), many were found wanting and did not survive the crisis. Fund raising had been difficult in the years after the GFC, during which only the larger more established global funds were able to raise money more readily. However, in the last few years, fund raising activities have risen significantly indicating the return of confidence by investors in private funds. Preqin reported funds raised in 2014 stood at US$710 billion, a significant rebound from the post-GFC quantum of US$195 billion in 2009.

The amount of funds raised in the Asia-Pacific region showed a similar upward trend rising from just over US$3 billion in 2008 to US$21.8 billion in 2014.

During this growth period, Singapore real estate companies also saw the potential of the private fund management business as an extension of being managers of public REITs. The first Singapore-based fund was SEAPAC, a three-party joint venture between US Prudential, Jones Lang Wotton and GIC, formed in 1994. In 2003, Keppel Land's fund management arm, Alpha Investment Partners, set up a close-end fund, the Asia No. 1 Property Fund and CapitaLand launched its first private equity fund, the Raffles City China Fund, in 2008. Many more funds were launched in

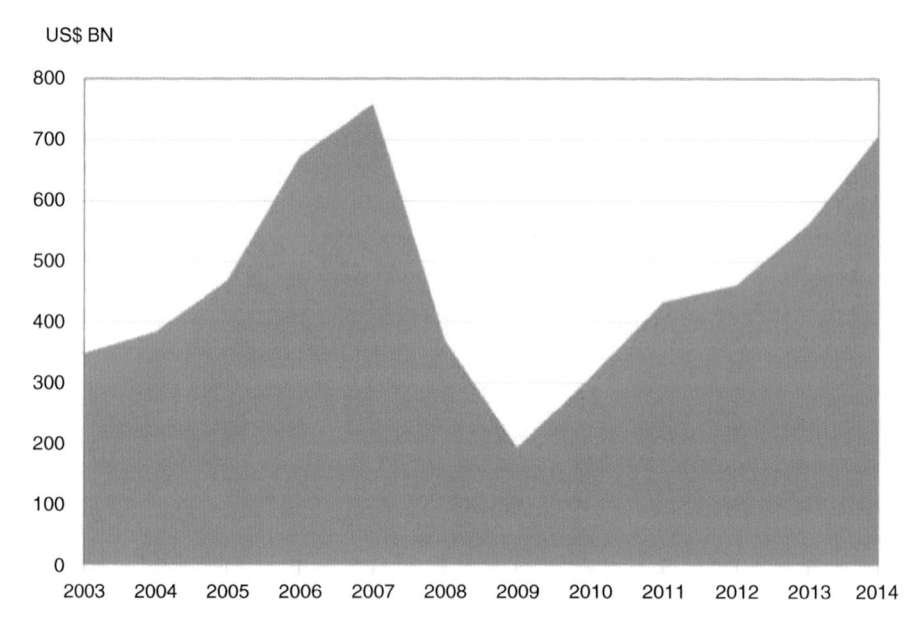

Figure 7. Global capital raised by private equity funds. (US$ billion).
Source: Preqin Ltd.

subsequent years in Singapore, including ARA Asset Management, Pacific Star Financial, Perennial Real Estate, Prudential Real Estate Investors Asia Pacific and Global Logistic Properties.[33] Preqin reported that whilst the number of real estate fund managers based in Singapore increased from three to six between 2003 and 2015, the aggregate capital raised grew by eight times and their average size quadrupled. Given the size of the Singapore market, most of these funds adopted a mandate of investing beyond Singapore, covering markets largely in Asia.

Conclusion

In 50 years, the Singapore real estate market has transformed into one of the most developed and sophisticated in the world. In the first 30 years, it lagged behind the developed markets, but rapidly caught up in the last 20 years, in spite of the many constraints and disadvantages. Constrained by a small local market and a lack of capital, but helped by strong economic growth and public sector support with world class soft and hard infrastructure, the real estate industry demonstrated its resilience, agility and adaptability to changing local and international conditions.

---

[33] Preqin Ltd.

In the early years, when developers were deprived of capital without the participation of home-grown institutional investors, as in the more developed markets, they innovated by selling commercial strata-titled units to recycle capital. As the market evolved, many decided to tap on public capital by becoming listed public companies, which enabled them to hold their developments for longer terms. The real estate industry overcame many constraints over the years but continued to enhance the design and construction of the buildings, to the extent that today, Singapore has some of the state-of-the art buildings comparable to the best in the world.

As real estate globalised and became integrated with the capital markets, Singapore adapted to and leveraged on these transformational changes in the global arena. Its home-grown institutions, like GIC and Temasek, were amongst the pioneering cross-border institutional investors in real estate. Singapore developers also expanded overseas in search of better opportunities as the domestic market became more competitive. While Singapore was exporting capital, it was at the same time attracting foreign capital flows into its real estate. Foreign investors and developers invested directly into bricks-and-mortar as well as indirectly through S-REITs. The success of the Singapore REIT market is another testimony of the effective partnership between the private sector and the government. The former identified the opportunity in securitising real estate in line with the global trend of integrating real estate with the capital markets and the latter provided the institutional support to make it possible. Because of the increased interest in Asian real estate and its status as a key financial centre in Asia, Singapore has also become a regional hub for fund managers to service the needs of such global investors.

In the last 50 years, Singapore has overcome many challenges and transformed itself from its humble beginning as a port city in the third world to a world-class metropolis with a real estate market which is mature, sophisticated and hopefully as adept at meeting new challenges in the future as in the past.

CHAPTER 6

Exporting Singapore's Experiences in Real Estate Development and Urban Planning

Sing Tien Foo and Yu Shi Ming

1. Introduction

Since the 1990s, the Singapore government has embarked on a regionalisation strategy to build an external wing for the economy. Constrained by its resources and market size, the strategy sought to grow its economy through establishing Singapore companies and businesses in the Asian region, especially in areas where her expertise would be highly sought after. In terms of real estate, this would include consultancy services in urban planning, development of industrial parks as well as townships and other infrastructure projects. This chapter traces Singapore's experience in exporting her expertise in real estate development and urban planning. It first explores the key phases of Singapore's economic development and reasons for spreading the "second economic wing". It then discusses the major government-to-government (G2G) initiatives which began in the late 80s and are still ongoing. The implementation of these initiatives was typically led by the Singapore government linked companies and other multi-national corporations (MNCs). The chapter also traces the regionalisation and expansion of Singapore-based developers and highlights some of their major projects and developments overseas.

2. Spreading the Second Economic Wing

Singapore's economy has undergone rapid expansion and growth since gaining independence in 1965. The earlier export-led manufacturing-centric economic activities were deliberate to not just serve the national interest in job creation, but most importantly to transform Singapore's economy — hinged so closely to entrepot trades — into an industrialised entrepreneurial economy.[1] There are three key features in the

---
[1] Chia, S. Y. (1997), "Singapore: Advance production base and smart hub of the electronic industry." In W. Dobson and S.Y. Chia (Eds.), *Multinationals and East Asian Integration*, Canada: IDRC, pp 31-61.

economic development and capital accumulation in Singapore: heavy dependence on foreign direct investment for industrialisation; active involvement of government linked companies; and regionalisation.[2] First, the early phase of economic development in 1960s and 1970s was largely driven by influx of foreign direct investment. Many foreign firms set up their labour-intensive and export-oriented manufacturing plants and facilities in Singapore because of the FDI-friendly policies and low cost production during the period. In the mid-1970s to 1980s, rising wage and labour shortage pushed the government to undertake industrial restructuring to move export-led activities to more capital-intensive activities in the production chain. In the 1980s and 1990s, knowledge-intensive and technology driven investments continued to move Singapore's economy up the value chain. In the 2000s, the shift to innovative entrepreneurship, research and development (R&D) will be the next engine to propel the economic growth of Singapore.[3]

Second, the Economic Development Board (EDB) is an agency set up in 1961 with the mission of attracting foreign direct investment and shaping economic growth of Singapore. The government has, via its statutory boards and agencies, played key roles in providing good infrastructure, such as road, electricity, transport and communication, which create a conducive environment for foreign firms to set up their manufacturing and production facilities in Singapore. Statutory boards, such as Jurong Town Corporation (JTC) and Housing and Development Board (HDB), with given autonomy in specific roles and functions, have been set up to provide industrial space and public housing for firms and their employees. In terms of finance and regulatory framework, the Monetary Authority of Singapore (MAS), the *de-facto* central bank of Singapore, has been set up to supervise and regulate the financial services industry in Singapore. The Development Bank of Singapore (DBS) was established in 1968 to support industrial financing activities in the earlier years of industrialisation in Singapore. It has since expanded into one of the largest banks in Asia with its footprint spreading across many cities. Like DBS Bank, which is a key government linked company (GLC), the government has invested and set up many GLCs or state owned enterprises to help boost growth and competitiveness in selected industries and sectors.[4] The two largest publicly listed real estate companies

---

[2] Yeung, Henry Wai-chung, "Regulating Investment Abroad: The Political Economy of the Regionalization of Singapore Firms," Antipode 31:3, 1999, pp 245–273.

[3] History of Singapore's Economic Development (Source: https://www.edb.gov.sg/content/edb/en/about-edb/company-information/our-history.html).

[4] According to Huff (1995), the government of Singapore had invested in 58 diverse companies with a total paid-up capital of S$2.9 billion as in 1983. [Source: Huff, W.G. (1995), "The developmental state, government, and Singapore's economic development since 1960." *World Development*, 23: 1421–1438.] Some of the state-owned enterprises have grown significantly into conglomerates with businesses spanning across different regions and countries, such as DBS Bank, Keppel Corporation, Singapore Telecommunications (SingTel), Sembawang Group, and many others.

linked to the government's investment arm, Temasek Holdings, are CapitaLand and Keppel Land.[5]

The third key feature of Singapore's economy took place after the 1985 recession. The government convened the Economic Committee, which recommended the regionalisation strategy as the new engine of growth for the country. The offshore investments and regionalisation drive were stepped up by Mr Goh Chok Tong after taking over as the second Prime Minister of Singapore in 1990. The regionalisation 2000 (R2000) blueprint was developed to strategise the effort to develop the country's "external wing" of economic growth.[6] The R2000 is a national thrust to create economies of scale for Singapore-based companies recognizing the constraints of a small domestic market with limited resource.[7] The Trade Development Board (TDB) set up in 1983 was restructured and renamed as International Enterprise (IE) Singapore in 2002 and has been tasked to grow globally competitive companies for Singapore.

The Singapore government took the lead in driving the regionalisation effort by taking an active role in promoting various government-to-government (G2G) collaborative projects. The SIJORI "growth triangle" was proposed in 1989 by Mr Goh Chok Tong, the then Deputy Prime Minister, as a partnership arrangement between Singapore, Malaysia (Johor) and Indonesia (Riau Islands) that aimed to leverage on different comparative strengths of the three countries, and enhance the regional division of labour and skills.[8] The G2G initiative was subsequently expanded by exporting urban and township technical know-how to countries like China, India, and Vietnam among other Asian countries that underwent rapid phases of urbanisation.

Many of the G2G projects especially those involving industrial parks and township developments have high risks and long pay-back periods. The government forms joint-venture consortia comprising GLCs and foreign state-owned entities to pool together capital and entrepreneurship skills and share risk. The industrial parks and township projects were marketed to many multi-national corporations (MNCs) as Singapore's brand developments, which were known for its reliability, efficiency and good planning, and these projects provide springboards for these MNCs to open up business opportunities in these new markets.

---

[5] CapitaLand is a public company listed on the Singapore Exchange; and Keppel Land was also a publicly listed company till 18 May 2015, when the parent company, Keppel Corporation, took it private through a voluntarily unconditional cash offer delisting exercise.

[6] Yeoh, Caroline, Koh, Chee Sin and Cai, Jialing Charmaine (2004), "Singapore's Regionalization Blueprint: A Case of Strategic Management, State Enterprise Network and Selective Intervention," working paper of Singapore Management University.

[7] Ministry of Finance (1993), *Final Report of the Committee to Promote Enterprise Overseas*, Singapore: SNP Publishers.

[8] Ho, K.C. (1994), "Industrial restructuring, the Singapore city-state, and the regional division of labour. Environment and Planning A, 25: 47–62.

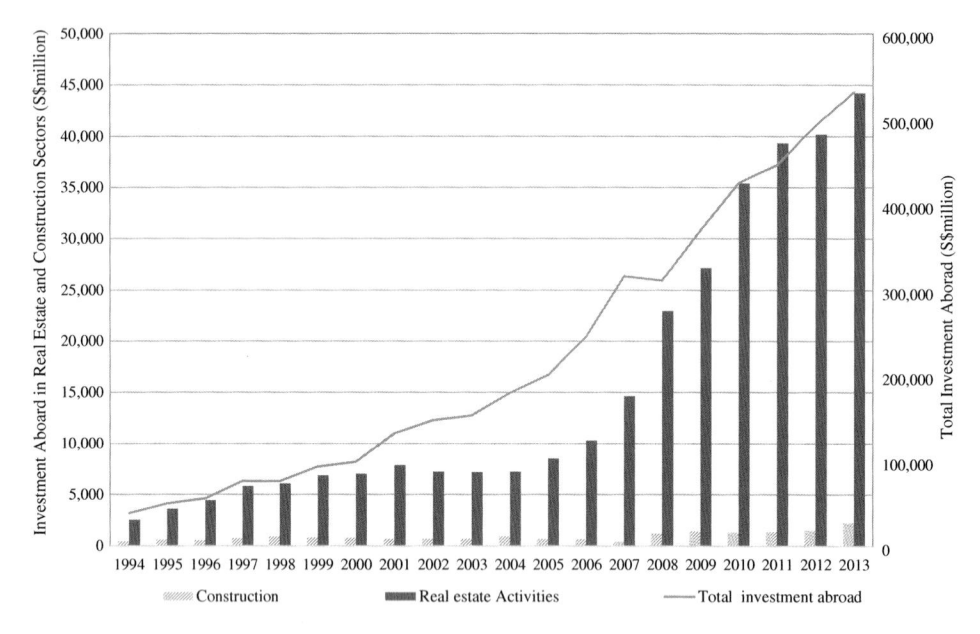

Figure 1. Singapore's investment abroad, 1994–2013 (S$ million).
Source: Department of Statistics, Singapore.

The regionalisation effort has borne fruit, and the Singapore's investments abroad have grown by nearly 14 times over a 20-year period from S$38.37 billion in 1994 to S$531.69 billion in 2013 (Figure 1). The real estate and construction investments abroad grew from S$2.97 billion to S$46.46 billion over the same period. By sector distribution based on the total oversea investment as in 2013, Figure 2 shows that financial and insurance services is the largest of outward investment constituting 45.96% followed by the manufacturing sector constituting 20.68% of the total investment. The combined share for real estate and construction investments is third largest with an estimated 8.73% of total outward investments in 2013.

3. Major Government-to-Government (G2G) Projects

Singapore's land constraint was one of the primary reasons for exporting the country's development expertise. In the late 80s, as the economy underwent a restructuring to move from labour-intensive manufacturing to more technology-focused industries, a critical requirement was land. Faced with land constraint, it was difficult to continue to attract industries to Singapore and expand her economic space. The EDB, which was driving the whole process of economic growth and investment promotion, began to look at the neighbouring countries which have a lot more land. This led to one of the early forays overseas — albeit not very far — the development of the Batam

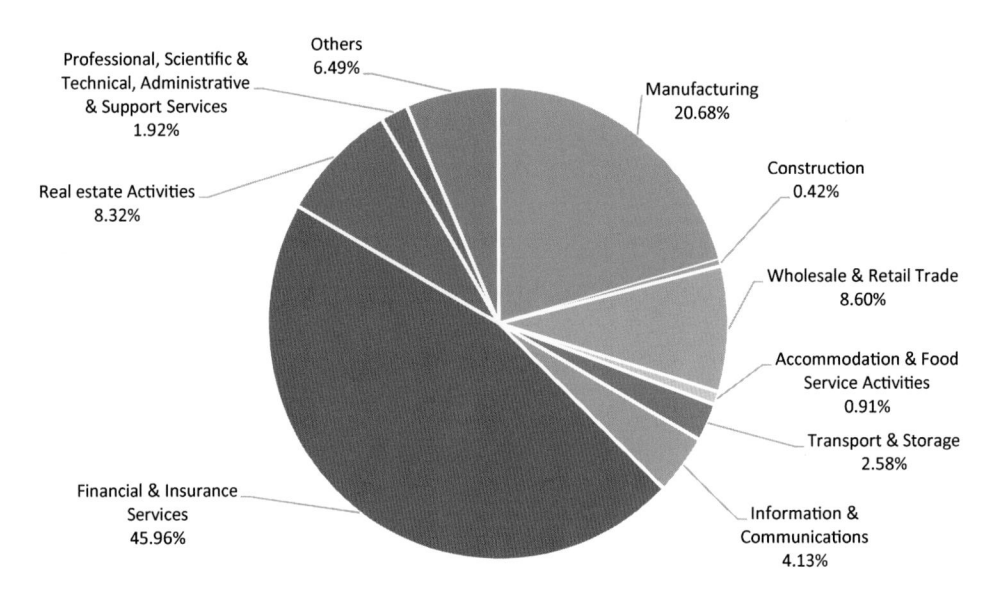

Figure 2. Sector distribution of total Singapore's investment abroad (as in 2013).
Source: Department of Statistics.

Industrial Park. This had helped to create the additional industrial and economic space for Singapore. It allowed the EDB to continue to promote and seek investments in Singapore with the option of locating the land-intensive industries in Indonesia, which would still be very much connected to Singapore. Being in proximity to Singapore, firms could leverage on Singapore's infrastructure in international trade and finance. The initial success led to developments in Bintan and then to Karimun, all part of the Indonesian Riau islands which the host country was happy to develop with Singapore's help. Malaysia, the other close neighbour to the north also had land to develop, and this led to the establishment of the growth triangle partnership named Sijori (Singapore-Johor-Riau). Over the years, however, little was developed in Johor under this partnership while Bintan and Batam continued to attract investments from Singapore, especially in resort developments. Nevertheless, the lessons learnt from the first G2G initiatives would be useful as Singapore continued to look for development opportunities overseas.

The next wave of regionalisation took its roots in the 1990s as part of the government's strategy to build an external economic wing. Mr Goh Chok Tong, who took over as Prime Minister in 1990, encouraged Singapore companies and Singaporeans to seek opportunities overseas especially for destinations that could be reached within a seven-hour flying time zone. China and India, as the two largest developing countries in Asia and within this perimeter of a seven-hour flying time zone, naturally offered the best opportunity for the Singapore government to work with. It was envisaged that

Singapore with its industrial and economic development expertise could help these countries in their initial developments such that both Singapore and the host country would mutually benefit, clearly a win-win model. China, for example, was going through its first phase of industrial development and opening up its economy. They needed good infrastructure to attract investments in industry, as well as investment promotion expertise to attract the industries. When Deng Xiao Ping visited to Singapore in 1978, he suggested that Singapore could be a good model for China's developing economy especially for the special economic zones on the east coast and southern China. This subsequently led to the idea for the two countries to jointly develop an industrial park to build a system of "software" transfer such as urban planning, fiscal policies and local governance and administration. The location was finally decided to be in Suzhou, a city near to Shanghai.

The Suzhou Industrial Park (SIP) launched in 1994 was the first major G2G initiative between the governments of China and Singapore. Although it is called an industrial park, it included township development as both countries wanted to create a sustainable model where the industries offered employment to workers who could live close by. It was very much a work-live-play concept although at the time of SIP's development, the concept was yet to be fully established. Like in most partnerships, there would be hiccups but the eventual completion and the handing over of the project from Singapore to the local government, signified a successful G2G project. That Singapore left its imprint in the areas of urban planning, township management and even local governance meant that this expertise could be transferred and replicated. Following the success of SIP, both the Singapore and Chinese governments decided to work together again with the development of the Tianjin Eco-city in 2008. Both countries would share expertise and experience in areas like urban planning, environmental protection, resource conservation, water and waste management and sustainable development. A Joint Steering Council (JSC) co-chaired at the Deputy Prime Minister-Vice Premier level charts the strategic directions of the project. A Joint Working Committee (JWC), co-chaired by Singapore's Minister for National Development (MND) and China's Minister of Housing and Urban-Rural Development, and comprising senior representatives from both sides, oversees the implementation of the Eco-city project and the achievement of its key milestones.

The success of the G2G initiative has led to the set-up of several new projects between China's provincial authorities and the Singapore government or Singapore companies. The results include the Knowledge City project in Guangzhou and the Sino-Singapore Jilin Food Zone in Jilin. There is also ongoing discussion of a third G2G project to help the development of western China.

Besides China, India also provides opportunities for Singapore to market its planning and development expertise. While the focus is still the sharing of expertise at the G2G level, there are some differences between the two countries. India, like

Singapore, was under British rule and therefore shares a common commercial language (English) and many aspects of the legal system. However, unlike China, it is very much driven by the private sector. So while the initial contact was G2G, Tata Corporation, the giant Indian conglomerate, spearheaded the first project with Singapore's Ascendas in the development of the Bangalore IT Park. This meant that the scale was different — SIP is a township whereas BITP is an integrated development, a mixed-use development of a denser but smaller scale. As a comparison, SIP would be like Singapore's JTC and the BITP would be like the Science Park (although housing is provided in the BITP). These differences account for the generally low-key publicity for the BITP unlike the SIP. Nevertheless, the successful completion of the BITP similarly spurred the interests of other cities such as Hyderabad and Chennai. Ascendas subsequently developed IT parks in these and other places in India. More recently, the state governments in India have sought the Singapore government's help in master planning cities and other infrastructural projects, such as the planning of a new capital city in the Southern state of Andhra Pradesh.

4. Leading the way by Government Linked Companies

In the G2G projects discussed above, the implementation and operation of the projects were mainly undertaken by government agencies or government linked companies. In the development of the Batam Industrial Park, for example, JTC was one of the key players responsible for the Master Plan, drawing on its experience with the master plan for the Jurong industrial estate, while Sembawang Corporation, a government linked company worked with JTC to implement the plan.

Similarly, JTC was involved with the initial development of the Suzhou Industrial Park before the establishment of the China-Singapore Suzhou Industrial Park Development Company (CSSD) which is jointly owned by a consortium from both countries. In the initial years, the Singapore consortium had majority ownership of 65% which was then reversed in 2001 with the Chinese consortium having the majority. A joint steering committee was overall responsible for the development and operation of the SIP. In the case of Tianjin, six working-level sub-committees, comprising officials from various Singapore agencies and Chinese officials from the Tianjin Eco-city Administrative Committee (ECAC), have been formed to focus on public housing, water management, urban planning and transport, environmental management, economic promotion and social development in the Eco-city. The Singapore agencies which are involved in the Tianjin Eco-city include the Urban Redevelopment Authority (URA), Housing and Development Board (HDB), Building and Construction Authority (BCA), National Environment Agency (NEA), Public Utilities Board (PUB), Land Transport Authority (LTA) and IE Singapore. At the private sector-level, the Sino-Singapore Tianjin Eco-city

Investment and Development Co. Ltd (SSTEC) which is formed by a Singapore consortium and a Chinese consortium, each with a 50% stake in the joint venture company, is the master developer for the project. SSTEC also undertakes economic promotion of the Eco-city. That the project is undertaken with the private sector helps to ensure its commercial viability and enhance its scope for replication. Keppel Corporation, a GLC, leads the Singapore Consortium, while the Chinese consortium is led by Tianjin TEDA Investment Holdings Co. Ltd. It should be noted that both the SIP and Tianjin Eco-City projects are large undertakings requiring substantial financial commitment with long gestation period; hence, the need for government backing and sizeable companies such as GLCs to take the lead. Subsequent projects between the two countries such as the Guangzhou Knowledge City (GKC) are being led by the private sector but are still backed by the government; in fact, the GKC will be upgraded to a state-level strategic project in the near future. Initiated in 2010, the GKC occupies a 123 sq km site for the development of knowledge industries and is designed to attract high-tech and creative start-ups. The project is a joint venture between Temasek-owned Singbridge International and Guangzhou Development District Administrative Committee.

The projects with India were somewhat different in that they were largely owned and operated by the private sector. While JTC, RSP (a Singapore-based architecture and planning consultancy) and L&M (a Singapore construction company) were involved initially in the BITP, Ascendas, a subsidiary of JTC, became the main developer. Tata Corporation was the main Indian partner as it owned some land in Bangalore. Given India's strength in IT, both governments agreed to go ahead with the BITP with the Indian government and Tata Corporation providing the land while Ascendas provided the expertise. Although backed by the government, the private sector-led partnership faced many difficulties with bureaucracy in securing infrastructure such as roads, water and electricity. To overcome the problems, Ascendas decided to build their own power plant, which proved to be critical as IT operations require uninterrupted power supply and public power plants in India were not as reliable. It was also decided that the industrial park should include housing so that workers need not spend too much time in commuting. These decisions plus the effort to ensure proper follow-up maintenance proved to be significant factors in the successful operation of BITP. The success in Bangalore led to other Indian cities inviting Ascendas to also implement similar projects in their cities.

Ascendas eventually expanded IT and business park developments into other countries in Asia, including the Philippines, Thailand, Vietnam, Korea, Japan and even Australia. This foray into new markets was firstly driven by the need to balance the risks of being overly exposed to developing countries. So, in order to have a more balanced risk portfolio, Ascendas felt the need to increase their expansion in more developed countries such as Korea and Japan.

5. Motivations for Regionalisation Drives of Developers

"*Location, location, location,*" a mantra that is closely associated with real estate, seems to imply that real estate is a local business, where knowledge of local culture and preference of house buyers is important. Evidence from the study of US investment homes shows that out-of-town buyers are misinformed about local housing market condition, and they misprice local markets, driving up local house prices.[9] Some researchers argue that real estate is "*the only game in town*" because of the locally-based and home-biased real estate investments. In cities with few public firms, households are more likely to own a second (investment) home nearby. "*The only game in town*" demand causes the housing prices to rent ratio to increase in these cities with fewer alternative investment options (few local stocks).[10]

The domicile nature of housing markets gives local developers comparative advantages, because they not only have direct access to information to local market and better knowledge about local buyers' preference; they can also establish their reputation easily through their local presence. Therefore, it is common to find a high concentration of a few oligopoly developers with a large market share contributed by these developers in the local markets. For example, in the private non-landed housing market in Singapore, the top 10 largest developers control 76.04% of the new condominium and apartment supply in the market for the period from 1995 to 2009.[11] Large local developers, such as City Development Limited, Far East Organization, CapitaLand, Fraser Centrepoint, Keppel Land, and others are able to establish their home-turf advantages against foreign developers, because of their local presence and proven track records in delivering quality houses in the local markets. There are also big name developers in other local markets, such as China Vanke Co., Ltd (万科企业股份有限公司), Evergrande Group (恒大地产集团), Poly Real Estate Group Co., Ltd (保利房地产（集团）股份有限公司), Dalian Wanda Group Corporation Ltd (大连万达集团股份有限公司) in China; Sun Hung Kai Properties, Cheung Kong, Henderson Land Development and New World Development in Hong Kong. It is, however, unusual to find the equivalents of "Microsoft", "Apple" in the computer software industry or "Coca Cola" and "Pepsi Cola" in the soft drink industry, in the real estate markets.

---

[9] Chinco, Alex and Mayer, Chris (2015), "Misinformed speculators and mispricing in the housing market," *Working paper, University of Illinois Urbana-Champaign, College of Business.*

[10] Choi, Hyun-Soo, Hong, Harrison, Kubik, Jeffrey D., and Tompson, Jeffrey P., (2013), "When Real Estate is the Only Game in Town," *Working paper, Singapore Management University.*

[11] See Chapter 3 of this book. (Source: Coulson, N.E., Dong, Z. and Sing, T.F. (2015), "Estimating Hedonic Cost Functions: Case of Singapore's Private Residential Property Markets," Working Paper, National University of Singapore, Institute of Real Estate Studies.

Lack of knowledge, high risk in new markets and resource constraints are possible barriers that prevent real estate developers from stepping out of their home market. There are other "push" and "pull" factors that motivate them to expand their "wings" outside their home ground. The small size of the domestic market is one "push" factor that motivates many Singapore-based developers to go abroad. Risk diversification and expanding an efficient frontier are some "pull" factors that motivate developers to search for new business opportunities outside Singapore. These pull factors may seem to be consistent with the standard textbook story advocating *"not putting all your eggs in one basket."* However, executing a diversification strategy across different real estate markets is not as simple as one may think. Unless developers are able to generate higher risk-adjusted returns in foreign markets than from the domestic market, it makes no sense to diversify for its own sake or just to overcome market size constraint.

Economic and business considerations are possible drivers for developers to expand their business outside their home markets. *"Brick and mortar"* businesses are not difficult to duplicate in foreign markets. Developers can create differentiated products through transporting and replicating established development concepts in the new markets. The Raffles City Brand of CapitaLand, which is an integrated development idea, is one example where a new development concept has been successfully replicated in gateway cities in China (See Case Study 1).

Scale economics can shorten learning curve, hasten technology adoption cycle and reduce costs, if they can deploy their technology know-how to development projects in other countries. Exploiting technology advantages is evident in motivating large construction firms in Japan, such as Shimizu, Taisei, Obayashi and Kajima, and Korea, such as Samsung, Hyundai, and Daewoo, to go internationally. However, for developers, the motivation to go abroad is correlated with the need to attract capital from institutional investors, who are more likely to invest in firms of global scale and diversified portfolios. The size advantage is useful for developers to attract talents, and broaden their managerial pool and expertise. In businesses like logistics and hospitality, it is strategic for developers to expand real estate portfolios across different countries to create necessary network effects. The Ascott Residence of CapitaLand and the Millennium & Copthorne Hotels of CDL are examples of how an internationalisation strategy is essential for the business operations.

Stakes are high if developers misread their oversea investments. Developers that go regional need a clear vision, bold entrepreneurial spirit and a risk-taking mindset to step out of their comfort zone in the home market, and compete in the world stage. To have staying power is also essential.

Development skills, management and technology are portable, but market knowledge is learnt. Foreign developers who are prepared to immerse in the local markets tend to become more successful. Understanding local culture and adapting

Case Study 1: CapitaLand's Raffles City Brand in China

1986 — Raffles City Singapore

Completed in 1986, Raffles City Singapore was built on the original site of the Raffles Institution, which is located next to the historic Raffles Hotel. An iconic development designed by the world-renowned architect I.M. Pei, Raffles City Singapore was conceptualised to be "a city within a city" that integrates retail, commercial, hotels and convention centre space into a single development. The integrated development consists of the 73-storey Swissôtel The Stamford, which was the world's tallest hotel when it was completed, a 28-storey hotel known as the Fairmont Singapore, a rectangular 42-storey office block — Raffles City Tower, and a seven-storey podium housing the Raffles City Shopping Centre and the Raffles City Convention Centre. The Raffles City Convention Centre when opened in 1986 was the Singapore's first convention centre.

Raffles City Shopping Centre is linked directly to the City Hall MRT interchange station and the Esplanade MRT station along the Circle Line. The integrated Raffles City Singapore was sold to two of CapitaLand's REITs in a deal that valued about S$2.1 billion on 19 March 2006. CapitaLand Commercial Trust (CCT) and CapitaLand Mall Trust (CMT) jointly own the Raffles City Singapore in a 60%:40% joint ownership structure.[1]

Exporting the Raffles City Brand to China

The **success** formula of the 1986 Raffles City Singapore development has been recognised by the CapitaLand Group that developed and continues to own and manage the integrated development, and the development concept has been adopted and replicated in several projects located in gateway cities in China. The Raffles City brand, according to the CapitaLand Group,[2] *"is synonymous with a series of signature integrated developments. The word 'City' is representative of both the prime locations that the developments occupy as well as their multi-functional 'city within a city' concept."* "A city within a city" integrates multi-functional uses, such as shopping malls, Grade A office buildings, serviced apartments, premium residential apartments and 5-star hotels into a single development. Designed by world-renowned architects, the Raffles City-branded developments create iconic landmarks symbolising urbanisation of a city.

The CapitaLand Group first exported the Raffles City brand to China in 2004 with the official opening of the first Raffles City Shanghai in the Puxi area, which is opposite Shanghai's historic People's Square. Raffles City Shanghai comprises a 40,000-square-metre retail podium and a 200-metre tall office tower with 87,000 square metres of prime Grade A commercial space. CapitaLand has since developed seven other Raffles City projects in gateway cities, such as Shanghai, Beijing, Chengdu, Ningbo, Hangzhou, Shenzhen and Chongqing

---

[1] Fiona Chan, "CapitaLand's Reits buy Raffles City in $2.1b deal -CapitaCommercial will take a 60% stake while CapitaMall will hold the remaining 40%," The Straits Times, 20 March 2006.
[2] The Raffles City brand website by CapitaLand: http://inside.capitaland.com/spaces/city/859-replicating-the-raffles-city-dna and http://www.rafflescity.com.cn/en/about.aspx.

(See Table CS6-1 for details of each of the projects). The eight developments in China offer over 3.1 million square metres of construction floor area and will have an estimated total value of about S$12 billion when completed.

Table CS6-1: The Raffles City developments of CapitaLand in China.

No	Name	Status/Target completion date	Location	Gross floor area (Sqm)	Components	Architect
1	Raffles City Shanghai	2004	Huangpu District, Shanghai	139,593	Grade A Office and Shopping Mall	P&T Group
2	Raffles City Beijing	2009	Dongcheng District, Beijing	110,996	Grade A Office, Shopping Mall, Serviced Residences	Stephen Pimbley
3	Raffles City Chengdu	2012	Wuhou District, Chengdu	240,514	Grade A Office, Serviced Residences, Shopping Mall, Premium Residential Apartments	Steven Holl
4	Raffles City Ningbo	2012	Jiangbei District, Ningbo	101,405	Grade A Office, Shopping Mall, Residences	Stephen Pimbley
5	Raffles City Hangzhou	2016	Qianjiang New Town, Hangzhou	296,336	Grade A Office, Shopping Mall, 5-star Hotel, Serviced Residences, SOHO	UNStudio
6	Raffles City Shenzhen	2017	Nanshan District, Shenzhen	200,980	Grade A Office, Shopping Mall, Serviced Residences, Residences, SOHO	Benoy
7	Raffles City Changning	2015	Changning District, Shanghai	261,011	Grade-A Office, Shopping Mall	P&T Group
8	Raffles City Chongqing	2018	Yuzhong District, Chongqing	817,000	Grade A Office, Shopping Mall, 5-star Hotel, Serviced Residences, Residential Apartments	Moshe Safdie

Sources: http://www.rafflescity.com.cn/en/about.aspx and the authors.

local practices into business models are also important to avoid pitfalls in oversea ventures. During an interview, Mr Philip Ng, the CEO of Far East Organization in Singapore, described the significance of integrating into local living in Hong Kong: *"... my brother (Robert Ng) and his family run the real estate business in Hong Kong (via the family-owned vehicle — the Sino Group). They have lived in Hong Kong for the last 40 years, and they understand what the market is about, and the culture of the buyers in Hong Kong. They have become localised over time."*

The half-hearted approach is not likely to help them to succeed in opening new frontiers on foreign soils. They should raise their ante, and bring their best minds to develop new markets. The former President and CEO of CapitaLand, Mr Liew Mun Leong, comments on its regional strategy[12]: *"...we have always made it a point to send only our A-graders to manage and lead our overseas operations and this is an important contributing factor behind CapitaLand's success in expanding overseas. This philosophy of sending A-graders overseas is adopted from Singapore Airlines. However, besides competency, it is important to note that one should be both bilingual and bicultural in the host country in order to do well overseas. Our experience has taught us that it is not sufficient to be just bilingual."*

6. Going Places by Singapore's Developers

Entering into a new market requires large capital outlays, and an oversea venture also entails high risks, which, if not managed properly, could have significant impact on developers' financial positions. Given resource constraints, it is not uncommon for developers to first build a firm foundation in the home market, before moving into a new market. However, Far East Organization is one of few developers that took a bold step in building their businesses concurrently on both the home turf and a new foreign market — Hong Kong.

Far East Organization (FEO) is the first Singaporean developer to start expanding its real estate business into Hong Kong. In 1970, Mr Ng Teng Fong, the company's founder, saw the development potential in the transformation of the Tsim Sha Tsui East area in Hong Kong, and seized the first mover advantage by aggressively acquiring some waterfront lands reclaimed around the Hung Hom Bay. It built the first commercial building, Tsim Sha Tsui Centre, in 1980, which houses the Headquarters of Sino Group. The Sino Group has established itself as one of the largest developers in Hong Kong, and whose real estate businesses are managed through three publicly listed companies and other privately held companies (Case Study 2). Far East's move into Hong Kong's property market *"was driven by my father (the late Mr Ng Teng Fong).*

---

[12] Lu Na, "Top 10 Property Developers in China in 2013," April 3, 2013, China.org.cn. [Source: http://www.china.org.cn/top10/2013-04/03/content_28429461_9.htm]

Case Study 2: Moving into Hong Kong — Sino Land

In 1970, Mr Ng Teng Fong, the founder of Far East Organization, established the Sino Group through Hong Kong-incorporated vehicle "Cherith Land Investment Co Ltd",[1] to build its Hong Kong real estate business. Sino Group's portfolio of companies include three public-listed companies, namely, Tsim Sha Tsui Properties Limited, Sino Land Company Limited and Sino Hotels (Holdings) Limited, as well as other private companies owned by Mr Ng's families. Tsim Sha Tsui Properties Limited was listed on the Hong Kong Stock Exchange in 1972, and Sino Land Company Limited in 1981. Sino Land was included as one of the constituent stock of Hang Seng Index in 1995.

Sino Group was among the earliest property developers who were instrumental in transforming Tsim Sha Tsui East from a desolate waterfront into a vibrant retail and commercial centre. In 1980, Sino Group completed Tsim Sha Tsui Centre, the first building in the area known as Tsim Sha Tsui East, once a land fill carved out of the former Hung Hom Bay. An important office-cum-retail centre, Tsim Sha Tsui Centre is conveniently located near the Tsim Sha Tsui and Tsim Sha Tsui East Stations and the Cross Harbour Tunnel. It serves as the headquarters of Sino Group. Surrounded by five-star hotels, the Alfresco Lane of Tsim Sha Tsui Centre offers a fine dining experience amid the stunning views of the Harbour.

Mr Ng via his Sino Group continued to invest in the Hong Kong property markets in 1980s and after, despite the uncertainty over the colony's post-Handover future. After more than four decades of active participation in all aspects of property development in Hong Kong, Sino Group has established itself as among the top three property developers in Hong Kong. It is also one of Hong Kong's largest landlords, owning a sizeable retail and office property holdings in Hong Kong.

Some of the development projects by Sino Group in Hong Kong are summarised in the following table (the listing is not exhaustive):

Residential projects	Commercial projects
The Hermitage, Lake Silver, The Palazzo, One SilverSea, Mount Beacon, Vision City, The Dynasty, Three Bays, Bowen's Lookout, Residence Oasis, Island Resort, Sky Horizon, Dynasty Heights, Hong Kong Gold Coast, Pacific Palisades and The Mayfair.	Central Plaza, The Centrium, Sino Plaza, Olympian City, tmtplaza, Citywalk, China Hong Kong City, Exchange Tower, Skyline Tower and Tsim Sha Tsui Centre.

Information was extracted from "Landmarks", a 50th year anniversary book published by Far East Organization in 2010.

---

[1] Cherith Land Investment Co. Ltd. (基立地产投资有限公司) was incorporated in Hong Kong on 5 January 1971. It was subsequently renamed Sino Land Company (信和置业有限公司) on 16 January 1981, and listed in the same year.

He has a lot of confidence in Singapore. However, because of the small size of the market, he chose Hong Kong as a good place to further grow the business. It is a Chinese dominant market, and a market that he understood. Like Singapore, it has the British style of planning, high density and with a large hinterland." Mr Philip Ng describes why his late father, Mr Ng Teng Fong, decided to enter Hong Kong's market in the 1970s.[13]

Following the earliest overseas move by the FEO, there were generally two subsequent waves of regionalisation by Singaporean real estate companies, which expanded their real estate business footprints overseas in the 1990s and 2000s. In the late 1980s and 1990s, the government took pro-active step to open the "second economic wings" through various government-to-government projects. They opened doors by bringing along government linked companies, such as Sembawang Group, Keppel Group, Ascendas, and others to form consortia with state-owned entities of the foreign counterparts. These consortia are involved mainly in large scale township projects.

During this period, two other developers have also made significant expansion overseas without riding on the government's "wing" — Hong Leong Group/CDL and CapitaLand (through its predecessor Pidemco). Hong Leong/CDL entered into the hospitality business with the first hotel acquisition — King's Hotel, at Havelock Road in Singapore in 1971. After the recession in 1985, it started to diversify its real estate business by acquiring Orchard Hotel in 1986. It has since grown its hotel portfolio dynamically through a series of acquisitions of hotels outside Singapore. In 1989, it listed its hotel arm, CDL Hotels International Limited, on the Hong Kong Stock Exchange, and raised more capital to support its expansion drive. In 1996, it listed Millennium & Copthorne Hotels plc (M&C), a subsidiary of CDL Hotels International Limited, on the London Stock Exchange. M&C has grown in a short span of time into one of the largest hotel owners and operators in the world, owning/operating more than 36,000 rooms in over 150 hotels across 24 countries (Case Study 3).[14]

CapitaLand Group makes its foray into the China market via its wholly owned subsidiary, CapitaLand China, set up in Shanghai in 1994. It has grown to become one of the leading foreign developers in China. The group focuses its key businesses on integrated developments, shopping malls, serviced residences, offices, homes and real estate fund management. CapitaLand China manages seven real estate funds in China. Mr Lim Min Yang, the current President and Group CEO, CapitaLand, who was also the CEO of CapitaLand China for nine years, shares his experience in build-

---

[13] Liew Mun Leong, (2011) "Building People, Training CEOs," Building People 2: Sunday Email from a CEO, John Wiley & Sons (Asia) Pte Ltd, pp288.
[14] An interview with Mr Philip Ng, the CEO of Far East Organization, was conducted by the editorial team (Sing Tien Foo and Jeanette Yeo) at Mr Ng's office at Far East Plaza on 22 January 2015.

Case Study 3: CDL's M&C Acquisition

CDL's foray into hotel property started in 1986 with the acquisition of Orchard Hotel. It expanded its hotel portfolio through a slew of acquisitions of hotels including Grand Hyatt Taipei, and other hotels in Malaysia, Hong Kong and the Philippines. Mr Kwek Leng Beng, CDL Executive Chairman, listed CDL Hotels International Limited on the Hong Kong Stock Exchange in 1989 to raise further capital for further expansion of hotel portfolios. The new hotel vehicle of CDL acquired many established hotels in the US and Europe, which include London's Gloucester and Bailey's Hotels, New York's Millennium Hilton and the Macklowe at Times Square (now Millennium Broadway).

In 1992, CDL started acquiring several hotels in New Zealand and eventually established the Group as New Zealand's largest hotel chain. In 1995, CDL partnered Saudi Arabia's Prince Al-Walled to purchase the world-famous Plaza Hotel on New York's Fifth Avenue. In the same year, Mr Kwek negotiated the acquisition of the Copthorne chain and added hotels in Britain, Germany and France, which led to the successful launch of CDL's new global brand, Millennium Hotel and Resorts. In 1996, Millennium & Copthorne Hotels plc (M&C), a subsidiary of CDL Hotels International Limited, became the first Singapore-controlled company to be floated on the London Stock Exchange.

The Group's expansion continued. In 1999, M&C acquired the five-star Seoul Hilton (now Millennium Seoul Hilton) as well as the Regal chain of 17 hotels in the US, which included the famous Biltmore Hotel in Los Angeles, the Knickerbocker in Chicago and Bostonian in Boston. From a small stable of six properties in 1989, M&C has since grown into one of the world's largest hotel groups — owning, asset managing and operating over 110 hotels at key gateway cities in 20 countries, from New York to Los Angeles, London to Paris, Dubai to Doha, Hong Kong to Singapore and China, and beyond.

For the distinctive achievement, Mr Kwek won the coveted " Businessman of the Year" title at the Singapore Business Awards by the Business Times and DHL Worldwide Express.

Information extracted from CDL's 50th year book — A Lasting Impression

ing up the China business: *"(t)he market was skeptical of our strategy to expand overseas post-merger (in 2000)*[15]. *When I was sent to Shanghai in 2000 to set up and lead CapitaLand's China operations, people were unfamiliar with us. It was very challenging at first, but we worked hard to build trust and confidence in the company. Today, we are well-recognised as one of the largest foreign-funded real estate developers in China, with S$20.7 billion of investment in China (as at June 30, 2015)"*.[16]

---

[15] Ann Williams, "Kwek Leng Beng receives lifetime achievement award from hotel industry gathering," *The Straits Times*, Oct 15, 2015

[16] Pidemco and DBS Land were merged to form CapitaLand in 2000. See Case Study 1 in Chapter 3 of this book.

Table 1. List of Singapore's government-led industrial park projects overseas.

Country	Industrial park name	Year launch	Location	Site area (hectare)	Developer	Singapore consortium	Foreign partner	#
Indonesia	Batamindo Industrial Park	1990	Batam Island	320	Gallant Venture	Sembcorp Development	Salim Group	1
	Bintan Industrial Estate	1993	Bintan Island	270				
India	International Tech Park Bangalore	1992	Bangalore	28	Information Technology Park Ltd	Ascendas Group	Karnataka Industrial & Areas Development Board (KIADB) and TATA Industries	3
China	Suzhou Industrial Park	1994	Suzhou	8,000	China-Singapore Suzhou Industrial Park Development Group Co., Ltd	Singapore Suzhou Township Development Pte Ltd	Suzhou Industrial Park Stock Co Ltd and	4
	Wuxi-Singapore Industrial Park	1994	Wuxi New District	330	Wuxi-Singapore Industrial Park Development Co., Ltd	Sembcorp Developmetn	Economic Development Group Corporation of Wuxi New District	5
	Tianjin Eco-City	2007	Tianjin Binhai New Area	3,000	Sino-Singapore Tianjin Eco-city Investment and Development Co. Ltd (SSTEC)	Keppel Corporation	Tianjin TEDA Investment Holdings Co. Ltd.	6

(Continued)

Table 1. (Continued)

Country	Industrial park name	Year launch	Location	Site area (hectare)	Developer	Singapore consortium	Foreign partner	#
	Nanjing Eco Hi-tech Island	2009	Jiangxinzhou, Nanjing, Jiangsu Province	1,500	Sino-Singapore Nanjing Eco Hi-Tech Island Development Co	Singapore Intelligent Eco Island Development (Sembcorp, Yanlord and Surbana)	Nanjing Jiangdao Investment & Development Co., Ltd ("Jiangdao")	2
	Sichuan Hi-tech Innovation Park	2012	Chengdu's Tianfu New CityBottom of Form	1,000	Sino-Singapore (Chengdu) Innovation Park Development Co. Ltd. (SSCIP)	Singbridge Holdings and Sembcorp Development	Chengdu Hi-Tech Investment Group Co. Ltd.	7
	Jilin Food Zone	2013	between Changchun and Jilin	5,700	Sino-Singapore Jilin Food Zone Development and Management Co., Ltd (JVMC).	Singbridge Holdings	Jilin City Government	8
	Guanzhou Knowledge City	2014	northeast of Guangzhou City	6,000	Sino-Singapore Guangzhou Knowledge City Investment and Development Co., Ltd	Singbridge Holdings	Guangzhou Development District Administrative Committee (GDD)	9

Vietnam	Vietnam Singapore Industrial Park (VSIP) Binh Duong I	1996	Thuan An District, Binh Duong Province	500	Vietnam Singapore Industrial Park (VSIP)	Sembcorp Development, Mitsubishi Corporation Development Asia and KPM Vietnam Investment	Becamex IDC Corporation	10
	VSIP Binh Duong II	2006	New Binh Duong Township, Binh Duong Province	2,045				
	VSIP Bac Ninh	2007	Bac Ninh Province	700				
	VSIP Hai Phong	2010	Hai Phong City	1,600				
	VSIP Quang Ngai	2013	Quang Ngai Province	915				
	VSIP Hai Duong	2015	Cam Giang District, Hai Duong Province	150				
	VSIP Nghe An	2015	Hung Nguyen District, Nghe An Province	750				

#*Sources*: 1. *http://www.gallantventure.com/ubm/slot/u307/gallantventure.com.sg/www/history.htm.* 2. *http://www.sembcorp.com/en/src/docx/usrdocx/Facts&Figures2014English.pdf.* 3. *http://www.itpbangalore.com/.* 4. *http://www.sipac.gov.cn/english/.* 5. *http://www.vsip.com.cn/English/WSIP/nroduction/359.html.* 6. *http://www.tianjinecocitygov.sg/bg_intro.htm.* 7. *http://www.sscip.com.cn/en/.* 8. *http://www.ssjfz.com/.* 9. *http://www.sgkc.com/.* 10. *http://www.vsip.com.vn/about-vsip/company-backgound.html.*

The third wave of real estate regionalisation took place mainly in the 2000s. Some government-linked companies used REIT vehicles set up in Singapore to undertake large-scale acquisitions of foreign commercial assets, which include warehouses, logistics properties, hotels, serviced apartments, shopping malls, office buildings and industrial properties. They also brought foreign assets into Singapore through the listing of cross-border REITs. Ascott Residence Trust, Ascendas India Trust, Ascendas Hospitality Trust, CapitaLand Retail China Trust, Mapletree Logistic Trust and Mapletree Greater China Trust are examples of Singapore's REITs that invest and own cross-border assets.[17]

In February 2015, the merger of four government-linked companies consisting of JTC's Ascendas and Jurong International Holdings (JIH) and Temasek's Surbana and Singbridge[18] took place through a 49:51 partnership structure between JTC and Temasek. The four companies have already established strong track records in township and industrial planning and development across the region. They are organised into two units that include the Ascendas-Singbridge unit as the asset investment and holding arm, and the Surbana-JIH unit offering construction and engineering services. This integrated company with an aggregate value of around $5 billion creates a new platform to compete and undertake large-scale and complex urban development projects in the region. This is expected to become a new model for Singapore's firms to export their urban and township planning expertise to countries outside Singapore.

7. Conclusion

This chapter traces the export of Singapore's development expertise to regional countries. The regionalisation strategy was adopted largely due to Singapore's land constraint. In the late 80s, as the economy underwent a restructuring to move from labour-intensive manufacturing to more technology-focused industries, a critical requirement was land. Faced with land constraint, it became more difficult to continue to attract industries to Singapore and expand her economic space. The regionalisation strategy was adopted as the country sought to develop a second "economic wing" via the establishment of Singapore-based businesses in the regional countries. Over the past three decades, this overseas expansion has gradually become a central part of local business strategy, even for the small and medium enterprises. Today, as businesses become more global and cross boundaries, the regionalisation efforts of the late 80s and early 90s have indeed helped to set the right direction for Singapore's continued economic growth. Three critical success factors can be identified.

---

[17] Kalpana Rashiwala, "Shaping the skyline here and overseas," *Property 2015, The Business Times*, October 22, 2015, page 2.
[18] See Chapter 8 of this book for more details on Singapore's REITs.

First, the government and private sector partnership stands out as the underpinning reason for success. The initial G2G agreements have helped Singapore companies to establish a foothold in the regional countries, especially China and India. This is further strengthened by the GLCs taking the lead in forming joint ventures with local companies.

Second, the clear identification of Singapore's unique expertise and the need for such expertise in the developing countries in the region help to frame the successful model for collaboration. The rapid transformation of Singapore's urban landscape can be largely attributed to the sound planning and management systems developed since independence. This "software", especially for urban planning, development and management expertise, is extremely useful for cities going through their early development. Such knowledge transfer was especially appreciated at the government level.

Last but not least is the understanding of the differences between the countries in terms of their culture, social and political environments. While Singapore is a multiracial society with a large Chinese majority, doing business with the Chinese in China has shown that differences do indeed exist and need to be given due consideration. Similarly, Malaysians, Indonesians and Indians have different perspectives from the Chinese and collaborations with them need to understand these differences in order to be successful. As these countries grow economically, the collaboration model needs to evolve for it to be sustainable.

Part C
Real Estate Capital Markets

CHAPTER 7

The Rise of Singapore's Real Estate Investment Trust (SREIT) Market

Sing Tien Foo

1. History and Evolution of REITs

Real estate investment trusts, or REITs, were created with the passage of the REIT act by the US Congress in 1960 to give retail investors an indirect channel to invest in large-scale income generating real estate. The three earliest REITs — Winthrop Realty Trust (formerly known as First Union Real Estate Equity and Mortgage Investments), Pennsylvania REIT (PREIT) and Washington REIT founded in 1960 and 1961, are still actively traded on the New York Stock Exchange (NYSE).[1] In Australia, REITs were called listed property trusts (LPTs) till March 2008. The first Australian LPT — the General Property Trust, was established in 1971 (See Case Study 1).

The REIT history in Asia is relatively short, and can be traced back to September 2001 following the debut of two Japanese REITs — Nippon Building Fund Inc. and Japan Real Estate Investment Corporation, on the Tokyo Stock Exchange. Singapore lost the *"race"* to be the first Asian REIT market after the failed attempt by CapitaLand Limited to list its retail mall REIT — SingMall Property Trust in October 2001. The retail mall REIT was subsequently repackaged and re-launched successfully under a new name — CapitaMall Trust — on the Singapore Exchange in July 2002. CapitaMall Trust was renamed CapitaLand Mall Trust (CMT) on 6 May 2015.

Korean REITs started in 2002 with the listings of three corporate restructuring REITs (CR-REITs). CR-REITs are close-end funds with finite life. CR-REITs invest in real estate disposed by financially distressed companies undergoing debt restructuring. The three earliest CR-REITs are Kyobo Meritz, KOCREF I and KOCREF III. In November 2005, Hong Kong's government listed the world's largest IPO for Link

---

[1] Source: the National Association of Real Estate Investment Trusts (NAREIT), www.REIT.com.

Case Study 1: The Rise of Australian REITs

(This case study is contributed by courtesy of Peter Verwer, CEO of the Asia Pacific Real Estate Association (APREA))

The evolution of Australian REITs followed several distinct phases, many of which are echoed in Asia's ongoing race to introduce REITs:

Property trusts — the early years

Unit trusts are an enduring feature of Australia's investment landscape, given the nation's early adoption of British common law trust principles. In 1956, Australia's High Court confirmed that unit trusts were entitled to significant tax advantages. In current terminology, this would be called "tax neutrality". That is, unit-holders are entitled to a proprietary interest in property assets and the income they generate. This court decision encouraged the formation of the first "prototype REIT" in 1959 — Hooker Investment Corporation's *Australian Lands Trust* — which was followed by dozens of other unit trusts in both the property and resources sectors.

The rise of institutions and developers

Institutional investors became interested in real estate ownership and development in the 1950s and 1960s. This trend was led by insurance companies searching for better and more diverse returns. After several false starts, real estate was viewed as an alternative to unattractive Commonwealth bond rates (then at 3.25%) and as a potential hedge against skyrocketing inflation, particularly after the onset of the Korean War. In short, insurance companies resolved to become more active investment managers. Fuelling these changes, Australian governments lifted bans on real estate investment by insurance companies and relaxed planning rules.

At the same time, major developers transformed their business models and sought closer links with institutional investors. The invention of curtain wall construction and air conditioning rendered entire swathes of Australia's pre-war stock obsolete. Plus, technological changes allowed for larger (cheaper) buildings that delivered scale (and bigger rent rolls). Australia's emerging services economy fuelled demand for office space. Meanwhile, the nation's huge post-war migration programme drove vast suburban building programmes. At the centre of these new suburbs were shopping centres, which became an institutional asset class almost immediately.

The launch of publicly traded REITs — servicing a growing middle class

The first Australian REIT (then called a "LPT") was listed in April 1971 by GPT — the fund management arm of developer Lend Lease. It was soon followed by *Darling Property Fund* in 1972, launched by the British Merchant Bank Darling and Co. These listed vehicles and a swathe of unlisted property trusts fed booming demand for high-yielding

(Continued)

(*Continued*)

investment products from Australia's newly wealthy middle class. A major attraction of property trusts was their tax neutrality. Nevertheless, property trusts competed with equities and resource-based unit trusts. Demand for property trusts ran hot and cold, often shaped by the latest boom or crash of resource stocks, such as nickel.

Incredibly, by the late 1970s, property accounted for around 72% of all unit trust allocations, compared to 16% for equities and 12% for other investments.

The modern REIT era — born of crisis

There is no distinct REIT code in Australia, unlike REIT markets in most other countries.

REITs (with their tax advantages) were a legacy of British trust law which was inserted into Australia's 1936 *Income Tax Assessment Act*. However, by the late 70s and early 80s, the collapse of several high-profile trusts led to calls for clearer ground rules.

In 1985, the Australian Government added Division 6C Part IIIA to the *Income Tax Assessment Act*. Division 6C established a rule that tax neutrality was available only to property unit trusts that existed to generate and distribute rental income — which became understood as "passive income" as opposed to the "active income" of trading companies.

The listed and unlisted trust industry then moved into overdrive — in 1987, there were already around 450 funds of all types in existence (with FUM of close to A$52 billion in today's dollars). Then came the perfect storm of the 1987 stock market crash, economic recession in 1990 and a financial crunch. The sputtering economy led first to a huge rotation into unlisted property and then a liquidity crisis as nervous investors tried to retrieve their savings.

The run on property trusts prompted the Australian Government to freeze redemptions for 12 months. Confidence in the unlisted property trust model was shattered. As a result, most property syndicates listed and many of the work-outs from distressed property businesses were established as new firms, most of which proceeded to list on the Australian Stock Exchange. The market mayhem also triggered a major overhaul of legislation for corporations, management investments and REITs, in particular. It also led to a bigger role for the Australian Securities Investment Commission (ASIC).

The birth of "managed investment scheme" rules, the concept of a "responsible entity", the embedding of Australia's unique "stapled security" structure and more transparent governance and disclosure practices all hail from this period. The Government's new legislative templates also clarified the concessional tax treatment of REITs, including lower withholding taxes. As a further spur, the Australian Government introduced compulsory superannuation in 1992. The modern REIT era had begun.

Growth, experimentation and re-booting

Two decades of REIT market growth in statistics:

- July 1996: a handful of REITs — fund under management (FUM) of A$10 billion
- July 2002: 45 REITs — FUM of A$42 billion

(*Continued*)

(*Continued*)

- September 2007 (pre-GFC peak): 70 REITs — FUM of A$148 billion, a 253% increase in five years
- March 2009 (post-GFC trough): 66 REITs — FUM of A$47 billion, a 68% peak to trough decline.

In July 2015, Australia's public REIT market manages A$121 billion in less than 50 funds. The early part of the century witnessed a growing appetite for higher returns driven by development activity, offshore investment and leverage. The GFC ended this experimentation. Since then, A-REITs have recapitalised and stabilised their income streams. REIT managers are also exploring the "real/alternative assets" arena — including, infrastructure, retirement living, child care and renewables, to name a few. In a final twist, industry and government are close to finalising new rules that will provide Australia's REITs with a distinct legislative home — a REIT Code within the nation's revised managed investment rules.

REIT, valued at US$2.5 billion, on the Hong Kong Stock exchange.[2] Despite having a head-start in listing Australian type LPTs on Malaysia's stock exchange in 1989[3], the Malaysian LPT market was stagnant with lukewarm responses from investors. In September 2005, the Malaysian government rebranded LPTs into modern REITs with tax-transparency status. It introduced the first Islamic REIT — Al-Aqar Healthcare REIT, on 10 August 2006 following the guidelines of the Shariah Advisory Council (SAC).

Taiwan established the first commercial REIT via the listing of the NT$ 6 billion (approximately US$200 million) Fubon 1 in March 2004. Fubon 1 REIT was structured as a close-end fund with an initial portfolio of four buildings in Taipei — Fubon Life Insuarance office building, Fubon Zhong Shan office building, Tien Mu Fubon office building and Lun Building shopping centre. The first REIT in Thailand, CPN Retail Growth Property Fund (CPNRF), was set up using a mutual fund structure by the Bangkok-based Central Pattana on 11 August 2005. On 11 October 2010, the Securities and Exchange Commission of Thailand (SEC) passed a new

---

[2] The initial portfolio consists mainly of shopping center and car parks owned by the Hong Kong Housing Authority. http://www.ft.com/intl/cms/s/0/4885b69e-5d62-11da-8cde-0000779e2340.html#axzz3aAtO0ib3

[3] Arab-Malaysian First Property Trust (AMFPT) was the first Malaysian LPT listed on the Kuala Lumpur Stock Exchange (KLSE) main board on 28 August 1989. Two other property trusts: the First Malaysia Property Trust (FMPT) and Amanah Harta Tanah PNB (AHTP) were respectively listed on 23 November 1989 and 28 December 1990. FMPT was subsequently delisted 16 July 2002 following a voluntary takeover offer by its substantial shareholder, Commerce Asset Holdings Berhad.

regulatory framework to path the way for REITs to replace the old property fund model. The first REIT IPO structured as a REIT, Impact Growth REIT, with total issued value of 20 billion baht (US$626 million), was offered to local investors in October 2014.

The REIT idea has also gained tractions in other new Asian markets. In August 2014, the Securities and Exchange Board of India (Sebi) gave the green light that may pave the way for REITs to be listed on Indian exchanges. In December 2014, the Chinese government selected four cities — Beijing, Shanghai, Guangzhou and Shenzhen, to set up pilot REIT programmes on affordable rental housing.

2. The Rise of Singapore REITs (SREITs)

The idea of introducing Real Estate Investment Trusts (REITs) to Singapore was first mooted by the Property Market Consultative Committee[4] in 1986, as part of the strategies to revitalise the sluggish property market. The government, via the Monetary Authority of Singapore (MAS), responded to the REIT idea 13 years later by unveiling the Guidelines on Property Funds on 14 May 1999, two years after the 1997 Asian Financial Crisis. However, the guidelines were slow to attract interests of private developers in Singapore. The ambiguity about the preferential tax treatment in the original Guidelines was one barrier for private developers to create REITs in Singapore.

In July 2001, the Inland Revenue Authority of Singapore (IRAS) cleared the hurdle on the tax treatment by allowing pre-taxed flow-through of income as dividends to REIT investors.[5] CapitaLand Limited tested the market by launching the first REIT IPO — SingaMall Property Trust (SPT), which owned three shopping malls (Junction 8, Tampines Mall, Funan the IT Mall) in November 2001. The S$530 million SPT IPO was the largest IPO exercise since the launch of the Singapore Telecommunications (SingTel) IPO in 1993. Unfortunately, the low book order of only 78% of the SPT IPO by retail and institutional investors led its sponsor, CapitaLand Limited, to scrap the IPO on 12 November 2001. In July 2002, the SPT was restructured and re-launched with the same three retail mall properties under the new name CapitaMall Trust (CMT), but with a smaller tranch size of 213 million units. The IPO units were oversubscribed by five times by retail and institutional investors (Case Study 2).

---

[4] The Property Market Consultative Committee was set up with representatives from the government and the private sector to look into ways to bolster the property market that was badly hit by the economic recession in 1985. The committee has come up with an action plan, with setting up REIT being one of the recommendations to stimulate the embattled property market.
[5] Rashiwala, Kalpana "REITs clear hurdle with IRAS" *Business Times*, July 24, 2001.

Case Study 2: CapitaMall Trust (CMT) — *Lessons from the first failed attempt*

CapitaLand Limited (CapitaLand) made the first attempt to list its maiden SREIT — SingMall Property Trust (SPT), on the mainboard of the Singapore Exchange in November 2001. However, only 80% of the 530 million SPT IPO units were subscribed, causing CapitaLand to abort the flotation of the SPT on 21 November 2001. The lack of investor education could be one reason for the poor acceptance for REIT, which is a relatively new product in Singapore. The unexpected surge in both debt and equity capital raisings by DBS group (a new share placement of $1.09 billion), Singapore Telecommunications (a $1.5 billion bond issue) and Singapore Airlines (a $437 million bond) during the SPT's initial price offering period could have drawn investors away from the relatively untested new REIT issues from the market.

CapitaLand Limited rebranded the failed retail mall trust and re-launched it under the CapitaMall Trust (CMT) in July 2002, which has been renamed as CapitaLand Mall Trust in 2015. CMT owns the same three major Singapore shopping malls — Tampines Mall, Junction 8 and Funan IT Mall (renamed as Funan DigitaLife Mall), but the properties were revalued in June 2002 at S$930 million, which increased by $35 million compared to valuation in October 2001 (Table CS1-1). A smaller public IPO tranch of 213 million units out of the total of 738 million issued units were offered to public and institutional investors. A book-running for a price range from S$0.90 to S$0.96 per unit exercise was conducted. The CMT IPO was five times over-subscribed, and the CMT units were priced at $0.96 per unit.

Table CS1-1. Initial portfolio of the three retail malls of CMT.

Independent valuer date of valuation initial property portfolio:	CB Richard Ellis 15 October 2001			CB Richard Ellis 01 June 2002		
	Net lettable area		Market value	Net lettable area		Market value
	sqf	sqm	($million)	sqf	sqm	($ million)
Tampines Mall	312,372	29,020	$409.00	312,526	29,035	$438.00
Junction 8	249,569	23,186	$295.00	248,471	23,084	$301.00
Funan the IT Mall	248,375	23,075	$191.00	248,622	23,098	$191.00
Sub-Total	810,316	75,281	$895.00	809,619	75,217	$930.00

Source: CMT IPO Prospectus, 2002.

The initial structure of CMT is shown in Figure CS1-1. It appointed CapitaMall Trust Management Limited (renamed as CapitaLand Mall Trust Management Limited)

(Continued)

(Continued)

("CMTML" or the "Manager"), an indirect wholly-owned subsidiary of CapitaLand, was appointed as the asset manager of CMT, and also the property management function is outsourced to another CapitaLand's wholly owned subsidiary, CapitaLand Retail Management Pte Ltd.

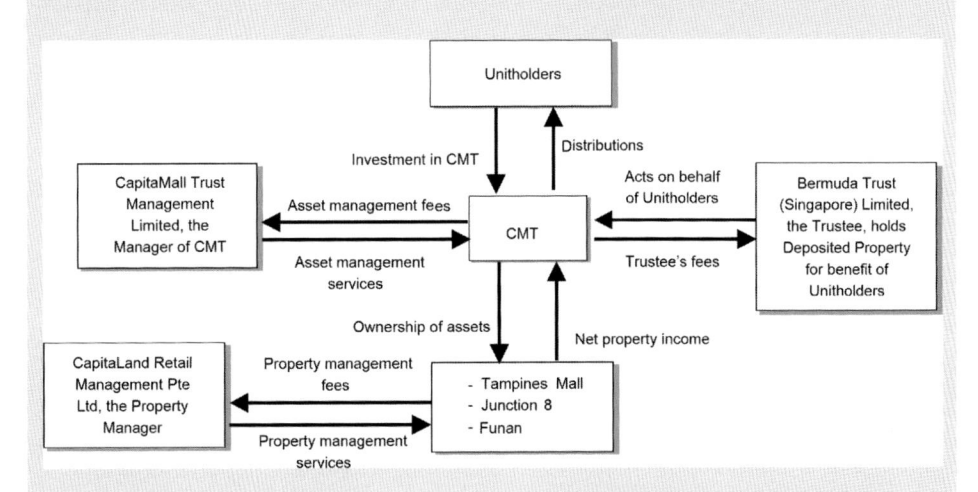

Figure CS1-1. The structure of CMT at IPO.
Source: CMT IPO Prospectus, 2002.

The success in the re-launch of CMT has laid an important foundation in the REIT chapter in Singapore. In the revamped CMT IPO, pricing of the CMT units was more attractive, estimated at 2% discount to the Net asset value (NAV) compared to the earlier attempt that priced the IPO at 2.7% premium. The forecast yields ranging between 7.06% and 7.73% have been improved. In addition, the sponsor, CapitaLand, has also articulated a convincing growth story in the IPO with a steady pipeline of new assets injection. The placement of the public tranch has been significantly reduced in the CMT IPO. 182 million units, which amount to 24.66% of the total issued units, have also been placed out to the cornerstone investors prior to the IPO. These key changes made to SPT offer valuable lessons for other REITs that plan for listing on the Singapore Exchange, and they are summarised in Table CS2-2.

(Continued)

(Continued)

Table CS2-2. Difference between SPT and CMT IPOs.

	SingMall property trust	CapitaLand mall trust	
Net Asset Value (NAV)	719.75[1]	729.605[2]	
Total issued units (million)	740	738	
IPO unit (million)	530	213	
Issue price (S$/Unit)	$1.00	$0.90	$0.96
Total issued value ($million)	$740.00	$664.20	$708.48
Premium (discount) to NAV	2.8%	−9.0%	−2.9%
Forecast earning yield:2002	5.75%	7.53%	7.06%
Forecast earning yield:2003	6.05%	7.73%	7.25%
Annual management fee	0.50%–0.70%[3]	0.25%[3]	
Performance fee		2.85%[4]	
Acquisition fee	1.00%[5]	1.00%[5]	
Divestment fee	0.50%[6]	0.50%[6]	
Cornerstone investors (units)	0	182[7]	

[1] Date of statement as on 16 November 2001.
[2] Date of statement as on 30 April 2002.
[3] Based on the value of deposited properties.
[4] Based on the gross revenue.
[5] Based on purchase price paid by CMT.
[6] Based on sale price (after deducting the interest of any co-owners or co — participants) of any real estate sold or divested.
[7] Unit owned before IPO (million) (does not include 65 million units owned by NTUC Investment Pte Ltd): NTUC Fairprice Co-operative (65 million); ING REIT Investments (Asia) B.V. (37 million); BT Funds Management Limited (30 million) and PGGM (50 million).
Source: SPT and CMT Prospectuses in 2001 and 2002.

Built on the success of CMT IPO debut, Ascendas Land (Singapore) Pte Ltd, a wholly-owned subsidiary of Jurong Town Corporation (JTC), partnered Australian-based Macquarie Goodman Industrial Management Pty Limited (MGIM) to launch the second Singapore REIT, Ascendas REIT (A-REIT), which owns a portfolio of eight business parks, light industrial and built-to-suit properties. The IPO raised S$240 million through the placement of 272.5 million units, which represent 50% of the total A-REIT issued units, at S$0.88 per unit.

The SREIT market has undergone a rapid phase of expansion with a large influx of new REIT IPOs into the SREIT market during the period from 2002 to 2008. The record number of new REIT IPOs was observed in 2006. The subprime

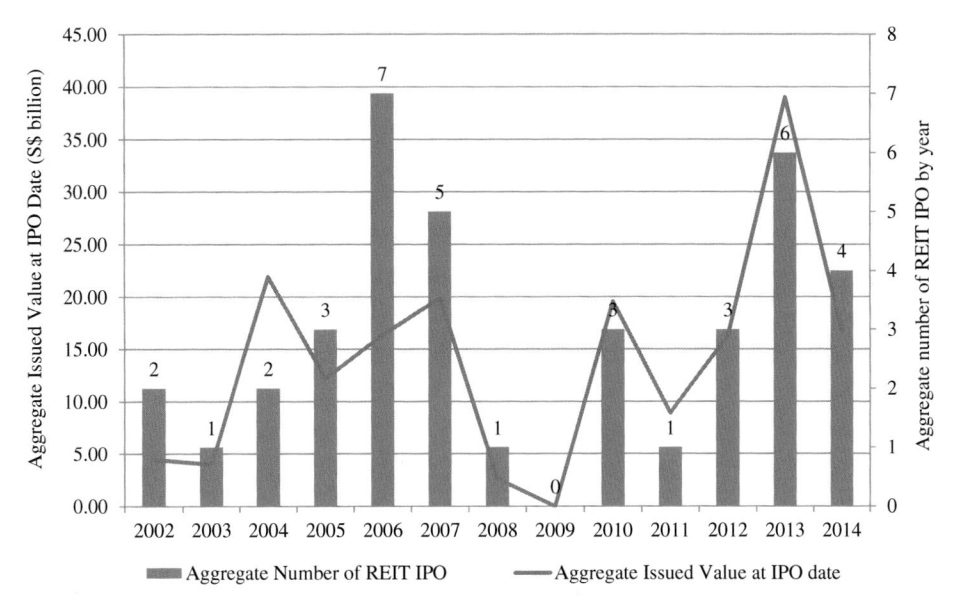

Figure 1. REIT IPOs in Singapore (2002–2014).
Source: Bloomberg and the Author.

crisis in 2007 brought a temporary respite to new REIT IPOs in 2009. The second REIT IPO wave started from 2010, and hit the peak of S$39.01 billion in terms of value raised through REIT IPOs in 2013 (Figure 1). As of 2015, there are 38 REITs and REIT-like securities (including five stapled securities and five business trusts[6]) listed on the Singapore Exchange with an aggregate market capitalisation of S$70.35 billion (as of May 2015). Figure 2 shows the aggregate market capitalisation for active listed REITs. Details of these securities are summarised in Appendix 1. By market capitalisation, Singapore is the second-largest REIT market in Asia, and third-largest in the Asia Pacific region, after Australia and Japan (Figure 3).

3. Reasons for Setting up SREITs

Most Asian real estate companies operate in the traditional asset-heavy model by developing and holding on to their commercial properties for long-term investment purposes. After the Asian Financial Crisis in 1997, many developers faced severe liquidity crunches. On the one hand, banks were reluctant to extend more loans to real estate projects. On the other hand, developers were not able to dispose of chunky

---
[6] Two business trusts — Perennial China Retail Trust and Forterra Trust (former Treasury China Trust), were de-listed from the Singapore Exchange in 2015.

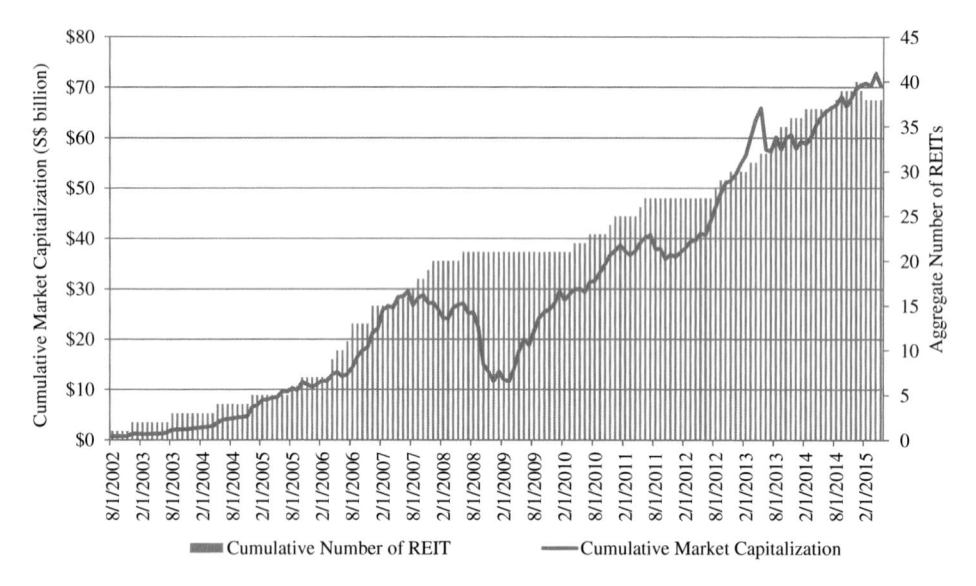

Figure 2. Aggregate market capitalisation of active REITs from 2002–2015.
Source: Datastream and the Author.

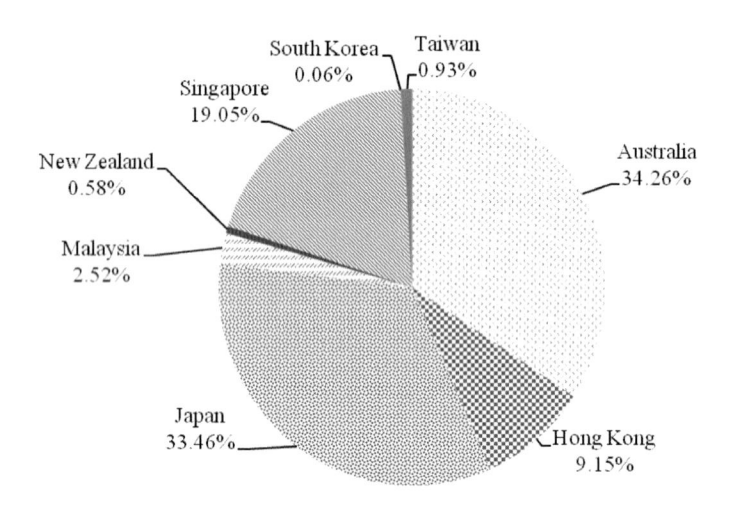

Figure 3. Asia-Pacific REIT markets by aggregate market capitalisation in 2014 (in US$)[#].
 # For SREITs, 34 REITs and Stapled Securities are represented in the sample.
Source: Bloomberg and the Author.

commercial real estate in the sluggish property markets. At that time, the Asian real estate capital market was thin and institutional funds were under-represented in the sector. In the late 1990s, firms owning large portfolios of commercial real estate used creative "*off balance sheet*" securitisation technology to raise capital abroad without being compelled to sell their real estate assets at significant discounts. The first commercial real estate backed securities were issued on the Neptune Orient Lines (NOL) Building at Alexandra Road in December 1998, and raised S$185 million. Other developers also issued commercial real estate-backed bonds on office properties and shopping malls, such as Raffles City Complex, Six Battery Road, 268 Orchard Road, Century Square, and Wisma Atria, to raise new capital and reduce gearing in their balance sheets.

MAS revised the guidelines on Asset Securitisation (note 628) on 20 August 2000 by imposing stricter clean sale and separation requirements on the "*off balance sheet*" structure. The changes significantly increase the costs of securitisation financing. Developers were compelled to consolidate the securitised properties back to their books. In 2001, developers started to explore the REIT vehicle as an alternative channel to unlock book values of commercial properties in their portfolios.

The successful listings of CMT and Ascendas REIT in 2002 paved the way for more developers to use REITs to liquidate commercial real estate assets. CapitaLand spun-off four office buildings (Capital Tower, 6 Battery Road, StarHub Centre, Robinson Point), 34 shop houses in the Bugis Street/Queen Street area and two carparks (Golden Shoe Carpark and Market Street Carpark) into its second REIT — CapitaCommercial Trust (CCT) in December 2003 (Case Study 3).[7] Developers use the REIT vehicle as an "*exit strategy*" to unlock the values of their commercial real estate assets.[8] By converting relatively illiquid real estate assets into liquid REIT securities, developers could operate in a more nimble and efficient "*asset light*" model with reduced assets in their balance sheets. By retaining controlling stakes in REITs,[9] developers continue to enjoy a stable income stream from commercial properties, while at the same time, substantially cutting down their debt burden in their balance sheets. They also generate recurring fees by providing real estate fund management services to REITs. Traditional "*brick and mortar*" developers, such as CapitaLand Limited, Mapletree Investment Private Limited, Fraser Centrepoint Limited and others, rode on the REIT bandwagon to aggressively grow their real estate financial services businesses. Third-party asset managers, such as ARA Asset Management Limited

---

[7] Keppel REIT was also established through distributions in specie of Keppel REIT units to the shareholders of the sponsor, Keppel Land, on 28 November 2005.

[8] The outbreak of severe acute respiratory syndrome (SARS) in Singapore in February 2003 adversely impacted both the stock market and property market in Singapore. Stocks prices of many of Singapore's publicly listed developers were traded at significant discounts to their net asset values (NAVs). The property market in Singapore was also in doldrums, which made it difficult for developers to sell their commercial real estate without taking large discounts to their values.

[9] In the US, the 5/50 rules, where the five larger shareholders should not hold more than 50% of interests in a REIT, which restricts large block holdings by limiting major shareholders' stake to not more than 10%. The rule is not applicable to SREITs.

Case Study 3: CapitaCommercial Trust (CCT) — *The establishment through distribution in specie of units*

CapitaCommercial Trust (CCT), which was renamed CapitaLand Commercial Trust in 2015, was established by way of a capital reduction exercise of the sponsor, CapitaLand, and also a distribution in specie ("Distribution in Specie") of CCT units to shareholders on 6 February 2004. In the first of its kind spin-off through the REIT structure, the sponsor, CapitaLand, distributed 60% of the issued units in CCT to its shareholders, who received 200 CCT units free of charge for every 1,000 ordinary shares they own in CapitaLand. CapitaLand would inject seven commercial properties (with an aggregate appraised value of S$2.018 billion) into CCT's portfolio upon establishment (see Table for details of the properties). Based on the estimated net asset value of S$1.469 billion as on 31 December 2003, and the total number of CCT units of 839,117, the CCT units were estimated at $1.75 per unit.

The distribution in specie was a win-win exercise for both the CapitaLand and its shareholders. The shareholders could receive separate REIT units that allowed them indirect access to investing in commercial real estate. The spin-off exercise generates benefits to the sponsor in the following ways:

- Achieving a more balanced portfolio of asset mix and income streams
- Enhancing capital productivity and improving return on asset (ROA) and return on equity (ROE)
- Increasing fee income from an expanded property fund management platform
- Potential re-rating of CapitalLand's share price

The financial impact of the distribution in specie is shown in Table CS3-1. The total asset value of the sponsor has reduced by 8.5%, but the earnings before interest and tax (EBIT) dropped by only 5.9% because the sponsor continues to receive partially the distributable income from CCT based on the 40% stake they retain in CCT. The total and net borrowing declined by 6.9% and 8.5%, respectively, and the spin-off exercise delivered positive wealth to CapitaLand's shareholders as reflected in the increases in ROA and ROE to 2.65% and 1.85%, respectively, compared to the ROA and ROE of 2.62% and 1.73%, respectively, before the distribution in specie exercise.

Table CS3-1. Financial effects of the distribution in specie.

	Before the distribution in specie	After the distribution in specie	Changes
Profit and Loss Account	($'000)	($'000)	(%)
EBIT	595,591	560,720	−5.9%
PATMI	105,254	94,558	−10.2%
EPS (basic) (cents)	4.2	3.8	−9.5%
EPS (fully diluted) (cents)	4.2	3.7	−11.9%

Table CS3-1. (Continued)

	Before the distribution in specie	After the distribution in specie	Changes
Balance Sheet			
Asset value (S$ billion)	17,600,000	16,100,000	−8.5%
Property value (S$billion)	14,500,000	13,300,000	−8.3%
Issued share capital	2,517,350	2,517,350	0.0%
Share premium account	3,429,376	2,539,369	−26.0%
Shareholders' funds	6,077,579	5,159,271	−15.1%
NTA	6,041,438	5,123,130	−15.2%
NTA per Share (S$)	2.4	2.04	
Total borrowings	7,548,334	7,027,278	−6.9%
Cash and cash equivalents	1,476,486	1,450,754	−1.7%
Net borrowings	6,071,848	5,576,524	−8.2%
Financial Ratios[#]			
ROA	2.62%	2.65%	0.03%
ROE	1.73%	1.85%	0.12%
Debt equity ratio	0.75	0.78	0.03
Interest cover ratio	3.67	4.02	0.35
Interest servicing ratio	5.52	5.85	0.33

[#] Changes in the ratios are computed as the difference before and after the distribution in specie

Legend:
EBIT   Earnings before interest and tax
PATMI   Profit after tax and minority interest
EPS   Earnings per share
NTA   Net tangible asset
ROA   Return on assets
ROE   Return on equity
Source: CCT and the Author.

and Pacific Star Group, have emerged to offer independent real estate asset and fund management services to REITs.

Real estate assets are usually priced at significant discounts to their net asset values (NAVs), when they are held in developers' books.[10] By separating real estate with

---

[10] Lee, N.J., Sing, T.F. and Tran, Dinh Hoang (2013), "REIT Share Price and NAV Deviations: Noise or Sentiment?" *International Real Estate Review*, Vol. 16, No. 1, pp. 28–47.

stable income streams from the more volatile development businesses of developers, real estate assets could be more fairly priced by the market. In addition to accessing lower cost capital, developers who set up REITs could also generate additional fee-based income by offering asset management and property management services to REIT investors. For investors, REITs offer an alternative option to invest in income generating commercial real estate.

4. REIT Growth Strategies

Structured as closed-end funds, SREIT unit prices are directly determined by the market. They can either be traded at discounts or premiums to NAVs. As asset management fees are pegged to asset NAVs, SREIT managers have incentives to pursue active growth strategies to create values for REIT unit-holders. Two growth strategies — organic growth and dynamic growth, are commonly used by REIT managers to expand asset portfolios. SREIT managers fund the asset growth strategies by using new debt and/or issuing new equity units via secondary public offers to existing unit-holders and new investors.

REITs pursue dynamic growth strategies by acquiring yield-accretive assets. The market timing is essential in the acquisition of new properties. During the recovery phase of the property cycle from 2003 to 2008, the supply of fairly valued commercial and industrial real estate was strong because sponsors were eager to raise new capital through divestments of assets in their portfolios, and manufacturers were also open to sell and lease-back their properties to generate new operating capital. Rising stock prices were an important factor in driving acquisition activities, because SREITs were able to raise new capital in equity markets at relatively low costs. SREITs took the opportunity to aggressively expand their portfolios through yield-accretive acquisitions. Ascendas REIT (A-REIT) added 78 new properties to its initial portfolio of eight properties during the period of 2002–2008, with an estimated acquisition price of S$2.86 billion (Case Study 4). CapitaMall Trust (CMT) grew its portfolio through acquisitions of 11 new malls at aggregate prices of S$3.93 billion during the same period.

Organic growth to existing SREIT portfolios is conducted via asset enhancement initiatives (AEIs). The scope of AEIs is not confined to sprucing up physical structure and adding new features to existing buildings. REIT managers find creative ways to enhance the yield of existing real estate space. Tearing down and redeveloping an existing structure into a new building is one, but it is a costly option. CMT redeveloped one of its existing malls — Jurong Entertainment Center (JEC), into a new mall called JCube, which has an Olympic-size ice rink and an IMAX cinema. The new building doubled the leasable space to 210,000 square feet upon completion in

Case Study 4: Ascendas REIT (A-REIT) — *Aggressive Dynamic Growth Strategies*

On 05 November 2002, Ascendas Land (Singapore) Pte Ltd ("Ascendas") and Australian based Macquarie Goodman Industrial Management Pty Limited ("MGIM") jointly launched the IPO of the first business space and industrial REIT on the Singapore Exchange. The IPO offered a total of 272,500,000 units of A-REIT units (before the over-allotment option) to public and institutional investors representing 50% of the total A-REIT issue of 545,000,000 units at an issue price of between S$0.83 and S$0.88 per unit. The balance of units would be issued to cornerstone investors (15%) and the Sponsors (35%). The public tranch of the IPO was over-subscribed by five times on the closing of the offer on 13 November 2002. A-REIT units started trading on the Singapore Exchange on 19 November 2002. Based on the upper range of the unit price of $0.88 per unit, the forecast annualised yields were 8.0% and 8.2% for the FY2003 and FY2004, respectively.

The initial portfolio of A-REIT at IPO date comprising eight properties: four buildings at the Singapore Science Park — The Alpha, The Aries, The Capricorn, and The Gemini; three hi-tech/light industrial buildings — Techlink at Kaki Bukit and Techplace I and II at Ang Mo Kio; and the built-to-suit Honeywell Building at Changi Business Park. The initial portfolio was valued at approximately S$607.2 million (as at 1 August 2002). A-REIT is managed by Ascendas-MGM Funds Management Limited, which is a 60%:40% joint venture by Singapore-based Ascendas Investment Pte Ltd, a related company of Ascendas Land (Singapore) Pte Ltd, and Australian-based Macquarie Goodman Industrial Management Pty Limited. Ascendas acquired the 40% stake of Macquarie Goodman in the REIT manager on 12 March 2008, and has since managed the largest industrial REIT under the 100% wholly owned subsidiary, Ascendas Funds Management (Singapore) Limited.

As at 31 March 2014, A-REIT remained the largest business space and industrial property REIT in Singapore with a total asset value worth S$7.4 billion. As in the financial year ended on 31 March 2014, the number of A-REIT's properties has increased from 8 to 105, and the total value of assets has grown by 11.6 times from $636.4 million to S$7,400 million.

Based on the properties in A-REIT's portfolio as in the annual report FY2013/14, business and science park properties (including two business park properties in China) constitute 41% of the portfolio. The remainder of the portfolio is made up of high specification industrial properties and data centres (25%), logistics and distribution centres (19%) and light industrial properties/flatted factories (15%). A-REIT has aggressively expanded its portfolio through yield-accretive acquisition, organic growth and development investments. A-REIT's portfolio increases from eight at the IPO stage to about 105 through new acquisitions and developments (Figure CS4-1). The most rapid phase of growth in A-REIT's portfolio occurred in

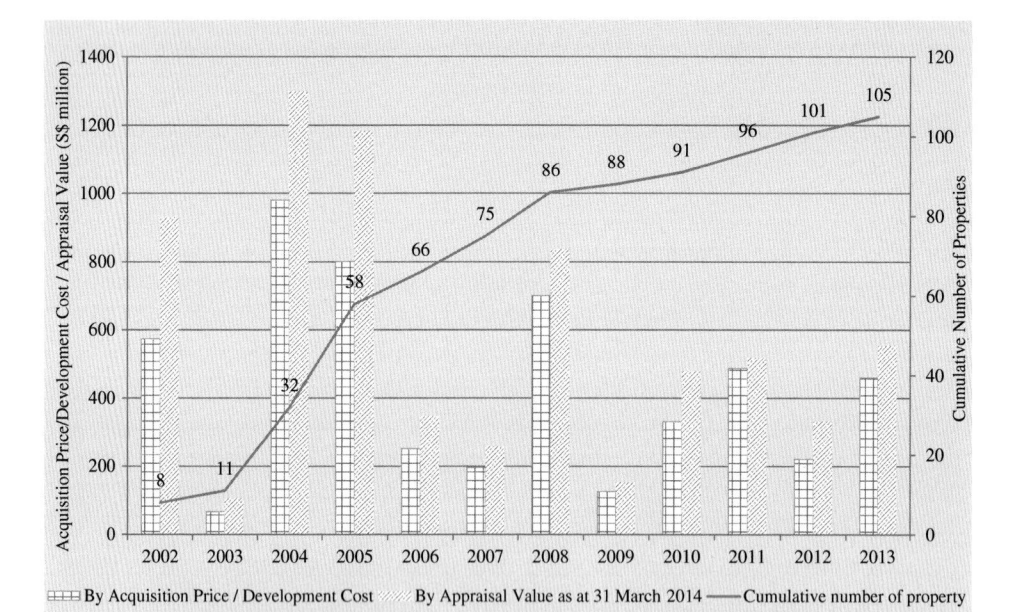

Figure CS4-1. Growth in real estate portfolio of A-REIT (2002–2013).
Source: A-REIT's Annual Report for the Financial Year 2013/2014.

2004 and 2005 with a total of $97 acquisitions at an aggregate acquisition cost of S$1.80 billion. Based on the valuation as at 31 March 2014, the value of the portfolio of 105 properties (including the 8 initial IPO properties) was estimated at S$6.991 billion, which accrued a 34.6% capital gain on the book, compared to the total costs of S$5.195 billion incurred for all the acquisitions and development projects till March 2014.

Following the revised Property Guidelines in 2005 that allow SREIT to undertake development activities of not more than 10% of the deposited property value, A-REIT embarked on its first development project in 2006 with the Courts Megastore, a warehouse cum retail store at Tampines. It has since completed 12 development projects with a total estimated cost of S$985.2 million. It achieved a cumulative unrealised development gains of S$320.9 million (32.6% over cost of development) based on the revaluation of the projects as at 31 March 2014 (Table CS4-1). A-REIT started to diversify geographically with the acquisition of two business park properties, Ascendas Z-link located in Beijing, China, from its sponsor, Acendas Group, in 2011, and A-REIT City @Jinqiaoa located in Shanghai, China, in 2013.

Table CS4-1. Changes in real estate portfolio size and financial performance.

	FY2013/2014	FY2012/2013	FY2002/2003*
No of Properties	105	103	8
Total Assets (S$ million)	$7,400.0	$7,000.0	$636.4
Net Lettable Area (sqm)	2,376,565	2,262,081	245,179
Tenant Base (local and international Companies)	1,300	1,200	300
Gross Revenue (S$ million)	$613.6	$575.8	$22.8
Net Property Income (NPI) (S$ million)	$436.0	$408.8	$16.5
Distribution Per Unit (DPU) (cents) (after performance fee)	14.24	13.74	2.78 (Annualized: 7.63 cents)

*Based on A-REIT's Annual Report 2003 for the period from IPO on 19 November 2002 to 31 March 2003, a period of 133 days
Source: A-REIT's Annual Report for the Financial Year 2013/2014.

2012. Redevelopment causes disruptions of income streams. A more popular strategy with only partial interruption to cash flows is by carrying out AEIs in phases. Value creation is made through decanting low-yielding space or space in less prime location to give way for high-yielding space. IMM Building is one example of an AEI that has generated positive returns to unit–holders (Case Study 5).

Dynamic and organic growth strategies generate positive economies of scale effects that allow SREITs to operate more efficiently and deliver positive returns to shareholders.[11] The results were evident in the significant premiums to NAV during the rapid growth phase (2005-2008) (Figure 5).[12]

Small REITs are potential targets for takeover by hostile acquirers.[13] Mergers and acquisitions (M&A) allow acquiring REITs to aggressively expand asset portfolios in

---

[11] Sham, Hiu Ting, Sing, Tien Foo and Tsai, I-Chun, (2009), "Are there efficiency gains for larger Asian REITs?" *Journal of Financial Management of Property and Construction*, Vol. 14, No. 3, pp. 231–247.

[12] Lee, N.J., Sing, T.F. and Tran, D.H. (2013), "REIT Share Price and NAV Deviations: Noise or Sentiment?" *International Real Estate Review*, Vol. 16, No. 1, pp. 28–47.

[13] From the corporate governance perspective, REIT managers may use acquisitions as an "empire building" exercise to entrench their roles and prevent potential takeovers. See Shleifer, A. and Vishny, R. W. (1997), "A Survey of Corporate Governance," *Journal of Finance*, Vol. 52, No. 2, pp. 737–83.

Case Study 5: IMM Building — *Organic growth through asset enhancement initiatives (AEI)*

REIT managers find various creative asset enhancement initiatives (AEI) to increase values of properties in the portfolios and deliver wealth to unitholders. CapitaLand Mall Trust (CMT), as the largest retail landlord in Singapore, enhances the retail environment and improves the attractiveness of the malls to keep abreast with stiffer competition in the retail market. Some strategies commonly adopted in the mall AEI include:

- Decantation of lower-yield space and conversion of the space into higher-yield space
- Reconfiguration of retail units to optimise space efficiency
- Maximising the use of common areas, such as bridge space, and converting mechanical and electrical areas into leasable space
- Upgrading amenities, adding play and rest areas, providing advice on shop front design and creating better shopper circulation to enhance the attractiveness of our malls

About CMT's acquisition and AEIs on IMM Building

Opened in 1991, IMM Building, located in the western part of Singapore, was originally intended to be used as an international merchandise mart, run by a consortium led by Yaohan. In 2000, IMM underwent a major revamp to reposition itself as a family entertainment and lifestyle centre. As at 31 January 2003, it attracted a diverse mix of 535 tenants with anchors such as Giant hypermarket (124, 138 square feet (sqf)), leading electronics store Best Denki (27,722 sqft) and Daiso, a trendy Japanese discount store (37,590 sqft). These anchors, together with over 100 specialty shops dealing in furniture and home appliances, provide the mall with a competitive point of difference to attract shoppers island-wide.

On 26 June 2003, CMT completed the acquisition of IMM for $264.5 million, which was at 5.5% discount to the appraised value of S$280 million as of 1 February 2003. The acquisition was financed through a combination of equity fund raising and additional borrowings. On 30 January 2004, CMT paid S$55.7 million to JTC as the upfront land premium for the lease term of 45 years ending 22 January 2049 for IMM.

IMM had a gross floor area of 1,426,504 square feet (sqf) as at 31 December 2014. More than 80% of IMM's gross rental income is derived from its retail space, which was predominantly on Levels 1, 2 and 3.

The mall embarked on a major AEI in 2006, spending $92.5 million. The upgraded IMM, opened in 2007, saw major enhancements, which include adding a new two-storey extension annex with a rooftop landscaped plaza on the former open carpark area, which was relocated to Level 5 after transferring decanted warehouse space an Level 5 down to Levels 2 and 3 (Figure CS4-2).

The AEI yielded an additional 53,700 square feet (sqf) of retail space on Levels 1 and 2 of the new extension annex. The AEI, costing about S$92.5 million, was completed in

(*Continued*)

CHAPTER 7 | The Rise of Singapore's Real Estate Investment Trust (SREIT) Market   179

(*Continued*)

Before AEI

After AEI

Figure CS4-2. IMM Building — Before and After AEI.

Photos courtesy of CapitaLand

the first quarter of 2008. The entire scope of work contributed to an incremental net property income (NPI) of $10.0 million per annum to achieve an ungeared Return On Investment (ROI) of 10.8%.

In May 2012, IMM underwent the first phase of major renovation to reposition itself as an outlet mall. Upon completion of this phase of renovation works in June 2013, IMM increased its total number of outlet brands from 19 to over 55, making it the largest outlet mall in Singapore. To further enhance its attractiveness as an outlet shopping destination, IMM started the second phase of its repositioning exercise in June 2014 to create space for more outlets. This round of AEI is complete with IMM now housing 85 outlet stores.

the shortest time. The subprime crisis has made small REITs more vulnerable to M&A. In 2008, Fraser & Neave (F&N) group acquired a 17.7% stake (125.6 million shares) in Allco Commercial REIT at $0.83 per share, and paid S$180 million for the entire stake in Allco REIT manager.[14] F&N renamed the REIT to Frasers Commercial Trust upon the acquisition. YTL Corporate Berhad, a Malaysian conglomerate, took over the control of Macquarie Prime REIT from Macquarie Bank in October 2008 through the acquisition of a 26% stake in Macquarie Prime REIT (MP REIT) and a 50% stake in the REIT manager, Prime REIT Management Holdings, for S$285 millon. MP REIT, which owned partial interests in two prime retail malls at Orchard Road — Wisma Atria and Ngee Ann City, was renamed to Starhill Global REIT following the acquisition. The third M&A involves AMP Capital's takeover of a 16.11% stake in MACARTHURCOOK Industrial real estate investment trust (MI Reit), and 50% in the REIT management and property management companies. The acquired REIT was traded in its new name — AIMS-AMP Capital Industrial REIT (AA REITs) on the Singapore Exchange with effect from 24 December 2009.

5. Code on Collective Investment Scheme (CIS) — Property Funds Guidelines

The Monetary Authority of Singapore (MAS), the *de-facto* Central Bank of Singapore, issued a set of Guidelines for Property Funds on 14 May 1999. The Guidelines laid down ground rules facilitating the establishment of SREITs. When announcing the 1999 Guidelines, the MAS stated that no special tax treatment was granted to property funds, and that they would be taxed according to the general tax principles as ordinary companies or trusts. On 23 May 2002, the MAS issued the Code on Collective Investment Scheme (CIS Code) pursuant to Section 321 of the Securities and Futures Act (Cap. 289), and the Property Fund Guidelines were subsumed under **Appendix 2** of the CIS Code.

When the Property Fund Guidelines were appended to the CIS Code in 2002, which was meant to regulate open-ended investments, SREITs were given two special exemptions under the CIS Code. First, SREIT managers were not required under the 2002 CIS Code to be licensed by MAS. Second, SREITs were not subject to the Singapore Code on Take-over and Merger. The Security

---

[14] Allco Commercial REIT was listed in March 2006 on the Singapore Exchange with an initial portfolio of S$683.9 million. Source: Reuters, "Singapore F&N buys Allco REIT stake, manager for $132mln," 7 July 2008.

Industry Council (SIC) extended the ambit of the Take-over Code to REITs on 8 June 2007.[15]

Since the introduction of the first Property Fund Guidelines in 1999, MAS has made various revisions to the Property Fund Guidelines contained in the CIS Code.[16] The major changes are found in 2005, 2007 and 2009. In October 2014, the MAS also published a consultative paper on "Enhancements to the Regulatory Regime Governing REITs and REIT Managers", and some of the recommendations have been adopted in the revised Property Fund Guidelines with effect from 2 July 2015 (See Appendix 2).

6. Features of SREITs

6.1 *Tax Treatment*

REITs pool capital from retail and institutional investors to invest collectively in income-producing properties. REITs are given tax transparency status subject to compliance with the investment and distribution conditions. Tax transparency is not automatically granted. REITs are required to apply for the favourable tax treatment from the Inland Revenue Authority of Singapore (IRAS) to exempt tax at source on distributable income for "Qualifying Unitholders".[17] In Singapore's Financial Year (FY) 2004/2005 Budget, tax exemptions on dividends received from SREITs were granted to individual investors, local or foreign, which give them double tax concessions. For foreign non-individual investors, dividends distributed from SREITs were subject to withholding tax at a reduced rate of 10%. In the same year, the government waived the stamp duty on the instruments of transfer of Singapore properties into REITs to be listed, or already listed on the SGX. In the FY2006/2007 Budget, the government further enhanced the Singapore's competitiveness as a listing hub for cross-border REITs by extending tax exemption

---

[15] The Take-over Code is applicable to SREITs after 2007, which indicates that a controlling unitholder who acquires 30% or more of the total SREIT units, and/or an existing unitholder holding between 30% and 50% of the total share, who intend to acquire more than 1% new shares in a SREIT, are obligated to make a general offer for the REIT.

[16] For more detailed discussions on the legal issues in relating to the changes to the Property Funds guidelines, refer to Lee, Suet Fern and Foo, Linda Esther, 2010, "Recent Legal and Regulatory Developments and the Case for Corporation," *Singapore Academy of Law Journal*, 22, pp. 36–65.

[17] These Qualifying Unitholders include Singapore residents, permanent residents, Singapore incorporated companies, town councils, statutory boards, registered charities, cooperative societies, trade unions, management corporation, clubs, and trade and industrial associations) and Singapore branch of a foreign company with special IRAS' waiver.

to foreign source of income received by SREITs. The tax concessions were subject to *"the sunset clause"*, which set an expiry date on the tax concessions only for income received on and before 31 March 2015.

In FY2015 budget, the government extended the income tax exemption to local and foreign sources of SREIT income received by individual investors for another five years with effect from 1 March 2015. However, the stamp duty remission for REITs on the purchase of local properties was not extended after 31 March 2015.[18]

6.2 Investment and Distribution Requirements

Based on the Property Fund Guidelines, SREITs must invest at least 75% of the total assets in income-producing real estate, which includes properties with leasehold or freehold interests, in or outside Singapore. Investments in real estate also take the forms of direct ownership or shareholding in an unlisted special purpose vehicle (SPV) constituted to hold real estate, and/or other listed REITs. These real estate assets in one form or another constitute a substantial proportion of portfolios of SREITs.

Investments in other non-core real estate assets are permitted, which may include investments in asset backed securities, listed or unlisted debt securities, listed or unlisted shares of local or foreign non-property corporations, government securities and securities issued by supra-national agencies or Singapore statutory boards; and holdings of cash and cash equivalent items. Revenue from the non-core real estate assets must not exceed 10% of the total revenue.

On the distribution requirement, SREITs must distribute at least 90% of their income back through dividends to individual unit holders in order to qualify for IRAS' tax concession at source. In the 2007 revisions to the Property Fund Guidelines, provision was made to allow REIT managers to distribute income in excess of profits subject to proper certification that excess distributions will not affect REITs' ability to fulfill their liabilities.

6.3 Development Activities

SREITs can undertake development activities, either on their own or jointly with others or by investing in unlisted property development companies, if they intend to acquire the developed property upon completion for investment purposes.

---

[18] Goh Eng Yeow, "Dropping REITs' stamp duty concessions helps level playing field," *The Straits Times*, 27 February, 2015.

However, SREITs are prohibited from undertaking development activities, and invest in vacant land and mortgages (except for mortgage-backed securities). This restriction does not prevent SREITs from investing in either real estate to be built on vacant land or uncompleted property developments.

The total contract value of property development activities undertaken and investments in uncompleted property developments should not exceed 25% of the deposited property value of SREITs with effect from July 2015. Property development activities do not include refurbishment, retrofitting and renovations.

CMT entered into a joint venture arrangement[19] with its sponsor — CapitaMall Asia, and CapitaLand Commercial Limited (a wholly owned subsidy of CapitaLand), to acquire a parcel of commercial land via the government's land tender at S$969 million for the Westgate, an integrated development located at Jurong Gateway, which consists of Westgate, a seven-storey lifestyle mall with 410,000 square feet (sqf) of net retail space, and Westgate Tower, a 20-storey office building with net space 304,963 sqf when completed in late 2014.[20]

Ascendas REIT completed 13 development projects, which were estimated at approximately S$985.2 million by the aggregate development costs (Table 1). Based on the valuation as on 31 March 2014, Ascendas REIT achieved an unrealised cumulative return of 32.57%.

6.4 *Aggregate Leverage Limit*

In the 2005 revisions of the Property Fund Guidelines, the aggregate leverage limit was set at 35% of the total asset in SREIT portfolio (based on the latest valuation). However, SREITs are allowed to increase the limit above 35% but not exceeding 60%, if a credit rating from one of the rating agencies — Fitch Inc., Moody's or Standard and Poor's, is obtained and disclosed to the public. The 2005 revisions categorise deferred payments into the total borrowings, which restricts REITs in financial engineering their cash flows to prop up yields in new acquisitions.[21]

---

[19] CapitaMalls Asia holds a 50% stake in the joint venture established via two special purpose vehicles — Infinity Mall Trust and Infinity Office Trust, while HSBC Institutional Trust Services (as trustee of CapitaMall Trust) holds 30% and CapitaLand hold the remainder 20%.

[20] Westgate Tower was sold to a consortium comprising Sun Venture Homes Private Limited and Low Keng Huat (Singapore) Limited for S$579.4 million on 23 January 2014.

[21] Borrowings should include bonds, notes, syndicated loans, bilateral loans or other debts. Deferred payments for acquired assets whether to be settled in cash or in REIT units are also included in the computation of aggregate leverage.

Table 1. Development projects undertaken by A-REIT.

No.	Development	Sector	Development cost (S$ million)	Revaluation as at 31 Mar 2014 (S$ million)	Date of completion
1	Courts Megastore	Warehouse Retail Facility	46.0	65.9	Nov 2006
2	Giant Hypermart	Warehouse Retail Facility	65.4	87.3	Feb 2007
3	HansaPoint @ CBP	Business Park	26.1	86.1	Feb 2008
4	15 Changi North Way	Logistics	36.2	48.4	Jul 2008
5	Pioneer Hub	Logistics	79.3	115.0	Aug 2008
6	1,3 and 5 Changi Business Park Crescent	Business Park	200.9	316.7	Feb 2009, Sep 2009, Dec 2010
7	71 Alps Avenue	Logistics	25.6	30.5	Sep 2009
8	38A Kim Chuan Road	High-Specs Industrial (Data Centres)	170.0	184.7	Dec 2009
9	90 Alps Avenue	Logistics	37.9	49.7	Jan 2012
10	FoodAxis @ Senoko	Light Industrial	57.8	78.1	Feb 2012
11	Four Acres Singapore	Science Park	58.7	57.3	Apr 2013
12	Nexus @one-north	Business Park	181.3	186.4	Sep 2013
TOTAL			**985.2**	**1,306.10**	

Source: A-REIT's Annual Report for the Financial Year 2013/2014.

The global financial crisis starting from end-2007 significantly reduced credit supply in the REIT markets. Banks and financial institutions were reluctant to extend credit facilities to REITs. SREITs with a large fraction of maturing debt faced serious delinquency risks. The refinancing risks have loomed large in the REIT markets in Singapore and other Asian countries in the aftermath of the 2007 crisis. In Japan, New City Residence Investment, a residential REIT, filed for bankruptcy under the Civil Rehabilitation Act (2000) with liabilities totaling US$1.1 billion (112.4 billion yen).[22] In Singapore, REITs affiliated with strong sponsors were able to weather through the liquidity crunches through short-term injection of new funds by sponsors. For example, Fraser Centrepoints, the sponsor

---

[22] Despite having a portfolio of properties with healthy occupancy rates, the Japanese REIT was forced to file for bankruptcy and was de-listed on 10 November 2008. Source: Taku Kato and Mari Murayama, "New City REIT Files Bankruptcy with $1.1 Billion Debt", Bloomberg News, October 9, 2008.

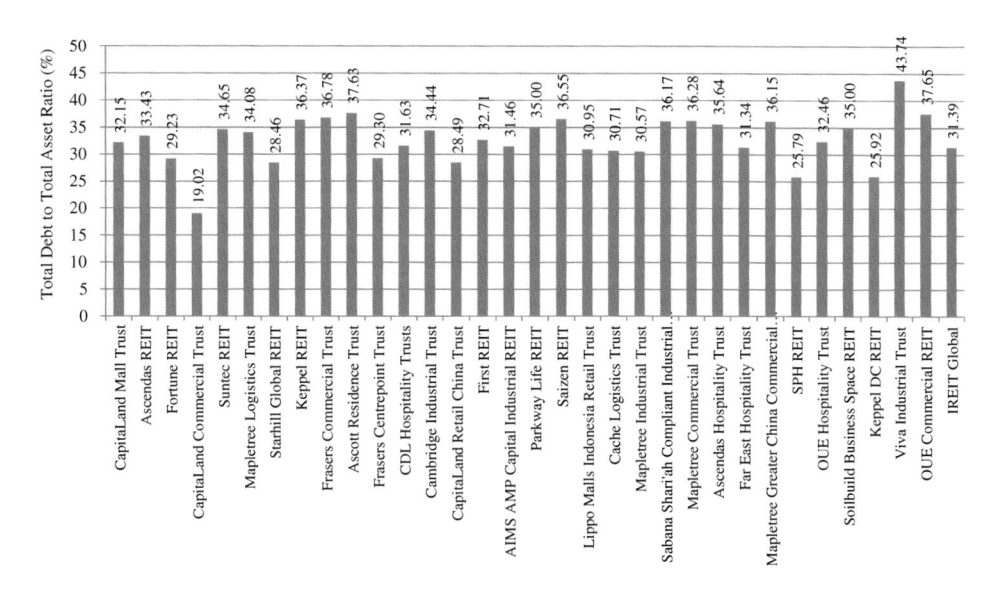

Figure 4. Total debt to total asset ratio as of June 2015.
Source: Bloomberg and the Author.

of the renamed Frasers Commercial Trust (FCOT) (the former Allco Commercial REIT), has helped to refinance $70 million short-term loans of the REIT expiring in November 2008, which was only five months after the REIT had been acquired.

During the subprime crisis period, declines in REIT asset values in the annual re-valuation exercise caused aggregate leverage limits of some SREITs to increase above the stipulated 35% level. On 9 January 2009, MAS issued a circular[23] to relax the aggregate leverage rules for SREITs when refinancing of mature debt. Increases in aggregate leveraging limit caused by decline in deposited property values during the revaluation process or refinancing of existing mature debt were not construed as a breach of the borrowing rules. SREITs were allowed to raise new debt earlier than the maturity of existing debt. The new funds raised solely for refinancing purposes would not be counted towards the aggregate leverage limit.

On 2 July 2015, MAS replaced the two-tiered aggregate leverage limit of 35% or 60% for SREITs with a single-tiered limit of 45% (See Appendix 2). Figure 4 shows that the total debt to total asset ratio of REITs (excluding business trusts) was averaged

---

[23] MAS circular No: CMD 01/2009, "Treatment of refinancing under the aggregate leverage limit."

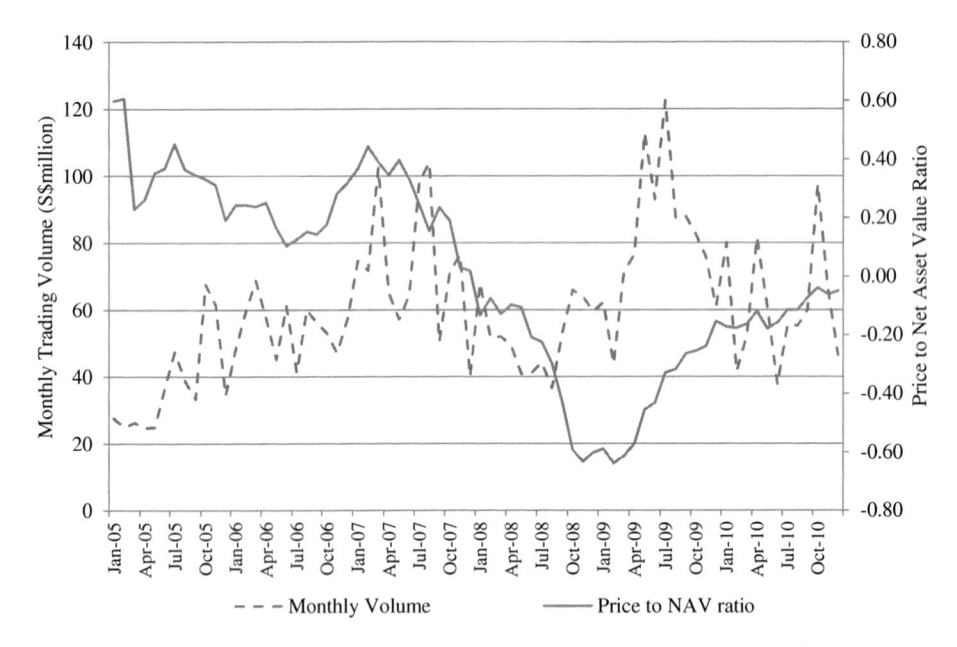

Figure 5. Price to net asset value ratio and trading volume of sample REITs.
Source: Lee, Sing and Tran (2013).

at 32.76%. Viva Industrial Trust has the highest debt ratio of 43.74%, which still falls below the 45% limit set in the new guidelines.

7. Cross-Border REITs

Diversification is not the main motivation of many REITs when they expand asset portfolios through acquisitions. Studies show that cross-border Asian REITs have higher risk premiums than REITs focusing on domicile real estate markets. REITs are more likely to achieve internal scale economies by specialising. However, REIT managers are required to have a broader range of expertise and knowledge to manage geographically diversified portfolios. Geographically diversified REITs may incur higher informational and operating expenses, because of diseconomies-of-scale from inefficiencies in operations.[24]

Sector-focus is the predominant strategy adopted by SREITs. Most commercial and industrial REITs exploit their home turf advantages by concentrating their acqui-

---

[24] Capozza, D. R., & Seguin, P. J., (1999). "Focus, transparency and value: the REIT evidence." *Journal of Real Estate Economics*, 27(4), 587–619.

sitions in local markets. However, for logistics and hospitality (serviced apartments) REITs, diversifying asset portfolios across regions is essential to offer efficient logistics and network solutions for potential tenants and clients. Mapletree Logistics Trust (MLT) started with an initial portfolio of 15 Singapore-based warehouses and industrial properties in 2005, and has since grown into a pan-Asian logistics REIT with 111 properties distributed across seven geographical markets (Singapore, Malaysia, Hong Kong, China, Japan, South Korea and Vietnam). The asset values have increased by 10 fold from S$422 million at the IPO to S$4.2 billion as of 31 March 2014. Ascott Residence Trust (ART) is a hospitality REIT that has invested in a geographically diverse portfolio of 86 properties including serviced residences, rental housing properties and other hospitality assets. ART's assets valued at about S$4 billion are spread across 36 cities in 13 countries in Asia Pacific and Europe.

Based on a sample of 245 properties in the portfolios of 17 SREITs with an estimated market value of US$20.17 billion as in 2006 and 2007, 55 of the assets, or 21.14% by net asset values in US$ terms, are located outside Singapore.[25] As at 2015, there were 22 SREITs holding foreign real estate, and they could be broadly divided into two categories (Table 2). The first group consists of Singapore-based REITs with geographically diversified portfolios. The small size of the local real estate market has driven these local REIT to diversify geographically. REITs in industrial and commercial real estate sectors, such as Ascendas REIT, Starhill Global REIT, and REITs in healthcare and nursing sector, such as Parkway REIT and First REIT, have started venturing overseas for new acquisitions, especially after the global financial crisis in 2008.

The second group of REITs, also known as cross-border REITs, holds mainly foreign real estate in the portfolios. Singapore's government has created a favourable tax environment since 2005[26] to actively attract foreign REITs to list in Singapore. These REITs bring a diverse range of foreign commercial real estate, which includes industrial parks in India (Ascendas India Trust), and retail malls in China (Capitaland Retail China Trust), Hong Kong (Fortune REIT), Indonesia (Lippo Malls Trust) and Japan (Croesus Retail REIT) to the markets (Table 2). In March 2013, Mapletree Investment, a Temasek-linked company, sponsored and launched the largest Singapore REIT IPO of 776,636,000 units in Mapletree Greater China Commercial Trust (MGCCT), a cross-border REIT, at an offering price of S$0.93 per unit (Case Study 6).

---

[25] Source: Cheok, S.M.C., Sing, T.F. and Tsai, I. (2011), "Diversification as a Value-Adding Strategy for Asian REITs: A Myth or Reality?" *International Real Estate Review*, Vol. 14, No. 2, pp. 184–207.

[26] It announced the waiver of stamp duties for properties acquired by REITs over a period of five years.

Table 2. Geographically diversified REITs and cross-border REITs.

No	REIT and other securities	Trust structure	Asset type	Regional distribution
1) Geographically Diversified SREITs				
1	Ascendas-Hospitality Trust	Stapled Securities	Hotels	Singapore, Australia, China, and Japan
2	Ascott Residence Trust	REIT	Serviced Apartments	Singapore, Australia, Belgium, China, France, Germany, Indonesia, Japan, Malaysia, Philippines, Spain, United Kingdom, Vietnam
3	CDL Hospitality Trust	Stapled Securities	Hotels	Singapore, Australia, Japan, Maldives and New Zealand,
4	Frasers Hospitality Business Trust	Business Trust	Serviced Apartments	Singapore, Australia, Europe, Japan and Malaysia
5	Cache Logistics Trust	REIT	Industrial	Singapore, Australia and Shanghai
6	Mapletree Logistics Trust	REIT	Industrial	Singapore, China, Hong Kong, Japan, Malaysia, South Korea and Vietnam
7	Ascendas REIT	REIT	Industrial	Singapore and China
	AIMS AMP Capital Industrial REIT	REIT	Industrial	Singapore and Australia
8	Fraser Commercial Trust	REIT	Retail and Office	Singapore and Australia
9	Keppel REIT	REIT	Office	Singapore and Australia
10	Starhill Global REIT	REIT	Retail and Office	Singapore, Australia, China, Japan and Malaysia
11	First REIT	RIET	Hospital, Hotel and Nursing Home	Singanpore, Indonesia and South Korea
12	ParkwayLife REIT	REIT	Hospital and Nursing Home	Singapore and Japan
2) Cross-border REITs				
13	CapitaRetail China Trust	REIT	Retail	China
14	Accordia Golf Trust	Business Trust	Golf courses	Japan
15	Croesus Retail Trust	Business Trust	Retail	Japan
16	Fortune REIT	REIT	retail	Hong Kong

(Continued)

Table 2. (*Continued*)

No	REIT and other securities	Trust structure	Asset type	Regional distribution
17	Indiabulls Properties Investment Trust	Business Trust	office and retail	India
18	IREIT Global	REIT	Office	Germany
19	Lipppo Malls Trust	REIT	Retail	Indonesia
20	Mapletree Greater China Commercial Trust	REIT	Retail and Office	Hong Kong and China
21	Religare Health Trust	Business Trust	Hospitals	India
22	Saizen REIT	REIT	Residential	Japan
23	Ascendas India Trust	Business Trust	Information Technology Park	India

Case Study 6: Mapletree Greater China Commercial Trust (MGCCT) — *Singapore's largest REIT IPO*

Mapletree Greater China Commercial Trust (MGCCT) is a Singapore-listed cross-border REIT that invests directly or indirectly in income-producing commercial real estate in the Greater China region. MGCCT was the largest SREIT IPO when launched on 7 March 2013. It successfully raised S$1.6.8 billion by placing out a total of 1.809 billion units comprising 1.73 billion base offer units and 0.79 billion over-allotment units at an offer price of S$0.93 per unit. Despite the subdued IPO environment in 2013, the IPO debut of MGCCT, a cross-border REIT with two commercial properties in Hong Kong and Beijing, was overwhelmingly received by attracting a total demand of S$19.9 billion from both institutional investors and retail investors. The institutional tranch and the retail tranch were over-subscribed by 38.1 times and 8.9 times, respectively. It recorded 10.8% gain on the first-day trading on the Singapore Exchange on 7 March 2013. The offer yields were projected at 5.6% and 6.1% for the first year (FY2013/14) and the second year (FY2014/15) of the listing, respectively.

MGCCT is managed by Mapletree Greater China Commercial Trust Management Ltd., a wholly-owned subsidiary of Mapletree Investments Pte Ltd. MGCCT's initial portfolio comprises Festival Walk, a premier retail and office building in Hong Kong, and Gateway Plaza, a premier Grade "A" office development with a retail atrium in Beijing. The two properties cover an aggregate gross floor area of approximately 2.4 million square feet and total lettable area of 1.9 million square feet (Table CS6-1).

(*Continued*)

(*Continued*)

Table CS6-1. Details of properties in the initial portfolio of MGCCT.

Property	Festival walk		Gateway plaza		Portfolio	
Property type	Office and retail		Office and retail			
Floor area (square feet)	Gross	Lettable	Gross	Lettable	Gross	Lettable
Overall	1,208,754	793,728	1,145,882	1,145,882	2,354,636	1,939,610
Office	228,665	213,982	1,019,503	1,019,503	1,248,168	1,233,485
Retail	980,089	579,746	126,389	126,389	1,106,478	706,135
Number of tenant	216		71		287	
Car park lots	830		692		1,522	
Gross revenue FY13/14 (S$ million)	$176		$58		$234	
Net Property Income FY13/14 (S$ million)	$137		$49		$186	
Appraised value as at 31 December 2012:						
Independent Appraiser:	Knight Frank	DTZ	Vigers	CBRE		
in Singapore dollar (S$ million)	$3,296	$3,344	$1,016	$1,017	$4,312[#]	
in Local currency ($million)	$20,700	$21,000	$5,165	$5,170		
Purchase price (S$ million)	$3,296		$1,013		$4,309	

[#] Based on the lowest of the two appraised values.
Source: IPO Prospectus of MGCCT.

The Acquisition of Festival Walk

Festival Walk is a premier retail and lifestyle mall comprising a seven-storey retail mall with a four-storey office and three floors of underground car parks. Centrally located in Kowloon Tong, it enjoys excellent connectivity to various parts of Hong Kong as well as mainland China. It is a multi-modal transportation hub directly linked to Kowloon Tong Mass Transit Railway (MTR) station, which is the interchange for Kwun Tong MTR Line, a bus interchange, local taxis and the East Rail Line linking Hong Kong directly to Shenzhen.

Mapletree Investments Pte Ltd (Mapletree), the sponsor of MGCCT, acquired Festival Walk from Swire Properties Limited at an agreed price HK$18.8 billion or about S$2.9 billion in August 2011. Festival Walk is Mapletree's first commercial property acquisition in Hong Kong. Hong Kong's property was injected into the initial portfolio when MGCCT was set up in February 2013 at a price of S$3.296 billion, which yielded a net capital gain of nearly 13.66% for Mapletree.

8. Alternative REIT Models — Business Trusts Stapled with REITs

In 2004, MAS introduced the business trust model, which is an investment vehicle that combines the roles of a trustee and an asset manager into a single entity, known as the "trustee-manager", to hold and operates business enterprises for the benefit of its beneficiaries who are unit-holders. The fiduciary responsibility to beneficiaries is placed squarely on a single trustee-manager. Investors or unit holders receive a steady dividend stream, but they do not have any operational control or shareholders' rights. The trustee-manager is professionally managed, and reports to a board, which comprises primarily independent directors. As of 2015, there are 24 registered business trusts, of which 13 have the REIT-like structure and hold income-producing real estate from overseas (Table 3A).

In some cases, issuers set up a business trust to run the active asset management business that generate recurring fee-based income, and a separate REIT vehicle to concurrently hold real estate assets that generate passive rental income. "Stapled securities" are created to link the passive income security (REIT) with the business trust that provides active income. In a stapled structure, the two securities are bound together, and treated as one security. Stapled securities are traded in the same way as ordinary shares, but they will be traded under one trading name. As of June 2014, there were six stapled securities listed on the Singapore Exchange, and five of them are REIT-related stapled securities (Table 3B).

CDL Hospitality Trust (CDL H-Trust), listed on the Singapore Exchange on 19 July 2006, was the first to staple a REIT, CDL Hospitality Real Estate Investment Trust (CDL H-REIT), which owns 14 hotels and two resorts, and a business trust, and CDL Hospitality Business Trust (HBT), which is the manager operating the hotel and resort businesses. CDL H-Trust is both the legal owner of the assets of the CDL H-REIT and the decision-making body of the trust. It performs both "trustee" and "manager" roles for the trust (Case Study 7).

9. Asset Management Model — Fee Based Income

SREITs are all externally-advised, which implies that they appoint a third-party REIT manager to manage real estate assets on behalf of unit-holders. Other than ensuring the compliance of REITs as public listed entities, REIT managers carry out three broad management functions: investment management, capital management and asset portfolio management. REIT managers identify investment opportunities and execute acquisition strategies to grow REIT portfolios. On capital management, REIT managers ensure that the aggregate leverage does not exceed the permitted limit, which is currently set at 45% (after July 2015), if a REIT obtains credit rating from an approved rating agency. They undertake prudent debt maturity and interest

Table 3. Alternative REIT models — Business trusts and stapled securities.

No	Name of business trust	Registration number	Date of registration	Name of trustee-manager	Listing status
A) Business Trusts					
1	Accordia Golf Trust	2014002	21-Jul-14	Accordia Golf Trust Management Pte. Ltd.	1 August 2014
2	Ascendas Hospitality Business Trust	2012004	11-Jul-12	Ascendas Hospitality Trust Management Pte Ltd	27 July 2012
3	Ascendas India Trust	2007004	3-Jul-07	Ascendas Property Fund Trustee Pte. Ltd.	1 August 2007
4	CDL Hospitality Business Trust	2006002	12-Jun-06	M&C Business Trust Management Limited	19 July 2006
5	Croesus Retail Trust	2013004	2-May-13	Croesus Retail Asset Management Pte. Ltd.	10 May 2013
6	Far East Hospitality Business Trust	2012005	13-Aug-12	FEO Hospitality Trust Management Pte. Ltd.	27 August 2012
7	Forterra Trust (FKA "Treasury China Trust")	2010001	19-May-10	Forterra Real Estate Pte., Ltd	21 June 2010
8	Frasers Hospitality Business Trust	2014001	27-Jun-14	Frasers Hospitality Trust Management Pte Ltd	14 July 2014
9	Indiabulls Properties Investment Trust	2008001	7-May-08	Indiabulls Property Management Trustee Pte. Ltd.	11 June 2008
10	OUE Hospitality Business Trust	2013006	17-Jul-13	OUE Hospitality Trust Management Pte Ltd	25 July 2013
11	Perennial China Retail Trust	2011002	28-Feb-11	Perennial China Retail Trust Management Pte. Ltd.	9 June 2011
12	Religare Health Trust	2012006	25-Sep-12	Religare Health Trust Trustee Manager Pte. Ltd.	19 October 2012

(*Continued*)

Table 3. (*Continued*)

No	Name of business trust	Registration number	Date of registration	Name of trustee-manager	Listing status
13	Viva Industrial Business Trust	2013007	25-Oct-13	Viva Asset Management Pte Ltd	4 November 2013

No	Stapled security	Code	REIT	Business trust	Date of listing
B) Stapled Securities					
1	Ascendas Hospitality Trust	Q1P	Ascendas Hospitality REIT	Ascendas Hospitality Business Trust	27 July 2012
2	CDL Hospitality Trust	J85	CDL Hospitality REIT	CDL Hotel Business Trust	19 July 2006
3	Far East HTrust	Q5T	Far East Hospitality REIT	Far East Hospitality Business Trust	27 August 2012
4	OUE Hospitality	SK7	OUE Hospitality REIT	OUE Hospitality Business Trust	25 July 2013
5	Viva Industrial Trust (VIT)	T8B	Viva Industrial REIT	Viva Industrial Business Trust	4 November 2013

Case Study 7: CDL Hospitality Trust — *A model of stapled securities*

The first hotel REIT under the CIS, which is stapled with a business trust, has been successfully listed on the Singapore Exchange on 19 July 2006. This is an important step forward in cementing Singapore as the Asian hub for REITs. City Development Limited (CDL), through its hotel vehicle, Millennium & Copthorne Hotels plc, an international hotel group listed on the London Stock Exchange, sponsored the first hotel REIT, which is known as CDL Hospitality REIT (CDL H-REIT) in Singapore. CDL H-REIT is set up to invest and hold a diversified portfolio of properties primarily used for hospitality and/or hospitality-related purposes. CDL H-REIT is stapled with the CDL Hospitality Business Trust (HBT), which is a dormant business trust at the listing date. It will take over the role as "the master lessee of last resort" if CDL H-REIT is unable to appoint a master lessee for any of the Hotels in its portfolio at the expiry of the relevant master lease agreement or for a newly acquired hotel. HBT can also undertake hospitality and hospitality-related development projects, acquisitions and investments, where CDL H-REIT is prohibited under the Property Fund Guidelines.

A total of 425 million stapled securities, known as CDL Hospitality Trust (CDL H-Trust), which constitute about 60.9% of the total securities, were offered to the public via the IPO process at the offering price of S$0.83 per stapled security. The remainder

(*Continued*)

(*Continued*)

39.1% or 273 million stapled securities were subscribed by the sponsor and its subsidiaries. The CDL H-REIT and HBT must be traded as a single stapled security on the stock exchange. The annualised distribution yields are forecasted at 6.37% and 6.69% for the years 2006 and 2007, respectively.

The initial asset portfolio owned by H-REIT comprises Orchard Hotel, Grand Copthorne Waterfront Hotel, M Hotel and Copthorne King's Hotel, all of which are located in Singapore, with a total of over 1,900 rooms at the date of IPO. Orchard Hotel Shopping Arcade and Orchard Hotel Shopping Arcade are also included as part of CDL H-REIT's portfolio (Table CS7-1). As in 2015, CDL H-Trust owns 14 hotels and two resorts with a total of 4,709 rooms, distributed across five countries, Singapore, Australia, New Zealand, Japan and Maldives.

The structure of CDL H-Trust is shown in Figure CS7-1. M&C REIT Management Limited and M&C Business Trust Management Limited, the subsidiaries of the sponsor, Millennium & Copthorne Hotels Plc, are appointed as the manager of CDL H-REIT and the Trustee-Manager of HBT, respectively. The REIT manager charges a base fee of 0.25% per annum of the value of the deposited properties, and a performance fee of 5.0% per annum of the net property income (NPI) of the CDL H-REIT. The manager will also levy 1.0% and 0.5%, based on the transaction price, for any acquisition and divestment completed on behalf of CDL H-REIT.

Table CS7-1. Details of properties in initial portfolio of CDL H-REIT.

Property	Orchard Hotel	Grand Copthorne Waterfront Hotel	M Hotel	Copthorne King's Hotel	Orchard Hotel Shopping Arcade	Total
Location	Orchard Road	Havelock Road	Anson Road	Havelock Road	Orchard Road	
Gross floor area (square meter)	49940.9	46662.6	32379.3	17598.3		146581.1
Number of available rooms	653	539	413	310		1915
Carpark lots	454	287	237	77		1055
Hotel Revenue Per Available Room	112	96	110	88		
Gross Revenue for FY2005 (S$million)	16.1	11.7	9	5.3	3.4	45.5
Purchase price ($million)	330.1	234.1	161.5	86.1	34.5	846.3

Source: IPO prospectus of CDL H-Trust.

(*Continued*)

(Continued)

Figure CS7-1. Structure of CDL H-Trust.

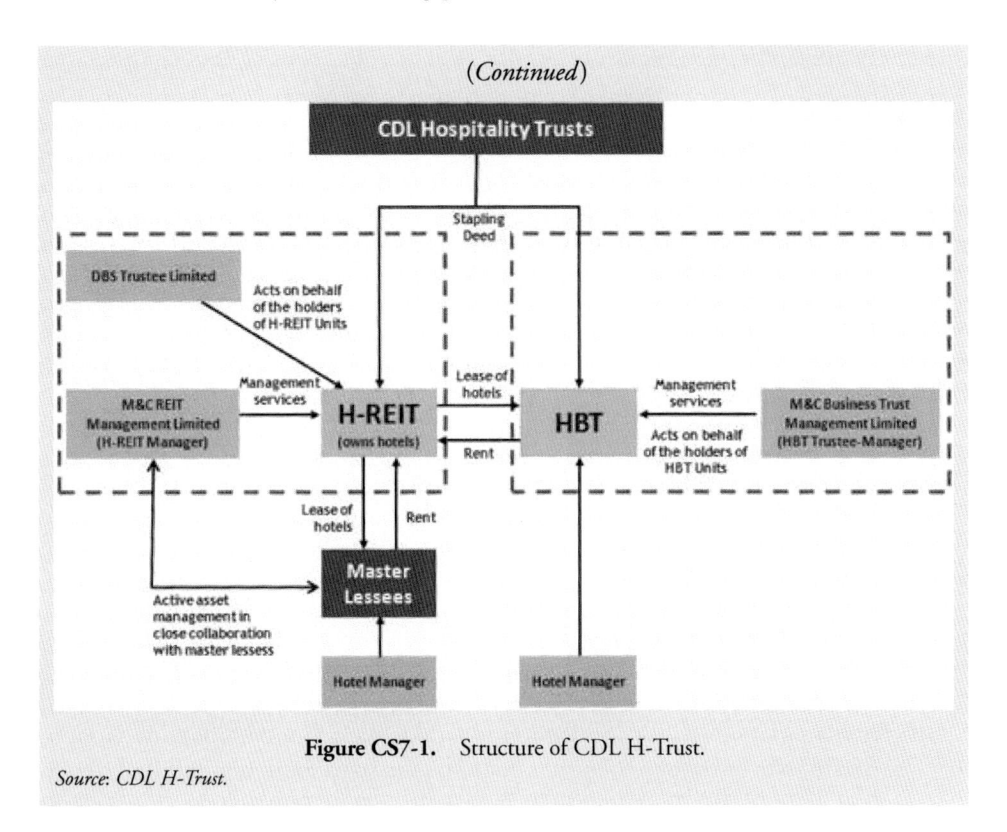

Source: CDL H-Trust.

risk management. Asset management covers activities that enhance occupancy and rental rate through holding well-diversified property portfolios with balanced tenant base. REIT managers also plan and execute asset enhancement initiatives (AEIs) to growth values of asset portfolios for REIT unitholders.

For their responsibilities and services in asset management, REIT managers are compensated with two types of fees, which include a tiered asset management fee (a base fee and a performance fee) based on deposited property value and income growth, and an activity-based fee, which include acquisition and divestment fee. The base fee could vary from 0.10% to 0.50% of the deposited property value. Newer REITs, such as Mapletree Greater China Commercial Trust, IREIT Global, Viva Industrial Trust, Soilbuild Business Space REIT, move away from using the property value in computing base fees to linking the base fee to distributable income. The performance fees vary widely across REIT managers; and they are paid the fees only if they deliver growth, which is measured in terms of either distribution per unit (DPU) or net property income (NPI), above predetermined targets. Acquisition fee is usually levied at 1% of the acquired property value, and divestment fee is set at 0.5% of the divested property value. In the revised guidelines announced by MAS in July 2015, asset managers are required to provide justification and disclosure on the structure and type of fees charged (See Appendix 2).

The routine property management and maintenance works are separately outsourced to third-party property managers. In Singapore, third-party asset managers and property managers are mostly wholly-owned by REIT sponsors. For corporate governance purposes, independent directors are appointed to the boards to monitor the roles of the asset managers. REIT sponsors' affiliations via their controlling stake in REITs and ownerships in asset managers bring positive benefits to shareholders by giving the first rights of refusal for properties put up for sale to captive affiliated SREITs.[27]

Asset managers, who generate steady streams of fee-based revenues, are attractive business ventures in Singapore. In 2008, four takeovers of REIT asset managers were completed:

- Ascendas acquired the 40% stake of Goodman in Ascendas-MGM Funds Management Limited; the manager of Ascendas REIT became the sole owner of the manager on 12 March 2008
- Fraser's acquisition of 17.1% of Allco Commercial REIT ($104.3 million) and 100% of REIT manager ($75.7 million) for S$180 million on 8 July 2008
- The subsidiaries of Oxley Group and National Australia Bank Limited (nabInvest) acquired 80% interest in Cambridge Industrial Trust Management Pte Ltd, the REIT managers of Cambridge Industrial Trust, on 20 February 2008
- YTL Corporation acquired 26% of Macquarie Prime REIT (S$202.62 million) and 50% of Prime REIT Management Holdings Pte Ltd (the asset manager) ($82.38 million) from Macquarie Bank Limited for S$285 million on 31 December 2008

Independent managers, who are not affiliated with REIT sponsors, emerged with the mushrooming of SREITs. After Cambridge Industrial Trust Management Pte Ltd was acquired, ARA Asset Management Limited (ARA) is the sole independent asset manager in SREIT markets. It was established in 2002 to manage asset portfolios of Fortune REIT, which was listed in 2003 in Singapore. ARA has become a public firm listed on the Singapore Exchange since November 2007. It has since expanded rapidly by providing independent asset management to seven REITs listed on the exchanges in Singapore, Hong Kong, Malaysia and South Korea (Case Study 8).

---

[27] Kudus, Syahzan Sani and Sing, Tien Foo, (2011) "Interest Alignment and Insider Shareholdings in the Emerging Asian REIT Markets," *Journal of Real Estate Portfolio Management*, Vol. 17, No. 2, pp. 127–138.

Case Study 8: ARA Asset Management — *A third-party asset manager*

In Singapore, most of the REIT managers are wholly-owned entities of the sponsors, which generate recurring income for the sponsors. ARA Asset Management Limited (ARA) is the first third-party real estate fund management company that has been publicly listed on the Singapore Exchange. Its core businesses involve offering the third-party management services to public-listed REITs and private real estate funds. ARA was established in 2002 by Mr John Lim Hwee Chiang, the current Group Chief Executive Officer, and a subsidiary of Cheung Kong (Holdings) Limited. ARA's real estate assets under management (AUM) have since grown from S$663.3 million (US$433.5 million) as of 31 December 2003 to S$7,233.4 million (US$4,727.7 million) as of 30 June 2007, prior to its public listing.

ARA's foray into REIT management business started with obtaining the first asset management contract from Fortune REIT, the first cross-border REIT listed in Singapore, which owns retail malls and properties in Hong Kong. It was then appointed the REIT manager for the Suntec REIT, which was created as a result of the divestment of the office and retail properties in Suntec City owned by a group of Hong Kong tycoons, among them Mr Li Ka-Shing, the Founding Chairman of Cheung Kong Holdings. It also advised the listing of the first private REIT in Hong Kong, Prosperity REIT, in 2005. Its REIT management business subsequently expanded to Malaysia, as the manager for the largest office REIT in Malaysia, AmFIRST REIT in 2006. Prior to its listing in 2007, the total REIT real estate AUM increased to S$6,922.2 million (US$4,524.3 million) as of 30 June 2007.

The two founders (Mr John Lim and Cheung Kong Holdings) launched the IPO for ARA on 25 October 2007 by issuing a total of 205,176,000 offering shares comprising 73,000,000 new shares and 132,176,000 existing share (vendor shares), with an over-allotment option for 36,000,000 additional vendor shares, at an IPO offering price of S$1.15 per share. A total of 37,824,000 shares have been allotted to three cornerstone investors, which include Fidelity Hong Kong, Mercury and Indopark, which collectively hold about 6.5% of the aggregate shares. Upon selling a total 279,000,000 shares via IPO placement and the exercised over-allotments, Mr John Lim's and Cheung Kong Holdings' shareholdings were pared down from the original shareholdings of 70% and 30%, respectively, to 36.40% and 15.60%, respectively.

ARA's core business comprises three primary segments: REIT management, private real estate fund management, and specialist equity fund management and corporate finance advisory services. As of 2015, ARA manages six REITs in Singapore, Hong Kong, and Malaysia, and two privately-held REITs in South Korea (ARA-NPS Real Estate Investment Company and ARA-NPS REIT No. 2). Details of the assets and AUM are summarised in Table CS8-1. As of March 2015, the total AUM of ARA is S27.2billion, of which about 79% comes from real estate in the portfolios from the stable of REITs under its management (Figure CS8-1). The revenue contributions from the REITs division come from three sources:

- Base fees as a percentage of the gross property value of the assets under management;

Table CS8-1. ARA's stable of REITs under management as of 2015.

REIT	Listing country	Listing year	Property	Property value[#] S$ million (US$ million)
Fortune REIT	Singapore	2003	Suburban retail properties in Hong Kong	S$6,020.89 (US$4,467.53)
Suntec REIT	Singapore	2004	Prime office and retail properties in Singapore and Australia	S$8,674.00 (US$6,436.15)
Prosperity REIT	Hong Kong	2005	Office & Industrial properties in Hong Kong	S$1,719.06 (US$1,275.55)
AmFIRST REIT	Malaysia	2006	Commercial properties in Malaysia	S$487.05 (US$361.39)
Cache Logistics Trust	Singapore	2010	Logistics properties in the Asia Pacific region	S$1,212.00 (US$899.31)
Hui Xian REIT	Hong Kong	2011	Commercial properties in China	S$9,063.34 (US$6,725.04)
ARA-NPS REITs[&]	South Korea (Private REIT)	2007, 2010	Office properties in South Korea	S$760.12 (US$564.01)

& *Two closed-end privately-held REITs with a finite term of 10 years.*
# *Based on publicly announced valuation as at 31 March 2015.*
Source: ARA Asset Management's 1Q2015 Annual Report.

- Variable (performance) fees as a percentage of the annual net property income of the assets under management; and
- One-off acquisition or divestment fees as a percentage of the gross property value of the assets acquired or divested.

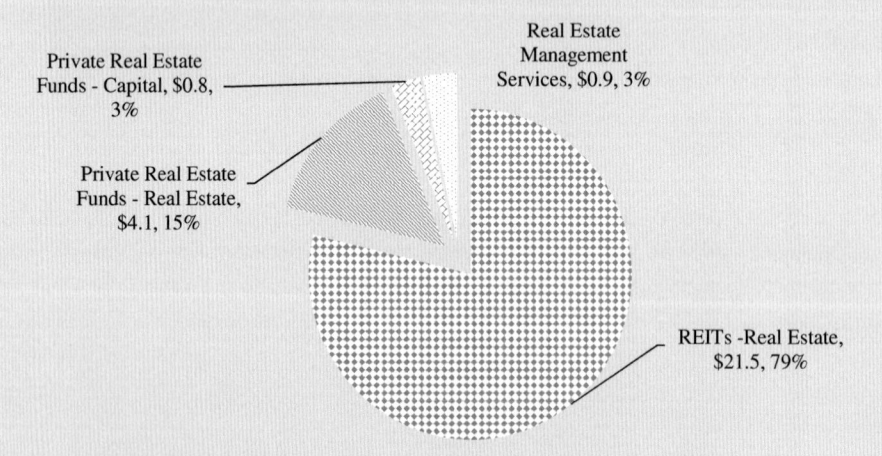

Figure CS8-1. Composition of ARA's group AUMs as at 31 March 2015.

- Private Real Estate Funds - Capital, $0.8, 3%
- Private Real Estate Funds - Real Estate, $4.1, 15%
- Real Estate Management Services, $0.9, 3%
- REITs - Real Estate, $21.5, 79%

Source: 1Q2015 Annual Report of ARA Asset Management.

10. Investing in SREITs

An REIT is a securitised vehicle that converts real estate assets into liquid tradable securities. REITs serve as a bridge to facilitate efficient flows of fund from regions with surplus-supply of fund to regions with abundant supply of real estate investment opportunities. Owners of real estate in Asia and the Europe have adopted the US REIT model to monetise physical real estate assets since the early 2000s.

REITs are defensive stocks, which distribute 90% or more earnings on a regular interval to investors as dividends. They enjoy tax transparency at the corporate level. Tax exemptions are extended to dividend payouts by REITs to individuals and qualified non-individual investors of REITs. REITs offer an indirect channel for investors to own income-producing real estate, which includes shopping malls, office, industrial properties, warehouses and others. As REITs are a collective investment scheme, investors can invest in a small denomination of REIT units without having to fork up large equity upfront. Like stocks, REITs are liquid investments freely traded on the stock market at low transaction costs. However, REIT prices are subject to stock market volatility.

From the above features, REITs can be viewed as a hybrid instrument that combines the features of real estate, stock and bond. "*REITs smell like real estate, look like bonds and walk like equity,*" says Greg Whyte, who heads up Morgan Stanley's REIT research unit.[28]

REITs appeal to both retail investors and institutional investors as an indirect channel of real estate investments. Based on historical prices of 40 SREITs (including business trusts) over the period from 2002 to 2015, the simple weighted quarterly price return series is computed for REITs. The quarterly return series of Straits Times Index is used to proxy stock returns, and URA price returns are computed for industry, office and shop. The descriptive statistics and correlations for different asset classes are summarised in Table 4. REIT has the highest quarterly return of about 1.5%. The return series for the five asset classes are plotted in Figure 6. The results show that REIT returns are highly correlated with the stock return in Singapore (0.876). Stock and REIT returns are much more volatile than returns of commercial real estate assets. The quarterly REIT returns during the subprime crisis period in 2007–2008 could decline by more than 60%, and subsequently rebound by more than 40% in 2009 and 2010.

11. Conclusion

The SREIT market has gone through a phase of rapid expansion from the period from 2002 to 2007, and the same growth rate is not sustainable for the SREIT

---

[28] Source: Ari Weinberg, "Liquid Properties," *Forbes*, May 22, 2002.

Table 4. Historical returns and correlations for different assets (September 2002– March 2015).

	Stock	Bond	REIT	Industry	Office	Shop
Mean	0.014	0.006	0.015	0.015	0.008	0.007
Median	0.026	0.006	0.027	0.009	0.010	0.007
Maximum	0.465	0.010	0.526	0.085	0.085	0.045
Minimum	−0.390	0.003	−0.694	−0.107	−0.128	−0.049
Standard Deviation	0.117	0.002	0.151	0.040	0.038	0.019
Correlation:						
Bond	0.042					
REIT	0.876	0.066				
Industry	0.132	−0.226	0.137			
Office	0.219	0.018	0.142	0.763		
Shop	0.220	0.064	0.223	0.697	0.849	

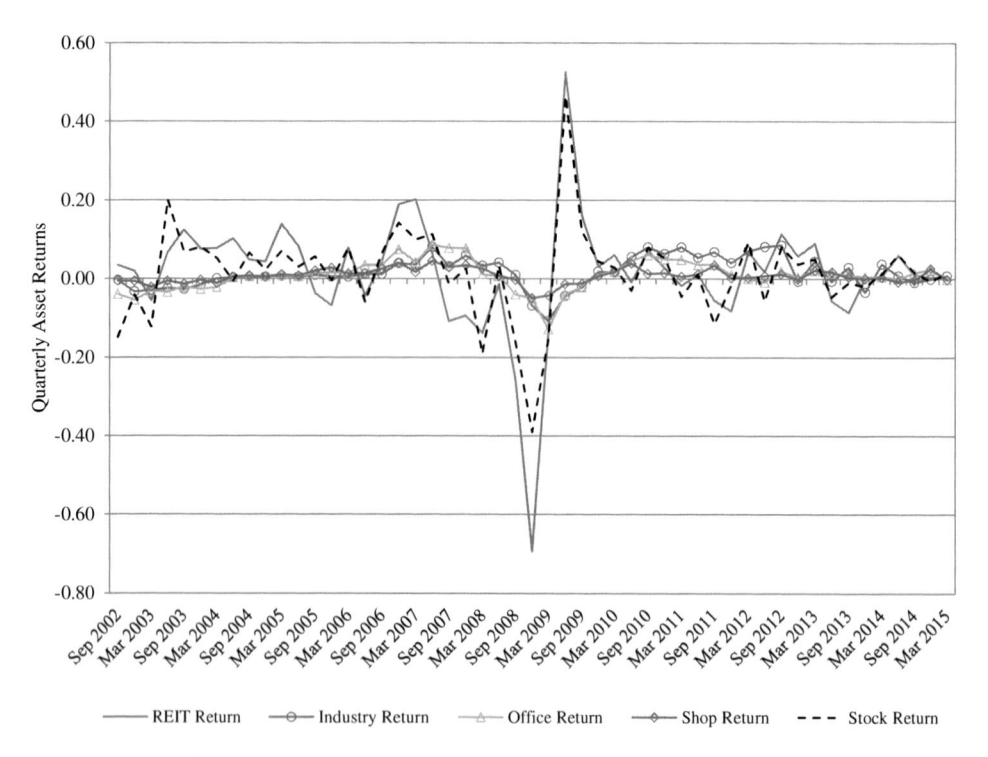

Figure 6. Quarterly asset returns (September 2002–March 2015).
Source: Datastream and the Author.

market. Moving forward, the SREIT market may face keen competition from other Asian REIT markets including potential new REIT markets in China and India. Therefore, differentiating growth strategies are essential to continue transforming the SREIT market into the most attractive and efficient REIT hub, outside the US. Government-linked REITs will continue to form the backbone of the SREIT market, which will serve as the magnet to draw more cross-border REITs to list in Singapore. They are expected to take the market leadership role in setting good corporate governance and practices in the SREIT markets.

New Model for SREITs

Will an internally-advised model, which has been the preferred model vis-à-vis the externally-advised model in the US REIT market in the 1990s, be adopted by SREITs? Internally-advised REITs, set up either as a c-corporation or a trust, directly appoint their CEO and other management staff, and pay their remuneration as general and administration expenses from REIT accounts. With strong sponsors' presence and influence, especially since 39.4% of the SREITs are affiliated with government-linked firms (sponsors),[29] the externally-advised structure is viewed more positively in forging interest alignment, and is expected to stay with SREITs in the near term. The small talent pool of CEOs in Singapore implies that unit-holders of small size REITs may not have scale economies to compete with large sponsor-affiliated REITs in finding experienced CEOs to create the US-styled internal model.

---

[29] Ditto

Appendix 1. Details of REITs actively traded on the Singapore exchange.

No	REIT name	REIT type	Property type	Total debt to total asset ratio (%)	Unit price at IPO (S$)	Total IPO unit issued (billion)	Listing date
1	CapitaLand Mall Trust	REITS	Shopping Centers	32.15	0.96	213.00	17-Jul-2002
2	Ascendas REIT	REITS	Diversified	33.43	0.88	272.50	19-Nov-2002
3	Fortune REIT	REITS	Shopping Centers	29.23	1.08$ (HK$4.75)	473.00	12-Aug-2003
4	CapitaLand Commercial Trust	REITS	Diversified	19.02	1.75	839.12	06-Feb-2004
5	Suntec REIT	REITS	Diversified	34.65	1.00	722.00	09-Dec-2004
6	Mapletree Logistics Trust	REITS	Diversified	34.08	0.68	310.88	28-Jul-2005
7	Starhill Global REIT	REITS	Shopping Centers	28.46	0.98	581.92	20-Sep-2005
8	Keppel REIT	REITS	Office Property	36.37	1.82	240.51	28-Nov-2005
9	Frasers Commercial Trust	REITS	Diversified	36.78	1.00	321.26	30-Mar-2006
10	Ascott Residence Trust	REITS	Hotels	37.63	0.68	340.50	31-Mar-2006
11	Frasers Centrepoint Trust	REITS	Regional Malls	29.30	1.03	261.93	05-Jul-2006
12	CDL Hospitality Trusts	Stapled Securities	Hotels	31.63	0.83	425.00	19-Jul-2006
13	Cambridge Industrial Trust	REITS	Diversified	34.44	0.68	206.11	25-Jul-2006
14	CapitaLand Retail China Trust	REITS	Regional Malls	28.49	1.13	193.30	08-Dec-2006
15	First REIT	REITS	Health Care	32.71	0.71	140.40	11-Dec-2006
16	AIMS AMP Capital Industrial REIT	REITS	Warehouse/Industry	31.46	1.20	247.33	19-Apr-2007
17	Ascendas India Trust	Business Trust	Industrial Park	22.05	1.18	423.38	01-Aug-2007
18	Parkway Life REIT	REITS	Health Care	35.00	1.28	373.06	23-Aug-2007
19	Saizen REIT	REITS	Apartments	36.55	1.00	196.74	09-Nov-2007
20	Lippo Malls Indonesia Retail Trust	REITS	Shopping Centers	30.95	0.80	645.47	19-Nov-2007

CHAPTER 7 | The Rise of Singapore's Real Estate Investment Trust (SREIT) Market 203

21	Indiabulls Properties Investment Trust	Business Trust	Commercial/Residential	20.59	1.00	262.48	11-Jun-2008
22	Cache Logistics Trust	REITS	Warehouse/Industry	30.71	0.88	531.01	12-Apr-2010
23	Mapletree Industrial Trust	REITS	Warehouse/Industry	30.57	0.93	917.49	21-Oct-2010
24	Sabana Shari'ah Compliant Industrial REIT	REITS	Diversified	36.17	1.05	605.80	26-Nov-2010
25	Mapletree Commercial Trust	REITS	Diversified	36.28	0.88	1015.09	27-Apr-2011
26	Ascendas Hospitality Trust	Stapled Securities	Hotels	35.64	0.88	521.94	27-Jul-2012
27	Far East Hospitality Trust	Stapled Securities	Hotels	31.34	0.93	705.71	27-Aug-2012
28	Religare Health Trust	Business Trust	Health Care	11.22	0.90	567.46	19-Oct-2012
29	Mapletree Greater China Commercial Trust	REITS	Diversified	36.15	0.93	1730.11	07-Mar-2013
30	Croesus Retail Trust	Business Trust	Shopping Centers	51.69	0.93	392.77	10-May-2013
31	SPH REIT	REITS	Regional Malls	25.79	0.90	559.88	24-Jul-2013
32	OUE Hospitality Trust	Stapled Securities	Hotels	32.46	0.88	681.82	25-Jul-2013
33	Soilbuild Business Space REIT	REITS	Diversified	35.00	0.78	586.53	16-Aug-2013
34	Keppel DC REIT	REITS	Diversified	25.92	0.93	551.45	12-Dec-2014
35	Viva Industrial Trust	Stapled Securities	Office	43.74	0.78	468.15	04-Nov-2013
36	OUE Commercial REIT	REITS	Office	37.65	0.80	433.00	27-Jan-2014
37	Frasers Hospitality Trust	Business Trust	Hotels	41.06	0.88	418.01	14-Jul-2014
38	IREIT Global	REITS	Office	31.39	0.88	499.01	13-Aug-2014

$ Exchange Rate in March 2003: S$1.00: HK$4.42.
Source: Bloomberg.

Appendix 2: Property Fund Guidelines and Various Revisions

20 October 2005[30] — The revisions aimed to enhance the SREIT managers' responsibilities and corporate governance, were comprehensive, covering the following areas:

i) *The presence of asset manager in Singapore* — The third-party asset manager must have minimum shareholder funds of S$1million. It must also set up physical office in Singapore, coupled with a Chief Executive Officer and at least two professional staff who are based in Singapore and also meet MAS' "fit and proper criteria".

ii) *Removal of an asset manager* — An asset manager could be removed by way of a resolution passed by a simple majority of unitholders present and voting at a general meeting.

iii) *Interested party transactions* — When transacting with interested persons, either sponsors or Trustees, two independent valuations for the acquired or disposed properties, of which one of the valuations must be commissioned independently by the Trustee. For acquisition from and disposal of properties to interested persons, asset managers are paid fees in the form of SREIT units based on prevailing market price.

iv) *Joint ownership of properties* — When an SREIT invests in a property as a part-owner, the joint venture arrangement should be structured through acquiring shares or interests in an unlisted special purpose vehicle (SPV).

v) *Restrictions in development activities* — SREITs' exposure to development activities is limited to not more than 10% of the value of deposited properties of SREITs.

vi) *Aggregate Leverage Limit* — SREITs are subject to an aggregate leverage limit, which includes borrowing and deferred payments, of 35% of the total deposited property value. SREITs are, however, allowed to increase the borrowing limit subject to a cap of 60%, if a credit rating is obtained from a credit rating agency, and disclosed to the public.

vii) *Disclosure of tenant profile* — SREIT managers are required to disclose detailed information on tenant profiles in property portfolios, which include total number of tenant, top 10 tenants, percentage of total gross rental income contributed by each of the top 10 tenants, trade sector mix of tenants, lease maturity profile of tenants by total gross rental income.

viii) *Valuation of property portfolio* — If a new equity raising exercise is planned and the valuation of properties in the portfolios of SREITs are more than six months old, the manager could choose to conduct a desktop valuation of the property portfolio in lieu of full valuation.

---

[30] Reference: Rodyk & Davison LLP.

March 2007 — The second major review to the Property Fund Guidelines was revealed by MAS on 28 September 2007. Some changes are summarised below:

i) Enhancing the disclosure requirements on the use of short-term yield-enhancing arrangements, which include financial engineering structures used to boost short-term yields.
ii) Providing guidance on permissible fixed-term management contracts to prevent SREIT managers from putting restrictive terms that prevent unit-holders from terminating the management contracts.
iii) Disallowing discounts to institutional investors for subscriptions made at the time of listing of an REIT;
iv) Specifying safeguards for SREITs that intend to pay dividends in excess of current income;
v) Requiring an SREIT to invest at least 75% of its assets in income-producing real estate; and
vi) Removing the 5% single party limit for investments in real-estate related securities.

11 November 2009 — Mandatory Annual General Meeting (AGM) requirement for SREITs

The major change in the 2009 revision was to mandate SREITs to hold an AGM once every calendar year and not more than 15 months from the last preceding AGM, with effect from 1 January 2010.

2 July 2015 — MAS has solicited feedback through a Consultation Paper on "Enhancement to the Regulatory Regime Governing REITs and REIT Managers" published on 9 October 2014.[31] On 2 July 2015, changes in three key areas were introduced to accord REIT unit-holders better protection and greater accountability while providing REIT Managers increased operational flexibility.[32]

(a) Strengthen corporate governance
 • Managers and their directors will be bound by a statutory duty to prioritise the interests of REIT unit-holders over the interests of the Managers and their shareholders, in the event of a conflict of interest.
 • At least half of the Manager's board of directors must be independent directors if unit-holders do not have the right to appoint the Manager's directors.

---

[31] Refer to the Consultative Paper (PO23-2014) published by MAS for details of recommendations.
[32] Source: "MAS Responses to Consultation Feedback on Strengthening the REITs Market." 2 July 2015.

- Managers will be required to disclose their remuneration policy and procedures in the REITs' Annual Reports.

(b) Increase transparency of fee structure

Managers are required to disclose the justification on the structure of fees or types of fees charged. Managers will also have to explain the methodology for computing performance fees, and justify how this methodology takes into account unit-holders' long-term interests.

(c) Allow greater operational flexibility
- The development limit of a REIT will be increased from 10% to 25% of its deposited property.
- The leverage limit imposed on a REIT will be increased from 35% to 45% of the REIT's total assets, but a REIT will no longer be allowed to leverage up to 60% with a credit rating.
- Stapled securities structures with a REIT component to operate without group operational limits are allowed. The REIT component will be subject to existing limits.

CHAPTER 8

Bridging the Gap between Capital and Real Estate Markets

Sing Tien Foo

1. Introduction

The investment model of building and/or buying commercial real estate assets to hold for rental income has remained unchanged for a long time. Real estate investments are invariably financed by a combination of private equity and bank loan, which is no different from how most individuals finance their homes. This funding structure is still prevalent. However, with financial innovations, the underlying capital structure of real estate has decomposed into parts which can be separately securitised and traded in both private and public markets. The financial innovations have expanded the range of real estate investment instruments in capital markets. Instead of buying and selling physical assets, new innovations in the capital markets allow institutional investors to specifically allocate funds in their portfolios to equity and debt components of the capital structure.

This chapter aims to examine the emergence of real estate securitisation markets in Singapore. Section 2 discusses the concepts and motivations of real estate securitisation. Section 3 covers three key development phases of real estate securitisation in Singapore. Section 4 illustrates various forms of real estate securitisation in Singapore, which include mortgage backed bonds, commercial real estate asset backed securities, and residential and commercial mortgage backed securities. Selected case studies in Singapore are included for illustration. Section 5 concludes the chapter with some remarks on future development of the securitisation markets in Singapore.

2. Securitising Real Estate Cash Flows

Real estate securitisation is a creative financing arrangement whereby debt/equity instruments backed by real estate cash flows, such as interest and principal payments from mortgages or rents, are created in the capital market. It involves a multi-stage process starting by pooling together cash flows generated from real estate mortgages

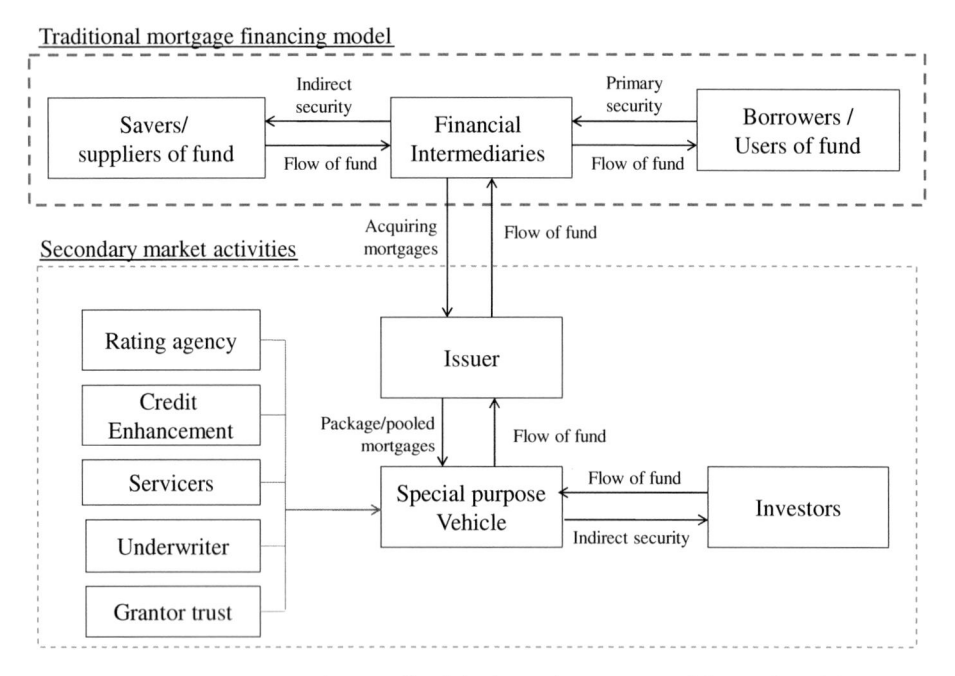

Figure 1. Disintermediation of banks' roles in the conventional financial model.

and assets, enhancing credit, structuring and tranching cash flows into tradable securities, and lastly distributing the securities to investors via capital markets. Various real estate backed securities can be created depending on the cash flow type (residential mortgages versus commercial mortgages) and the security structure (pay-through versus pass-through).

Banks and financial intermediaries with a high concentration of real estate mortgages can mitigate their real estate market risks through securitisation. The securitisation process unbundles roles of financial intermediaries into a range of specialised activities including packaging/pooling of assets, structuring of cash flows into tradeable securities, credit rating, debt servicing, underwriting, credit enhancement and grantor trust and others (Figure 1). While the roles of banks and lending institutions as intermediaries of capital are diminished, specialised types of fee-based services are created, which include credit rating and enhancement, and distributing asset backed securities to investors. The new structure through divisional and specialisation of duties in the secondary market enhances efficiency and reduces transaction costs of financing over time. Securitisation also bridges the gap between users of funds and suppliers of funds. By creating secondary market products that match investors' risk preference, funding costs can be reduced for buyers and investors in real estate markets.

In the traditional *on-the-balance sheet* financing arrangement, real estate assets remain in the books of the owners. However, in Singapore, real estate owners have increasingly used securitisation as a form of *off-the-balance-sheet* financing. In the process, they transfer the legal rights of their real estate assets to a special purpose vehicle (SPV) at open market value. The outright sales separate real estate assets from the owners' book, which is a key feature in creating the *off the balance sheet* financing structure. The SPV is set up as a bankruptcy-remote vehicle to hold real estate assets and also separate real estate from owners' business risks. In this structure, credit risks of real estate backed securities can be assessed based on quality of real estate assets and their cash flows, which are independent of the owners' own financial and business risks. In a typical real estate development lifecycle, a spectrum of cash flows ranging from land financing, pre-completion sale proceeds, and construction financing at the pre-completion stage to rental income and sale proceeds at the post-completion stages can be technically securitised.

3. Motivations for Real Estate Securitisation in the US

3.1 *Residential Mortgage Backed Securities (RMBS) Market*

The RMBS history in the US can be traced back to the 1930s, when the US government intervened in the housing finance market in the aftermath of the Great Depression.[1] The US Congress established two key agencies — Federal Housing Administration (FHA) in 1934, and the Federal National Mortgage Association (FNMA) (Fannie Mae) in 1938, which have played an instrumental role in the creation of RMBS markets.

FHA provides mortgage insurance on loans originated by approved lenders throughout the United States and its territories. FHA mortgage insurance protects RMBS investors against losses caused by homeowners' default on mortgage payments. FHA has introduced standardisation to housing loans by adopting a fixed rate, self-amortising, long-term maturity structure. Fannie Mae creates a secondary mortgage market by acting as a buyer for FHA-insured mortgages from originators. The process allows new funds to be injected into the housing mortgage markets. Fannie Mae obtains its capital by issuing bonds at the beginning, and subsequently by selling RMBS in the secondary mortgage markets after being privatised in 1968.

Fannie Mae was split into two entities under the Fair Housing Act of 1968. The first one is a privatised entity which retained the same "Fannie Mae" (FNMA) name and has been given the mandate to purchase private mortgages not insured by FHA and other government-guarantee programmes. The second entity is a public agency that has a new name — Government National Mortgage Association (GNMA)

---

[1] Green, Richard K., and Susan Wachter (2005) "The American Mortgage in Historical and International Context." Journal of Economic Perspectives, Vol. 19, No. 4, pp. 93–114.

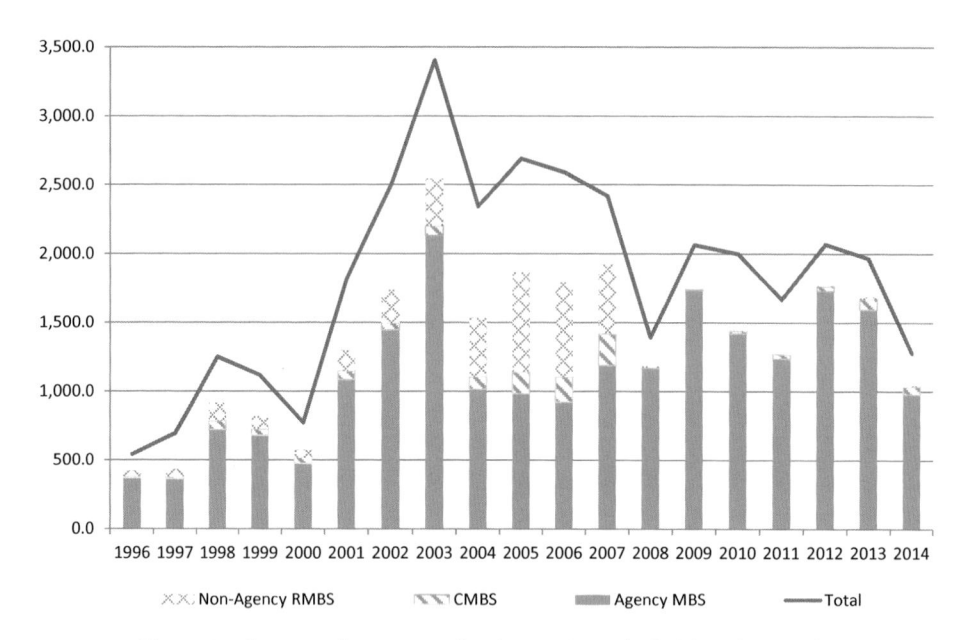

Figure 2. Issuance of mortgage related securities in the US (1996 to 2014).
Source: The Securities Industry and Financial Markets Association (SIFMA).

(Ginnie Mae). It is entrusted to provide guaranty backed by the full faith and credit of the US government for timely payment of principal and interests on FHA-insured loans. The FHA mortgage insurance and Ginnie Mae's guaranty are two key factors underpinning the RMBS development in the US.

Ginnie Mae guaranteed the first mortgage pass-through security in 1968. In 1970, the US government created the Federal Home Loan Mortgage Corporation (FHLMC) (Freddie Mac), another government-sponsored enterprise, to purchase and securitise non-FHA-insured loans made by savings and loans associations. Freddie Mac issued its first mortgage pass-through, called a participation certificate, in 1971. In 1981, Fannie Mae issued its first mortgage pass-through, called mortgage backed securities. The agency-RMBS issuance reached a peak of US$2.13 trillion (S$3.62 trillion) in 2003.[2] However, the market share of the agency-RMBS declined from 67.8% in 1996 to 43.3% in 2003 because of the large increases of other mortgage-related issuance during the period (Figure 2). However, after the subprime crisis in 2008, the new issuances of private-label (non-agency) RMBS and CMBS were nearly dissipated. New issuances of the agency-RMBS constituted more than 70% of the market share after 2008.

The early efforts of Ginnie Mae and the two quasi-government agencies (Fannie Mae and Freddie Mac) in the development of the secondary mortgage market created

---

[2] Exchange rate: US$1: S$1.7008 as in 2003 (Source: The MAS).

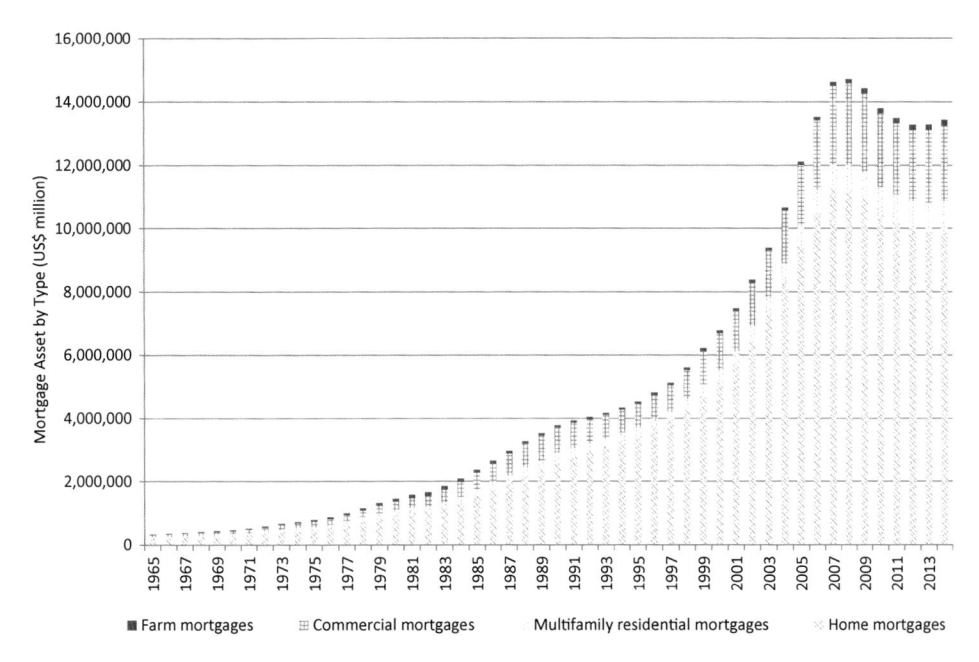

Figure 3. Total mortgage assets by type in the US — 1965–2014.
Source: Federal Reserve System.

an important channel to provide new capital for the US lending institutions. The securitisation of mortgages improves the efficiency of fund flows from supply-surplus regions to demand-surplus regions. It also reduces financing institutions' exposure to various risks related to residential lending such as interest rate risk, credit risks, funding risks, liquidity risks and sectoral concentration risks. The RMBS market increases liquidity and lowers financing costs for the housing markets in the US. The total home mortgage assets have grown by more than 42 times from US$263 billion (S$804.89 billion)[3] when the first RMBS was issued in 1968, to US$11.20 trillion (S$16.20 trillion) at the peak in 2007. As in 2014, home mortgages are the biggest mortgage assets constituting about 73.44% of the total mortgages in the US market (Figure 3).

3.2 Commercial Mortgage Backed Securities (CMBS) Market

Unlike the RMBS market that was motivated by the need for liquidity, the Savings and Loans (S&Ls) crisis in the US precipitated by the property market bust in the late 1980s was the key factor driving the development of the CMBS market.

---

[3] Exchange rate: US$1: S$3.0612 in 1968 (Source: © 2015 by Prof. Werner Antweiler, University of British Columbia) and US$1: S$1.4412 (Source: the MAS).

The US Congress set up the Resolution Trust Corporation (RTC) under the Financial Institutions Reform, Recovery and Enforcement Act (FIRREA) of 1989 to purchase the ballooning non-performing loans owned by insolvent S&Ls. After acquiring a large portfolio of assets from insolvent S&Ls, the RTC looked to the capital markets for innovative solutions. By creating a subordinated structure[4] to enhance risk protection for senior CMBS tranch investors, the RTC was able to sell the non-performing loan assets to investors on Wall Street. The RTC's liquidation of the non-performing loans contributed to the rapid expansion of the CMBS market between 1991 and 1993. After accomplishing the objective of recapitalising the distressed thrifts and banks and liquidating the non-performing commercial loan assets, the RTC was disbanded in 1995. Based on a report by Ernst & Young Leventhal Group, the RTC issued in excess of US$17.8 billion of CMBS between 1991 and 1995.[5]

This CMBS innovation turned out to be a major breakthrough, opening up a whole new dimension for commercial real estate investment and financing. The RTC's model of CMBS continues to be adopted by other commercial real estate lenders to tap into capital sources in the CMBS markets. The strong demand coupled with attractive yield spreads for the CMBS issued by the RTC further boosted investors' confidence in the instruments. The growth of the CMBS market was driven by conduit mortgage lenders[6] after the mid-1990s. Diversified portfolios of "*jumbo-grade*" commercial mortgages with asset values in the range of US$1 million (S$1.4 million) to US$10 million (S$14 million) provide a stable supply of the conduit-CMBS (Han, 1996). The new CMBS issuance increased from US$12.8 billion (S$18.0 billion) in 1996 to the peak of US$229.6 billion (S$330.8 billion)[7] in 2007, an increase of nearly 17.9 times by issuance value (Figure 3). The market share of new CMBS issuance has expanded from 2.36% in 1996 to 9.49% by the total issuance value of mortgage related securities. The subprime crisis that originated in the RMBS market in 2007 has spilled over to CMBS, causing new issuance to plunge to a trough of US$4.5 billion (S$6.5 billion) and US$8.7 billion (S$12.2 billion)[8] in 2008 and 2009, respectively. The market confidence recovered

---

[4] The senior-subordinated structure of CMBS distributes the cash flows received in a top-down direction, whereas the losses, if incurred, are allocated in the reversed direction, with the junior tranche holders being put in the first loss position (Harding and Sirmans, 1997).

[5] Nueberg, S.E.D., (2008), "The Anatomy, History and Future of Commercial Loan Securitisation," Commercial Mortgage Insight, July 2008.

[6] Conduit lenders are commercial or investment banks that originate and warehouse commercial loans with the intention of securitizing them into CMBS. They are active in providing financing to the small and low-quality commercial property owners, which are largely neglected by conventional lenders.

[7] Exchange rate: US$1: S$1.3998 in 1996 and US$1: S$1.4412 in 2007 (Source: The MAS).

[8] Exchange rate: US$1: S$1.4392 in 2008 and US$1: S$1.4034 in 2009 (Source: The MAS).

CHAPTER 8 | Bridging the Gap between Capital and Real Estate Markets 213

gradually in 2010 with new CMBS issuance recovering to US$79.7 billion (S$100.9 billion)[9] in 2013.

3.3 *The Subprime Crisis*

Mortgage-related securities[10] grew by leaps and bounds to a sizeable market with a total outstanding debt of US$8.73 trillion as of the end of 2014.[11] During the peak in 2007, mortgage related securitisation was the largest user of debt financing, covering nearly 30% of the total outstanding debt value in the US market, and surpassing the commercial debt (16.5%) and the treasury (14.2%) as shown in Figure 4.

The surge in mortgage related securitisation fuelled by strong housing prices in the early 2000s exposed the vulnerability of the financing markets in the US. The cracks started to surface when exuberance in the housing market sentiment faded. The straw that broke the camel's back occurred in 2006, when housing prices declined, and liquidity constraint households started to default on their mortgage payments. When the "music" stopped, the collapse of the "houses of cards" could no longer be contained to the housing markets.[12] The housing bubble burst and

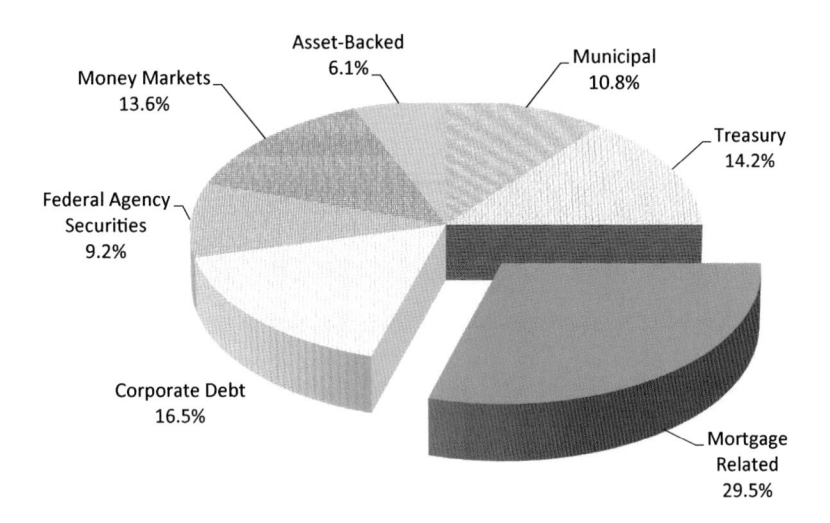

Figure 4. Outstanding bond market debt as in 2007.
Source: The Securities Industry and Financial Markets Association (SIFMA).

---

[9] Exchange rate: US$1: S$1.2653 in 2013 (Source: The MAS).
[10] Agency RMBS, private-label RMBS and CMBS collectively represent about 87% of the outstanding mortgage-related debt in US as in 2014.
[11] Source: The Securities Industry and Financial *Markets Association* (*SIFMA*).
[12] Stiglitz, J., (2007), "House of Cards," guardian.co.uk, 9 October 2007.

triggered one of the biggest financial market meltdown in the US economy since the Great Depression in 1930s, and also brought the world economies into deep recession.

Securitisation, which has helped lubricate the housing financing market by making mortgages more affordable in the US since the 1970s, has created incentive distortions between originators, home borrowers and capital suppliers (investors) in the markets.[13] As originators can pass on credit risks of loans to investors through securitisation, more subprime loans have been granted to high risk borrowers, whose loan applications would have had been previously rejected by banks. More aggressive investment bankers invented complex products, such as collateralised debt obligations (CDO), and marketed them aggressively to investors. When mortgages went sour, securities of investors at the lower end of the "securitisation-chain" (the first loss pieces) became worthless. Investors' confidence dissipated quickly, causing sudden "shut-down" to the supply of capital stifling both the housing and financing markets.

There are many lessons to be learnt from the subprime crisis in the US. A major "overhaul" to the securitisation market is needed to restore investors' confidence and bring about more transparent and efficient securitisation markets. The securitisation vehicle is temporarily down, but not completely out of the market. Agency-RMBS has supported the mortgage issuance activities in the US. As in 2014, the mortgage backed securities remain one of the largest issuers constituting 22.4% of the total outstanding bonds after the crisis.

4. Real Estate Securitisation Activities in Singapore

Unlike in the US where the secondary real estate mortgage market has developed and thrived, real estate mortgages are primarily retained by banks and finance companies in Singapore for long-term investment purposes. The real estate secondary market in Singapore is still at its infancy. Real estate developers, who are the major users of real estate fund, are the main drivers of securitisation activities in Singapore.

4.1 *Real Estate Mortgage Markets in Singapore*

As of 2014, the outstanding real estate loans, comprising building and construction loans and housing and bridging loans originated by banks, amounted to S$281.15 billion. This represents over 46.3% of the total loans and advances (including bill financing) granted by banks in Singapore (Figure 5). The housing loans grew, steadily buoyed by strong growth in the private residential property market from

---

[13] Blinder, Alan S., "Six Fingers of Blame in the Mortgage Mess," *The New York Times*, September 30, 2007.

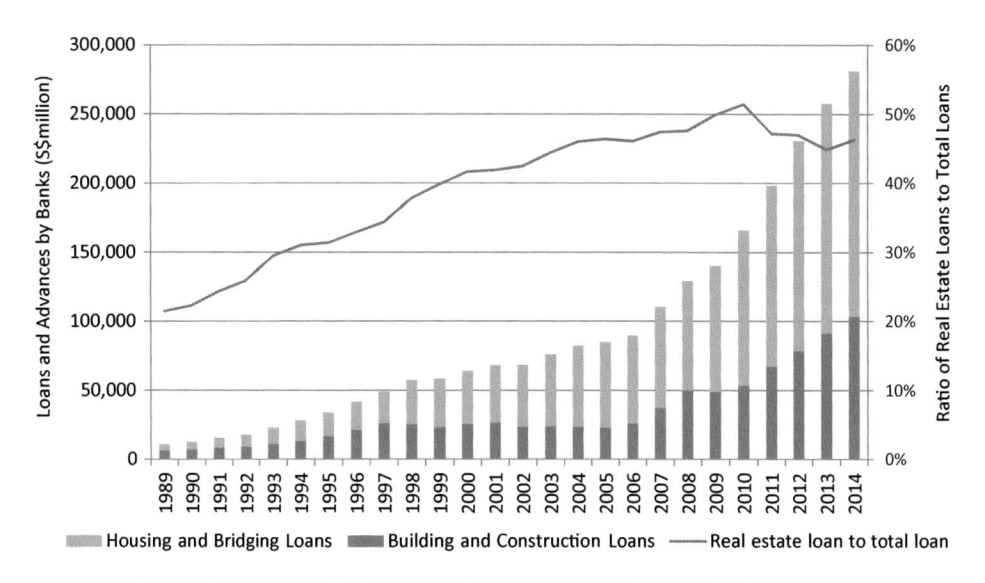

Figure 5. Loans and advances by Singapore's banks (domestic banking units).
Source: *The Monetary Authority of Singapore and the Authors.*

1993 through 1997. A large increase of S$8.85 billion in housing loan was reported in 1998, whereas the business sector loans for the construction and building sector declined by S$0.65 billion in the same year. The real estate loans comprising building and construction loans to businesses and developers and home and bridging loans to consumers have exceeded the Monetary Authority of Singapore's (MAS) prescribed limit of 30% since 1994.

The outbreak of the Asian Financial Crisis in 1997, which started with the devaluation of currencies of some Asian countries including South Korea, Thailand, Indonesia and Malaysia, spilled over to real estate markets, causing housing prices to rapidly spiral downward. Singapore's property market was not spared from the crisis, with private residential property prices declining by 41.7% from the peak in the second quarter of 1996 to the trough in the fourth quarter of 1998. Banks cut down the flows of fund into the real estate markets after the crisis, causing a severe liquidity crunch to both individual homebuyers and developers. The crisis-induced housing recession also brought a sharp correction in the new housing loans issued by banks, which declined by 61.99% from the peak of S$8.85 billion in 1998 to S$3.36 billion in 1999 (Figure 6). The new housing loan growth was stable, fluctuating around the S$5.0 billion mark for the next six years.

For the commercial market, the Urban Redevelopment Authority (URA) office price indices declined by more than 42% between the second quarter of 1996 and the third quarter of 1999. There was a dearth of commercial property transactions during

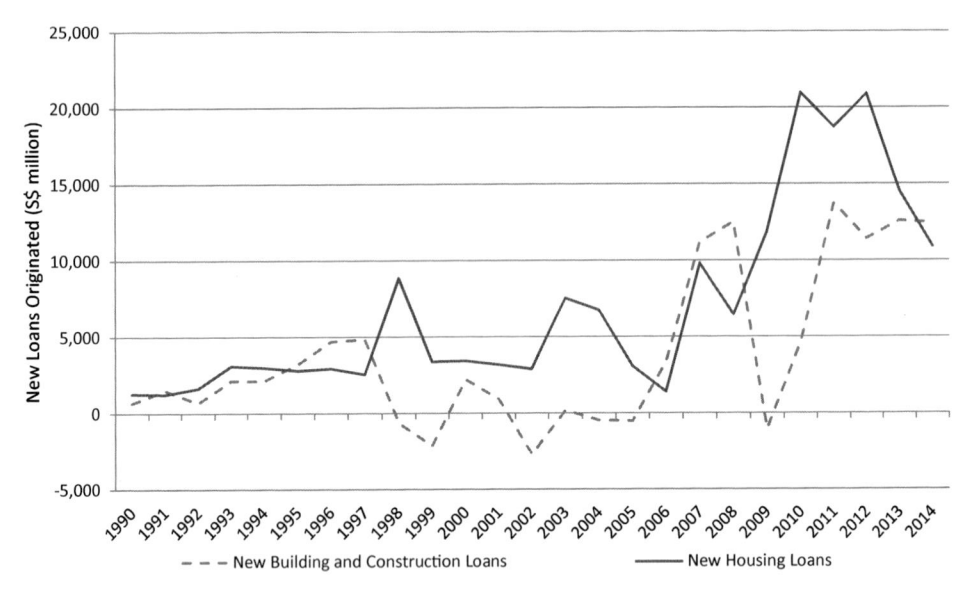

Figure 6. New real estate loans originated by banks (1990–2014).
Source: The Monetary Authority of Singapore and the Authors.

the post-crisis periods. New construction and building loans to developers and other businesses experienced a sharper decline by more than 144% in the two years between 1997 and 1999. The new real estate business loan origination remained weak in the post-crisis period with net negative loan origination of S$2.61 billion from 2001 to 2005.

The crisis has exposed the vulnerability of the real estate market that has overly relied on bank loans. The Monetary Authority of Singapore, the de-facto central bank of Singapore, formulated strategic plans to deepen and broaden the debt capital market. Real estate mortgage securitisation has been identified as a strategy to diversify the financing source in Singapore.[14] The MAS subsequently introduced policy changes aimed to ease banks' operational flexibility, such as lowering the minimum cash balance from 6% to 3% in July 1998, and reducing the Tier-1 Capital Adequacy Ratio (CAR) from 12% to 8% in September 2000. In the Banking (Amendment) Act in 2001, it replaced the 30% prescribed real estate loan limit with the revised Section 35, which adopts a more discretionary approach toward regulating banks' exposure to real estate risks. The changes increased liquidity of banks, which disincentives them from securitising mortgages off their books.

---

[14] This was expressed in the keynote address "*Opportunities in Asian Debt Markets — Strategies to Deepen the Singapore Debt Market,*" by the Second Minister for Finance, Singapore, Mr Lim Hng Kiang, at the Finance Intelligence Asia (FIA) — Asian Financial Markets Conference (02 May 2000).

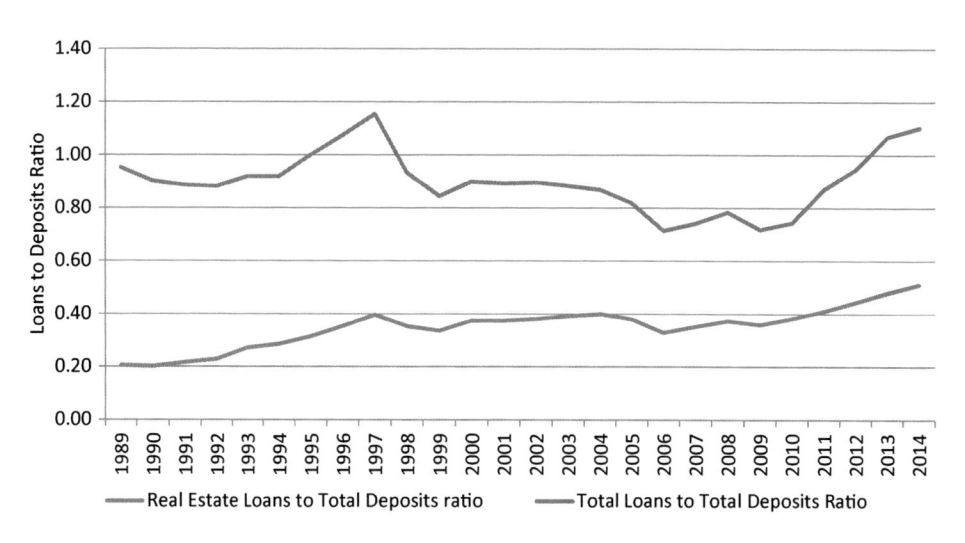

Figure 7. Loans to deposit ratio of banks (1989–2014).
Source: The Monetary Authority of Singapore and the Authors.

Banks have increased their real estate loan share after the 1997 crisis. Figure 7 shows that the total loans to the total deposit ratio has declined from the peak of 1.15 in 1997 to 0.714 in 2006. However, the growth momentum of real estate loans (comprising both loans to businesses and consumers) has been positive, where the total real estate loans to the total deposits ratio was estimated at 0.376 on average from 2000 to 2006. The ratio of real estate loans to total loans hit the peak of 51.4% in 2010.

4.2 *Real Estate Securitisation Activities in Singapore*

Securitisation of residential mortgages was not found in Singapore.[15] Real estate securitisation activities, however, took place mainly in real estate asset markets (including both commercial properties and residential development projects) in Singapore. There were broadly three distinct waves of real estate securitisation activities in Singapore. The earliest wave of commercial real estate mortgage securitisation started in 1986, when Citicorp Investment Bank (Singapore) arranged to securitise mortgage pledged on Hong Leong Building valued at S$280 million. The earlier securitisation deals were relatively small and piecemeal, covering mortgages on a single real estate project. Banks worked with some developers to securitise loans pledged on residential development projects (Case Study 1) or commercial buildings via issuance of mortgage

---

[15] Sing, T.F. and Ong, S.E. (2004), "Residential Mortgage Backed Securitization in Asia: The Singapore Experience," Journal of Real Estate Literature, Vol. 12 Issue 2, p. 159–179.

Case Study 1: Mortgage Backed Bonds (MBB) Issued by Goldenview Properties Limited

In June 1994, Goldenview Properties Limited (GPL) issued S$88 million Mortgage Backed Bonds (MBB) secured on the first mortgage of Orchard Scotts Deluxe Serviced Apartments (the property) in 1993. The property, comprising 80 apartments and 116 maisonettes, was completed in 1982. The property was built on a 99-year leasehold (lease commencing on 31 August 1989) site with a total area of 24,427.2 square metres (262,932 square feet). The property, located in a prime residential district in Singapore, bounded by Clemenceau Avenue, Anthony Road and Peck Hay Road, was leased out as service apartments for senior expatriate executives of foreign firms. The property has an occupancy rate of 93 per cent, yielding a gross rental income of around S$11 million. Knight Frank Cheong Hock Chye & Ballieu (Property Consultant) Limited was appointed to conduct a valuation of the property. As on 12 May 1994, it estimated the open market value at S$160 million on the basis as the current use as serviced apartments, and at S$170 million on the basis as a vacant development site with a gross plot ratio of 2.486.

The GPL first mortgage MBB, bearing a fixed coupon of 5.125 (5 1/8) percent per annum payable annually, were arranged and underwritten by the Citicorp Investment Bank (Singapore) Limited. The MBB were offered by way of private placement to financial institutions and private investors in the denomination of S$250,000 each. The bonds are redeemable at par after five years in 1999, but issuers are not obliged to redeem the bonds earlier prior to the maturity. The first legal mortgages on the property were pledged and the rental income generated from the properties was assigned to the Trustee to guarantee timely payments of coupons and redemption of bond at par for bondholders.

GPL was incorporated as a fully-owned subsidiary of Golden Development Pte Ltd (GDPL) to hold the property and serve as the issuer in connection with the fund-raising exercise. GDPL, a company controlled by Mr Ng Teng Fong's Far East Organization, serves as a guarantor on the MBB issuance. On top of the first mortgage on the property, the parent company, GDPL, unconditionally and irrevocably guaranteed timely payments of interest and principal due to MBB investors. The structure of the MBB is represented diagrammatically in Figure A1.

Unlike the MBB in the US where credit enhancements in the forms of third-party guarantee or over-collateralisation are used, the current MBB were guaranteed by the parent company GDPL through the first charge on the mortgage. In addition, the guarantor also through the trust indenture assigns rental income from the property to the Trustee for the purposes of meeting the coupon obligations due to the bondholders. Based on the "open market value" of $170 million for the property, the total issued MBB of $88 million was translated into an equivalent loan to value of approximately 51.76%. For the investors, the bond offered a relatively higher interest rate than the prevailing domestic interest rate of less than 3%. The issue was fully subscribed with institutional investors forming 90% of the subscribers and wealthy individuals taking up the balance.

(Continued)

(*Continued*)

The fund raised through the five-year MBB issuance was used to partially repay the existing bank borrowing, and also to fund additional working capital of the Guarantor, GDPL. As at 28 February 1994, the total bank borrowing of GDPL stood at approximately S$203.9 million.

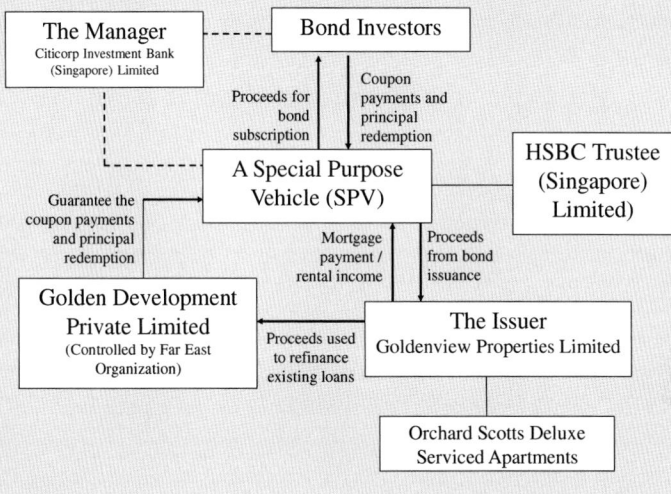

Figure A1. The structure for Goldenview Property Limited MBB.
Source: The Authors

backed bonds (MBBs). Developers used the fund raised from MBBs to refinance their existing loans. Banks were able to reduce loans secured by immobile property in their books via the MBB issuance. Prior to the 2001 amendment to the Banking Act (Chapter 19), Singapore-based banks were required to keep their real estate loans below a prescribed limit of 30% of the total value of its Singapore's deposit under the Section 34(1) of the Act.

Prior to the 1997 crisis, listed real estate developers/owners of commercial real estate relied mainly on stock market and bank lending to fund their business activities. Developers/owners faced double whammy when sourcing for new capital for their projects. On the one hand, they were not able to raise funds via secondary equity offerings in the depressing equity market. On the other hand, they had difficulty obtaining new loans from banks. Banks, despite having more liquidity, were hesitant to inject more funds into real estate markets, which were in doldrums after the 1997 downfall. The liquidity crunch had pushed the second wave of securitisation, where real estate developers/owners were forced to find creative ways to obtain new financing outside the traditional sources. The advancement in securitisation technology enabled developers/owners to take their commercial real estate *off-the-balance-sheet* via setting up a special purpose vehicle (SPV). The first commercial real estate backed securitisation was arranged for the 26-storey headquarter building of Neptune Orient Line (NOL) at Alexandra Road in 1999.

The third wave of securitisation was akin to the US model of CMBS, but the initiative was spearheaded by private real estate funds and real estate investment trusts (REITs). In 2012, the first CMBS was set up by CapitaMall Trust, now renamed CapitaLand Mall Trust (CMT), to create a revolving credit facility to refinance their existing loans. CapitaRetail Singapore Limited (CRS) (Case Study 2), a private fund set up by CapitaLand Limited, issued CMBS to raise funds from investors in capital markets in both Europe and Singapore in 2004 to finance their acquisitions of three retail malls, which have yet been injected into a REIT. Prior to the

---

Case Study 2: The Robinson Point CREBB by Visor Limited

In the case of commercial real estate backed bonds (CREBB) issued by Visor Limited, an SPV was set up by the sponsor — Birchvest Investments Private Limited, a wholly owned subsidiary of DBS Land (now CapitaLand), for bond issuance purposes. The bonds were backed by cash flows generated from Robinson Point (the property), a prime office building located at 39 Robinson Road. The CREBB issuance raised a total of S$193.00 million (US$121.97 million) in July 1999. In the securitisation process, Robinson Point Private Limited, a holding company that owns the property, was transferred *off-the-balance-sheet* of Birchvest Investment Private Limited, the originator of the CREBS deal. The structure of the CREBS is represented diagrammatically in Figure A2.

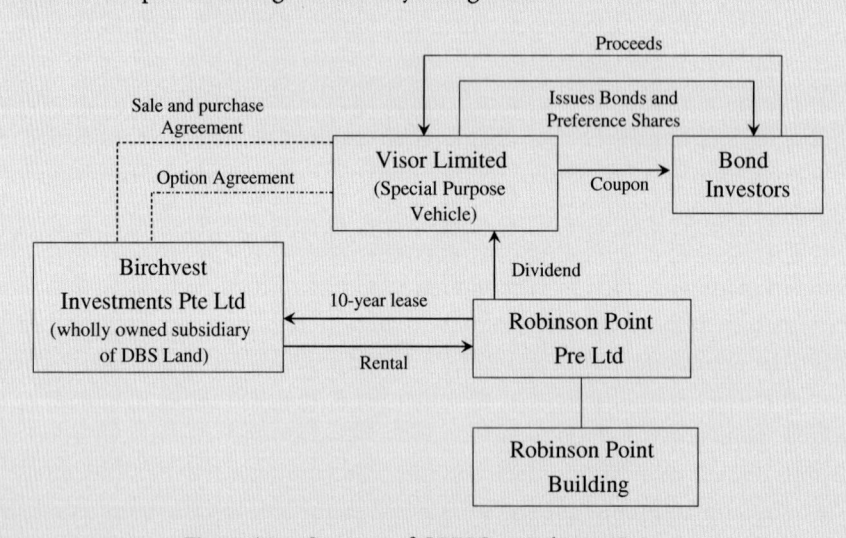

Figure A2. Structure of CREBS on Robinson Point.
Source: Sing, Ong and Sirmans (2003) and *Prospectus of Visor Limited CREBS Bond Issuance*

(*Continued*)

(*Continued*)

In the sale and purchase agreement, the originator obtained a lease-back option and a buy-back option on the properties with the SPV. Pursuant to the lease-back agreement, the originator assumed the role of a master lessee of the property for a period of 10 years, and in return it guaranteed to rental income that was sufficient to meet the coupon payments due to the bondholders. The buy-back option gives the originator the right to re-purchase the property at the purchase price plus a premium that will be staggered according to the option exercising date.

Visor Limited, the SPV, issued a total of S$193 million (US$121.97 million) of 10-year fixed rate bonds comprising S$125 million of senior bonds together 12,500 "A" preference shares and S$68 million junior bonds together with 6,800 "B" preference shares to fund the purchase of the prime office property. The Senior Bonds carry a fixed rate coupon of 6% per annum, whereas the Junior Bonds carry a fixed rate coupon of 2% per annum, and both coupons are payable semi-annually in arrears.

In the transaction, there are complex buy-back and sell-back options being structured into the agreement. The SPV is given call options that are exercisable any time after year three, but up to six months before the expiration of the bonds. The options, if exercised, give the SPV the right to re-purchase the property at par value plus a premium. The premium is only shared with bondholders via the preference shares, if the property value exceeds the par value of bond of S$193.00 million (US$121.97 million). The SPV is also entered into a put option agreement with bondholders to allow bondholders to sell back the property to the SPV, after the call options lapse but the bonds are not redeemed. The sale-back option is only exercisable in the last six months leading to the bond expiration.[1]

---

[1] For more details on the option features and pricing of the options, please refer to Sing, T.F., Ong, S.E. and Sirmans, C.F. (2003), "Asset-Backed Securitization in Singapore: Value of Embedded Buy-Back Options," *Journal of Real Estate Finance & Economics*, Vol. 27, No. 2, pp. 173–180.

2007 subprime crisis, CMBS have been a popular vehicle for Singapore-based REITs to tap on capital sources, especially in the European markets, as a way of diversifying their funding risks.

5. Commercial real estate securitisation Vehicles in Singapore

Three securitisation vehicles have been used by Singapore's real estate companies to tap funds in secondary real estate markets: mortgage backed bonds (MBB), commercial real estate backed securities (CREBS), and commercial mortgage backed securities (CMBS). For CREBS, cash flows generated from rental income of commercial properties are used to support coupon payments to bond investors. The CREBS structure has been used by developers to securitise cash flows generated from progress payment receivables from sales of residential development projects under construction. In recent years, a pass-through structure has been used to create profit participation securities in Singapore.

5.1 *Mortgage Backed Bonds (MBB)*

The earliest form of securitisation in Singapore was structured as pay-through bonds backed by mortgages on single commercial assets.[16] The MBB securitisation allows banks to take commercial real estate mortgages off their balance sheet, and reduce their exposure to real estate market risks.[17] The arranging banks could earn fee-based income by providing supports in structuring and servicing MBB issuance.

The first Singapore dollar MBB of S$185 million was issued in November 1986 by Hong Leong Holdings Limited on the legal mortgage pledged on the Hong Leong Building, an office building in the Central Business District. This property, with 45,000 square metres lettable area held under a 999-year leasehold title was valued at S$280 million by the valuer, Richard Ellis Limited. Citicorp Investment Bank (Singapore) was the MBB arranger and Bank of Tokyo provided the guarantee on the MBB. The five-year MBB on Hong Leong Building carried a semi-annual coupon at 7.125%. The second MBB of S$51 million was issued six years later in 1992 by Orchard Parade Holdings, the listed vehicle of Far East Organization. Buoyed by rising property prices, MBB activities expanded quickly with 16 MBB issued between 1994 and 1997. Far East Organization and CDL/Hong Leong groups were the two most active MBB issuers, which collectively constituted 55.89% of the MBB issued by value in the market. MBB with pledge on mortgages of investment residential projects and serviced apartments, such as Orchard Scott Deluxe Serviced Apartments owned by Goldenview Development Private Limited, a wholly owned subsidiary of Far East Organization (Case Study 1), was used by developers to raise funds. Table 1 lists the MBB issued since 1986, which have a total estimated value of S$ 2.70 billion.

5.2 *Commercial Real Estate Backed Bonds (CREBB)*

Unlike the MBB that use an *on-the-balance-sheet* structure, a more sophisticated *off-the-balance-sheet* financing structure was adopted for commercial real estate securitisation deals in Singapore after 1999. It moved one step closer to the US-style pay-through securitisation model, where the separation of ownership of assets is an

---

[16] Ong, S.E., Ooi, J., and Sing, T.F. (2000) "Asset Securitization in Singapore: A Tale of Three Vehicles," *Real Estate Finance*, Summer, pp. 1–10.

[17] Banks are restricted under the Singapore's Banking Act, Chapter 19 (1999 revised edition) to grant real estate loans in excess of 30% of the total Singapore's deposits.

Table 1. MBB issued in Singapore.

S/No	Issuer	Issue Year	Term	Principal	Coupon (%)
1	Hong Leong Holdings Ltd	1986	5	185,000,000	7.25
2	Orchard Parade Holdings Ltd	1992	5	51,000,000	5.625
3	Avenbury Property Ltd	1994	5	50,000,000	4.7
4	Goldenview Properties Ltd	1994	5	88,000,000	5.125
5	Orchard Parade Holdings Ltd	1994	5	93,000,000	6.09
6	Orchard Parade Holdings Ltd	1995	5	150,000,000	5.7
7	Branbury Investment Ltd	1996	5	210,000,000	4.93
8	CDL Properties Ltd	1996	5	280,000,000	5.5
9	Eunos Link Technology Park Ltd	1996	5	100,000,000	5.625
10	PLPM Properties Ltd	1996	7	350,000,000	5.06
11	Seasons Green Ltd	1996	5	60,000,000	6.5
12	Century Square Development Ltd	1997	5	146,000,000	5.06
13	Dover Rise	1997	3, 4	130,000,000	6.07–6.20
14	Guthrie GTS	1997	5	75,000,000	3.02
15	MCL Land (RQ) Ltd	1997	5	90,000,000	5.09
16	Orchard 290 Ltd	1997	5	270,000,000	4.6
17	Orchard 300 Ltd	1997	5	180,000,000	4.875
18	Superbowl Holdings Ltd	1997	5	30,000,000	3.53
19	Leonie Condotel Ltd	1998	5	162,000,000	7.12

Source: Ong, Ooi and Sing (2000)

important feature in the securitisation structure. A special purpose vehicle (SPV) is set up to facilitate the transfer of legal rights of commercial real estate from the books of developers/owners. The SPV holds commercial real estate assets in trust of investors. As a bankruptcy remote entity, it insulates investors of commercial mortgage backed securities (CREBB) against business and bankruptcy risks of originators and enhances credit rating of CREBB. It raises funds in capital markets by issuing bonds that guarantee fixed rate coupons. Rental streams generated from the securitised commercial real estate are used to meet the coupon obligations of CREBB. Figure 8 gives a diagrammatic representation of a typical CREBB deal.

5.2.1 *Commercial Real Estate Securitisation*

The first CREBB was issued in 1999 by Neptune Orient Line (NOL), involving the sale of NOL's 26-storey headquarter building located at Alexandra Road, for S$185 million. An SPV — Chenab Investments Limited, issued 10-year fixed rate commercial

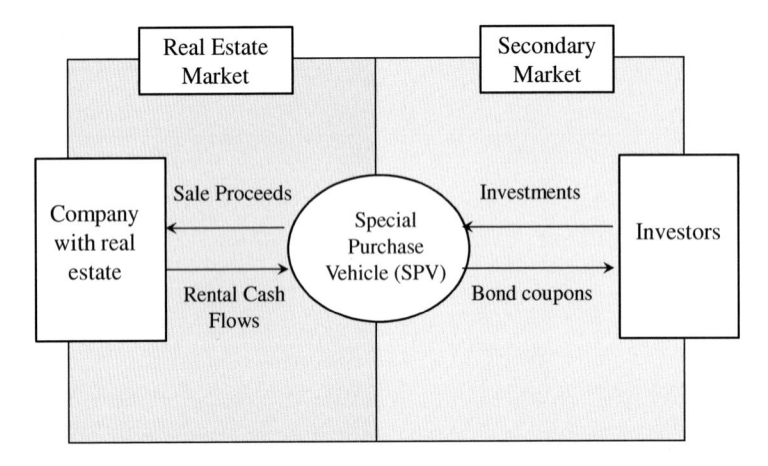

Figure 8. The model of a typical CREBB deal.

real estate backed bonds to fund the transaction. From 1999 to 2002, 10 CREBS deals were arranged, raising a total of S$4.095 billion through issuance of fixed rate bonds backed by commercial real estate (CREBB) (Table 2). The largest CREBB issuance by value of S$945 million was created in June 2001 on the office and shopping centre components of the Raffles City. The commercial real estate made up 55% stake of the Raffles City (Private) Limited, which also owns the convention facilities and hotels in the mixed use development. Tincel Limited, an SPV, funded the acquisition through the issuance of two tranches of 10-year fixed rate secured bonds.

In a typical CREBB (Case Study 2), a simple subordination structure is adopted by partitioning the CREBB tranch into senior class and a junior class bonds. Senior bonds are the "last loss" pieces that are subordinated by junior bonds in the case of default. They have a higher priority of claims on distributable cash flows. CREBS bonds are issued up to the market value of the commercial real estate. Third party guarantee and over-collateralisation are not used for credit enhancement purposes in the CREBB.

Buy-back and lease-back options are built into the terms and conditions of sale.[18] The buy-back option gives the first right for the originator to buy back the securitised property at the original price plus a premium, which is staggered over time. The originators (owners) retain the upside potentials of the property via the buy-back option. The lease-back option, if exercised, allows the originator to assume the role of a master lessee for the securitised property. It guarantees rental cash flows that are sufficient to meet the bondholder's debt obligation. As an exit option, the SPV is given a sell-back option, which gives the SPV the rights to sell back the securitised property to the

---

[18] Sing, T.F., Ong, S.E. and Sirmans, C.F. (2003), "Asset-Backed Securitization in Singapore: Value of Embedded Buy-Back Options," *Journal of Real Estate Finance & Economics*, Vol. 27, No. 2, pp. 173–180.

Table 2: List of commercial real estate backed securitisation deals in Singapore.

Property securitised	Property type	Sponsor/owner	Special purpose vehicle	Bond issued (S$mil.)	Senior bonds	Junior bonds	Bond tenure	Issue date
Neptune Orient Line HQ	Office	NOL	Chenab Investments Ltd	$185.00	6.75%	7.25%	10-year	Mar-99
Robinson Point	Office	Birchvest Investment Pte Ltd. (DBS Land)	Visor Limited	$193.00	6.00%	2%	10-year	Jul-99
Century Square Shopping Mall	Shopping Centre	First Capital Corporation	Pemberton Development Ltd	$200.00	N.A.		7-year	Jun-99
268 Orchard Road	Office	RE Properties (DBS Land)	Baronet Limited	$184.00	5.50%	6.50%	10-year	Sep-99
Tampines Centre	Shopping Centre	DBS Bank	Tampines Assets Limited	$180.00	5.63%	6.00%	7-year	Dec-99
Six Battery Road	Office	Birchvest Investments Pte Ltd (DBS Land)	Clover Holdings Limited	$878.00	6.00%	6.50%	10-year	Dec-99
Raffles City	Shopping Centre cum office	Raffles Holdings	Tincel Limited	$984.50	5.00%	7.40%	10-year	Jun-01
Wisma Atria	Shopping Centre cum office	Al Khaleej Investment/Wisma Development	Upperton (Aspinden) Holdings	$451.00	4.94%	7.0% (A)/ 8.85% (B)	5-year	May-02
Compass Point Shopping Cenre	Shopping Centre	Fraser & Neave Ltd	Sengkang Mall Limited	$335.00	4.88%	8.00%	10-year	Nov-02
Capital Square	Office	Keppel Land	Queensley Holdings Limited	$505.00	4.50%	N.A.	7-year	Nov-02

Source: Compilation by the author.

originator at the market price, at the maturity of the bond. This ensures that the outstanding bonds can be fully redeemed at the maturity. After the Institute of Certified Public Accountants of Singapore (ICPAS) revised and aligned the Singapore Statements of Accounting Standards (SAS) with the International Accounting Standards (IAS) in 2001, the embedded options in the CREBB transactions do not qualify the "true" sale requirements.[19] Commercial real estate assets "sold" in the earlier CREBB are consolidated back into the sponsors' books.[20] The stricter accounting rules on removing real estate assets *off-the-balance-sheet* reduce the economic benefits for developers/owners to securitise their commercial real estate using the CREBB structure.[21]

5.2.2 *Residential Development Project Securitisation*

The US-version of residential mortgage backed securities (RMBS) does not exist in Singapore because banks are not prepared to dispose their home mortgages off their books. However, developers use a creative financing engineering vehicle to securitise cash flows generated from the pre-completion sales of their residential projects. The cash flows come in the form of progress payment receivable from buyers of units in the residential projects under construction. This securitisation is sometimes referred to RMBS in Singapore, though the collaterals are not home mortgages but payments made in stages by individuals. The progress payments, which are usually paid into a project account following the progress of construction, are "sold" by developers to an SPV. The SPV in turn issues bonds backed by the cash flows to fund the acquisition. The RMBS term is usually tied to the project completion time. The lump sum proceeds received upfront will be used by developers to finance construction costs for the projects, and thus reduce the financing costs.

The first securitisation was created in 1999 on progress payments from a single residential project — The Clearwater, located at the Bedok Reservoir area, which was developed by Pidemco (the predecessor of CapitaLand). The Clearwater RMBS bonds with a total issued value of S$100 million for a three-year term with a fixed coupon of 4.75% per annum were arranged and managed by Tokyo-Mitsubishi International (Singapore) Limited. The residential project securitisation model was extended to include multiple projects in 2001 by CapitaLand Residential, which securitised the progress payments from the three residential projects under construction: SunHaven, Palm Grove and The Loft (Case Study 3). The proceeds from the

---

[19] SAS 33 establishes conditions for determining when control over a financial asset or liability has been transferred to another party. For financial assets, a transfer normally would be recognised if (a) the transferee has the right to sell or pledge the asset and (b) the transferor does not have the right to reacquire the transferred assets.

[20] Rashiwala, Kalpana, (2002), "CapitaLand seen buying back 2 more securitised buildings," *Business Times*, 22 November, 2002.

[21] Fan, G.Z., Sing, T.F., Ong, S.E. and Sirmans, C.F. (2004) "Governance and Optimal Financing for Asset-Backed Securitization," *Journal of Property Investment & Finance*, Vol. 22, No. 5, pp. 414–434.

Case Study 3: Securitisation of Progress Payments from Residential Projects under Construction

CapitaLand uses the collateralised mortgage obligation (CMO) model to securitise progress payment receivables from three of their residential projects under construction: The Loft, Palm Grove and Sunhaven. It set up an SPV, Peridot Investment Limited (Peridot), to facilitate *the off-the-balance-sheet* transfers of the progress payments of the projects from Capitaland. Peridot issued S$200 million fixed rate semi-annual coupon RMBS bonds on 15 June 2001 to fund the acquisition. There are four tranches of bond issued with "AAA" rated bonds, constituting about 80% of the total issued, having a par value of $160 million. The details of the multi-tranch bond structure are summarised in table below:

Tranch	Bond type	Rating	Bond Value (S$ mil.)	Coupon (%)
Class A	Fixed Rate	AAA	160	3.71%
Class B	Fixed Rate	AA	18	3.83%
Class C	Fixed Rate	A	12	4.09%
Class D	Fixed Rate	BBB	10	4.79%

Source: Information Memorandum of Peridot Investment Limited.

Peridot's RMBS are secured on the progress payments from three residential projects under construction. The three projects are expected to generate a total project value, if fully sold, of S$504.20 million. At the time of issuance, only 71.1% of the project units have been sold with an estimated aggregate sale value of $358.60 million. The details of the collaterals (residential projects) are shown in the Table below:

	The loft	Palm grove	Sunhaven	Total
Location	Nassim Hill	Palm Grove Avenue	Upper Changi Road East	
Leasehold	99 years	999 years	freehold	
Land Area (Sqf)	81,095	130,528	242,502	454,125
Allowable Plot Ratio	1.4	1.4	1.6	
Net Saleable Area (sqf)	108,000	167,000	391,000	666,000
Total Number of Units	77	111	295	483
Units Sold	34	77	251	362
% Sold over Total Units	44.2%	69.4%	85.1%	
Launch Date	Mar-2000	Jun-2000	Jun-2000	
TOP Date	Mar-2003	Dec-2002	Jun-2004	
Legal CSC Date				
Current Sales Value ($ mil.)	$59.20	$74.60	$224.80	$358.60
Estimated value of unsold units ($ mil.)	$75.80	$30.90	$38.90	$145.60
Expected Project Value ($ mil.)	$135.00	$105.50	$263.70	$504.20

Source: Information Memorandum of Peridot Investments Limited.

The RMBS deal was managed and arranged by Bayerische Hypo-und Vereinsbank AG, Singapore Branch. The six-year bonds matured in June 2007. The originator, CapitaLand, used the fund raised from the bond issuance to refinance loans on the project and also fund construction costs for the three projects. Figure A3 shows a diagrammatic representation of the securitisation structure of RMBS on progress payments on the three residential projects under construction.

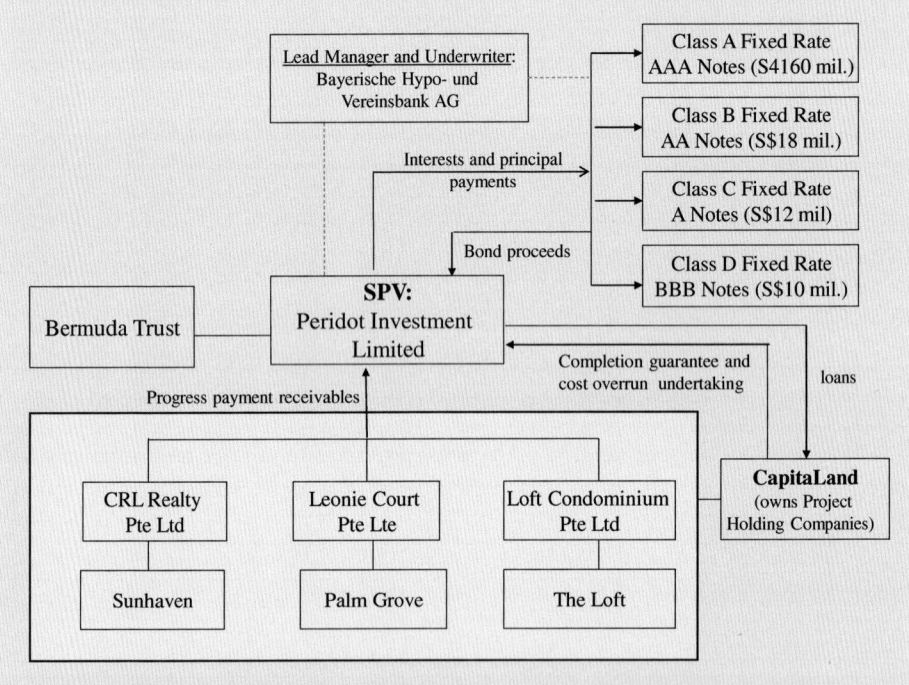

Figure A3: Structure of securitisation on progress payments of a residential project.
Source: The Authors.

RMBS were used to finance land and construction costs. Table 3 shows the list of residential projects that have been securitised in Singapore. Developers raised a total of S$2.82 billion from the 10 residential project securitisation deals.

5.3 Commercial Mortgage Backed Securities (CMBS)

After the successful listing of the two real estate investment trusts (REITs) — CapitaMall Trust (CMT) and Ascendas REIT (A-REIT) on the Singapore Exchange in 2002, REITs have replaced CREBB as a new and more popular vehicle for developers to raise funds in the capital market. The REIT market grew rapidly

CHAPTER 8 | Bridging the Gap between Capital and Real Estate Markets   229

Table 3. Residential development project cash flows securitisation.

Issuer	Originator	Issue date	Maturity date	Collateral assets	Issue Value (S$/US$ million)	Issue Value (S$ million)
Silverlac Investment Ltd	Pidemco Land	July 1999	July 2002	The Clearwater	S$ 100.00	S$ 100.00
Brizay Property Pte Ltd	Tan Chong International	September 2000	Not known	Wilby Residence	S$ 146.00	S$ 146.00
Peridot Investment Corporation	CapitaLand Residential Limited	June 2001	June 2009	The Loft, Palm Grove, Sunhaven	S$ 200.00	S$ 200.00
Jasmine Investment Corp	Keppel Land	June 2002	December 2007	Edgewater, Butterworth8 and Amaranda Garden	S$ 302.00	S$ 302.00
Aragon Investment Corp	Capitaland Residential	January 2003	December 2009	Waterina Project	S$ 121.00	S$ 121.00
Riviera Investment	Centrepoint Properties	August 2003	August 2006	Cote d'Azur	US$ 162.00	S$ 275.53[#1]
Arwen Investment Corp	CapitaLand Residential	April 2004	December 2006	Botanic on Lloyd and The Imperial	S$ 155.60	S$ 155.60
Faramir Investment Corp	CapitaLand Residential	March 2006	March 2009	Citylights and Varsity Park	S$ 332.70	S$ 332.70
Okeanos Investment corp	CapitaLand/Hwa Hong Corp	January 2007	June 2009	Rivergate	US$ 477.00	S$ 687.45[#2]
Vesta Investment Corp	CapitaLand Residential/ Lippo Resources China	July 2007	October 2009	Metropolitan, Scotts HighPark	US$ 346.00	S$ 498.66[#2]

#1 Exchange Rate US$1: S$1.7008 as in 2003 (Source: the MAS).
#2 Exchange Rate US$1: S$1.4412 as in 2007 (Source: the MAS).
Source: CapitaLand and the Authors.

through new REIT listings and expansion of the existing REITs' real estate portfolios. Despite having relatively conservative leverage ratios,[22] REITs actively explore ways to manage their capital structures, especially in hedging against their interest rate risks. REITs securitise floating rate mortgages on real estate assets via issuing medium- to long-term fixed coupon CMBS bonds. In the process, they swap floating rate obligations in commercial real estate mortgages into fixed rate obligations in CMBS bonds.

Unlike the single-asset CREBB, the collateralised mortgage obligation (CMO) model is adopted in the CMBS issuance by REITs, which involves pooling multiple commercial mortgages into an SPV and issuing securities in multiple tranches. The multi-tranch CMBS is no different from the US CMBS, but instead of banks, the roles of issuers are assumed by REITs in Singapore.

Public REITs and private real estate funds, such as CapitaRetail Singapore Limited (Case Study 4), are the main issuers of CMBS in Singapore. CapitaLand Mall Trust (CMT) issued CMBS via an SPV — Silver Maple Investment Corporation Limited (SMICL), to obtain S$172 million of term loans and S$28 million of revolving credit facilities secured on three retail properties in the CMT portfolio in February 2002. Three other tranches of US dollar-denominated term loan facilities amounting to SG$ 797.96 million (US$522.6 million) were obtained through CMBS issued from June 2003 to October 2005. The CMBS were backed by nine retail properties in the CMT portfolios. Ascendas REIT issued CMBS via the SPV — Emerald Assets Limited, with a total issued value of EUR$309.00 million (S$623.56 million) in two different tranches, which were backed by mortgages on 40 industry properties, in 2004 and 2005, respectively. As of September 2006, 31 tranches of CMBS with a total bond value of S$5.91 billion have been created (Table 4).

CMBS bring several advantages to private real estate funds, developers, REITs, the secondary real estate market, and institutional investors. For users of fund, the CMBS market offers an alternative avenue for REITs to tap on capital outside Singapore, especially the European money markets that have strong demand for these senior rated real estate backed instruments. REITs can secure a stable long-term source of funding via CMBS and hedge against interest rate fluctuations by matching their asset cash flows with coupon obligations of CMBS bonds. The funding option is attractive when the spread between long-term senior bond yield and the risk-less instrument is small. Economies of scale can also be created via mortgage pooling, which further reduces the funding costs. For institutional investors, CMBS broaden the investment options in real estate assets with fixed income characteristics.

---

[22] REITs are subject to a borrowing limit of 35%, or 60% if credit rating reports are obtained, under the Property Fund guidelines.

Case Study 4: A CMBS issued by CapitaRetail Singapore (CRS)

The CMBS issued by CapitaRetail Singapore (CRS) is a typical structure used by Singapore's REITs in securitising mortgages on commercial real estate. CRS is a private property fund set up by CapitaLand Limited to hold three suburban malls that were acquired for S$500 million in September 2003. CRS issued two tranches of Euro-dollar denominated four-year CMBS bonds and three tranches of Singapore-dollar bonds to raise a total value of S$296.17 million (excluding Class E bonds retained by the issuer).[1] The scheduled maturity of the CMBS is on 27 February 2008 with a possible extension to a final maturity date of 27 August 2009 at stepped up interest rates. The senior class A and class B bonds of €81 million (S$180.17 million) are floating rate tranches, whereas the junior tranch consists of three classes of fixed rate bonds, where two of class D and class E bonds are not rated. The CMBS tranches are summarised as follows:

CMBS bonds	Issue value	Interest rate	Credit Rating Moody's	Standard & Poor's
Class A	€67.5 million	Floating rate	Aaa	AAA
Class B	€13.5 million	Floating rate	Aa2	AA
Class C	S$33.0 million	Fixed rate	A2	A
Class D	S$83.0 million	Fixed rate	Not rated	Not rated
Class E	S$213.0 million	Fixed rate	Not rated	Not rated

Source: Moody's and Standard & Poor's.

The CMBS were secured on loans on three suburban retail malls — Lot 1, Bukit Panjang Plaza and Rivervale Mall, in Singapore. The property details are described below:

Property	Property type	Tenure	Gross floor area (sqf)	Net lettable Area (sqf)	Mortgage loan (S$ mil.)	Independent valuation% (S$ mil.)
Rivervale Mall	A 4-storey suburban shopping centre in Sengkang New Town	99-year w.e.f. 6 Dec 1997	109,244	80,686	$40.674	$67.80
Lot One Shoppers Mall	A 7-storey suburban shopping centre in Choa Chu Kang	99-year w.e.f 1 Dec 1993	301,516	207,961	$152.00	$253.30
Buiking Panjang Plaza	A 3-storey suburban shopping centre in Bukit Panjang	99-year w.e.f 1 Dec 1994	215,259	146,030	$100.54	$167.60

% independent valuation by CB Richard Ellis.

---

[1] Based on the exchange rate of €$1: S$2.2243 as in 2004 (Source: The MAS).

The total loan value of the three mortgages was estimated at S$293.17 million, which was translated into a loan to value ratio of 60% based on the open market valuation of the three suburban shopping malls. The subordination structure offers credit protection against default risk for senior-tranch bond investors (classes A to D), who have priority of claims on the collateralised properties over the unrated class E bondholders. The three loans are cross-collateralised to give further credit enhancement to the CMBS. The originator, CMT, subscribes to the 30% E-class bonds at S$60 million using a combination of equity ($45 million) and debt ($15 million). The indirect route via the acquisition of the class E bonds without injecting the three CRS properties into the portfolio reduces the impact on the gearing of CMT, which rose only marginally from 29.7% to 31.2%.[2] The class E CRS-CMBS tranch acquisition was also yield-accretive, delivering returns in excess of 8.2% to CMT.

Figure A4 shows the structure of the CRS-CMBS. As the two tranches of Class A and Class B bonds are issued in floating rates that are pegged to Euro-zone interbank offered rates and coupons are paid in European currency. The cash flows received by the CRS SPV are protected against currency and interest rate risks through the swap contracts provided by BNP Paribas and Overseas Chinese Banking Corporate (OCBC) before the distribution.

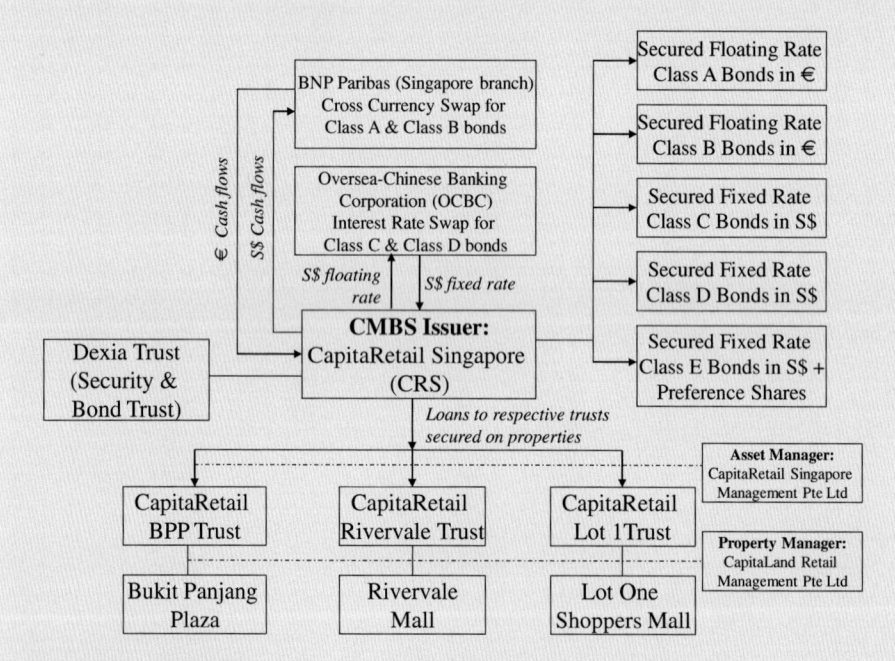

Figure A4. Structure of CMBS of CapitaRetail Singapore (CRS).
Source: Sing, Ong and Ng (2004).

---

[2] "CapitaMall Trust – An Indirect Route to Asset Acquisition," *Asia Pacific Equity Research Report* published by investment bank, J.P. Morgan Securities, on 10 September 2003.

CHAPTER 8 | Bridging the Gap between Capital and Real Estate Markets 233

Table 4 (A). List of commercial mortgage backed securities (CMBS) deals in Singapore.

CMBS issuer	CRE mortgagor	Issue date	Term of notes	Tranches/ classes of notes	Currency	Issue size ($ mil.)	Aggregate value (SGD$ mil.)	Commercial properties
Silver Maple Investment Corporation Limited#1	CapitaMall Trust (CMT)	26-Feb-02	5 years	Series 001: Fixed Rate Notes	SGD	$ 172.00	S$ 969.96	3 retail malls in CMT portfolio: Funan the IT Mall, Junction 8, Tampines Mall
		26-Jun-03	7 years	Series 018: Floating Rate Notes	USD	$ 72.10		The IMM Building
		2-Aug-04	5 years	Series 022: Floating Rate Notes	USD	$ 195.00		Plaza Singapura
		31-Oct-05	7 years	Series 025: Floating Rate Notes	USD	$ 255.50		Parco Bugis Junction, Hougang Plaza, Jurong Entertainment Centre, Sembawang Shopping Centre
CapitaRetail Singapore Ltd	3 Single Purpose Trusts (SPTs) that hold the 3 assets	27-Feb-04	4 years	Class A: Floating Rate Notes	EUR	$ 67.50	S$ 492.46	3 retail malls: Rivervale Mall, Lot One Shoppers Mall, Bukit Panjang Plaza
				Class B: Floating Rate Notes	EUR	$ 13.50		
				Class C: Fixed Rate Notes	SGD	$ 33.00		
				Class D: Fixed Rate Notes	SGD	$ 83.00		
				Class E: Fixed Rate Notes	SGD	$ 213.00		
Silver Loft Investment Corporation Limited	CapitaCommercial Trust (CCT)	16-Mar-04	5 years	Class A1: Floating Rate Notes	USD	$ 90.00	S$ 520.06	Capital Tower, 6 Battery Road, StarHub Centre, Robinson Point, Bugis Village, Golden Shoe Car Park, Market Street Car Park
				Class A2: Floating Rate Notes	USD	$ 147.00		
				Class A3: Floating Rate Notes	USD	$ 47.00		
				Class A4: Floating Rate Notes	USD	$ 56.60		

Table 4 (B). List of commercial mortgage backed securities (CMBS) deals in Singapore.

CMBS issuer	CRE mortgagor	Issue date	Term of Notes	Tranches/classes of notes	Currency	Issue size ($ mil.)	Aggregate value (SGD$ mil.)	Commercial properties
Emerald Assets Limited	Ascendas REIT	5-Aug-04	5 years	Floating Rate Notes	EUR	$ 144.00	S$ 623.56	17 properties: business park properties (6), light industrial properties (4), hi-tech industrial properties (2) and distribution and logistics centres (5)
		12-May-05	7 years	Floating Rate Notes	EUR	$ 165.00		23 properties: logistics and distribution centres (6), hi-tech industrial properties (6), light industrial properties (10), and business and science park (1)
Winmall Ltd	Jurong Point Reality Ltd	27-Oct-04	5 years	Class A: Floating Rate Notes	SGD	$ 73.00	S$ 520.00	Jurong Point Shopping Centre
				Class B: Fixed Rate Notes	SGD	$ 86.00		
				Class C: Fixed Rate Noes	SGD	$ 9.00		
				Class D: Fixed Rate Notes	SGD	$ 36.00		
				Unrated Notes (Fixed/Floating & Subordinated Floating)	SGD	$ 316.00		
Platinum AC1 Ltd	Suntec REIT	30-May-05	4.5year	Floating Rate Notes	EUR	$ 320.00	S$ 645.76	Suntec City Mall & Suntec Office Towers (strata floors)
Triumph Assets Ltd	Fortune REIT	28-Jul-05	5 years	Class AAA: Floating Rate Notes	HKD	$ 1735.00	S$ 466.27	11 retail properties in Hong Kong
				Class AA: Floating Rate Notes	HKD	$ 360.00		
				Class A: Floating Rate Notes	HKD	$ 290.00		

CHAPTER 8 | Bridging the Gap between Capital and Real Estate Markets   235

Table 4 (C). List of commercial mortgage backed securities (CMBS) deals in Singapore.

CMBS issuer	CRE mortgagor	Issue date	Term of notes	Tranches/ Classes of notes	Currency	Issue Size ($ mil.)	Aggregate value (SGD$ mil.)	Commercial properties
Orion Prime Ltd	Prime REIT	20-Sep-05	5 years	Floating Rate Notes	EUR	$ 186.20	S$ 375.75	Ngee Ann City & Wisma Atria Shopping Centre (Strata floors)
Blossom Assets Ltd	K-REIT Asia	17-May-06	5 years	Tranche A: Floating Rate Notes	EUR	$ 80.40	S$ 192.52	4 Office building: Keppel Tower, GE Tower, Bugis Junction Tower, Prudential Tower (strata floors)
				Tranche B: Floating Rate Notes	EUR	$ 15.00		
Silver Oak Limited	CapitaMall Trust & CapitaCommercial Trust	7-Sep-06	5 years	Class A1: Floating Rate Notes	USD	$ 427.00	S$ 844.60	Raffles City: office towers, hotels, shopping centers and conventional center and carpark
				Class A2: Floating Rate Notes	EUR	$ 30.00		
				Class B: Floating Rate Notes	USD	$ 86.50		
Star Topaz Limited	Frasers Centrepoint Trust	19-Sep-06	5 years	Floating Rate Note	SGD	$ 260.00	S$ 260.00	3 Shopping Malls: Causeway Point, NorthPoint and AnchorPoint

Note:

Asia1 currency converter	SGD	USD	EUR	HKD
Exchange Rate (as on 28-Feb-07)	1.000	1.5269	2.018	0.1955

Source: The author's compilation, Fitch Rating, Moody's and Standard & Poor's Reports & Annual Reports of Mortgagors

The rating requirement and monitoring mechanism of bond markets improve information efficiency in the secondary real estate market.[23]

5.4 *Property Participation Securities*

In December 2014, CDL securitised the Quayside Collection valued at S$1.5 billion using a pass-through securitisation structure.[24] The mixed-use development on Sentosa Island comprises a 240-room luxury hotel, 44,121 square feet (sqft) of retail space and 228 residential units. CDL (37.5%), Blackstone (48.9%) and CIMB (13.6%) jointly own an SPV that issues S$750 million Profit Participating Securities (PPS). The securities guarantee an annual yield of 5% for five years backed by cash flows from the Quayside Collection. If the residential assets in the development are sold after five years, the sale proceeds will be distributed to the PPS investors.

6. Conclusion

In Singapore, securitisation efforts have mainly been driven by the users of fund including real estate developers, commercial property owners and REITs. Banks, however, focus predominantly on businesses of loan origination in the primary market. Some banks play active roles in supporting and structuring secondary real estate market deals. They are involved in a whole range of specialised supports and services ranging from pooling of assets, setting up of SPVs and tranching to distributions of securities to investors, and collection and disbursement of cash flows.

Compared to the US markets, Singapore's securitisation market is relatively new and still in its infancy. Liquidity crunch after the economic recession in 1985 and the Asian Financial Crisis in 1997 has put pressure on Singapore's real estate developers to use securitisation as an alternative source of funding. The developers have made some progress in embracing financial innovations after the first MBB was introduced in 1986. From a simple MBB issuance backed by mortgages pledged on a single commercial building, the securitisation model used in Singapore has evolved over time to a more sophisticated multi-asset, multi-tranche structure. CMBS have been used by some real estate funds and REITs since 2002 as a capital management tool to manage financing risks, especially the interest rate risks.

The sub-prime crisis in 2007 has significant spill-over effects onto the CMBS markets in Singapore. The CMBS markets have been temporally halted with no new

---

[23] Sing, T.F., Ong, S.E. and Ng, K.H. (2004), "Commercial Mortgage Backed Securitization in Singapore: The Challenges Ahead," *Real Estate Finance*, pp. 14–27.
[24] Khoo, Lynette (2014), "CDL ties up with Blackstone, CIMB to monetise Sentosa Cove assets," *Business Times*, 17 December 2014.

CMBS issuance. The low interest rate environment coupled with the large influx of liquidity resulting from the expansionary monetary policies in the US and other developed countries eased the access to relatively cheap funding in the primary lending markets. Singaporean developers face no pressure and urgency to tap new capital in the secondary markets. However, the return of CMBS to Singapore's real estate market is imminent. The secondary real estate market activities are expected to pick up steam again in Singapore, when funding costs increase and commercial banks tighten their lending to real estate markets.

Part D
50 Years of Grooming Real Estate Talents

CHAPTER 9

Real Estate Education

Yu Shi Ming

This chapter traces the evolution of real estate education globally and specifically in Singapore, given its role in nurturing the talent required to support the evolving real estate industry. As the real estate landscape in Singapore has evolved over the last 50 years, the real estate degree programme has also undergone significant changes to meet the constantly-changing needs of the industry. Indeed, as the only real estate degree programme offered in Singapore, the National University of Singapore (NUS) Department of Real Estate has been producing graduates for the real estate industry since its inception in 1969, four years after Singapore's independence. Today, these graduates can be found in both public and private sectors. Many are leaders in professional consultancy firms, real estate investment trusts and funds, development and other real estate-related companies and various government agencies.

The concluding chapter of this book compiles the opinions and comments on Singapore's real estate industry from key leaders who are alumni of the Department. Some of them were from the founding batch in 1969 and they all continue to contribute to every segment of the real estate industry. This reflects the close connection and network between the industry's key leaders and their alma mater, the University.

Growth and Development of Global Real Estate Education

Real estate education offered at universities can be traced as far back as the early 20th century in the UK and even before the turn of the century in the US. Through the years, real estate degree programmes developed under two main schools of thought: the UK and the US models. In the nascent stages of real estate education, the UK model placed professional technical skills and knowledge of physical property at its core, whereas the US model focused on the broader management and administration of real estate. Today, there is cross-convergence between the two models as educators become increasingly responsive to the firms' need for graduates with strong knowledge of both property and business management.

In the UK, full-time education for the surveying profession existed for many years with the establishment of the College of Estate Management, which received its Royal Charter in 1922. From 1918, the BSc degree in Estate Management from the University of London was available through either full-time or part-time study, generally with the aid of the College's correspondence notes. This was supplemented in 1919 by an estate management degree at Cambridge University. For many years, these were the only degrees of their kind until the creation of the Council for National Academic Awards in 1964, which paved the way for development in tertiary education through polytechnics and colleges. Comparatively, real estate education started much earlier in the US.

In the US, the first course in real estate at the collegiate level was taught at the University of Wisconsin in 1892. In 1927, Arthur Mertzke, Director of Education and Research of the National Real Estate Boards (now the National Association of Realtors) observed that special higher-level training was required for persons entering the real estate business.[1] Some 52 universities and colleges offered such real estate specialisation at that time.

A traditional UK chartered surveying discipline focused on five main areas: valuation, law, economics, building construction and planning. Over time, new areas such as management, finance and information technology were introduced to these core subjects in order to keep pace with the needs of industry. This model aimed to provide a set of core professional skills required by a chartered surveyor from a technical as well as a project development perspective. It ensured that graduates not only obtained the requisite knowledge and skills, but also a deeper understanding of the role of the chartered surveyor vis-à-vis other real estate professionals like the architect, land surveyor, engineer and so on. Such a multi-disciplinary approach further equipped the trained chartered surveyor with a broad appreciation of legal and planning frameworks and even building construction techniques.

In contrast, the US model developed as part of business management. Weimer (1956) argues that a more appropriate approach to the teaching of real estate course is that of the business or administrator.[2] He stresses that greater emphasis should be given to such topics as the place of the real estate function within the organisational structure of the modern business firm, the relationship between the administration of real estate and other functions performed by the firm and the techniques of analysis which may be used to reach sound managerial decisions involving real estate problems. Dasso (1976) further asserts that the financial management framework is the vehicle best suited for real estate's recognition as an academic discipline.[3] Similarly,

---

[1] Mertzke, A. (1927) "Status of real estate education in the United States", National Real Estate Journal, June 1927.
[2] Weimer, A. (1956) "The teaching of real estate and business administration", Land Economics, Feb 1956.
[3] Dasso, J (1976) "Real estate education at the university level", Recent Perspectives in Urban Land Economics, University of British Columbia.

Graaskamp (1976) sees the curriculum for real estate at a major university as being centred in a school of business administration.[4] While the origin of the development of the US model is distinctly different from that of the UK, both share a common multi-disciplinary approach, although the mix of the disciplines may differ.

In between these two schools of thought, the real estate degree programme in Singapore has taken an eclectic approach by combining components of the two. For instance, the curriculum includes modules in planning and law as with the UK model, but also has a substantial coverage of finance and business management, almost to the same extent as the US real estate programmes.

Internationally, real estate education is now well-developed and established at the university level. The ongoing maturity of the discipline has seen increased stature and recognition in both developed as well as developing economies. In China, the proliferation of real estate degree courses at universities reflects the demand that has fuelled residential property prices and rapid urbanisation over the last two decades.

The development of real estate programmes at the universities in other countries took place mainly after the end of World War II. Commonwealth countries, in particular, introduced degree programmes as a natural progression from technical-level and vocational diplomas. For instance, the BSc Estate Management offered at the then University of Singapore started in 1969 when the Department of Building and Estate Management was set up at the Singapore Polytechnic at Prince Edward Road. Besides a full-time programme, the Department also offered two part-time professional diploma-to-degree conversion courses in the early 70s. In Australia and New Zealand, real estate degrees were introduced in the late 70s and early 80s, although they had very established diploma courses in valuation and land economics for a much longer period.

Major Milestones of Real Estate Education in Singapore

Early tertiary real estate education in Singapore was offered primarily via the UK College of Estate Management, the local polytechnic and the diploma in valuation from New Zealand universities under the Colombo Plan scholarship scheme, sponsored by New Zealand to help Singapore as a young nation develop its professional expertise in valuation. In the 60s and 70s, given the small cohorts in the early years of the Estate Management degree course, degree holders from the Colombo Plan scholarship returned to serve as valuers at the Inland Revenue Authority. Local university enrollment only started to grow to more than 50 from the early 80s and gradually expanded to its current size of about 150 in the last decade.

Real estate education was formally introduced at the university level in Singapore when the Faculty of Architecture, comprising the School of Architecture and the

---

[4] Graaskamp, J. (1976) "Redefining the role of university education in real estate and urban land economics", The Real Estate Appraiser, Mar-April, 23-6.

Department of Building and Estate Management, was instituted in 1969 at the former Singapore Polytechnic Campus at Prince Edward Road. In 1970, the Faculty moved to Kinloss House at Lady Hill Road. It moved again in 1976 when the new Kent Ridge campus of the then University of Singapore was ready. In fact, it was among the first Faculties to move to its present location at Kent Ridge. The Department of Building and Estate Management offered two basic degree courses: the BSc (Building) and the BSc (Estate Management). Both are four-year direct honours degree programmes.

Shortly after the University programme was introduced in 1969, a part-time professional diploma-to-degree conversion course was offered for a few years, catering to the students doing the diploma course at the Polytechnic then. Indeed, it has to be acknowledged that training in real estate first started at the Polytechnics and continues to do so today. When the demand from the Polytechnic graduates for university degrees increased, the Department offered two part-time degree courses in Property Management and Valuation from 1999 to 2006. Today, the Polytechnics continue to offer real estate or real estate-related diploma courses, while the National University of Singapore continues to be the only university offering a real estate degree in Singapore.

Initial cohorts of the BSc (Estate Management) programme each comprised of approximately 20 students, who were taught by a few full-time faculty members (predominantly expatriates) supplemented with local practitioners as part-time staff. The intake for the BSc (Estate Management) programme more than doubled in the late 70s/early 80s. When the then University of Singapore was merged with Nanyang University to form the National University of Singapore in 1980, recruitment of local full-time faculty members increased. In the same year, the Council of Professional and Technical Education paved the way for the expansion of the Department of Building and Estate Management, to increase its intake. Both the number of students and faculty grew significantly through the 1990s to reach the current level of more than 25 full-time faculty members with a student enrollment of around 700; these numbers qualify the department as one of the largest real estate academic institutions in the world today.

A major milestone was the renaming of the BSc (Estate Management) degree to the BSc (Real Estate) in 1996. This was to reflect the shift in focus from the narrow field of estate management to a wider scope encompassing a range of professional disciplines in the real estate industry. Another key development took place 10 years later in 2006 — the real estate degree had its own direct admission when the BSc (Building) was changed to the new BSc (Project and Facilities Management). For more than 30 years, the degree programmes shared a common first year as it provided advantages in terms of sharing resources in conducting lectures which were required for both degree courses. It also provided a platform for the students to establish relationships that could be useful in their future careers given the close proximity of the construction and real estate industries. Indeed, the Building and Estate Management Alumni (BEMA) was established in 1993 as an NUS Alumni Chapter and has since remained as one body for graduates from both Departments.

A key feature of professional degrees is the need for accreditation by professional bodies. This means that graduates can become members of such bodies upon graduation, subject to obtaining the requisite work experience. The BSc degree has been accredited by the local Singapore Institute Surveyors and Valuers (SISV) since the 80s and by the UK's Royal Institution of Chartered Surveyors (RICS) in 1989. Membership of these bodies provides a rich network for professional and career development as well as opportunities to work in overseas countries where these memberships are recognised. In addition, the membership of the local body is a prerequisite for obtaining an appraiser's licence in Singapore.

A postgraduate degree intended as a higher degree for practitioners in property and estate management — the MSc in Property and Maintenance Management — was offered in 1986; this was subsequently replaced by the MSc (Real Estate) in 1992, which aimed to serve a broader range of real estate industry practitioners with a non-real estate first degree by enhancing their theoretical and conceptual knowledge of real estate. Since 2004, the Department of Real Estate also offers an MBA (Real Estate Specialisation) with the NUS Business School, and from 2013, the Masters in Urban Planning with the Department of Architecture.

The Department of Real Estate also runs postgraduate research degrees at the Masters and PhD levels. The number of applicants for these research degrees has also increased significantly in the last 15 years as the Department's reputation in research grew, especially in the Asia Pacific region. In fact, the Centre for Real Estate Studies was first set up in 1991 and was subsequently elevated to a University Institute to become the Institute of Real Estate Studies in 2007. The Institute has served to help both staff and student research pursuits, in particular by leveraging on its international platform.

Evolving Curriculum

In 1969, the BSc (Estate Management) was launched with the purpose of producing graduates capable of entering managerial and executive positions in the building industry and the allied professions of quantity surveying, valuation and estate management. The curriculum was largely based on the UK model and was designed for a relatively narrow job market. In the 70s, when the first batch of students graduated, the emerging real estate market in Singapore was small and lacked sophistication. The course then catered to Ministries, statutory boards and a small number of developers, consultants and corporations with large property holdings. Since then, the job market has grown considerably as real estate activities have expanded in the traditional areas, both within Singapore and in the Asian region and into the sphere of finance, banking and investments.

Changes in the marketplace have necessitated changes to the curriculum, which has undergone regular major revisions over the last four decades. These reviews were major exercises where industry feedback was obtained and the restructuring subjected to scrutiny and approval at the different levels of the university system, culminating with approval from the University Senate. As the process takes six to 18 months, major reviews are only carried out every five-seven years; this allows the changes to be introduced gradually over the four-year cohort. Obviously, industry changes such as major government policies which have major impact on the real estate market and practice occur much more frequently and these need to be reflected in the curriculum when they emerge.

Global trends have also shaped and influenced changes to the real estate curriculum in NUS. First, increase in securitisation activity by real estate owners has created a demand for real estate professionals who are equipped with knowledge in real estate finance and securitisation. Second, regional expansion by Singapore real estate development companies and rapid urbanisation of emerging economies like China, India and Vietnam have generated employment opportunities for graduates with expertise to formulate urban planning policies for new townships and city-scale developments in Singapore and the region. The last curriculum review in 2010 introduced two specialisation tracks in real estate — finance and urban planning — to address these demands.

In terms of the mode of teaching, university education in Singapore has also witnessed tremendous change over the last 50 years. First, the system of assessment based on final year examinations was replaced by a modular system in 1995. The modular system allows students to elect cross-faculty modules as a means to widen their academic interests. This had significant impact on professional degrees such as engineering, architecture and real estate, where the focus was to ensure that graduates are well-equipped with professional competencies. It meant that to cater to a broader and a more general education, some core modules needed to be redefined and reduced.

In summary, five key paradigm shifts in the real estate education have taken place:

1. A broader knowledge base. Apart from learning technical fundamentals of real estate development, students are exposed to general education modules in science and technology as well as the humanities and social sciences. They are also required to read a Singapore Studies module to appreciate of the history and development of Singapore.

2. Flexible cross-faculty modular-based learning. The transition to a modular-based programme has enabled students to extend their learning beyond real estate-based subjects.
3. Increasing awareness of the role of real estate. Rapid urbanisation and the growth and globalisation of capital markets have made students more aware of the role and significance of real estate. To cater to this growing interest, the Department offers two minor tracks in real estate and urban studies.
4. Increasing emphasis on the financial aspects of real estate. As the real estate market shifts away from a simple brick-and-mortar play to a more capital market-centric business model, there has been a need to incorporate more in-depth modules on finance and the capital markets to equip graduates with the relevant knowledge base in both real estate and finance.
5. Shift in emphasis from local to global. From the 1990s, regionalisation and globalisation brought an influx of foreign developers and funds into Singapore. This pushed local firms to seek greater economic space outside of Singapore. From an educational perspective, it meant that students needed exposure beyond Singapore. Changes to the curriculum were made to teach students global best practices and exchange programmes were put in place to enable them to spend time at overseas academic institutions. For example, the NUS Real Estate Department offers exchange programmes for overseas students to gain insight into Singapore's business environment and policies, while third-year NUS real estate undergraduates have the option of taking a graded elective module under a Summer Programme to gain a deeper understanding of a foreign country's socioeconomic, demographic and political issues, which underpin real estate transactions in that country.

Today, the BSc (Real Estate) course aims to train real estate professionals who are able to understand the physical, economic, institutional and social aspects of the built environment and who are equipped with professional knowledge and competency in real estate wealth creation and management, in local and global contexts. While the core disciplines of real estate — comprising planning, law, economics, finance, valuation and management — have remained largely intact, technical subjects such as the theory and practice of buildings, building services and surveying were replaced with commerce-centric modules relating to investments, market analysis and research in response to the changing demands of the real estate industry. The following table compares the curriculum of 1969 and 2015 in the core areas of Building and Construction, Law, Planning, Economics, Valuation, Finance and Management. Notwithstanding the several major reviews in between these years, clearly the focus of the curriculum has changed. While technical expertise was emphasised in the early development years with many building and construction subjects, the current curriculum has more modules in management and finance, given the changes in the job market.

Table 1. Curriculum in 1969 and 2015.

Core areas	1969	2015
Building and Construction	History of Building	Understanding Design and Construction
	Surveying and Levelling	
	Theory of Design of Structures 1–2	
	Building Sciences 1–3	
	Theory and Practice of Building 1–4	
	Earth Sciences	
	Building Services and Equipment	
	Quantity Surveying	
Law	Elements of Law 1–4	Land Law
		Real Estate Finance Law
		Real Estate Development Law
Planning	Town and Country Planning	Urban Land Use and Development
		Urban Planning
		Advanced Topics in Urban Planning
		Urban Design and Conservation
		Urban Planning Seminar
		Advanced Urban Planning Theories
		Public Policy and Real Estate Markets
		Urban Planning in Asian Cities
Economics	Economics of Industry	Principles of Economics
	Real Estate Economics	Introduction to Statistics
	Construction Economics and Cost Planning	Real Estate Market Analysis
		Real Estate Economics
		Real Estate Development
Valuation	Valuation of Land and Buildings 1–2	Principles of Real Estate Valuation
		Property Tax and Statutory Valuation
		Advanced Real Estate Valuation
Finance	Finance Theory	Fundamentals of Real Estate Finance
	Principles of Accounting 1–2	Real Estate Finance

(*Continued*)

Table 1. Curriculum in 1969 and 2015.

Core areas	1969	2015
Management	Theory of Management Estate Management 1–2	Real Estate Investment Analysis Corporate Investment in Real Estate Real Estate Finance Seminar REIT Management Real Estate Securitisation Real Estate Risk Analysis and Management Property and Facilities Management Professional Communication Real Estate Marketing and Negotiation Real Estate Practice and Ethics Research Methodology Quantitative Methods in Real Estate Advanced Real Estate Marketing

Graduates for the Industry

The major real estate consultants and developers we interviewed all mentioned that the availability of trained professionals was and continues to be a key strength for Singapore. From the early Polytechnic years to the establishment of the estate management course at NUS, employers were able to have access to graduates with real estate-focused backgrounds. This proved to be a distinct advantage given that even today, there are countries in Asia that do not have tertiary institutions producing real estate professionals. In fact, an emerging trend over the last decade has been the recruitment of NUS real estate graduates by developers with projects in developing countries such as China and Vietnam — in particular, Chinese or Vietnamese graduates trained in NUS who have the advantage of being local and possessing the training of an established international institution. The growth in the number of foreign students from the developing countries in Asia also means that NUS is indirectly helping to train graduates for these countries' developing real estate markets.

The other area of growth has been in finance, as employers typically highlight the changing demand for graduates with knowledge in investment and finance. Blending the core understanding of real estate with finance is seen as a powerful combination that is highly sought-after in today's marketplace.

Practical training, regarded as a cornerstone of professional degrees, has always been an important component of the course. In the early years when the intake was small, students typically were able to seek attachments with private sector companies during the long vacation period. When the professional bodies granted accreditation, practical training was made compulsory and the Department had to arrange industry placements with both public and private sector companies. However, as student enrollment increased, it became impractical to continue with compulsory placements. Hence, the introduction of the Real Estate Internship Programme (REIP) as a graded elective module offered only to third-year undergraduates on a competitive basis. Despite the limitations of the REIP, most if not all undergraduates are able to obtain internship experience at least once during their second- or third-year vacation period. This has certainly helped to prepare graduates for the industry.

Besides being ready for the job market, employers today also seek graduates who are able to communicate effectively. Take the example of the real estate consultancy business which has gone from one which principally represented owners and provided traditional real estate services, to one that is now split 50-50 between representing both owners and tenants, with a much broader basket of services. Such evolution requires graduates to have a broader base of knowledge and the ability to adapt to changes. They must also be able to communicate effectively with all stakeholders, including the public sector, owners, tenants, clients and occupiers.

To produce all-rounded graduates who are not only competent professionally but are also able to articulate and communicate, the Department has also put in place a number of initiatives such as the Real Estate Leadership Programme as well as student ambassadors. These initiatives are designed to allow students who have demonstrated leadership potential to be invited to specially arranged sessions with industry leaders and other industry seminars.

Real Estate Research and Executive Education

Real estate education has indeed played an important role in a country's physical and economic development. It has provided the necessary professional manpower for the development, use and management of the built environment. The emphasis on technical skills and knowledge in preparing graduates for the profession has helped Singapore to industrialise and transform the urban landscape. As Singapore shifts to a service-oriented and knowledge-based economy, real estate education also shifts its emphasis to focus more on management and finance. Besides being the only university providing real estate education for the industry, the department has also made significant contributions in research and executive education.

Research, which has always being the other important part of a university, has become even more significant as universities' reputation increasingly hinges on their research output. In this regard, the Department, with the establishment of the Institute of Real Estate Studies (IRES), has emerged among the top universities in real estate research globally, and the leading university in Asia. This rise in reputation has led to key partnerships with other reputable universities such as Tsinghua University in China, Hong Kong University, University of Maaschritt and the Massachusetts Institute of Technology (MIT). It has also helped to draw PhD graduates from the top US universities to the Department.

Besides formal education, the Department has also conducted many executive courses and programmes over the years. Typically, the courses are designed for clients who range from Singapore's Ministry of Foreign Affairs, statutory boards and local companies to foreign governments, institutions and companies. Singapore has been a sponsor for developing countries that sent senior civil servants to attend courses on urban management, including public housing and town councils, run by the Department. There are also tailor-made real estate courses at the basic or advanced level for government statutory boards such as the Housing Development Board (HDB), JTC, NParks and the Singapore Land Authority (SLA). The Department has also conducted special real estate courses for foreign institutions such as the Vietnamese Ministry of Pricing, local authorities from various provinces and cities of China and even university staff from Indonesia developing their own real estate degree course. In the last few years, the Department has also launched a very successful Graduate Certificate in Real Estate Finance programme, focusing on bridging the real estate and capital markets.

Future Challenges

An ongoing challenge for real estate education has been public perception. Although real estate news occupies a sizeable stage in the media, the typical lay person associates real estate with agencies. The rest of the professional activities in the real estate spectrum somehow do not come into the picture. One possible reason for this could be that since real estate is part of the environment, it has been taken for granted. This ignorance or a lack of better understanding of what real estate really is has been a challenge in attracting school leavers to apply for the real estate degree programme.

Constant change is probably the most significant challenge to education today. As seen in the growing influence of real estate expertise in the growing fund management industry, flexible educational curriculum is needed to meet the needs of an ever evolving real estate industry. For now, a modular system provides the best means for customised broad-based learning; yet, universities need to ensure that core competencies of the profession are not compromised. Another evolving and increasingly important issue is environmental sustainability. This has a direct impact on real estate education as it seeks to find a solution to address the challenges brought about by rapid urbanisation and globalisation.

Another key challenge facing the industry in Singapore is keeping pace with the rapid changes wrought by technological innovation. The impact of digital technologies and the power of mobile communications have been felt by every sector of the real estate industry. From the looming challenge retailers face against the ease and economy of e-commerce to the runaway success of Airbnb as a serious competitor to the hospitality industry, graduates need to understand how technology impacts the end-user and how it influences human behaviour and interaction in order to assess the repercussions on physical real estate and its values. They also need to embrace technology to enhance communication, for example, by leveraging on software and applications to increase the sophistication and responsiveness of property management services. Real estate practitioners should also be vigilant of emerging competition from data aggregators such as Real Estate Exchange and PropertyGuru. While they remain real estate data providers today, they have the ability to use their online platforms to replace the role of real estate intermediaries like consultants and agents in services like property sales and leasing.

From the academic perspective, mobile communication technologies have also expanded the reach of academic institutions in an unprecedented way. Online teaching and virtual classrooms have replaced or supplemented the traditional lecture and tutorial systems; off-campus learning in some instances means that students do not even need to leave their home to obtain a degree. These new methods of delivering academic content mean that learning can be done anywhere, any time, and that the real estate educator has to think of innovative ways to facilitate access to content. There is an urgent need for universities to leverage these new technologies in order to engage a younger, more mobile, more demanding generation of potential real estate professionals. This is especially relevant since students seeking to join the real estate profession will struggle to put together a bespoke learning programme on their own and will still require the rigorous and holistic real estate training which university-based learning provides.

Fundamentally, the key challenge for real estate education is staying relevant in a world with less borders and more technology. The curriculum needs to be at once flexible and also focused to ensure professional competence through the core disciplines while at the same time being able to adapt to changes in the market place. Similarly, educators need to keep pace with changes not only in the industry but also the mindsets of their students as they continue to shape the minds of the future generations.

Chapter 10

Transforming Singapore's Real Estate: Building on Firm Foundation

Sing Tien Foo and Yu Shi Ming

1. Introduction and the Real Estate System

The late Professor James A. Grasskamp at the University of Wisconsin-Madison defines real estate "… *generally as space delineated by man, relative to a fixed geography, intended to contain an activity for a specific period of time. To the three dimensions of space (length, width, and height), then, real estate has a fourth dimension — time for possession and benefit. This can be referred to as a space-time characteristic. The space-time concept is illustrated by the terms apartment per month, motel rooms per night, square footage per year, and tennis courts per hour. A fundamental element in real estate is that any space-time unit has a corresponding monetary value. While many of the value judgments and debates about real estate projects relate to elusive criteria of what is good and beautiful, in a money economy the ultimate criterion is cash.*"[1]

Professor Grasskamp further describes real estate development as a process of creating space time units. Three groups of people involved in the real estate development process include space producers (developers), space users (households and firms), and infrastructure and services providers (the government).

In a real estate capital market, a business enterprise undertakes the conversion of space-time to money-time units. The real estate system is diagrammatically represented by the space-time and money-time markets, which are connected by a government in the centre (Figure 1). The government's roles involve regulating the money-time market activities and supporting the space-time unit creation process by providing infrastructure and services (see Chapter 2 for more details). In Singapore, the government is also responsible for building affordable public housing and selling lands to private developers for building new commercial and residential space (space-time units). Developers obtain capital, either through bank borrowing or security

---

[1] Grasskamp, J.A. (1981) "Fundamentals of Real Estate Development," Urban Land Institute, Development Component Series, Washington DC.

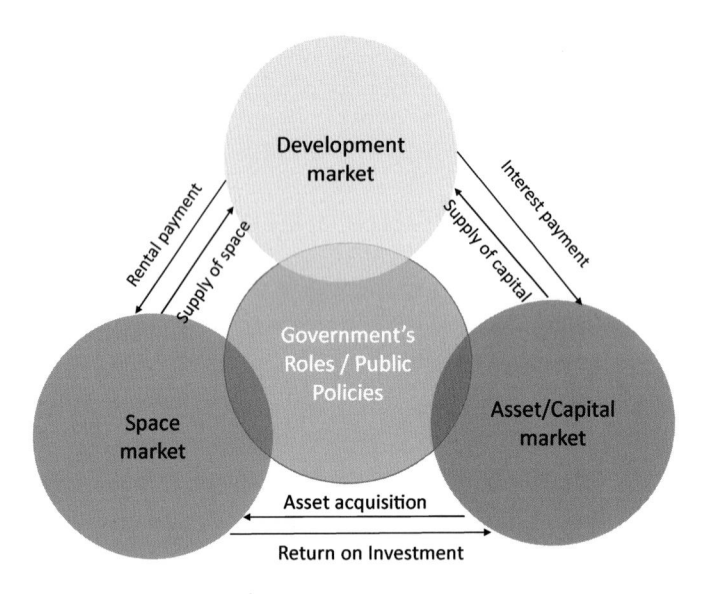

Figure 1. Real estate market system.

Source: The Authors.

issuance in the capital market. The space created in the market is used to satisfy the housing, business and production needs of various users. They pay rents for the use of space, which can then be translated into property value (money-time units) that can be monetised by investors in the asset market. The conversion of space-time and money-time, together with the government's regulatory roles to ensure fair-play, complete the real estate system.

The interactions of different groups and the inter-connectedness of different markets as represented by the circles in Figure 1 ensure smooth functioning of the real estate system. The outcomes of an efficient real estate system are an organised and sustainable urbanisation, wealth creation, and quality space for live-work-play. In the last 50 years, Singapore has undergone rapid urbanisation, evolving from a third-world to a first-world city. This success could not have been possible without the farsighted vision and the strong will of political leaders. The collaborative efforts of various stakeholders in the real estate system in Figure 1 are also an essential factor. The government lays down the long-term urban planning roadmap; developers bring their entrepreneurial and risk taking spirit, together with capital from a well-functioning financial market; and lastly, a healthy economy generates demand for real estate space. All parties in the system contribute in one way or another on the road of nation building and urban growth of Singapore.

The Department of Real Estate at the National University of Singapore was established in 1969 as the Department of Building and Estate Management. The objective was to provide tertiary education and formal training to produce real estate professionals to support early nation building in the post-independence years. The Department was subsequently renamed the School of Building and Real Estate in 1995, which, together with the School of Architecture, formed the Faculty of Architecture, Building and Real Estate. In June 2001, a reorganisation at the Faculty level led to the change of the Faculty's name to the School of Design Environment. In the same year, the School of Building and Real Estate was split into two independent departments: the Department of Building and the Department of Real Estate. In 2006, the Institute of Real Estate Studies (IRES), a university-level research institute, was set up to spearhead high impact real estate research and elevate the profile of NUS Real Estate, which collectively represents IRES and the Department of Real Estate.

In the last 46 years, NUS Real Estate has produced many batches of real estate professionals, who have made significant contributions, in one way or another, to the transformation of Singapore into one of the world's most liveable cities[2] and one of the top business cities[3] in the last 50 years. Many NUS Real Estate alumni and graduates also apply their real estate skill sets and expertise to create space-time and money-time units in real estate markets outside Singapore. It is therefore appropriate and fitting to devote this concluding chapter to the collation of some thoughts and reflections on the past and future real estate and urban developments in Singapore from some of the NUS Real Estate alumni, many of whom are industry leaders in Singapore. The rest of the chapter is organised into three sections. Section 2 discusses the sustainable eco-system in NUS real estate education that has trained and continues to produce real estate professionals and leaders. Section 3 collates the reflections of some of the distinguished alumni on the last 50 years of transformation in the real estate industry, and their expectations of the future of the real estate market. Their views and comments are organised into themes, which are aligned with the book structure. The last section sums up the discussions with forecasts of some mega trends that are likely to affect Singapore's real estate market.

2. Real Estate Professionals and Education

Figure 2 shows the NUS Real Estate eco-system that plays pivotal roles in grooming and producing real estate professionals and leaders. As a tertiary institution, one of its roles is to support the country's manpower needs in the urbanisation and development

---

[2] According to the ECA survey, Singapore is the most liveable place in Asia for expatriates and also the most favoured city in the world for Asian expats. Source: Rachel Boon, "Singapore remains the most liveable place in Asia for expatriates: Poll," *The Straits Times*, 23 January 2015.
[3] The World Bank Group ranked Singapore as the top city in the "*Doing Business*" Surveys for two consecutive years in 2005 and 2006. (Source: http://www.doingbusiness.org/data/exploreeconomies/singapore#close)

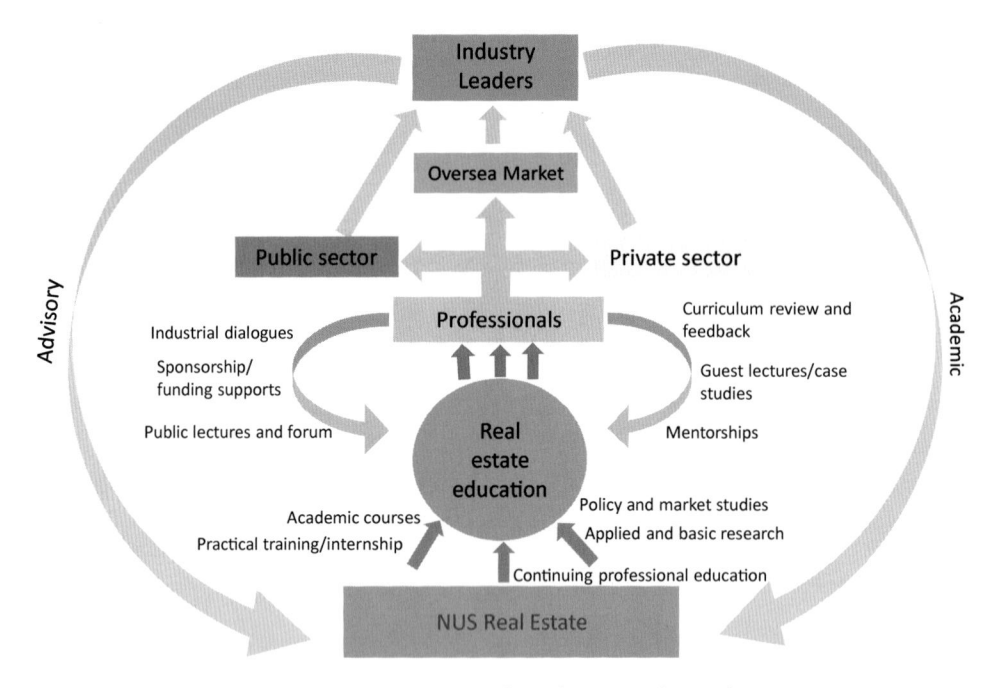

Figure 2. An eco-system for real estate professionals.

process. Through this, it has also made significant contributions in various ways in transforming Singapore into a liveable and sustainable global city.

The influence and presence of NUS Real Estate alumni can be found in the private, public and oversea sectors covering a wide spectrum of activities from urban development, built environment and real estate business. It has produced many prominent industry leaders, who have played a key part in building Singapore into a modern garden city. NUS Real Estate constantly engages the industry and alumni via platforms and channels, such as industry dialogues, public forums, seminars, mentorships and others. Alumni and industrial practitioners are invited to give guest lectures, share experiences, and provide career advice to students. Their views and feedback in curriculum review exercises are solicited to ensure that real estate curriculum, content, and pedagogical methodology are up-to-date and relevant with changing times.

Many graduates who took up leadership positions in the industry have reconnected with their alma mater by contributing their time and resources in various ways. Some have returned to contribute in advisory roles and even in leadership positions. Some contribute directly in the grooming of the next generation leaders by taking up academic positions, which include part-time, full-time and adjunct teaching faculty roles.

Dr Lim Lan Yuan, who was among the early batches of graduates, joined the university and became the Head of School of Building and Real Estate from 1987 to 2000. Dr Seek Ngee Huat, a co-author of this book, was a graduate from the pioneer cohort of the real estate (estate management) course at NUS. He is currently serving as the Chairman of the NUS Institute of Real Estate Studies and a Practice Professor at the Department of Real Estate, following his retirement as President of GIC Real Estate Pte Ltd. Dr Amy Khor (1981) was a faculty member with the NUS Real Estate Department before returning to industry. She is now serving as the Senior Minister of State for the Ministry of Health, and Ministry of Environment and Water Resources. Associate Professor Muhammed Faishal Ibrahim is a faculty member of the Department, and is currently seconded to serve as Parliamentary Secretary for the Ministry of Education and Ministry of Social and Family Development.

Many graduates have taken up leadership positions in the private sector in various fields, such as valuation, urban planning and consultancy; and in the public sector with statutory boards such as IRAS, HDB, URA, JTC, SLA, AVA. etc. Some prominent industry leaders have returned to serve on the Department's Consultative Committee, including Chia Ngiang Hong (1972), who chairs the committee, and other members including Chong Siak Ching (1981), Pauline Goh (1981), Tan Poh Hong (1981), Gerard Lee (1984), Pua Sek Guan (1988) and Kwok Wai Keong (1973).

3. Reflections on the Last 50 Years of Transformation

This section presents the views and perspectives of 30 prominent NUS Real Estate alumni on the transformation of Singapore's real estate industry over the last 50 years (Table 1 shows the names and current affiliations of the 30 prominent alumni). In keeping with the organisational structure of the book, this section is organised into the following sections (*the views of the individual alumni do not represent the views of their organisations and firms*).

3.1 *From a Third-World to a First-World Economy*

Since gaining independence in 1965, Singapore, with no endowment of natural resource, has adopted an industrialisation strategy to generate economic growth and create employment. In a short span of 50 years, Singapore's industrialisation strategy has moved up rapidly in the value chain from labour-intensive industries in the 1970s, capital-intensive and high-technology industries in the 1980s, and high value-added manufacturing industries with emphasis on technology and investment in the 1990s, to knowledge-based industries that leverage on R&D and innovation

Table 1. List of Alumni.

No	Title	First name	Designation	Organization	Graduation year
1	Ms	Chang Yoke Ping Frances	Property & Projects Director	Dairy Farm Singapore	1992
2	Mr	Chia Ngiang Hong	Group General Manager	City Developments Limited	1977
3	Mr	Chng Shih Hian	Executive Director	Suntec Real Estate Consultants Pte Ltd	1988
4	Ms	Chong Siak Ching	Chief Executive Officer	National Gallery Singapore	1981
5	Dr	Choo Kian Koon Steven	Chairman	VestAsia Group	1974
6	Dr	Chua Yang Liang	Head of Research & Consultancy, Singapore/ Head of Research, South East Asia	Jones Lang LaSalle Property Consultants Pte Ltd	1995
7	Ms	Goh Pauline	Chief Executive Officer (Singapore and South East Asia)	CBRE Pte Ltd	1981
8	Mr	Kwok Wai Keong	Managing Director	GIC	1973
9	Mr	Lee How Cheng Gerard	Chief Executive Officer	Lion Global Investors Ltd	1984
10	Mr	Leong Hong Yew	Director, Corporate, Policy & Planning Group (CPG), Policy & Research Division (PRD)	JTC Corporation	1992
11	Mr	Lim Swe Guan	Chairman	Asia Pacific Real Estate Association (APREA)	1979
12	Mr	Lim Tong Weng Eugene	Key Executive Officer	ERA Realty Network Pte Ltd	1991
13	Dr	Liow Kim Hiang	Professor	Department of Real Estate, School of Design and Environment, National University of Singapore	1985
14	Dr	Muhammad Faishal Ibrahim	Parliamentary Secretary and Member of Parliament (Nee Soon GRC)	Ministry of Education and Ministry of Social and Family Development	1993

15	Mr	Ng Seng Tat Michael	Group General Manager	UIC Limited and Singapore Land Limited	1988
16	Ms	Ong Choon Fah	Chief Executive Officer	DTZ Debenham Tie Leung (SEA) Pte Ltd	1981
17	Dr	Ooi Thian Leong Joseph	Dean's Chair Associate Professor	Department of Real Estate, National University of Singapore	1988
18	Mr	Phua Jimmy	Managing Director, Head of Real Estate Investments Asia	Canada Pension Plan Investment Board (CPPIB) Asia Inc.	1991
19	Mr	Poh Boon Kher Melvin	Managing Director	Fission Development Pte Ltd	1997
20	Mr	Pua Seck Guan	CEO & Executive Director	Perennial Real Estate Holdings Pte Ltd	1988
21	Ms	Sum Siok Chun Patricia	Managing Director	The Real Advisory Pte Ltd	1985
22	Ms	Tan Bee Kim	Senior Executive Director	Wheelock Properties (Singapore) Limited	1986
23	Ms	Tan Chew Ling	Group Director, Estate Administration & Property Group	Housing & Development Board	1990
24	Mr	Tan Swee Yiow	President (Singapore)	Keppel Land International	1985
25	Mr	Tan Tin Kwang William	General Manager (North China)	Keppel Land China Limited	1993
26	Mr	Tan Wee Kiong Augustine	President (REDAS) / Executive Director (Property Sales & Corporate Affairs)	Real Estate Developers' Association of Singapore (REDAS)/ Far East Organization	1983
27	Mr	Tay Kah Poh	Executive Director, Head of Residential Services	Knight Frank Pte Ltd	1983
28	Mr	Yap Neng Tong Jonathan	Chief Investment Officer	Ascendas-Singbridge Pte Ltd	1992
29	Mr	Yeo Eng Ching Danny	Group Managing Director	Knight Frank Pte Ltd	1980
30	Mr	Yeo Huang Kiat Dennis	Managing Director, Asia Industrial and Logistics Services	CBRE Pte Ltd	1988

in the 2000s. The industrialisation strategies have propelled economic and per capita income growth, moving Singapore from a third-world to a first-world economy.

"The transformation of Singapore from a simple entrepot to a thriving metropolis within a short span of five decades is simply remarkable."

— Chia Ngiang Hong

"Over the 50 years of development, the industrial property landscape has changed many times. This evolution was inevitable as Singapore progressed in her transformation from Third-World to First. Benefitting from an advantageous strategic location, Singapore started out as a humble entrepot trading centre from the 1950s. Capital-intensive industrialisation in the 1960s and 1970s steadily progressed towards knowledge-based industries in the 1980s, forming the precursor of today's current technology-based manufacturing sector. In tandem, similar strides were made in the supporting and complementary logistics, warehouse and transportation."

— Dennis Yeo

Given the limited land resource, the government realises the need to make careful and long-term land use and transportation planning. The first Master Plan was approved on 8 August 1958 to guide the land use and development of Singapore. It is important to ensure that after setting aside lands for housing, commercial and industrial uses, there are enough lands to provide for other infrastructure and green space. However, the static nature of the Master Plan was inadequate to deal with the dynamic social and economic changes, which led to the government seeking the United Nations' (UN) technical assistance in the State and City Planning Project (SCP) in 1967. The SCP recommendations led to the formulation of the long-range urban land use and development plan, which was the first Concept Plan for Singapore, in 1971.

"In 50 short years, Singapore has made the remarkable journey from a sleepy fishing village to a global top six city with one of the greenest and most liveable environments in the world today. This is the result of the far-sighted efforts of the government in long-range planning, creation of a world-class business climate, investment in physical infrastructure, liveability and quality of life."

— Augustine Tan

The multiple 20-year long-range plans[4] together with the statutory land use Master Plans (reviewed every five years) are the blueprints that collectively shape

---

[4] The first Concept Plan is a 20-year long-range plan, and it has been revised in 1991, 2001, and 2011.

the visions of making Singapore a *"thriving world-class city"* and *"a city in a garden."*[5]

"In just 50 years and in tandem with its leap from a third-world to a first-world economy, Singapore's real estate landscape has transformed from mud-tracks, swamps and kampungs to flyovers and expressways, bustling financial districts and thriving public housing estates."

— Chong Siak Ching

"Singapore has marched in double-quick time, transforming from Third-World to First-World within one generation, and real estate has followed in tandem. Swamps and slums have been replaced with world-class R&D facilities, while majestic commercial edifices house global multinationals from all over the world."

— Ong Choon Fah

3.2 *A Strong Public and Private Partnership*

The long-range Concept Plans have guided several major public infrastructure developments in Singapore, such as the world-class Changi Airport, the world's-busiest seaports, the MRT networks, and the new Marina Downtown Business Districts. The government via the JTC Corporation develops modern and innovative industrial facilities, such as Cleantech Park, Jurong Island, Science Park I, II and III, Fusionopolis, Biopolis, Aerospace Park and more to support world class knowledge-based industry clusters.

"Singapore's industrial property has evolved with and catalysed the transformation of its economy. This is evident in the changing industrial landscape from the early pre-independence days of basic low-rise factories to a bustling industrial township in Jurong, as well as the development of industrial estates in other parts of Singapore in the 1970s/1980s. This was followed by the development of specialised parks, such as the Wafer Fab Parks and Jurong Island in the 1990s to support a capital intensive economy. In more recent years, we have seen the development of one-north and business park such as Changi Business Park and Mapletree Business City to accelerate the development of a knowledge- and innovation-intensive economy. With the industrial property market becoming more transparent and less speculative, I believe it will be more stable and sustainable moving forward."

— Leong Hong Yew

---

[5] *"A thriving world-class city"* and *"a city in a garden"* have been the visions painted in the URA revised Concept Plans in 2001 and 2011, respectively.

The private sector plays an important role in bringing in capital and participating in the developments of commercial and industrial space that meets the needs of multi-national corporations, and high-quality living space in the private residential market to meet the rising aspiration of residents.

Chia Ngiang Hong describes the contributions of private developers in the process of translating the plans into reality. *"In the early years, besides the government, the property development business was dominated by a few major pioneer developers who played a key role in building up the real estate industry and, to a large extent, transformed Singapore's skyline. Back then, satisfying the basic needs of business and living accommodation was the main focus. But as the nation develops, higher expectations and demands, coupled with rapid changes in businesses and lifestyles, have presented new challenges. To ensure stability and growth, the public and private sectors forged a collaborative and consultative partnership and worked hand in glove to propel our built environment to greater heights. Moving forward, as Singapore progresses, real estate development opportunities are expected to get more competitive. Developers would have to be much more entrepreneurial and creative to stay ahead of intense competition, both locally and overseas. Developers will continue to play a crucial role in forging ahead with the push for innovative, sustainable and technological excellence to enhance our built environment and complement Singapore's vision to be a Smart Nation."*

"REDAS and its members look forward to furthering Singapore's long term approach to innovative urban planning, good governance and strong public-private partnership to build a healthy and stable property market and a 'future-ready' real estate industry," said Augustine Tan, the President of Real Estate Developers' Association of Singapore (REDAS) 2015, reiterating the private developers' commitment.

Economic growth and employment are the engines to drive the rapid urbanisation and transformation of the island-state. The urban blueprints and the visions envisaged would not be releasable without the close collaboration between the public and private sectors.

"The 3P — Public Private Partnership model — has worked very well for Singapore in the last 50 years. The real estate sector has benefitted enormously from the government's push to position Singapore as a gateway city on the world map."

— Pauline Goh

Some argue that forward land use planning and the real estate market are closely intertwined. The growth of Singapore into a global real estate marketplace would not have been possible without the government's pro-business and market-oriented approach in urban development. A flourishing and *laissez-faire* private real estate sector has formed an important component in the economic growth and employment of the nation.

"*Our infrastructure is world-class, our business operating environment is first-rate. Under these conditions, the real estate sector in Singapore has transformed to be the global playground it is now, having caught the attention of investors around the world. A key success factor for the future lies in leveraging wider economic communities such as ASEAN. With full integration, Southeast Asia is projected to be the 7th-largest economy in the world. As a key member, Singapore's status as an investment destination will be enhanced. For one, the level of capital flow is set to increase when regulatory barriers are removed, paving the way for an increase in real estate investment activity. With a boost in GDP, employment growth will be accelerated as production of goods and services increases, leading to an increase in demand for commercial and industrial/logistic properties.*"

— Pauline Goh

"*Working alongside the public sector, real estate developers have played a vital role in the transformation of our urban landscape. Real estate remains a key pillar of the Singapore economy. Of the country's top 20 listed companies, a quarter comprises property companies, or businesses offering real estate-related services. Real estate accounts for about half of the total fixed capital formation. One in five persons in the workforce is employed by the real estate and construction industry.*"

— Augustine Tan

"*The property business was dominated by well-known local developers and high net worth families as well as a few government linked companies. Activities focused on the domestic market and assets were fairly tightly held. Occasionally a few Japanese or Indonesian groups would make forays into residential and commercial development or buy into existing investment properties. Over time, with the metamorphosis of Singapore into an international gateway city in a rapidly growing Asia, the real estate landscape has undergone a tremendous transformation. The demands of a rapidly growing population along with the influx of MNCs in various fields of banking and finance, oil and gas, technology, biosciences, medical and pharmaceuticals, etc. have seen major changes not only in the physical developments across all asset classes, but also in the caliber of the participants and the way real estate projects and investments are undertaken and funded.*"

— Michael Ng.

3.3 *Homes for the Nation*

Providing affordable housing and promoting home ownership have all along been an important thrust in Singapore's nation building since gaining self-government in 1959. Today, more than 80% of Singaporean households live in public housing, and more than 90% of residents own their public housing flats, which is one of the highest rates of home-ownership in the world.

"In 1965, Singapore public housing was barely a year into its "Home Ownership for the People Scheme" — a scheme which stemmed from the vision of our founding PM Mr Lee Kuan Yew, who firmly believed that home ownership was vital for our migrant society. Some 1,600 units of 2-/3-room flats in Queenstown were sold in the first batch. Today, more than 900,000 flats have been sold, and about 92% of the households live in flats which they own. A third generation of Singaporeans has embarked on their homeownership journey where new flats come with greater design variety and can be mistaken for private condominiums. New flats are also taller, greener and smarter. They are served by modern facilities, and they remain affordable. There is also an established resale market which forms an integral part of our housing market. Public housing policies are more sophisticated -- they reach out to different segments of our society without losing sight of families, especially those who are buying their first homes."

— Tan Chew Ling

With growing affluence of Singaporean residents coupled with changing demographics and lifestyle, better quality housing and diverse housing options in the public and private markets are needed to meet the aspirations of the younger and more mobile residents.

"The residential property market has changed significantly over the past 50 years. For many of us, our first home is the Housing and Development Board (HDB) flat. While this provided basic housing when we started our families, these HDB flats have also provided the base for many of us to upgrade to private housing. Today, it is not uncommon to see HDB flat owners who also own private properties for investment."

— Eugene Lim

"Going forward, public housing will continue to evolve to stay relevant. There will be new and better developments, estate rejuvenations and stronger communities living cohesively in the heartlands. While there may be volatility from time to time, the public housing market in the long run would be a stable and sustainable one."

— Tan Chew Ling

Housing is no longer just a roof over the head for many Singaporeans. It is their home that brings many fond memories of growing up and experiences to the minds of the residents.

"In neat contrast, public and private housing, gardens and other public spaces serve as poignant reminders that Singapore is home. On top of bricks and mortar, we have built software: concepts such as place management, precursors of the internet of everything and the like."

— Ong Choon Fah

For senior citizens, it is a familiar environment with many friends to allow them to *age-in-place*, as Muhammad Faishal Ibrahim commented, "*the real estate landscape in Singapore is expected to change as we journey into an ageing society and our continuous quest to make Singapore an exceptional Nation for our people. For example, real estate developments and amenities will have to respond and meet the needs of a rapidly ageing society. This will be in the form of more senior friendly amenities, such as housing, health, retail, transport, etc. Features that facilitate the lives of the seniors may contribute more to property values when such demand is high.*"

The home ownership scheme has been used by the government as a policy tool from the onset to help residents sink their roots into the country. Many new immigrants today have been attracted to make Singapore their home, where they can raise their families safely and comfortably.

"*Singapore has become an established global city and attracts many international talents who work, live and play here. Many have become permanent residents and citizens, and have made Singapore their home, to build their lives and raise their families here.*"

— Eugene Lim

3.4 "A Great City to Live, Work and Play"

Given limited land resources, Singapore has to optimise and intensify land use on the one hand, and safeguard green, open space and water catchment areas on the other. Augustine Tan explains: "*Singapore's future urban planning and physical development will have to balance economic growth with societal well-being and environment quality, to achieve a high quality, sustainable and liveable environment for all.*" Decentralisation and high-density housing are strategies adopted by planners to ensure lands are optimally used to provide a high quality and sustainable environment for housing, leisure and work. "*Greater emphasis will be placed on decentralisation to create more offices, retail and recreation options closer to homes in trans-urban locations, which will drive unprecedented opportunities for commercial, industrial, retail and mixed-use development. On the back of population growth and evolving consumer lifestyle, there will be greater scope to spawn innovation in residential real estate to redefine living space and inspire better lives.*"

Collective sales, or en bloc sales, take place where owners of two or more property units come together to sell their units, usually with an existing underdeveloped structure, to a developer who redevelops the land into higher density developments. Melvin Poh explains how the collective sales help expedite land intensification and urban renewal. He says: "*In the last 50 years, Singapore has seen rapid urbanisation. Old properties near the city centre that were built 30–40 years ago* were of low intensity, became economically obsolete and thus ripe for redevelopment. At the same time, URA's progressive release of the Development Guide Plans (DGPs) provided greater transparency and clarity on the higher planning intensity that could be allowed. The combination of these two factors, together with rising land prices, enabled collective sales to happen which directly contributes to urban renewal and optimisation of scarce land resources in Singapore. Recognising the benefits of the redevelopment of old buildings to facilitate urban rejuvenation, the Government made its legal framework more transparent to facilitate Collective Sale transactions. Hence, in 1999, the Land Title (Strata) Act was amended to promote fairness and transparency in the collective sale process. More importantly, in order not to allow minority groups of landowners to hold the rest of the owners at ransom, the Act also allows a sale to proceed if 80% of the owners agree to the sale."

With the relocation of the City Terminals (Tanjong Pagar, Keppel and Brani) and Pasir Panjang Terminal by 2030, more than 1,000 hectares of land, which is equivalent to three Marina Bays, will be free for future development and land use needs. Muhammad Faishal Ibrahim said: "...*the economic restructuring and new development areas, such as the Greater Southern Waterfront will set new equilibriums in the Singapore Property Market.*" The Greater Southern Waterfront Development area will be developed into housing, commercial, entertainment and cultural use, which will further enhance Singapore's position as a world-class city to live, work and play.

The emergence of e-commerce and other IT-enabled workplaces will change consumption behaviours of shoppers and office workflows. "*Going forward, setting land use and building standards which commensurate with the emerging and evolving future trends that affect the way in which we work, live and play, can result in the pioneering development of efficient, well-designed buildings that will provide both benefits and synergy for all real estate users. An example is e-commerce. This will change the way in which we produce, store, move and transact goods and services within Singapore and beyond. The relentlessly growing appetite for storing, managing and harnessing data and information technology will be a major factor driving change in the industrial landscape.*"

— Dennis Yeo

Integrating work-live-play into construction is likely to be an important trend for commercial buildings in the future. Tan Bee Kim said: "*Future commercial buildings in Singapore may have a large connected subterranean footprint in addition to height, due to our limited land. Furthermore, our commercial buildings will have to evolve with the new economy as well as users' changing needs and preferences. Increasingly, successful commercial buildings have incorporated physical and social features not imagined in previous generations of buildings. Our new commercial buildings should be developed with facilities* to address the lifestyle and work-life balance preferences of the Millennials. These may include non-conventional spaces for chill-out and interaction, yoga studios and gyms, child care facilities, relaxation pods, as well as shower and cyclist facilities. With a progressively creative business environment that fosters a live, work and play ethic, organisations and employees will be more engaged to thrive in the workplace."

Public transport system and major road networks are essential parts of urban planning to promote more "car-lite" towns and neighbourhoods with better connectivity to MRT and bus interchanges. Muhammad Faishal Ibrahim comments: "*On the transport front, the move to get Singaporeans more connected will see many areas in Singapore being served by the MRT and buses. The new MRT lines and stations will stimulate more activities and development nodes around the stations. This will in turn affect property values and inject more nodal points across our island.*"

3.5 *Corporate Real Estate Services Providers*

Local and global named firms co-exist in the competitive markets of intermediating real estate deals and offering third-party professional real estate services to firms. The last decade witnessed the changing landscape in Singapore's real estate market with greater investment fund flows into real estate markets. Corporate real estate service providers therefore have to improve and broaden their scope to keep pace with the changes.

"*The formation of Real Estate Investment Trusts/Funds or REITs, whether from Institutional or Private Enterprises, know they require Real Estate professionals to be well-versed with Asset Management as well as knowledge of Financial Modeling. So the challenge facing the Real Estate Services Industry is not just being a brick and mortar services firm for Sales/Leasing, or Valuation. It is a whole gamut of real estate and financial-linked services under one roof, with presence in all major gateway cities to take care of every Real Estate need of a new generation of global investors; i.e., we need to transform and be a truly global service company.*"

— Danny Yeo

"*In the last 50 years, the real estate services have morphed alongside the growth of the country — from a traditional brick and mortar sector depending on local domestic capital to a highly securitised industry driven by local and global private funds and REITs. The real estate service offering has stepped up to meet this increasingly sophisticated landscape. As change is indeed the only constant, such transformation is inevitable. There are many forces existing today that are reshaping the market. A new era of change is unfolding, brought about by the tectonic shift in technology. Not only has it increased the accessibility to market information, it has enhanced the connectivity between consumer and supplier — simply with a click of the mouse or a touch on the smart phone. The traditional real estate industry, which rode on this information gap, is facing increasing competition. As the transparency of our market increases, likewise the nature of the real estate services must change. Embracing technology in our work is only a minor part, personalising the service for every client will be instrumental. Consumers are becoming more aware of their options and discerning about their wants. The real asset wealth advisor is one who can offer reliable advice with thought leading insight and a personality to match."*

— Chua Yang Liang

3.6 *From the Local to the Global Market Place*

The physical geographical borders dividing real estate markets have become blurred and less restrictive across countries. More real estate investors and developers have expanded their real estate businesses outside their home countries with the objectives of diversifying risks.

"The real estate sector worldwide has evolved over the years with the changing needs of businesses and people. As Singapore joins the league of global cities, we are increasingly open to new and bold development concepts."

— Tan Swee Yiow

"With Globalisation, investors are no longer bound by borders. Whether it's a Singapore Real Estate player or others, this phenomenon will accelerate as they expand and look for opportunities in key gateway cities around the world. Companies will continue to expand into new markets and the movement of people across continents will necessitate services from real estate professionals from one contact point. This will post challenges for real estate services firms having limited presence in key gateway cities, in supporting both inbound and outbound companies."

— Danny Yeo

"Global real estate players have descended into our little red dot. Now, developers and real estate funds of various origins have presence here or are actively looking at the Singapore market. The rapid development of REITs since their first listing on the SGX in 2002 has also opened up another whole new chapter in our real estate playbook. Homegrown property groups, both big and small, have also spread their wings boldly into major foreign markets across all continents in developed as well as emerging markets. Notable investments and developments carrying the Singapore flag are found in the UK, US, Europe, China, Korea, Japan, Australia, Vietnam, Malaysia, Indonesia, Myanmar and many other countries."

— Michael Ng

Patricia Sum agreed that more local family businesses look outward to expand their international real estate portfolios: "*Over the past 50 years, Singapore witnessed the architecture transformation of CK Tang, Farrer Court, Marco Polo Hotel and the open grass at Paterson into Tangs Shopping Centre/Marriot Hotel, D'Leedon Condominium, Grange Residences and ION, respectively. Behind these tidal changes are strong local family groups growing their businesses, participation with foreign investors, government-linked companies' initiatives, entry of global real estate funds and REITs.*"

"*International real estate exposure is becoming an essential activity for the performance oriented fund. Particularly amongst countries where significant wealth and savings are confronted with limited investment options at home, the motivation for going offshore is high.*"

— Lim Swe Guan

International real estate has attracted strong interest from institutional investors and funds, who have significantly increased allocation of funds into the real estate asset class. "*According to PERE (Private Equity Real Estate) Research & Analytics, the top 30 global institutional investors' real estate equity investment in 2014 was over $567 billion, an increase of over $100 billion in three years. This increase will continue as sweeping structural changes such as ageing demographics compel sovereign wealth funds, pension funds and insurance funds to allocate or increase their real estate weighting in search of higher returns. These global institutional investors will intensify competition, influence markets and shape their rules of engagement,*" said Jimmy Phua. He further explained that "*as a region, Asia is appealing for its relative higher growth and diversification benefits. But understanding and navigating the very diverse and complex Asian real estate markets is a major challenge for most. These investors are looking for strategic engagement with Asian partners with impeccable corporate governance, world class competence and visionary leadership to guide them through the rapidly evolving real estate landscape in Asia. Whilst some Singapore organisations have cognizance of this, few have been thoughtful and deliberate in engaging these investors. Tapping into this deep and long-term pool of capital could potentially be the next phase of growth for Singapore real estate organisations and spring board them to world-class status.*"

More investment opportunities are opening up with the development of real estate capital markets. "*In retrospect, the past 50 years were exciting times for investors who rode the real estate cycles as Singapore journeyed from third world to first. From an initial focus on investments in private equity in bricks and mortar in the early years, the investment landscape evolved, along with the changing skyline, to offer a broader range of real estate investment opportunities spanning equity and debt in both the private and public* space. Real estate also came into its own as an asset class in institutional investment portfolios."

— Kwok Wai Keong

Risks are increasingly higher in international real estate investments. Lim Swe Guan explains: *"Funds invest offshore both to obtain diversification and higher risk adjusted returns. Diversification comes from exposure to foreign currencies (particularly for the home country with an inherently weak currency) and economic sectors that are alien to the home economy. As well, because certain countries are growing faster or benefitting from favourable demographic trends and consumption patterns, good returns are obtainable from exposure to the right sectors. Obviously, investing offshore also comes with its share of risks. Some of these are specific to the sector, such as market maturity, transparency of information or operational factors and some are political or sovereign in nature such as changes in government policies that may dilute property rights or raise ownership costs."*

Therefore, risk management strategy is important for international real estate investors. Lim Swe Guan further comments: *"Apart from being able to quantify the risks and drivers of growth in the country, investors have to acquire a holistic understanding of how the property markets operate in the foreign country; for example, the important factors that affect value, the rights tenants have over landlords and vice versa. Flying in an investment officer with strong property evaluation and financial skills may be insufficient. That person has to be familiar with the nuances of investing in the particular local market and that may take years to perfect."*

Gerard Lee also cautions that being a global capital city, real estate prices here are expected to be more susceptible to market volatility: *"It is an amazing feat to be among the top few financial centres in the world from a third-world city just 50 years ago. However, this achievement is not without its problem. One of the characteristics of a top financial city is that real estate value increases at a rate faster than the population's rate of income growth. Even when stock markets were going through a bear phase, cities like New York and London saw very little depreciation in their real estate value."*

3.7 *Emergence of REITs and other Financial Innovations*

In July 2002, the listing of CapitaLand Mall Trust (previously known as CapitaMall Trust, CMT) marked an important milestone in Singapore's real estate market. Steven Choo comments: *"One of the most significant milestones in Singapore's real estate history was the birth of the REIT industry in early 2002. It was a classic case of 天时, 地利, 人和" (tian shi, di li, ren he) and of opportunities borne out of a crisis. At the time, Singapore was looking at ways to reflate its economy after the dot-com bust and 9/11. REITs were sanctioned by the ERC (Economic Review Committee) and the regulatory bodies as a means to grow and strengthen Singapore's position as a fund management centre, widen the investment base, as well as to create jobs for PMETs. On the ground, the real estate industry needed and was prepared to innovate and tap into the capital market on top of traditional debt financing to maintain its growth momentum, especially for its non-residential sectors. At the company level, leaders of pioneer REIT sponsors, namely CapitaLand and Ascendas, were determined to unlock value from their portfolio, be asset-light and grow their fee-income business, and had assembled teams of professionals ready for and equal to the task."*

The REIT market offers an alternative way for developers to monetise their income generating commercial real estate. It integrates the "brick and mortar" business with capital markets opening a new avenue for retail and institution investors to invest and hold real estate assets. The first chief executive officer (CEO) of CMT, Pua Seck Guan, comments that *"Singapore's REIT industry has flourished over the past 14 years, driving the growth of the industry's total market capitalisation and asset size tremendously. Sponsors/owners established REIT as an exit platform to monetise chunky real estate, while individual investors/retirees identified REIT as a relatively safe investment instrument which provides regular yield and diversification."*

Ascendas, which is now a part of the merged entity — Ascendas-Singbridge, listed the first business space and industry REIT in 2002, shortly after the listing of CMT. Jonathan Yap, who is the former CEO of Ascendas-India Trust, the second REIT sponsored by Ascendas-Singbridge and listed in 2007, comments that *"the introduction and development of REITs in Singapore ("S-REIT") not only created a new investment product for institutional and individual investors, it also helped to deepen the real estate market in Singapore. Firstly, it offered a new dimension to real estate developers' business model, thereby allowing income-producing assets to be held in a more capital efficient manner. In addition, it aided the development of the knowledge of real estate industry and professionals. Finally, it contributed to Singapore' relevance as an investment location in the region."*

Pua Seck Guan argues that the REIT market development attracts businesses and talents in fund management and other down-stream financial services: *"Less apparent is the creation of a sizeable community of REIT professionals, who have been supporting and growing with the REIT industry, ranging from investment and debt bankers, to legal advisers, asset managers and REIT managers. Alongside this development, real estate professionals have seen their work scope extend beyond just property management, to asset and capital management. The debt market also saw a rise in popularity and activity in a number of debt instruments."*

"By relentlessly creating, enhancing and unlocking real estate investment in a disciplined yet innovative manner, Ascendas-Singbridge integrates real estate investment, development and management with the capital market. As a committed sponsor to our listed and private funds, Ascendas-Singbridge looks to continue augmenting the growth of

the Singapore REIT sector as it advances from its position of strength," said Jonathan Yap, agreeing on the importance of the fund management expertise in REIT markets.

With more REIT listings, Singapore can position itself as the Asian REIT hub. *"As Singapore continues to enhance corporate disclosure and governance standards, investors can look forward to more quality international REIT listings on the Singapore Exchange. Consolidation and structural changes can also be expected as the market matures, much like the experience of more mature markets like the United States and Australia. Ultimately, Singapore's REIT market will only become more reputable and vibrant, with stronger local and international players and higher-quality assets in a well-governed environment."*

— Pua Sek Guan

For individuals facing rising housing prices when Singapore moves toward being a top global financial centre, other indirect investment options can be created to help preserve wealth. Gerard Lee said: *"This phenomenon, if left unchecked, will result in politics of envy. Unfortunately, in top financial centres, real estate investments are beyond the reach of the average person, including his home. REIT is a viable channel to partake in capital appreciation but its price volatility is quite high. Recently, the Government introduced the SSB — Singapore Savings Bonds. It's a bond where the investor can have his cake and eat it, that is, he does not suffer from price volatility and gets rewarded with higher interest rate if he keeps his investment longer.*

To address the politics of envy resulting from lofty real estate value, it is recommended that a real estate SSB equivalent be created for Singaporeans. It should have low volatility, reward those who hold their investment longer and, more importantly, enable the investor to participate in the huge appreciation of real estate values. Like the SSB, the private sector would not be able to structure such an investment — only the Government can. With huge exposure to properties, the Government can create an SPSS — Singapore Property Savings Security. The returns of this security can be linked to the value of the Government's real estate assets. To minimise volatility, the price of the SPSS should be linked to a long-term moving average of the Government's marked-to-market real estate value, for example a ten-year moving average." He added that *"Like the SSB, the SPSS will be uniquely Singaporean!"*

Sophisticated financial instruments are created to meet the demand of institutional investors, who look for yields in real estate. *"Supporting these changes are matching vigorous growth seen in the banking sector, which has moved from vanilla bilateral loan financing to syndicated project financing, bonds issuance, Medium Term Notes, mezzanine funding and Asset-Backed Securitization involving local banks as well as branches of foreign banks from Europe, Southeast Asia, Japan and the US. In like manner, investment options in real estate range expand from direct equity participation in projects to shares in listed real estate companies & REITs."*

— Patricia Sum

3.8 *Future Ready Real Estate Graduates*

Real Estate is not just about brick and mortar; it is a business of people, as Ong Choon Fah comments: *"Real estate practitioners have a significant role to play. The built environment has a profound impact on the well-being of our society. First, we build the city, then the city builds us. What kind of a city-state do we want for generations of Singaporeans to come? Each of us can make a difference. We must have the courage and vision to envisage a better tomorrow. As is often said, not everything that can be counted counts and often, it is what cannot be counted that counts. Ultimately, real estate is not about bricks and mortar, but about people."*

As NUS Real Estate is an institution that educates and produces "people" for the real estate industry, what type of skill-sets and knowledge should the future real estate professionals be equipped with? Some comments are summarised below:

"My wish is that all Singapore real estate graduates will be future-proof, globally astute, well-rounded, articulate, confident and capable real estate leaders who do not just make a lot of money for themselves and for the organisations they work for, but who are also socially sensitive, ethically grounded and environmentally aware."

— Tay Kah Poh

"Going forward, as Singapore plans to accommodate a population of 6.5 to 6.9 million by the year 2030, many more homes will be added to the current stock. Real estate needs and the demands of sellers, buyers, landlords and tenants will become increasingly sophisticated. It is therefore apt for future generations of real estate practitioners to take their education and training seriously with the objective of improving the residential property experience for all whom they serve."

— Eugene Lim

"Opportunities now have never been better for a career in Real Estate. I am confident the Department of Real Estate, NUS, will continue to rise to the challenge in spearheading the development of the industry, to be able to attract the best talents and prepare them to take on the demands of the global real estate marketplace and also champion the way forward in more environmentally friendly and sustainable practices."

— Michael Ng

"From Sino-Singapore Suzhou Industrial Park to Sino-Singapore Tianjin Eco-city, from Beijing to Shanghai to Nanning, Singapore developers/professionals are well recognised as a benchmark of Quality/Standard. This would not have been possible without a well-organised and disciplined real estate industry and the professionalism carried by our fellow real estate practitioners from Singapore. This is the greatest asset we possess, that enables us to arise to new heights. Despite the global competitive market, I strongly believe that with the core values we possess, Singapore real estate professionals will continue to be a benchmark others look forward to in the region."

— William Tan Tin Kwang

3.9 Innovations in Real Estate Education and Research

NUS Real Estate has offered formal tertiary education in real estate since 1969 and has continuously aimed to be amongst the best in the world, as described by Joseph Ooi: *"Singapore is well poised to be the hub for research and education on real estate in Asia. Through its flagship BSc (Real Estate) and MSc (Real Estate) degree programmes, NUS Real Estate has a rich history of training real estate professionals who have contributed significantly to Singapore's built environment and national development. On the research front, NUS continues to establish itself as a leading real estate research university in Asia."*

NUS Real Estate should constantly review its real estate curriculum and pedagogical approach that will keep abreast with the changes in the real estate markets. Some suggestions include:

"For my SG50 wish, let me focus on real estate education for the next decade — it's hard to look beyond five years, much less 50. My wish is that Singapore, and in particular, NUS, will be at the cutting edge of real estate education in Asia — always innovative in approach, always relevant in content, always practical in application, always global in perspective — mirroring how real estate has become an integral part of urban economies, corporate and household balance sheets everywhere in the world. My wish is that we will also develop the effective, the technologically appropriate pedagogy that will equip students with deep skills and tools for life-long learning in this exciting field."

— Tay Kah Poh

Liow Kim Hiang also suggests that *"real estate education at NUS has to impart deep knowledge and appreciation on the real estate market and the dynamics of capital market at national, regional and international levels. Accordingly, contemporary real estate education embraces a wide range of subjects including real estate and urban development, legal studies, valuation and appraisal, property and facilities management,* urban economics, portfolio and asset management, real estate capital markets and securitised real estate investment vehicles."

Joseph Ooi, who is currently the Deputy Head overseeing NUS Real Estate academic programmes, identifies some key challenges facing real estate education at NUS: *"Following the growth of REITs and fund management businesses, real estate business has become increasingly sophisticated and globalised. To keep abreast of the developments, NUS Real Estate continually reviews its course curriculum. For example, in line with the closer integration of the real estate and capital markets, BSc (Real Estate) students can now specialise in Real Estate Finance. To leverage on Singapore's expertise in urban planning, which is much sought after by many emerging economies, real estate students can also enrol in a concurrent degree programme which allows them to graduate with both the BSc (Real Estate) and a Master in Urban Planning within five years. The content of the M.Sc. (Real Estate) modules has also been updated, and strategic discussions to mount separate double-degree programmes with Renmin Business School and NUS Business School are ongoing. At the management level, the Graduate Certificate in Real Estate Finance (GCREF), which is a structured three-module senior executive programme to bridge knowledge in real estate and capital markets, has been running successfully since 2011.*

At NUS, we seek to train a new generation of real estate professionals who not only have deep knowledge and understanding of traditional "brick and mortar" real estate, but are also conversant with the dynamics of the capital markets. We value the strategic partnerships with our alumni and industry stakeholders in our continual efforts to better prepare and equip our graduates to face challenges and seize opportunities in the new real estate world."

"Research complements teaching," as Liow Kim Hiang puts it. He further argues for the importance of real estate research, where more emphasis should be devoted to understanding the interaction between space-time (urban economics) and money-time (financial economics) dimension in real estate markets. *"Real estate is a significant resource component of many national economies, as well as a major global capital asset that is comparable to the capitalisation of common stock and bond markets. Therefore, a good understanding of the characteristics of real estate with regard to its "urban economics" and "financial economics" attributes, as well as the contribution of real estate towards urban development, economic development and wealth creation/accumulation, underpin the changing landscape of real estate education and research and guide future scholarly pursuits at NUS.*

The four-quadrant model calls for an in-depth understanding and research expertise on the "space (urban economics)" and "asset (financial economics)" dimensions of real estate and their dynamic interactions in the globalisation context. The "wealth creation", "wealth management" and "risk management" themes of real estate and other investment assets means theoretical and applied research and innovations on "portfolio and asset management" will continue to gain momentum in global investing and consulting. Finally, research in housing will dominate the urban economic domain in the context of an ageing population, social wealth redistribution and technological advancements."

3.10 *Responding to Changing Future Needs*

"Singapore is limited in land, but never in space and ideas. Situated in a fast growing region, Singapore must continue to make itself relevant, amidst rapidly evolving geopolitics. Our challenges are different from those of our pioneers. How do we turn limited land to our advantage? How do we build on our racial, social and religious harmony in this increasingly global village? How do we harness technology? How do we look out and make ourselves valuable to the world around us?" Ong Choon Fah raised some challenges facing Singapore in driving future growth.

Moving forward, three demand factors that may be important game-changers and are expected to impact how real estate space is created, are: heart-ware (art-culture), software (information communications and technology), and sustainability and green movement.

First, after meeting the basic needs of housing, employment, and wealth accumulation of Singaporeans in the last 50 years, it may be time to enrich their pursuits for culture and art. Chong Siak Ching shares: *"In my view, Singapore's real estate landscape in the next 50 years will see greater arts and cultural drivers coming into play. In fast-developing countries, when the pursuit of wealth and material gains starts to divide the population, arts and heritage can be an important social glue. In our jubilee year, Singapore pursued and achieved the UNESCO World Heritage Site recognition for our Botanic Gardens. In November 2015, the new National Gallery, repurposed from Singapore's two most historically significant monuments — the former Supreme Court and City Hall — will be opened."* She added: *"We've seen a similar trend with the launch of arts institutions and cultural districts such as Louvre Abu Dhabi, UAE and M+ in West Kowloon Cultural District, Hong Kong. Even successful economic powerhouses are looking towards arts and cultural developments to stay relevant. As a city matures and ages, injections of new arts and cultural icons as seen with Guggenheim Museum Bilbao and Centre Pompidou-Metz in Bilbao, Spain and Metz, France respectively, have revitalised these industrial cities to newly-branded cultural destinations."*

Chong Siak Ching was optimistic that *"In the next 50 years, we can look forward to a Singapore where the landscape will be a good mix of financial skyscrapers, iconic arts and heritage institutions amidst our beautiful green spaces."*

Second, information communications and technology are likely to result in the reconfiguration of office workflows, retail delivery, and production process in the long term. Changes in behaviour of end users could drive how real estate space is used efficiently in the future. Dennis Yeo foresees: *"The internet and advanced* communication technologies have, in both big and small ways, altered the way Singaporeans live, work and play. With this change in trends, our built environment will change."

Kwok Wai Keong adds: *"Looking ahead, technological innovations such as 3D printing, advanced analytics, smart machines and the Internet of Things could conceivably change the way we work, shop and play. These developments will influence and reshape space markets, perhaps modify the way we think about location and may even disrupt long-established relationships between landlord and tenant. Figuring out the implications of these changes on investments will be challenging, but potentially rewarding for those who succeed in doing so."*

"The next lap in Singapore's future will be about creating an industrial landscape that will harness the accomplishments of the past with a mastery of today's advance communication technology and locational advantage; facilitating Singapore's continued growth and prosperity and a better life for her people."

— Dennis Yeo.

Real estate space needs to be re-designed and adapted to suit the new-age workforce and production processes. *"In terms of design, functionality, financial and ownership structure, these (Singapore's commercial and industrial property) sectors have to adapt constantly to remain relevant and viable. Industrial premises are no longer drab places for production or warehousing, but incorporate facilities for live, work and play, catering to the needs of a knowledge-based workforce for today's data intensive businesses in design, research and production. Today's warehouses are served by ramps on multiple-storeys, catering to a myriad network of high value and time sensitive logistics and production chains, having come a long way since the days of the godowns by the Singapore River."*

— Chng Shih Hian

The traditional "brick and mortar" retail model faces challenges from the "click and mortar" model, where firms integrate retail mall space and e-commerce capability to provide new shopping experiences. Chng Shih Hian notes: *"Retail amenities have also evolved in complexity, from resettling street vendors and businesses from old shophouses in the early years, to today's vast shopping complexes catering to different neighbourhoods and consumer tastes."*

Frances Chang shares a similar view: *"Having been in the retail real estate industry for many years, one cannot help but notice the landscape in retail brick and mortar industry fast changing. Real Estate vs Information Technology? What is the future for the retail property market with the onslaught of online shopping? We are all time-strapped consumers and shopping in the comforts of our home is attractive. E-commerce is growing rapidly and what does this mean for the future of retail real estate in Singapore? How does this affect the graduates from Department of Real Estate in their choice of career in the retail real estate industry? My opinion is that we will see a co-existence and retail malls here will take the shopping experience to a higher level and leverage on technology to assist retailers to make their retail channels seamless."*

Third, "sustainability" and "green" seem to become important buzz words in real estate developments in the coming years. With firms becoming more conscious about corporate social responsibilities, demand for "green" features and technology are expected to increase in real estate. *"Going forward, "green" considerations for environmental sustainability will be the next frontier."*

— Chng Shih Hian

"At the same time, concerns over the environment and cost of energy as well as government regulations are pushing the envelope for sustainability. Businesses today recognise that going green is no longer an option but a competitive necessity if they wish to future-proof their products and services. Property developers need to work closely with innovative vendors and suppliers as well as authorities to tap on technology and innovation for a more sustainable built environment. At Keppel Land, we see real estate as a life-touching, life-transforming business. We are in the business of realising dreams, building lives and shaping landscapes. We embrace the belief that thoughtful innovations lead to thoughtful experiences. It is this unwavering approach to think and see things differently that has enabled us to raise the benchmark for waterfront living with iconic residences at Keppel Bay and Marina Bay, and put Singapore on the global real estate map. Wherever we operate, we will strive to create vibrant live-work-play environments in premium properties of a distinguishable Keppel quality."

— Tan Swee Yiow

4. A Next Wave of Transformation of Singapore's Real Estate

In summary, Singapore's real estate industry has certainly made a big leap moving from a third-world to a first-world city in the last 50 years. The first mover advantage in creating a REIT market helps cement Singapore's position as one of the most established REIT hubs in Asia, where Singapore ranks second by market capitalisation after Japan. Real estate has indeed transformed not only in terms of the physical space, it has also become a global investment asset. Institutional investors, which include pension funds, sovereign wealth funds, insurance companies, hedge funds and many high net-worth investors, channel large foreign capital inflows into acquiring prime grade commercial and high-end residential properties in Singapore, especially in the most recent decades in the 2000s. The excess liquidity chasing for local real estate assets has, to some extent, caused significant price appreciation in the markets, prompting the Government to take swift actions to cool the overheating property market with a slew of macro-prudential measures and imposition of both the buyer's and seller's stamp duties starting from 2010.

The market landscape has become more integrated and intertwined (Figure 3). The introduction of REIT and other financial market innovations improves price and information discovery process in the market on the one hand; and stock market volatility could spillover into real estate space market via the REIT channel on the other. In the development market, competition from foreign developers and escalating land costs motivate developers to adopt a "soft-touch" approach in their marketing strategies aiming to build longer term seller-buyer and landlord-tenant relationships in the real estate markets. Reputation building could be amongst the key agenda to prepare developers for the long haul in real estate business in Singapore. When the market resumes its normality, and supply and demand stabilise, the government could assume facilitating roles to work hand-in-hand with the private sector to convert the long-term blueprint of making Singapore a thriving, liveable, city in a garden into reality.

Looking ahead, changes are inevitable where space producers (developers), space users, and capital suppliers/investors are required to formulate new real estate business models and re-examine the established theory about location, and the relationship between landlord and tenant. What will drive the next wave of transformation of Singapore's real estate? Based on the views collated above and the authors'

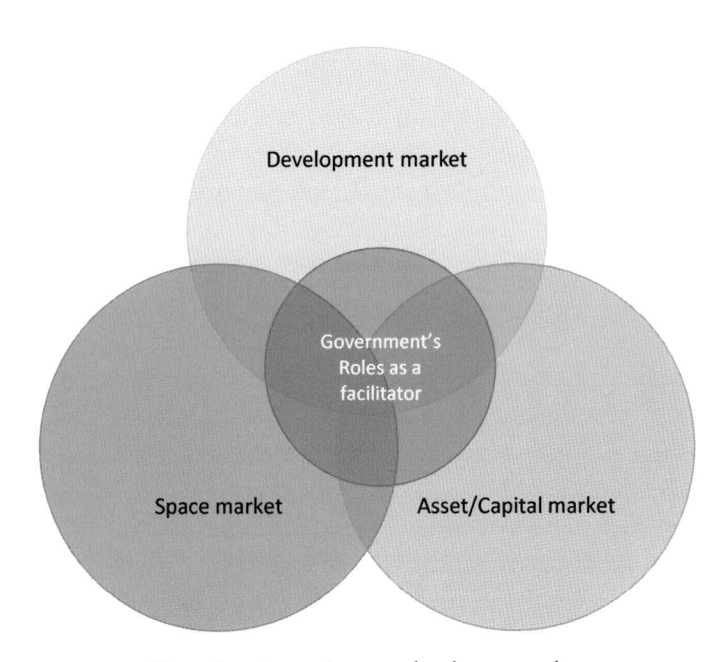

Figure 3. A more integrated real estate market.

observations, five mega irreversible trends are expected to influence the next phase of growth of Singapore's real estate market. They are summed up in the following themes:

- **Technology induced demand for space to work, live and play**

Proliferation of internet and wireless communication revolutionises the way workflows are organised in business space, online shopping search and match experience, agglomeration of knowledge clusters in R&D and value creation industries. In housing, preference for quality space with smart features, energy efficient devices, and greenery will dominate. As the city grows in sophistication, there will be more attention to the arts and culture, which can be infused into the space and activities of the community. In some residential developments, such as St Regis, the art and sculpture of famous artists have already been included as an integrated part of the development.

The advancement of order fulfillment and tracking technologies supported by logistics structure located close to various supply sources has significantly lifted the online capability of many big e-commerce firms, such as 淘宝网 (Taobao), Amazon, iTunes music etc, which have already shown significant impact in some businesses, such as books, music and others.

Advances in communication and information technology will shape new real estate space; and new real estate space should be adaptive to new technologies. The two are not, however, mutually exclusive, but complement each other in creating a smart building/home in a sustainable environment.

- **A city with a greener and more sustainable built environment**

The Ministries of the Environment and Water Resources and National Development jointly published "The Sustainable Singapore Blueprint"[6] in 2015, which outlines the national vision and plans for "A Liveable and Endearing Home", "A Vibrant and Sustainable City," and "An Active and Gracious Community". The government has been actively promoting green mark certified developments in Singapore, spearheaded by the Building and Construction Authority (BCA). Developers are motivated to embrace a "green" and "sustainable" approach in creating new real estate space. They use advanced building technology to improve energy, water, and circulation efficiency in buildings, and adopt alternative clean energy, such as solar panels, to show their commitments to creating a sustainable and liveable home and city in a garden. The "green" campaign should send home an important message to users — to adopt practices and change their behaviour towards reducing carbon footprints.

After the seaport terminals in the city and Pasir Panjang areas have been relocated, lands of more than thrice the size of the current Marina Bay will be freed up for the

---

[6] Source: http://www.mewr.gov.sg/ssb/files/ssb2015.pdf.

Greater Southern Waterfront developments. Private and public sectors can work together and harness the opportunity to create a viable model for the most "sustainable" and "liveable" city in the area, which will be enviable by the world.[7] Similarly, the relocation of the Paya Lebar airbase will free up much land for future development and remove the current height constraints in the surrounding areas.

- **Abundant local and global real estate opportunities**

The local development market has become increasing competitive and "crowded" with the entrance of many foreign developers. However, with continual economic growth, more capital inflows are required to support urbanisation and new development. Foreign developers' participation increases competition and flattens the real estate playing fields in the local market; at the same time, they also bring in new technology and new ways of creating real estate space in Singapore. Similarly, local developers, who have already spread their wings outside Singapore, making inroads into other real estate markets, could bring their overseas experiences and best practices back to inject creativity and raise the quality of real estate developments in Singapore. Joint ventures between local and foreign developers are expected to be formed to undertake large-scale and complex development projects.

The government continues to lead in the opening up of new investment opportunities outside Singapore via government-to-government (G2G) projects in countries like China, Vietnam, India, and further afield. The G2G projects, such as the Sino-Singapore Tianjin Eco-City, not only display Singapore's style of urban and township developments, the government can also experiment new urban living ideas with these projects, and bring home experiences for Singapore's urban and land use planning. The third Sino-Singapore G2G project in Chongqing, centering on the theme of *"modern connectivity and modern services"*, will stretch planning — thinking outside the box for new business solutions leveraging on smart technology and state-of-the-art supply-chain methodology. This project will be a catalyst and priority demonstrative project for China's One Belt, One Road initiative.[8]

On the capital market front, Singapore, as a financial hub in Asia, is an ideal gateway for international investors to tap on growing opportunities in Southeast Asia and beyond. Political stability, transparency, strong governance, and efficient financial systems are positive factors that will draw more financial institutions and investment funds via Singapore to the region. With institutional funds allocating more investments into real estate, more "money" will chase after quality assets in and outside their

---

[7] In 2011, a Siemens-Economist Intelligence Unit study ranked Singapore as Asia's greenest city.

[8] China's One Belt, One Road initiative aims at rejuvenating two ancient trade routes and knitting Eurasia into a single vast market. (Source: "Third G-to-G project to be in Chongqing," Today Online, 7 November 2015.)

home countries. Cross-border flows of investments could expose local real estate prices to volatility in international capital markets. More risk hedging instruments and financial innovations, such as derivatives and securitisation structures, will emerge to protect investors with international real estate assets from extreme financial risks, such as the subprime crisis. Data analytics, cloud computing and data storage are likely to change how financial and real estate market analysts, fund managers and institutions will analyse risks and predict future price trends.

- **Integrated real estate capital market**

With more institutional funds investing in REITs and other prime commercial real estate in Singapore, demand for yield accretive real estate assets will increase. Real estate securitisation could further increase to a level more akin to those in matured markets, such as US and Australia, where nearly half, if not more, of their income generating real estate is currently held by REITs and some private funds in the capital market space. Singapore as an Asian REIT hub could create a platform for regional REITs to tap funding sources from institutional investors outside the region. It is also in a good position to experiment with financial innovations and apply securitisation technology to improve liquidity and risk matching between suppliers (investors) and users (firms and homebuyers) of funds across regions.

Developers could explore the capital markets as an exit strategy to monetise their physical assets, and recycle the capital into more productive development and land acquisition businesses. CDL's Profit Participation Securities (PPS) is an example of how developers could use financial innovations to raise new capital. At the same time, developers could generate new sources of fee-based management revenues by providing asset management and property management services to REITs.

With the maturity of Singapore's REIT markets, corporate disclosure and governance standards of REITs could be further strengthened. The pool of professional asset and fund managers could be expanded, which is important to support more REIT listings in the local bourse. REITs with cross-border assets, different asset classes, different asset management models (internal versus external), performance-based fee structure, and others, are potential changes to widen options for investors.

- **Beyond real estate knowledge and professional skill-sets**

When the local real estate market becomes more "international", internationally accepted principles and practices will be adopted in valuation, investment feasibility analyses, and also financial structuring, and risk assessment of real estate. Corporate real estate service providers could leverage on their international networks and tie-ups to broker and facilitate large-scale cross-border transactions. Investment banks and other professional service providers, like accountancy and tax advisory firms, play increasingly dominant roles in brokering some of the international transactions. Real estate service providers should up their ante by scaling up their advisory services beyond simply focusing on "brick and mortar" deals to include due diligence, contract designs, and currency hedging issues in cross-border investments.

Developers should build up and integrate capability in development value-chains starting from development planning and project management to financial and asset management functions. CapitaMall Asia, a wholly-owned subsidiary of CapitaLand, is an example of an integrative retail-mall business model that encompasses retail real estate investment, development, mall operations, asset management and fund management capabilities.

The changing real estate landscape presents both threats and opportunities to real estate graduates and professionals in the future. Real estate education should be constantly reviewed to keep abreast with the market demand for new skill-sets and knowledge that go beyond "brick and mortar". Integrating "financial" rigours into real estate curriculum will equip real estate graduates with better financial knowledge to evaluate and analyse real estate deals with complex structures. With more international real estate investments flowing into and out of Singapore, real estate graduates should have perspectives that are more international, and always be ready to explore new opportunities outside Singapore. This new generation of real estate graduates will become industry leaders to chart new frontiers and break new paths in the next wave of transformation in the real estate industry!